Managing Madness

Sociology Editor Howard Newby
Professor of Sociology University of Essex

For Lindsay and Michael

Managing Madness
Changing ideas and practice

Joan Busfield

London
UNWIN HYMAN
Boston   Sydney   Wellington

Published by the Academic Division of
Unwin Hyman Ltd
15/17 Broadwick Street, London W1V 1FP, UK

Unwin Hyman Inc.,
8 Winchester Place, Winchester, Mass. 01890, USA

Allen & Unwin (Australia) Ltd,
8 Napier Street, North Sydney, NSW 2060, Australia

Allen & Unwin (New Zealand) Ltd in association with the
Port Nicholson Press Ltd,
Compusales Building, 75 Ghuznee Street, Wellington 1, New Zealand

First published by Hutchinson Education
Paperback edition first published by Unwin Hyman in 1989

British Library Cataloguing in Publication Data

Busfield, Joan
  Managing madness
  1. Psychiatry
  I. Title
  616.89   RC454

ISBN 0 09 164110 1
    0 04 445380 9 pbk

Library of Congress Cataloging in Publication Data

Busfield, Joan.
  Managing madness.

  Bibliography: p.
  Includes index.
  1. Psychiatry — Philosophy. 2. Psychiatric hospitals —
History. I. Title
RC454.4.B87   1986   362.2   86–3171

ISBN 0–09–164110–1
    0–04–445380–9   PBK

Typeset in Baskerville by Folio Typesetting Bristol
and printed in Great Britain at the University Press, Cambridge

Contents

Preface

Over the past three decades our ways of thinking about and treating the mentally ill have been the subject of much criticism. The attacks have come from numerous quarters – from pressure groups and politicians, from doctors and psychiatrists, from sociologists and psychologists and from patients and the public – and have raised many issues. Some have been concerned about the treatment of patients in mental hospitals, about the over-ready use of drugs, the use of ECT and psychosurgery and the deleterious effects of long-term hospital care, as well as about specific cases of maltreatment and neglect; some have pointed to the inequitable distribution of resources within the health service, to the low status of psychiatry within medicine, and to the fact that comparatively little is spent on community mental health services; others have expressed concern about the problems and dangers of compulsory detention and about the holding of criminal offenders in mental hospitals, while others have questioned the right and the capacity of professionals to judge behaviour as sick or disturbed. Indeed, the value and validity of the very notion of mental illness has been seriously questioned as has the whole discipline of psychiatry – the medical speciality which has major responsibility for the care and treatment of mental disorders.

Of course criticism of the social provisions for those considered mad, insane or mentally disturbed is hardly new. The institutions, policies and practices relating to the mentally disordered have never been short of critics and detractors. The practice of compulsory detention has long been a problem for liberal consciences fearful that some people were wrongfully detained. Indeed, it is this fear and the whole issue of legal safeguards for compulsory detention that has served as a major motive force underlying much of the mental health legislation in this country in the nineteenth and twentieth centuries. Concern, too, about the precise nature of the care given to the insane and mentally disturbed has been long standing. Scandals about the maltreatment of those living in asylums were no less a feature of the eighteenth and nineteenth centuries, when the first institutions for the insane were built, than they are today.

What is largely new, however, is the way in which the medical control of the care and treatment for the mentally disordered now bears the brunt of much of the more radical criticism. Since it is medicine that provides most of the services for the mentally disordered it is medicine that is held to be primarily responsible for all that is considered wrong with existing ways of treating mental disorder. Yet for many critics, especially those writing in the 1960s, the problem is less any inherent defects and deficiencies of medical practice than the application of medical ideas and techniques to this particular sphere: it is the appropriateness of the medical framework for the care and treatment of disturbances of mind that is called into question. The fundamental flaw, it is suggested, lies in the adoption of ideas based on the study and treatment of bodily processes, on which medicine is largely founded, to what is seen variously, according to the critic, as quintessentially mental processes, human behaviour or human action. The implication is that psychiatry, because of its distinctive object of attention, is unlike other medical specialities in certain important respects, and is consequently open to a whole range of unique objections. My own belief is that such a view is mistaken. While it is undoubtedly the case that there is much that is wrong with contemporary psychiatry, what is striking, once we locate it in its medical context, is the extent to which its deficiencies reflect those of medicine as a whole, and indeed the whole approach to human welfare in advanced capitalist societies. Psychiatry, far from being distinctive, is but a reflection of the standard response to problems and conflicts in contemporary society. To understand what is wrong with psychiatry and the ways in which it should be changed we need, therefore, to examine the forces and pressures that have determined the form and nature of psychiatry and of the mental health services in which psychiatric work is carried out. This is the first and overriding objective of this book.

My approach to the task of accounting for the nature and character of psychiatric work and of the mental health services combines both sociology and history, although it draws more heavily on the traditions of the former than the latter in its explanatory concerns and in its modes of argument and analysis. Nevertheless I take the view that any explanation of existing social ideas and practices, such as those that constitute the medical specialism of psychiatry, must analyse the development of the ideas and practices over time. Current ideas and practices incorporate the residues of past thought and action, and the social and economic conditions that gave rise to them; they are shaped by the past as well as by existing social conditions. In that respect, despite their own distinctive disciplinary traditions, history and sociology are inseparable and an analysis of the historical development of psychiatry is no less vital to a full understanding of its present-day form and character than an examination of contemporary forces and conditions.

However, any attempt to examine the factors, whether past or present, that mould psychiatry and the mental health services explicitly or implicitly involves the adoption of some theoretical framework that structures and shapes the explanation of psychiatry that is put forward. Such a framework involves assumptions about the way society is organized, about the way power is distributed, about the dynamics of social change and so forth, as well as incorporating value judgements as to the desirability of particular features of society. This applies as much to discussions and analyses of historical developments as to contemporary practice. It is necessary, therefore, when considering accounts of the contemporary features of psychiatry, not only to consider past and present conditions but also to attend to the different theoretical perspectives and the different assumptions on which particular accounts are based. It is these theoretical perspectives with their assumptions and values that also form the basis of contrasting evaluations of psychiatric work and so provide the key to many of the debates and controversies about psychiatry.

This book is, therefore, divided into two parts. Since theoretical assumptions are involved in any discussion of psychiatry, whether explanatory or evaluative, the first part of the book delineates the dominant ways of thinking that have structured and shaped discussions about psychiatry and the mental health services. The first two chapters locate psychiatry as a specialism of medicine and elaborate some of the key ideas and practices of that specialty and of medicine more generally, detailing the way psychiatrists and doctors typically think about their own practice. In Chapter 1, I delineate a liberal–scientific conception of psychiatry and medicine, I identify some of the dominant characteristics of modern medicinal work and I point to some of the salient differences between psychiatry and other areas of medicine. In Chapter 2 I turn to medical and psychiatric ideas about illness. I examine the way psychiatrists and other medical practitioners conceptualize illness and the different types of mental illness they distinguish. I also look at the social characteristics of patients identified as mentally ill, and at psychiatric diagnosis in practice. In Chapter 3 I then examine and assess some of the well-publicized criticisms of the liberal–scientific conception of psychiatry put forward in the 1960s by a diverse group of writers such as Thomas Szasz, R. D. Laing, and T. J. Scheff. These writers offered alternative ways of thinking about psychiatry and mental illness in which mental illness is generally viewed as a form of social deviance and psychiatry as an institution of social control. Chapter 4 then turns to look at ways of thinking about psychiatry and mental illness developed in the 1970s which are critical not of psychiatry in particular but of medicine more generally. I examine both theoretical perspectives that emphasize the professional power and professional interests of medical practitioners, including psychiatrists, and those that see medicine and the health services as shaped by the economic forces of capitalism. I also consider theories that have incorporated gender as a salient feature of discussions about medicine and the health services.

The second part of the book provides an historical account of the development of psychiatric ideas and practices into their contemporary form. It draws on the burgeoning scholarship in the history of medicine and psychiatry. Unlike much of that scholarship which is highly specific as to time and place, often, for instance, examining the history of a particular institution over a short period of time, I do not seek to examine particular features of psychiatric ideas and practices in great detail. Instead I provide an overview of some of the key changes that have occurred in the emergence of twentieth-century psychiatry and mental health services, focusing primarily on England. My aim is to bring together into an organized whole some of the findings of recent historical research in order to provide a sketch-map for those whose prime interest is in present-day psychiatry, whether they be sociologists, psychologists, psychiatrists, general practitioners, social workers or health service planners and administrators.

My historical account takes the sixteenth century as its starting point because it was in this period that the foundations of the Poor Law were laid, which provided the context within which the first state provisions for lunatics were made. It was also a period in which important early stages in the professionalization of medicine occurred. In Chapter 5 I begin by examining the key features of healing in this and the following century. I then look at the development of the first separate institutional provisions for lunatics in the form of the private madhouses. In Chapter 6 I consider the establishment of the voluntary general hospitals in the eighteenth century, and the parallel special wards and hospitals for lunatics. I also examine the ideas and philosophy of moral treatment that developed at the end of the eighteenth century. In Chapter 7 I turn to the activities of the state, considering first the development of the poor law from the sixteenth century onwards and then the factors that gave rise to the establishment of public asylums for lunatics in the first half of the nineteenth century. In the next chapter I outline the way in which, and the reasons why these public asylums developed into essentially custodial institutions.

Chapter 9 brings us to the twentieth century. In it I deal with strategies for the reform of the custodial asylums and their eventual introduction in the public sphere via the 1930 Mental Treatment Act. I consider the factors that led to legislative change, examining both twentieth-century changes in welfare provisions, and developments in psychiatry outside the asylums. In Chapter 10 the picture is brought up to date. I analyse the move to community care, the overall increase in service provision, and the changing balance of psychiatric and medical work in relation to mental illness, setting out the main factors that have given rise to these changes. In the concluding chapter I offer an overview of the development and character of psychiatry.

My interest in psychiatry and mental illness is long standing, dating from my training as a clinical psychologist at the Tavistock Clinic in the first half of the 1960s. In this period controversies about the concept of mental illness and its causes were just beginning to become more vocal and to receive wider public attention. My move into sociology and to university teaching in the second half of the 1960s deflected the dominant focus of my intellectual work for some time, although I continued for some years to work on a part-time basis as a clinical psychologist. It was sociology, however, that provided the tools which allowed me to come to grips with the questions and puzzles that I faced in thinking about psychiatry and mental illness – some of them first raised in the 1960s, others of more recent origin. Overall, therefore, this book represents the outcome of my ongoing intellectual endeavour to make sense of psychiatry and the phenomena of mental illness. It is, consequently, a book for those interested intellectually or practically in the field of psychiatry, of whatever disciplinary background or persuasion, who want to try and clarify their ideas and understanding of the character of psychiatry and the mental health services.

Given the length of time over which this book has had its gestation, my intellectual and personal debts are considerable. The Tavistock Clinic imbued me with psychoanalytic ideas which left an indelible and valued impression on my psychological understanding, though I often felt frustrated by the apparent reluctance of many of the psychoanalysts I encountered to question the intellectual foundations on which their practice was based. Severalls Hospital, Colchester, where I worked as a part-time clinical psychologist, gave me a greater knowledge of the realities of psychiatric institutions and psychiatric practice, as well as of the problems faced by large-scale, long-stay institutions. More recently my stimulus has come from sociologists and historians, particularly those connected at some time or other with the University of Essex. I owe an especial debt to Ludmilla Jordanova, Diana Gittins and Michael Lane for their personal and intellectual solidarity and support. Roy Wallis gave me some early though no doubt long-forgotten help with research materials, and Ken Plummer and Robert Broadhead some valuable comments on an earlier draft of the book. Mary Girling, Carole Allington and Teresa Edge all helped to transform my manuscript into a legible copy. To them and to Lindsay Lane and Jeffrey Vernon I would like to give my thanks.

part one
Theoretical Issues

1 Psychiatry and medicine: thought and practice

Controversy over the aims, methods and nature of psychiatry, and the organization and content of the mental health services, reflects a diversity of ideas and assumptions about the nature and causes of mental illness, about the efficacy and value of therapeutic techniques, about the power of professionals, and about the structure and organization of society and the distribution of power within it. The object of the first part of this book is to delineate and analyse some of the divergent strands of the debates and discussions concerning psychiatry and the mental health services, in order both to clarify the controversies that surround psychiatry and to serve as a first step towards providing an account of the factors that have shaped its development.

Psychiatrists as medical specialists carry out their work within a context of ideas about medical practice that permeate the whole of medicine. There are, of course, important differences between psychiatry and other areas of medicine, particularly in their historical trajectories, some of which are outlined briefly at the end of this chapter. There is, too, considerable diversity in the ideas and practices of different medical practitioners whatever their specialism. None the less, it is possible to identify a shared framework of beliefs and assumptions about the nature of medical and psychiatric work that dominates both psychiatry and medicine.[1]* Much of the conflict about the causes of mental illness, for instance, and about preferable treatments occurs within this framework and does not question its basic parameters. The framework constitutes, therefore, an ideology – that is, a set of ideas and assumptions and the related practices in which they are embedded – which is rarely called into question.[2] I have called this ideological framework as it operates within the psychiatric sphere the liberal–scientific conception of psychiatry rather than the 'medical' or 'psychiatric' conception, since such phrases, like the more fashionable term 'medical model', suggest a single, distinctively medical way of thinking about psychiatry, that is a necessary

* Superior figures refer to the Notes and reference sections following each chapter.

and unchanging foundation of medical and psychiatric work. The term medical model in particular has become a shorthand for a set of ideas about mental illness and psychiatry whose content is rarely specified. As a result its meaning has become extremely vague and imprecise. Goffman used the term to refer to the medical version of what he called the 'tinkering services' model. His concern was to specify the general characteristics of the service relationship between client and expert and to identify some of the problems of applying this model to medicine.[3] More commonly, however, the term is used, along with that of the 'disease model', simply to refer to a view of mental illness that locates its significant causes and treatment exclusively within the realm of the body, and to imply that this view is common to all medical practitioners.[4] Since there is considerable diversity of opinion among psychiatrists about the causes and treatment of mental illness, however, and no necessary symmetry between aetiological accounts and therapeutic practices; and since the conception that I shall delineate embraces both ideas about the tasks and methods of psychiatry and about the nature of mental illness, and is a particular historical product, I have preferred the characterization 'liberal–scientific', recognizing, thereby, that the ideological foundation of psychiatry, as of medicine, changes over time.

The liberal–scientific conception of psychiatry

The liberal–scientific conception of psychiatry has its immediate origins in Enlightenment thought of the eighteenth century and the value it placed on reason and scientific rationality.[5] The lineaments of that thought incorporated beliefs and values that structured and still continue to structure the form and content of medicine and the specialism of psychiatry as well as many practitioners' ways of thinking about their work. The conception of psychiatry, like others, incorporates basic assumptions about the nature and causes of mental illness, the role of psychiatry, the source and extent of its powers and the assessment of its value and efficacy, as well as about the distribution of power within society. Psychiatry, according to this point of view, is a specialty that has developed within medicine to provide help and treatment for one group of the sick: the mentally ill. More specifically it is a branch of clinical medicine – that is, of medicine whose object is the cure and treatment of sickness (the word clinical meaning 'of or pertaining to the sick bed').[6] As such the overriding obligation of the psychiatrist, as of other clinicians, is to provide help for the patient's sickness: as one author puts it 'the role of the physician centres on his responsibility for the welfare of the patient in the sense of facilitating his recovery from illness to the best of the physician's ability'.[7] This objective, associated as it is with the highest ideals of medicine, provides the *raison d'être* of psychiatry as of medicine.

However, within the liberal–scientific framework a commitment to helping the sick is not in itself sufficient to specify the exact nature of medical or of psychiatric activity. What helps to distinguish the clinician from others who seek to help and care for the sick is a further obligation that points to the methods that should be used in helping the patient. This is the obligation: 'to acquire and use high technical competence in "medical science" and the techniques based upon it'.[8] Although the aim is action, action should be based on science and scientific knowledge should be the foundation of clinical care. It is assumed, therefore, that psychiatric knowledge should, as far as possible, have its basis in science – a science that constitutes the pinnacle of human reason. Consequently the concepts, explanations and treatments offered by psychiatry can be contrasted with the non-scientific, less rational orientation towards the insane and mentally disturbed of other times and places. What others have called madness, lunacy and insanity are deemed to be illnesses; to be the consequence of natural processes (that is to say those that can be studied scientifically); to be best treated and eradicated by natural means; and their care and treatment to be placed in the hands of medical practitioners. The liberal–scientific conception rejects, for example, any idea that mental illnesses are the result of forces of evil or of some supernatural power, or that they should be dealt with either by exorcism or punishment. Moreover, it sees psychiatry, by virtue both of its objective and its methods, as more liberal and more humane in its approach to mental disorder than any alternative. Zilboorg, whose classic *History of Medical Psychology* provides an interesting exemplar of this perspective, conveys the ideas and imagery of the new humanism: 'Mental disease, which medicine finally wrested from the clutches of superstitious sadism, began to be looked upon as the misfortune of man as a person; the lunatic became as much an object of human concern as any sick man.'[9]

Science is, then, viewed as the lynchpin of psychiatric practice; it is science that permits the boundary to be drawn between the normal and the pathological; it is science that creates the possibility of accurate identification of the mentally ill; it is science that provides sound knowledge of the causes of mental illness; and it is science that provides effective methods of cure. Consequently, it is science that determines the essential content and form of psychiatric practice; what help is offered, where it is offered, and who receives it, within, of course, the constraints of the existing political order and its willingness to provide and finance the psychiatric services that science dictates.

If, moreover, science is the essential arbiter of the form and content of psychiatry, the psychiatrist serves as the repository and purveyor of this knowledge, the expert whose authority, power, status and prestige derive from his (or occasionally her) expertise, whose task it is to apply and use scientific knowlege in the interests of individual patients to cure their sickness. The psychiatrist is considered a professional; someone whose lengthy training is necessary to transmit the full range of relevant scientific knowledge, and whose socialization and professional status are the guarantee of integrity and altruistic concern.[10] And as a profession psychiatry has and must have autonomy – that is, independence and freedom from the control of outsiders – for only in this way will it be governed by disinterested science and protected from the contrary forces of the political arena. It is the profession that can and should control and police its own members in order to ensure high standards of conduct; and overall the profession, like any other group, will have no more power than the task requires.

Given this view of science as the moving force of psychiatry, and the psychiatrist as the purveyor and interpreter of a body of scientific expertise, the significant moments of the history of psychiatry are to be found in any movement towards a greater use and acceptance of science as the proper foundation of its practice, as well as in the developments and innovations in the relevant body of scientific knowledge.Psychiatry's history is viewed as basically linear and progressive, albeit at times halting (or even occasionally regressive), in which science and progress are seen as synonymous. Science is held to develop in a cumulative fashion and, as it accumulates, so scientific knowledge and psychiatry advance in an ever onwards march. Science is a matter of search and discovery in which the natural world is forced to give up its secrets, a struggle of reason against the forces of darkness and metaphysics. Zilboorg's chapter headings give a flavour of how that historic struggle has been characterized in this fashion: 'The Restless Surrender to Demonology', 'The Blow of the Witches' Hammer', 'The First Psychiatric Revolution', 'The Age of Reconstruction', and so forth.[11] And in this struggle in the name of reason, science and truth, psychiatry and humanism are in a common alliance. Victory comes from the subjugation of irrationality in the form of prejudice and sentiment. And the symbol of the historic moment in the development of psychiatry of the triumphal alliance of science and humanism is to be found in the liberation of the insane from the chains at Bicêtre.[12]

This is not to say that within the liberal–scientific conception all psychiatric systems are assumed to be perfect. But if there are failings, and they often exist, they are thought to be due either to an insufficient allocation of finance or resources to the system, or to lack of progress in the relevant areas of scientific knowledge, or to the fact that insufficient freedom has been granted to the psychiatric profession to follow what it considers scientifically necessary or desirable. We know the complaints well enough: too few hospital beds, old hospitals, poorly qualified personnel, low pay, too little new investment, the need for more research, too much outside interference, and so on.[13] If only these can be overcome then the system will work properly and effectively.

The liberal–scientific conception involves, therefore, an optimism and enthusiasm about what science has to offer and about what can be achieved with enough money, training, research and freedom; an optimism and enthusiasm that sociological and political discussions of science and psychiatry have seriously questioned. The importance of the perspective stems, however, not from the accuracy of its appraisal of psychiatry or its view of psychiatry's historical development, but from the fact that it commonly serves, as I have suggested, as the ideology of the psychiatric profession itself, and of medicine more generally. Hence, having initially served as the cognitive base on which the medical specialty of psychiatry was developed, it now constitutes the frame of reference by which many practitioners within the profession think about their work. Psychiatrists generally believe in the scientific, rational and humane basis of psychiatric work, and justify their demands for power and autonomy in these terms. However, in as far as the conception offers an inaccurate or inadequate model of the psychiatric system, as many authors have contended, it may also serve to mystify and distort perceptions of psychiatric practice.[14] In order to consider such arguments more fully it is necessary to separate out the basic assumptions of the liberal–scientific conception more clearly. They can be divided into three areas concerning the psychiatric task, psychiatric methods, and psychiatry as a profession respectively.

First, the psychiatric task. Psychiatry's purpose, like that of clinical medicine more generally, is assumed to be essentially altruistic. The doctor's job is to help the patient and the patient's interests (as the doctor interprets them) are held to be paramount. The doctor should side with the patient, if necessary against the interests of other individuals, groups or institutions, and should put the patient's interests before self-interest.[15] Moreover, the altruism which is built into the very definition of the clinician's work is held to be ensured both by medicine's commitment to the use of science as the means of gaining knowledge of sickness, and by the way in which it is organized as a profession.

Second, psychiatry and science. Mental illness is viewed as a natural phenomenon, the result of natural processes and hence amenable to natural intervention. Consequently psychiatry is and should be based, as far as possible, on science. By science is meant positive science, that is, science in which knowledge is based on empirical observations and conforms to the standards of objectivity that have been developed in the natural sciences.[16]

A number of other assumptions are linked to this basic premise and follow from additional ideas about the nature of science. One is that since science is assumed to be rational, objective, and value-free, so too is psychiatric knowledge. Psychiatric science is based on empirical observation and logical argument rather than on intuition and metaphysics. At this point the set of ideas incorporates an important contrast between science and ideology, with the presumption that the two are mutually exclusive.[17] If psychiatry is scientific, it cannot be ideological. This means, for instance, that its notions of sickness and disease are objective; they are based on statements of fact, not value, and are independent of the standards of any particular culture.

Another related assumption is that since science is the fount of new methods of detecting illness and new methods of cure, as well as of a new orientation to madness which does not assume moral culpability, then psychiatry must be essentially beneficial and humane. Its task is the care and treatment of sick individuals and scientific knowledge is the weapon it uses to alleviate pain and suffering and to restore the sick to health. A further assumption is that since scientific development is cumulative and progressive, so too is the development of psychiatry.[18] There may be periods of stagnation and temporary decline in which knowledge may be lost or fail to advance; however, overall there is a movement towards greater knowledge and better understanding of mental illness and more effective cures.

Third, psychiatry as a profession. The basic premise here is that psychiatrists are experts – the guardians and prophets of scientific knowledge.[19] This premise has a number of important corollaries stemming from additional assumptions about the acquisition and use of scientific knowledge. First, members of the psychiatric profession must be carefully selected and trained so that they acquire the necessary body of scientific knowledge on which good practice depends, otherwise the public might be the victim of inadequately trained 'quacks' (those who lack proper scientific knowledge). Second, the source and justification of psychiatrists' power, authority, status and prestige lie in their scientific knowledge.[20] It is because psychiatrists are experts that they are both given, and have the right to expect, deference from their patients and the professionals' rewards of pay, power and esteem. Third, and finally, only psychiatrists who are properly trained and qualified have the power and the right to judge the best form and content of psychiatric services, thereby serving the patient's interests.[21] It is the profession, by virtue of its highly specialized, scientific training, that can make the best-informed, scientific judgements and should be given independence and autonomy to do so. Similarly, the profession should be responsible for controlling entry into its ranks and regulating the conduct of its members. Both the professional status and the autonomy of psychiatrists are necessary and justifiable in the interests of science. Implicit, therefore, in the liberal–scientific conception is the assumption that power is broadly diffused throughout society and that psychiatrists constitute only one of a range of competing interest groups. Their power is no more extensive than required for the task in hand, and is counterbalanced by the power of other individuals and groups, including patients, in an essentially well regulated system.[22]

The paradigm of professional practice in medicine has historically been the professional working on an individual basis, offering a range of services that the client pays for according to the service given – the so-called 'fee-for-service' model.[23] The system is essentially entrepreneurial, and the provision of services for a fee in theory allows practitioners direct control over the organization and content of their work. The contract between practitioner and patient, arranged on a one-to-one basis, is treated as a free contract between both partners that either may terminate. This, it is argued, (in conjunction with the adequate training and licensing of practitioners) guarantees the quality of practice and ensures that the patient's interests will be served, since patients may turn elsewhere if they are dissatisfied.[24] Fee-for-service practice has generally been regarded as most consistent with the ideals and values of the liberal–scientific conception of medicine and psychiatry, and the stress tends to be put more on its supposed guarantee that patients will receive the services they desire and need, than on the entrepreneurial aspects of its character.

Of course, the organization of much of contemporary medicine does not conform to this simple model of professional practice. Almost invariably there is now some third party that intervenes in the relationship between practitioner and patient.[25] In private sector medicine there is often an insurance company covering some or all of the medical fees, and there may also be some business corporation involved in providing funds for the necessary investment in plant and equipment so essential to modern medicine.[26] In the public sector it is the state that funds and administers the medical services, whether practitioners retain some elements of the fee-for-service model as independent contractors or are salaried employees. However the fee-for-service model has tended to exert a powerful ideological influence on ideas about the organization of medical practice.

The characteristics of contemporary medicine

Within the liberal–scientific conception of psychiatry the fundamental altruism of psychiatry, the existence of a body of scientific expertise on which it can draw, and the professional character of its practice as a guarantee of responsible conduct by its practitioners are all assumed. Without attempting at the moment to call this conception into question (a number of major criticisms form part of the argument of the theorists discussed in Chapters 3 and 4), it is, however, necessary to examine in detail some of the actual characteristics of contemporary medical thought and practice that are not stressed by this particular conception. They relate to the task definition and prescribed methods embodied in the liberal–scientific conception, and apply to much of psychiatry as well as medicine. Some, too, provide the grounds on which psychiatry is criticized.

The medical task

The principal objective of clinical medicine, to help the sick, is associated with a number of important characteristics of contemporary medicine. First, its curative orientation. Clinical medicine directs attention to the cure of already existing sickness rather than to the prevention of ill-health; the first and immediate task is to treat illness rather than to keep the healthy in a fit condition. In his influential book, *Mirage of Health*, Dubos contrasts this strategy for achieving health with a preventive or public health orientation in terms of two opposing Greek legends:

The myths of Hygeia and Asclepius symbolize the never-ending oscillation between two different points of view in medicine. For the worshippers of Hygeia, health is a natural order of things, a positive attribute to which men are entitled if they govern their lives wisely. According to them, the most important function of medicine is to discover and teach the natural laws which will ensure to man a healthy mind in a healthy body. More skeptical or wiser in the ways of the world, the followers of Asclepius believe that the chief role of the physician is to treat disease, to restore health by correcting any imperfection caused by the accidents of birth or of life.[27]

As ways of approaching a common goal – health – the two orientations have little in common. The former usually demands a fuller exploration of the potential causes of illness, and consequently the recognition that many aspects of human life may affect health. Only in this way can it facilitate the development of strategies for the preservation and enhancement of health. The latter permits a much narrower perspective in which an understanding of the original causes of sickness may be of little importance, since the aim is to cure the already existing disease. Beveridge, in his plans for the welfare state, recognized the need for a broader vision in planning for health: 'Maintenance of health does not depend solely or primarily on health services, and still less on medical treatment. It depends even more on good food; on sufficiency of the other necessaries of life; on healthy homes . . . .'[28] However, as this passage indicates, in practice the major task of the so-called health services has been to treat sickness and disease, rather than creating a healthy society with all that entails in terms of food, housing and work. While the British National Health Service was supposedly set up to secure improvement 'in the physical and mental health of the people' and 'in the prevention, diagnosis and treatment of illness', only a small proportion of its resources are actually devoted to prevention.[29] In 1975/ 6 only 4 per cent of NHS current expenditure went on medicine that was explicitly preventive.[30] Health education, too, receives only little in the way of resources.[31]

A second important characteristic of modern medicine is its concentration on acute (that is, of recent onset) at the expense of chronic (long standing) sickness. Where cure is the goal, illnesses that are amenable to some form of treatment receive more attention and resources than those that are not. This is a marked tendency in contemporary health services. On a whole range of measures acute sickness is better provided for in the NHS than chronic sickness, and the same is true in other advanced industrial societies.[32] One example is given in Table 1; it shows that the amount of money spent per patient, even on basic services such as catering and heating, is far less in long-stay, chronic, mental illness and mental handicap in hospitals, than it is in acute and maternity hospitals. In the United States insurance schemes hardly touch chronic illnesses, and those who become chronically ill fall almost inevitably into the vagaries and inadequacies of the public sector.[33] In this respect a curatively oriented medicine might usefully be

Table 1   Cost per in-patient week of different services in different types of hospital as a percentage of the cost of those services in acute non-teaching hospitals, England 1971–2

Type of service	ACUTE HOSPITALS (OVER 100 BEDS)			Long-stay	Chronic	Mental illness	Mental handicap
	Amount (£)	per cent	Maternity				
Medical	4.48	100	65	27	13	26	13
Nursing	20.81	100	152	66	66	45	40
Domestic	3.76	100	143	58	60	27	27
Catering	7.39	100	100	55	48	45	43
Laundry	1.45	100	163	63	62	38	46
Power, light, and heat	2.43	100	115	65	57	50	42
Building and engineering maintenance	3.11	100	92	60	50	60	54
General cleaning	0.74	100	182	68	55	35	32
Total net costs	78.58	100	100	44	39	32	30

Source: DHSS and Welsh Office, National Health Service, Hospital Costing Returns, year ended 31 March 1972, HMSO (from Townsend, 1974, Table XII).

contrasted with a medicine whose first priority is with the care of patients rather than their cure, though the notion of care nowadays all too readily suggests the provision of treatment rather than the relief of pain and the alleviation of suffering. Nor should we suppose that the two are always compatible: treatments that prolong life and advance the objective of cure may well cause pain and suffering. Certainly the way in which the effectiveness of treatment is invariably measured in terms of the prolongation of life rather than the amelioration of misery and discomfort provides further evidence of how cure dominates care as the goal of medicine.[34] It is dealing with life-threatening conditions that counts, and the preservation of life, even a painful one, is the overriding objective. The battle between life and death epitomizes heroic medicine.

A third important characteristic of modern medicine is a strong individualism. Clinical medicine is structured around the one-to-one relationship of the doctor and patient and the clinician's task is to provide help for particular individuals who seek help. Consequently the doctors' first responsibility is to the individual patient and they are less likely to concern themselves with trying to improve the health of whole groups of populations. Their job is to treat individual patients, not to worry about the public's health, so that individualism is built into the very organization of medicine. Only community physicians are employed to serve a group or population rather than specific individuals, and they constitute only a small proportion of all medical practitioners.[35]

Individualism, moreover, permeates every aspect of the medical orientation to sickness, including the explanations and treatments it offers. The notion of disease itself refers to a process that unfolds and develops within the individual, and what occurs within the individual and what the individual does is the prime object of medical interest and endeavour, rather than the individual's relation to others or to the environment, or vice versa. And this is true of preventive as well as curative medicine. Preventive medicine, where it does exist, tends to focus on action at the individual level: vaccination and innoculation, and changes in personal life-style, such as improvements in diet and reduced alcohol and cigarette consumption, are the typical preventive solutions to the maintenance of health, rather than social changes that would affect the population's health, such as the changes in the production of food or in the labour process, or more stringent governmental controls on industrial pollution, or the redistribution of wealth.[36] It is the individual who is expected to stop smoking and to eat healthier foods, not the business corporations to stop making profits from cigarette advertising or the manufacture of highly refined and processed foods.[37] Self-help and self-control are the new panaceas.

The fourth key characteristic of modern medicine is its voluntarism. Clinical medicine is directed at those who ask for help and is not normally backed up by any legal compulsion to give or receive treatment. It is assumed that the patient will ask for the doctor's help if and when it is needed, and that in normal circumstances there will be no compulsion to receive any treatment that is offered. Doctors and others do have a range of powers that create both formal and informal pressures on sick individuals to seek treatment and to accept the treatment that is offered.[38] Nevertheless, not only is the doctor–patient relationship usually viewed and idealized as a free contract (with all that implies for the rhetoric of free choice, individual liberty and so on), but also, in practice, doctors treat only those who have decided, for whatever reason, to consult them. And this has important consequences for the nature of medical work. It means that although doctors may attract patients by the treatments they offer and so – wittingly or not – affect the supply of patients, in certain respects they do play a passive role in setting the boundaries of sickness, dealing only with those who come to them and with the problems they present.[39] It also means that the patients who do receive treatment are not necessarily those who by any objective criteria are most in need of help, but those who, depending on the organization of medical practice, can afford to consult a doctor, have better access to medical facilities, or feel themselves to be most in need of medical help.[40] Consequently there are large disparities in the use of medical facilities according to factors such as age, gender, occupation, religion, region and so on – disparities that often bear little close relation to patterns of sickness.[41]

The methods of medicine

The medical profession's commitment to the positive methods of natural science gives rise to a number of important features of medicine. First, its concentration on bodily processes at the expense of psychological and social ones. While medical science is not a single science but the application of a range of sciences which at times may include the psychological and social sciences, in practice the latter receive relatively little attention as is evidenced by the small part they play in the medical curriculum: 'Physics, chemistry, and biology are considered to be the sciences basic to medicine.'[42] Since the natural sciences offer the paradigm of 'real' science, it is by alliance with them that medicine can claim to be properly scientific and can legitimate its claims to special knowledge and expertise.[43] And the association is self-reinforcing. In so far as medicine relies on the natural sciences and accepts a positive epistemology, the social sciences, which find it harder to satisfy the criteria of positive science, are excluded. This concentration on physical processes has become the virtual hallmark of medicine and the terms medical and physical are at times used synonymously, as in the use of the term 'medical model', to refer to the assumption that mental illness can be explained, understood and treated in physical terms. In conjunction with its individualism, medicine's involvement with the physical realm has meant a special concern with what goes on within the body – with the internal rather than the external. It is the organism not the environment that receives most attention.[44]

Second, medicine has a mechanistic conception of human functioning. The approach to the human body adopts an essentially engineering model in which the body is seen as series of separate, independent systems; ill-health is viewed as the mechanical failure of some part of one or more of these systems; and the doctor's task is to repair this mechanical failure, which may be done without attention to the individual as a whole.[45] As a result the individual is rarely viewed as a whole person and a humanistic approach is made more difficult:

Most modern techniques of medical practice deal with some specialized, or limited, aspect or part of the organism. Each specialized technique is set in the framework of a relatively simple, or simplistic, mechanical philosophy of structure – function relationships more suitable to the nineteenth than to the twenty-first century. It inevitably follows that, for the moment at least, the student (and his teacher) sees the patient less and less as a person, more or less integrated and 'whole', and more and more as a somewhat fragmented collection of thousands of variables.[46]

Third, medicine is devoted to the use of technology. Where science is the ideal and the body is viewed as a machine, then inevitably the technologically sophisticated often appears superior to the simple and less complex. There are numerous examples of the way in which medicine has become increasingly technologized. Premature baby units, intensive care units, as well as kidney machines, heart transplants, foetal monitors and so on, provide ready evidence of the increasing role of sophisticated technologies in medical practice.[47] Technology has become the symbol of medicine's expertise and its devotion to science. The mechanization of medicine proceeds apace and is continually glorified and encouraged by the media.

However, medicine's commitment to science, with all that it entails for the methods it uses to deal with sickness, is not unqualified. The twin obligations of curative medicine – to help the sick person and to use scientific knowledge – create a tension between the concern to help the individual and the demands and procedures of positive science. As one author puts it 'the aim of the practitioner is not knowledge but *action*. Successful action is preferred, but action with very little chance of success is to be preferred over no action at all.'[48] Clinical medicine, therefore, displays a commitment to action that often overrides its scientific ideals. The obligation to help the sick person requires that the doctor do something, and something is almost always considered better than nothing, regardless of its proven value. This gives rise to a medical practice that is both interventionist and pragmatic. On the one hand doing something is all-important and can become an end in itself.

It is frightening, but expected, that when a specialised group is formed to perform certain actions, it is evaluated and continues to be supported because of the *number* of such actions it does, rather than by whether a problem is solved.[49]

On the other hand doctors often act in a pragmatic way and rely on intuition and personal experience rather than on scientifically established generalizations. The commitment to science is tempered and qualified. Freidson describes the effects as follows:

The practitioner is a fairly crude *pragmatist*. He is prone to rely on apparent 'results' rather than on theory, and he is prone to tinker if he does not seem to be getting 'results' by conventional means . . . the clinician is prone in time to trust his own accumulation of personal, *first hand experience* in preference to abstract principles or 'book knowledge', particularly in assessing and managing those aspects of his work that cannot be treated routinely . . . . And finally, the practitioner is very prone to emphasise the idea of *indeterminacy or uncertainty*, not the idea of regularity or of lawful, scientific behaviour.[50]

Medical practitioners' reliance on clinical experience allows them to appear to satisfy the dictates of positive science, with its empiricist leanings and demands for detailed observation, while ignoring the requirements of systematic observation over a range of cases with experimental controls that are supposed to be the basis of sound generalization. It is not surprising, therefore, to find that much medical treatment derives from clinical experience, has not been subject to systematic scientific test, and is sometimes unnecessary.[51] In many instances there is little clear evidence that particular treatments have value over and above their operation as placebos. When particular treatments are tested using randomized control trials, results surprising to the medical profession often emerge. Intensive care units for coronary patients apparently offer no better chance of survival than care within the home.[52] Other aspects of medical practice also stem from its essentially pragmatic nature: the use of treatments in a trial and error fashion in a search for one that is effective; the tendency to make diagnosis contingent on the response to treatment; the reluctance of the profession to stand back and analyse and assess its own practice.[53]

Medicine's use of science is therefore partial in two senses. On the one hand it pays more attention to certain sciences rather than others. On the other hand scientific standards are often subservient to clinical demands. The clinician wants action and results and these often come before the more abstract ideals of science.

Psychiatry and medicine

Psychiatry diverges from medicine more in terms of its object of interest and its institutional location than in its objectives, values and approaches. Definitions of psychiatry vary. According to one dictionary it is 'the medical treatment of diseases of the mind'; in contrast an influential text defines it as 'that branch of medicine in which psychological phenomena are important as causes, signs and symptoms, or as curative agents', thereby giving the specialism a broader scope than the dictionary definition suggests.[54] The definitions concur, none the less, in seeing mental or psychological processes as the special object of psychiatry's concern. Moreover, historically much of the specialism's work has been located in separate asylums or mental hospitals.[55] In general these distinguishing features have not prevented psychiatry from trying to model itself, where possible, on its parent medicine, and it has been imbued with many of the same ideas, beliefs and values. However psychiatry's involvement with certain types of problem in certain types of location has led to certain important differences between its work and that of medicine.

First, it must draw more or less heavily on psychology rather than the natural sciences proper (though some psychiatrists try to keep this to a minimum). While some theoretical approaches within psychology, most obviously behaviourism, have been developed in conformity with the canons of positive science, much of psychology and the social sciences on which psychiatry also draws is not considered properly scientific and has little part in the medical curriculum.[56]

Second, a great deal of psychiatry's work has been with chronic rather than acute sickness and there has been little prospect of achieving much in the way of cure. This is partly a reflection and even a measure of the limitations of existing knowledge and techniques of therapy, but it is also a function of the types of problem with which it has had to deal. This has often been a matter of concern to some psychiatrists.[57] More recently there has been something of a shift in the type of problems brought to psychiatrists and work with acute cases makes up a far higher proportion of psychiatric work, as we shall see in Chapters 9 and 10.

Third, where compulsory powers of detention are involved, psychiatric work does not conform to the voluntarism that is held to be paradigmatic of professional practice. Initially all those dealt with on an institutional basis in public asylums were detained under compulsory powers, and although the proportion of residents of psychiatric beds in England held under such powers at any one time is now small (around 5 per cent), a somewhat higher proportion are admitted as 'formal' patients (some 10 per cent in 1981).[58] While the existence of compulsory powers is not specific to the psychiatric field (there are compulsory provisions under public health legislation which may be exercised in relation to infectious illness), nevertheless, the routine departure from the principles of voluntarism in a proportion of cases is an important feature of psychiatric work.[59] To some extent it is a reflection of a fundamental difference in the historical development of the organization of psychiatry. Although there have been medical practitioners working in the private sector on a fee-for-service basis dealing with psychiatric problems, to a greater extent than the rest of medicine, psychiatry has developed around the work of medical practitioners employed by the state to deal with those compulsorily detained on grounds of insanity.[60] Hence it departed very early and very substantially from the organizational ideals of medical practice.

These divergences between psychiatry and medicine, which will emerge in more detail in subsequent chapters, account in part for the low status of psychiatry within medicine as a whole and the active hostility of many medical practitioners to it.[61] Psychiatry is an unpopular specialty, the first choice of few medical students, and it has difficulty in attracting good recruits, not least because they take over the negative values and attitudes of their seniors.[62] Psychiatry provides few opportunities for the heroic, technologically sophisticated, scientific medicine that is so esteemed by the medical profession itself. However, although many critics argue that psychiatry should try to become more like the rest of medicine, others want it to break its strong associations with medicine. Before considering such debates further, we need to examine psychiatric ideas about mental illness in more detail. This is the task of the following chapter.

Notes and references

1   Useful discussions of the shared assumptions and beliefs underlying medical work are to be found in Parsons, 1951, Chapter X; Freidson, 1970a *passim*; and Becker *et al.*, 1961.

2   For discussions of some of the meanings of the term ideology, see Plamenatz, 1970; see also Larrain, 1983.

3   See E. Goffman 'The medical model and mental hospitalisation: some notes on the vicissitudes of the tinkering trades', in his *Asylums* (1968).

4   This is, for instance, the basic model outlined by Wing in his *Reasoning about Madness*, 1978, Chapter 2. See also Siegler and Osmond, 1974, Chapters 2 and 4, and Coulter, 1973, Chapter 1.

5   Gay, 1973; Cassirer, 1955.

6   Shorter Oxford English Dictionary.

7   Parsons, 1951, p. 447.

8   ibid., p. 447.

9   Zilboorg, 1941, p. 280.

10   Issues concerning the professionalization of medicine are discussed more fully in Chapter 4.

11   Zilboorg, 1941.

12   The extent of this liberation is called into question by Foucault, in *Madness and Civilization*, 1967, Chapter 9.

13   The Government White Paper *Better Services for the Mentally Ill*, issued

by the Department of Health and Social Security in 1975, identifies many of the problems of existing services visible from this perspective.

14   See also the arguments put forward by Thomas Szasz which are discussed in Chapter 3.

15   See Parsons, 1951, Chapter X, and Becker *et al.*, 1961.

16   On positivism in science see Harré, 1972.

17   See also Durkheim's view of scientific knowledge; see Benton, 1977, pp. 94–9.

18   The cumulative view of science is challenged by Thomas Kuhn in *The Structure of Scientific Revolutions*, 1962.

19   The term quack is a derogatory one suggesting that the person in question claims knowledge he or she does not have.

20   Freidson, 1970a, *passim*.

21   ibid.

22   This pluralist conception of power is outlined and assessed by C. Wright Mills in *The Power Elite*, 1959, Chapter 11.

23   Johnson, 1972, especially Chapter 5.

24   Freidson, 1970a, pp. 31–2.

25   Johnson (1972) refers to the situation as one of mediation. See Chapter 6.

26   The role private companies play in the provision of supplies for the National Health Service is examined by Hyman, 1979. See also Thunhurst, 1982, Chapter 3.

27   Dubos, 1959, pp. 110 11.

28   Beveridge, 1944, p. 160.

29   Quoted in the *Report* of the Royal Commission on the National Health Service, 1979, p. 8.

30   Calculated from the figures in Annex 2, Table 1, Department of Health and Social Security, 1976a, p. 82.

31   Royal Commission, 1979, p. 44.

32   See Townsend, 1974. The term acute when applied to diseases means 'coming sharply to a point or crisis of severity'; chronic diseases are those 'lasting a long time, long-continued, lingering, inveterate' (Oxford English Dictionary).

33   Bodenheimer *et al.*, 1977.

34   Illich, 1977a, Chapter 1; McKeown, 1976a.

35   In 1978 there were some 765 community physicians (including trainees) in England and Wales out of a total of 58,053 doctors working within the NHS (Figures taken from the Royal Commission on the National Health Service, 1979, Chapter 14).

36   This is the focus of the Department of Health and Social Security's *Prevention and Health: Everybody's Business*, 1976.

37   See Thunhurst, 1982, Chapter 2; Doyal, 1979, Chapter 2.

38   Freidson, 1970b, especially Chapter 4.

39   This point is discussed more fully in Chapter 2.
40   Some of the inequalities in the availability and use of the health
      services are discussed in *Inequalities in Health: the Black Report*,
      (Townsend and Davidson, 1982, Chapter 4).
41   ibid.
42   McKeown, 1976b, p. 6; see also Parsons, 1951, p. 455.
43   McKeown, 1976b, *passim*.
44   ibid., Chapter 1.
45   ibid.
46   Towers, 1971, p. 165.
47   On technologies available to obstetricians in the mid-1970s, see
      Cartwright, 1979, p. 135. See also Thunhurst, 1982, Chapter 3; Royal
      Commission, 1979, pp. 379–80; Brighton Women and Science Group,
      1980; Hanmer and Allen, 1980.
48   Freidson, 1970a, p. 168.
49   Quoted in Cartwright, 1979, p. 2.
50   Freidson, 1970a, p. 169.
51   See Cochrane, 1972.
52   ibid., Chapter 6.
53   The use of electroconvulsive therapy (ECT) to aid diagnosis is touched
      on by Clare, 1976, p. 245.
54   Shorter Oxford English Dictionary; Slater and Roth, 1969, p. 6.
55   See Part Two below.
56   McKeown, 1976b, Chapter 8.
57   See Chapter 9.
58   Informal patients are those admitted or resident without legal
      formality – i.e. without the use of compulsory powers. Formal patients
      are those admitted or detained under one of the sections of the
      Mental Health Act that sets out the procedures for admission and
      detention on a compulsory basis. The figure of 6 per cent of residents
      is for the end of 1973 (MIND, 1976, p. 3) but according to MIND the
      figure has remained in this region since then (personal
      communication). Data on the legal status of those admitted to
      psychiatric beds, unlike that of residents, is routinely provided by the
      Department of Health and Social Security. The figure of 14 per cent is
      for 1981, the most recent year for which statistics have been published
      (Department of Health and Social Security, 1984, Table D4).
59   And has been much criticized as a result. See Szasz, 1970b, pp. 113–
      39.
60   Unfortunately there is little data that allows us to estimate the precise
      extent of private practice psychiatry in this country. However more
      NHS consultants in psychiatry have full time NHS posts than the
      average. In 1978, 74.1 per cent of consultants in mental illness had
      full-time posts compared with an average of 47.6 per cent. The figure

for mental handicap is even higher at 91.7 per cent (Royal
Commission on the National Health Service, 1979, Table E5, p. 430).

61   Zilboorg (1941) comments 'The history of twenty-four centuries of
medicine shows clearly there has always been a strong and deep-
seated antagonism between medicine and psychiatry' (p. 521). See also
Clare's comments in Shepherd, 1982, p. 15.

62   Clare, 1976, Chapter 9.

2 Conceptualizing and identifying illnesses

Deciding who is ill and who is healthy is considered a technical matter over which doctors have formal control: 'the medical profession has first claim to jurisdiction over the label of illness and anything to which it may be attached, irrespective of its capacity to deal with it effectively'.[1] In like manner psychiatrists have formal jurisdiction over the labels of mental health and illness: 'psychiatrists possess the ultimate power to assign one person to the status of being mentally ill, and to refuse the designation to another'.[2] In England and Wales this power is enshrined in mental health legislation which provides no formal definition of mental illness and makes it a matter of clinical judgement to decide on the correct application of the term, as well as on the severity of illness, the likelihood that treatment would be of benefit, and so forth.[3] Moreover, in addition to the formal, legal right to decide who is ill and who is healthy, medical and psychiatric practitioners help to constitute and create the boundaries of health and sickness through their own practice. Medical conceptualizations of illness, the development and delineation of new disease concepts, new ideas about the causes of illness, and the introduction of new treatments, all affect the way that people think about their bodily and mental states and come to decisions about whether they or others are or are not sick and in need of medical help, as well as having far wider implications for patterns of work, the rules governing sickness pay and sickness benefit, and so forth.

However, though viewed as a medical judgement, and though influenced by medical ideas and medical practices, medical practitioners' power to settle the boundaries of health and sickness is qualified. The ideological voluntarism of medicine helps to ensure that the way in which medical practice is organized, the availability of services, and the way in which they are funded, all affect the range of complaints and problems brought to doctors and, consequently, have an impact on medical notions of health and illness in general, and on psychiatric notions of mental health and illness in particular. Medical and psychiatric ideas and practices have been developed as ways of ordering, organizing and structuring the problems and difficulties with which clinicians are, for a variety of reasons, called upon to deal: their own ideas and practices constitute one factor affecting that flow.

In what way, therefore, do medical practitioners think about illness? How are their ideas about illness developed and applied to the realm of mental illnesses?

The conceptualization of illness

Medical and psychiatric practitioners rarely attempt any formal general definition of health or illness, and mental health legislation has followed medical convention in not providing any general definition of mental illness. Within medicine health is almost invariably defined negatively as the absence of illness, and few offer a positive definition, recognizing, no doubt, the problems and pitfalls in the way of vagueness and imprecision.[4] The oft-quoted positive definition attempted by the World Health Organization of health as a 'state of complete physical, mental, and social well-being and not merely the absence of disease or infirmity' illustrates the problems all too clearly.[5]

In turn, illness is itself not normally given a general definition, but is usually given meaning through the specification of a list of particular illnesses with their own characteristics: it is given an extensive rather than an intensive definition. To some degree this failure to define illness as a general term is due to the difficulty of the task, a point that Eysenck implies in his comment 'medical textbooks have too much sense to attempt such a definition'.[6] Certainly attempts by commentators to produce general definitions of ill-health have not been very successful. A recent analysis of concepts of disease identified the following range: disease as *1* suffering; *2* what doctors treat; *3* physical lesion; *4* adaptation to stress; *5* imperfection; *6* statistical abnormality; *7* abnormality that puts the organism at a disadvantage; and *8* a condition warranting action.[7] All have limitations and no single one covers all the conditions commonly regarded as diseases. But the failure to offer general definitions of illness is not simply a matter of the difficulty of the task. It also stems from the clinical context in which medicine usually operates and its characteristic voluntarism which I described in the last chapter. The typical patients seen by doctors are people who have already decided that something is wrong with them. The medical task is to decide what is wrong, not whether anything is wrong at all, although on occasions a clinician may come to question whether an individual is in fact ill at all. As a result clinicians tend to focus on diagnosing the particular illness not on specifying the general characteristics of illness.

Although general definitions of illness do not feature as an important component of medical thought, nevertheless medicine does tend to operate with an underlying biological model of the human organism that provides an overall conceptual structure for medical ideas about illness, gives some substance to the notion of illness, and in fact combines some of the criteria of illness mentioned above. In this biological model the body is viewed as a series of functioning systems whose efficiency is maintained by homeostatic mechanisms. Sickness or pathology exists when functioning deviates from normal efficient levels.[8] What constitutes normality is a matter both of statistical typicality and of the consequences of deviation. On the one hand states that are rare are more likely to be seen as pathological than those that are not. The norm is usually that for people in general, although the typical functioning of the particular individual, if it is known, may also be used as a standard.[9] On the other hand it is the consequences of a deviation that determine whether it is seen as pathological or not.[10] The boundaries of acceptable deviation are set by what follows from the change. Three types of consequence are of special importance. First, and perhaps most important, there is the individual's chances of survival. Conditions that hasten death are likely to be seen as pathological. Second, there is pain and suffering; this is often the main criterion for personal assessments of sickness.[11] Third, there is the issue of the body's adaptation to, or ability to cope with the environment.[12] This is obviously a far looser, more imprecise criterion than the first two, though even they are by no means unproblematic.

The biological model of functions and norms not only provides a rather loose, general conceptualization of illness, it also contributes to the idea that there are specific types of illness – the efficient functioning of the organism can break down in a variety of ways – and to the view that the concept of illness is relatively unproblematic and does not need to be formally defined. The smooth working of the organism is relatively easy to assess; the real skill comes in deciding what has gone wrong.

Medical ideas about particular illnesses are themselves structured by a second model. This is a typological model in which particular illnesses are viewed as discrete, distinctive entities, differentiated from one another in terms of their causes, symptom patterns, course and outcome. This typological conceptualization of illness owes much of its contemporary form to a model of infectious diseases associated with the germ theory of Louis Pasteur and Robert Koch.[13] The model, which came into ascendancy when infectious diseases were still the major cause of mortality, still plays a dominant part in medical thought, and provides a basis for describing, classifying, diagnosing, explaining and treating illnesses. Although the idea of disease entities has a long history in medicine, ways of thinking about disease have changed markedly over time. Germ theory provided a new paradigm of disease that still permeates much medical thought and practice, although its general validity has also been seriously questioned in academic medical circles.[14] Germ theory identified different germs – that is, living organisms – as the specific, distinctive and necessary causes of different infectious illnesses, for 'the researchers showed by laboratory experiments that disease could be produced at will by the mere artifice of introducing a single specific factor – a virulent micro-organism – into a healthy animal'.[15] The model can be expressed diagramatically for an illness such as tuberculosis in the following manner:

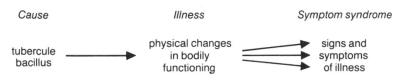

Cause　　　　　　　*Illness*　　　　　　　*Symptom syndrome*

tubercule bacillus ⟶ physical changes in bodily functioning ⟹ signs and symptoms of illness

Figure 1

This model of disease has a number of important features. First, it assumes that there are discrete, distinct illnesses, involving qualitative breaks in functioning between the healthy and the pathological. This assumption, which characterizes most typological models, can be contrasted with a dimensional approach that stresses a continuity between the normal and the pathological and attempts to locate individual differences in functioning along one or more of a series of dimensions.[16] While the typological model may be the most appropriate for infectious diseases, it is arguably of less value in other areas of medicine including psychiatry.[17] Second, it assumes that each illness has its own unique cause, which is the specific cause of the particular illness; for example, the tubercle bacillus in the case of tuberculosis. This presumption of a specific aetiology for each illness then serves as a basis for the differentiation and classification of illnesses. Illnesses may, however, also be distinguished by their symptom syndromes, their course and their outcome, for although single symptoms are not unique – raised temperature is a common sign of illness – the precise combination of symptoms, the syndrome, and their development over time is. By either means the categorization should be the same, but classification by aetiology is considered the ideal, since knowledge of causes should establish the specificity of an illness.[18] In practice, however, since the specific cause of an illness may not be established, categorization often proceeds on the basis of symptoms and may be modified over time. In some cases the problem is the inadequate knowledge of aetiology. In others, however, the whole assumption of aetological specificity is questionable.

Germ theory incorporates other important ideas that reflect the dominant characteristics of modern medicine and is, consequently, often referred to as *the* disease model. It assumes that the presence of some physical entity, the infectious micro-organism, is the cause of pathological bodily changes, and so this model contributes to and intensifies medicine's organic orientation. It assumes that the introduction into the body of this physical entity causes the illness and so directs attention to what goes on within the body rather than outside it. It focuses more on the mechanisms of disease than on its origins.[19] And it assumes that illness is to be understood at the level of individuals, by understanding what happens to them, rather than by consideration of environmental and social processes, such as the spread of infections, the level of exposure and resistance of a particular population to that infection, and so on.[20]

Of course germ theory as developed by Pasteur and Koch does not rule out a broader view of causation and treatment, and it is clear that the model as depicted in Figure 1 gives us a very oversimplified explanation of infectious diseases. It picks out a micro-organism as the cause of a particular illness for purposes of differentiation and treatment in the way that lawyers, for instance, may select some factor as the cause of an accident or an event.[21] They are concerned to identify the factor that 'makes a difference', not to specify all the factors and conditions that contributed to it. This is the justification that is offered for its use in the clinical context: identifying the specific cause of an illness allows the doctor to distinguish one illness from another, to decide why a patient has measles rather than whooping cough, and to prescribe the appropriate type of treatment; one directed at eradicating the noxious agent. Nevertheless, the approach does simplify and it does select. For many scientific purposes we want to know the set of conditions necessary for the occurrence in question, not just the one that makes the difference – to identify the causes, not only the specific cause, if there is one. And for an evaluation of medical practice we need to decide whether eradication of this specific cause at the individual level is the best solution.

In the case of tuberculosis while the presence of the tubercle bacillus is a necessary condition, it is not the only factor that contributes to the development of the illness. Infectious micro-organisms may be present within the body without the illness developing. The outcome depends on the resistance of the individual to the micro-organism, which is itself a function of bodily development, nutrition, past illness history and contact with the organism, psychological state, and so on. These factors are in turn accounted for by a range of inherited and environmental factors both biological and social such as diet, wealth, the production and distribution of food, employment, housing and so on. Equally the exposure of individuals to infectious micro-organisms, and consequently their chances of becoming ill, are affected by a number of environmental factors such as their social status, occupation, style of living, housing conditions, and so on, as well as the dispersal or concentration of micro-organisms in both the communities and households in which they live and work.[22] A somewhat more detailed model of infectious illness taking these factors into account is portrayed in Figure 2.

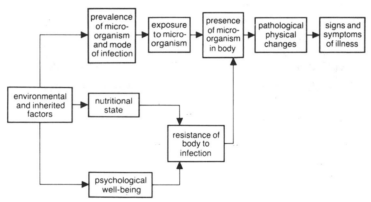

Figure 2

Yet even this aetiological model provides a poor conceptualization of many illnesses. It still attempts to portray the aetiology of an infectious disease at the level of the individual, and it still assumes a clear-cut qualitative distinction between health and illness. It is becoming increasingly clear that the aetiology of some illnesses is far more complex and depends not only on the interaction of a large number of factors but on their occurrence at different stages in the individual's life history. Some of the suggested explanations of different types of cancer could not be readily accommodated even into this expanded model.[23] Adequate accounts of many illnesses are likely to involve complex multifactorial models, and will have to be conceptualized not only at the level of the individual but also the level of the population or social group.

There can be few doctors, however, who would deny that the overall aetiology of disease is more complex than the simple germ theory of disease outlined in Figure 1, and there are some who would emphasize the point and act accordingly. What many would deny is the relevance of more complex models to the day-to-day activities of clinical medicine, especially so far as treatment is concerned. This is because the simple model fits in well with, and is encouraged by, the curative demands of clinical medicine. Clinical medicine demands the identification and treatment of specific illnesses in individual patients and the simple disease model provides a useful analytical framework for this task. It both facilitates and reinforces concern with the detection of specific illnesses in particular individuals – with the question 'what is wrong with this individual?', rather than with the question 'why is anything wrong?'. The existence of illness is treated as given, identifying its exact nature and doing something about it are the only important questions. The simple causal model derived from germ theory is also consistent with and reinforces the emphasis in clinical medicine on physical cures directed at the individual, such as drugs. As Dubos points out

Drugs provide the perfect complement to the idea of specific aetiology. Hence whatever the nature of disease, the most important task – so at least is the well nigh universal belief – is to discover some magic bullet capable of reaching and destroying the responsible demon within the body of the patient.[24]

The alternatives – reduction in the exposure to noxious agents by improvements in sanitation, cleanliness and conditions of work; increasing the resistance to and likelihood of illness by changes in diet and in the consumption of substances like alcohol and tobacco – which might be best achieved by radical changes in industrial and agricultural production, in government policies or by reductions in the stress of everyday life, are alien to the concerns of clinical medicine. As far as clinicians are concerned, to go beyond individual physical methods of treatment is to move beyond the task they have been allotted and their own sphere of special competence – to move outside the confines of the clinical gaze.[25]

A situation has arisen, therefore, in which there is a marked discrepancy between the existing diversity of ideas about the causes of health and illness, both within and outside the medical profession, and the limited character of the public intervention to maximize health. Research on the social and psychological causes of illness and the conditions for the maintenance of health, although less well funded and supported than that on the physical aspects of illness, has been relatively extensive; but there is little in the way of political or policy activity or commitment in response to this work, since the organizational and ideological structure of health services is restricted to clinical values and practices.[26] Instead new research findings about the social and psychological causes of illness are transformed and adapted to fit the clinical mould and become the basis not for social and political change but for demands for individual effort and self-control.

Types of mental illness and their classification

Psychiatrists, following medical convention, give meaning to the term mental illness by specifying a diverse range of distinctive and discrete mental illnesses, many of which seem to have little in common apart from their location within the psychiatric scheme. In so doing they generally adopt the medical assumption of disease entities and their differentiation in terms of specific aetiology, symptoms, course and outcome. For many aetiology is still the preferred and ultimately the definitive criterion of the distinctiveness of a particular illness. However, not only is the aetiology of a given condition often unknown, or a matter of dispute, but as we have already observed, the idea of aetiological specificity is problematic once we move away from infectious diseases. In practice, therefore, mental illnesses are largely distinguished descriptively in terms of symptom syndromes, although aetiological assumptions may be involved in making certain distinctions.[27] However, even when they are avoided in the initial differentiation of illnesses, the glossaries of mental disorders, which elaborate and give some content to the diagnostic categories, often refer to the presumed causes of some of the different illnesses.

Elaboration of diagnostic categories is much more detailed in psychiatric texts which often build up a picture of each mental illness. This not only involves specification of symptoms but also details the possible causes and the likely age (age of onset is, at times, an integral feature of the differentiation of certain mental illnesses), gender and social background of patients as an aid to the diagnostic process, as well as suggestions as to suitable treatment. Details about the social character of patients are obtained from the expanding body of work on the social epidemiology of psychiatric illness, which is discussed in the following section of this chapter, as well as from psychiatrists' own observations of their patients. Taken together all this material generates diagnostic sterotypes or typifications – characterizations of what are considered to be typical illness patterns and typical patients – whose content is part of the organizational and intellectual apparatus of psychiatric practitioners.[28] The typifications are not, of course, fixed, and as new ideas and new treatments are introduced they may change more or less gradually without any necessary change in nomenclature.[29]

Psychiatric classifications

Since differentiation by symptom syndromes is inevitably imprecise (few symptoms are specific to a particular illness); since psychiatrists differ in their theoretical approaches and their ideas about the causes of particular mental illness; and since they also do not agree about the precise value and desirable characteristics of classification schemes, it is not surprising to find that there is no single universally agreed list of mental illnesses or mode of classifying them. Most lists include many of the same illnesses but they do not always give them the same names or group them in a similar manner. Most typological classifications mention schizophrenia and anxiety states, but the precise delineation of these conditions in the glossary may well differ, as may the number and types of illness recognized and their location within the overall classification scheme.

Early categorizations of mental illnesses varied considerably.[30] On the whole they differentiated fewer illnesses and the ones that were mentioned seem to bear little precise resemblance to the types of mental illness now recognized. Hippocrates, whose ideas generally figure in histories of medicine, distinguished two basic types of mental disease: mania — states of abnormal excitement; and melancholia — states of abnormal depression.[31] But he also referred to other conditions, such as hysteria, then considered physical illnesses, which are now included in lists of mental disorders. Contemporary categorizations of mental illnesses derive from the so-called era of classification at the end of the nineteenth century when attempts were made to systematize the highly varied classifications used by practitioners.[32] The work of the German psychiatrist, Kraepelin, whose ideas were developed and publicized through several editions of his *Compendium of Psychiatry*, first published in 1883, is considered of particular importance in this period. He developed a classification of mental disorders on the basis of his clinical observations of the natural history of diseases: aetiology, onset, symptomatology, course and prognosis. It distinguished two basic types of mental illness: exogeneous psychoses – those with external causes – including febrile delirias, psychosis due to exhaustion, intoxications, thyrogeneous psychosis, general paresis, psychosis resulting from cerebral tumour or abscess and dementia praecox; and endogeneous psychoses – those with internal causes – such as degenerative psychosis, manic-depressive psychosis, paranoia, the neuroses, which included hysteria and epilepsy, psychopathic states, compulsive neuroses and homosexuality, idiocy, and imbecility.[33]

While attempts at systematization in the era of classification did not yield a single agreed classification scheme, there has been considerable progress in the development and acceptance of a uniform international schema during the last four decades. The current international classification of mental disorders forms part of the International Classification of Diseases, Injuries and Causes of Death, now in its ninth revision (ICD–9).[34] This is the classification used in England for statistical purposes, although most psychiatrists use various simpler schemes in their clinical work.[35] A classification of mental disorders was added to the ICD in 1948 when the sixth revision was introduced and the schema was broadened from a classification of causes of death to include diseases and injuries.[36] The ICD uses a typological classification of mental disorders along Kraepelinian lines and aims to achieve an international standardization of diagnostic categories both for statistical and clinical purposes. The main categories of the ICD–9 schema for mental disorders are set out in Table 2 (there are further subdivisions of these categories). It provides a comprehensive schema to allow any mental disorder or symptom to be classified and now has its own glossary that provides brief descriptions of the different illnesses. This is an innovation for the ninth edition, although there was a British glossary for the eighth.[37] While the regular revision of this classification schema prevents complete ossification, the concern to standardize (which has been fuelled by the desire for international statistical comparisons, as well as by concerns about diagnostic reliability) makes innovation more difficult.[38]

The United States has shown considerable reluctance to follow the international schema and continues to develop its own Diagnostic and Statistical Manual of Mental Disorders, the third edition of which was produced at the end of the 1970s (DSM–III).[39] Although this edition incorporates the usual typological categories, it makes no specific assumption that each mental disorder is a discrete entity with sharp boundaries, and it also adopts a 'multi-axial' approach to diagnosis with a view to incorporating more information into the initial diagnosis.[40] It uses five axes, the first two covering clinical psychiatric syndromes (Axis I) on the one hand, and personality disorders and specific developmental disorders (Axis II) on the other. The third axis is for physical disorders

---

Table 2   Mental disorders as classified in the International Classification of Diseases, ninth revision (ICD-9)

Organic psychotic conditions (290–4)

290   Senile and presenile organic psychotic conditions
291   Alcoholic psychoses
292   Drug psychoses
293   Transient organic psychotic conditions
294   Other organic psychotic conditions (chronic)

Other psychoses (295–9)

295   Schizophrenic psychoses
296   Affective psychoses
297   Paranoid states
298   Other nonorganic psychoses
299   Psychoses with origin specific to childhood

Neurotic disorders, personality disorders and other non-psychotic mental disorders (300–16)

300   Neurotic disorders
301   Personality disorders
302   Sexual deviations and disorders
303   Alcohol dependence syndrome
304   Drug dependence
305   Nondependent abuse of drugs
306   Physiological malfunction arising from mental factors
307   Special symptoms or syndromes not elsewhere classified
308   Acute reaction to stress
309   Adjustment reaction
310   Specific nonpsychotic mental disorders following organic brain damage
311   Depressive disorder, not elsewhere classified
312   Disturbance of conduct not elsewhere classified
313   Disturbance of emotions specific to childhood and adolescence
314   Hyperkinetic syndrome of childhood
315   Specific delays in development
316   Psychic factors associated with diseases classified elsewhere

Mental retardation (317–19)

317   Mild mental retardation
318   Other specified mental retardation
319   Unspecified mental retardation

Source: *Mental Disorders: Glossary and guide to their classification in accordance with the Ninth Revision of the International Classification of Diseases*, World Health Organisation, 1978, p. 19.

(Axis III), and the final two depart from the identification of illness categories and cover the severity of psychosocial stressors (Axis IV), and the highest level of adaptive functioning in the past year (Axis V). In so doing the schema has in the last two axes introduced a quantitative 'dimensional' component into the classification.[41] The introduction of multi-axial classification is seen by its proponents as a logical development of the procedure possible within previous versions of the

Table 3 Mental disorders as classified in the American Psychiatric Association's Diagnostic and Statistical Manual of Mental Disorders, third edition (DSM–III)

Disorders usually first evident in infancy, childhood or adolescence

Mental retardation
Attention deficit disorder
Conduct disorder
Anxiety disorders of childhood or adolescence
Other disorders of infancy, childhood or adolescence
Eating disorders
Stereotyped movement disorders
Other disorders with physical manifestations
Pervasive developmental disorders
Specific development disorders

Organic mental disorders

Section 1. Organic mental disorders whose etiology or pathophysiological process is listed below (taken from the mental disorders section of ICD–9–CM)
    Dementias arising in the senium and presenium
    Substance induced
Section 2. Organic brain syndromes whose etiology or pathophysiological process is either noted as an additional diagnosis from outside the mental disorders section of ICD–9–CM or is unknown

Substance use disorders

Schizophrenic disorders

Paranoid disorders

Psychotic disorders not elsewhere classified

Affective disorders

Major affective disorders
Other specific affective disorders
Atypical affective disorders

Anxiety disorders

Somatoform disorders

Dissociative disorders (or hysterical neuroses dissociative type)

Psychosexual disorders
Gender identity disorders
Paraphilias
Psychosexual dysfunctions
Other psychosexual disorders

Factitious disorders

Disorders of impulse control not elsewhere classified

Adjustment disorders

Psychological factors affecting physical condition

Personality disorders

V codes for conditions not attributable to a mental disorder that are a focus of attention or treatment

Additional codes

DSM for multiple categories to be coded for any one individual. The main categories for the classification of mental disorders on Axes I and II are set out in Table 3.

As these two classifications illustrate, the range of conditions falling within psychiatric schemas is very diverse and particular types of illnesses are grouped together into a number of basic types covering the full spectrum of disorders. Four distinctions have been of special importance in generating the various groupings of different classification schemas though their exact role varies from schema to schema.

Mental illness and mental retardation

Most psychiatric classifications incorporate a distinction between mental illness itself and what is variously called mental retardation, mental subnormality, mental defect, mental impairment or mental handicap, both coming under the more general term mental disorder. This is the contemporary version of the old distinction between madness and idiocy, and the distinction has been sufficiently fundamental in terms of service provision that from the middle of the nineteenth century, with the rapid growth of institutional provision for the mentally disordered, the two groups have been assigned to separate institutions.[42] Legislation, however, has often dealt with the two groups alongside one another, though distinguishing the two. In Britain mental subnormality was the term used in the 1959 Mental Health Act, but the recent revisions of mental health legislation have substituted the term mental impairment.[43] Severe mental impairment is defined as 'a state of arrested or incomplete development of mind which includes severe impairment of intelligence and social functioning and is associated with abnormally aggressive or seriously irresponsible conduct.'[44] The condition differs from mental illness in that it is characterized by arrested or incomplete development of intelligence. Senile dementia, for instance, which is categorized as a mental illness, also involves deficiencies of intellectual functioning but refers to an impairment of functioning that was previously normal. The label mental subnormality is applied to those whose intellectual functioning never reaches normal levels, and, consequently, largely to conditions initially present at birth or in early childhood. The question of whether mental subnormality is a medical problem is a matter of considerable debate, as is the question of whether it should be covered by the same statutes as mental illness. Many argue that the problems of mental subnormality are essentially educational rather than medical and therapeutic.[45] However, my concern in this book is primarily with mental illness.

Organic and functional mental illnesses

Following the principle that aetiology should be the preferred means of classification most psychiatric classifications give some prominence to a second distinction in their grouping of mental disorders. This is a distinction between mental illnesses that involve definite organic pathology and those that do not. The former are referred to as organic mental illnesses and the latter group, if they are given a general name, are often referred to as functional mental illnesses. (The eighth revision of ICD did not place organic mental illnesses together in a separate group.)[46] The psychiatrist Stafford-Clark, in a best-selling book, describes the contrast like this. There is

an organic group, embracing all those forms of mental illness which are directly related to and dependent upon some distinct bodily disorder, and a functional group in which the disorders, while still in many cases almost certainly due to some disturbance of bodily processes, display a form and pattern which is recognizable on psychological rather than a physical plane, and for which no characteristic structural basis has as yet been discovered.[47]

This passage implies that the basis of the contrast (reflected in the term functional), is between disorders of 'structure' and disorders of 'function', but this distinction is problematic.[48] The organic group comprises two rather different types of mental illness, and in only one is there clear evidence of 'structural' pathology. On the one hand there are the various chronic dementias such as senile and pre-senile dementia.[49] These involve a chronic and progressive deterioration of intellectual functioning, based on tissue damage to the brain itself, that if untreated is usually irreversible and terminal. On the other hand there are the various states of acute delirium that can be produced by toxic substances such as alcohol and drugs – alcohol and drug psychoses – or by infections.[50] These also involve 'impairment of orientation, memory, comprehension, calculation, learning capacity and judgement' – the classic symptoms of 'organicity', but they do not involve the same gross structural changes to the brain and are often completely reversible.[51] The common characteristic of dementia and delirium is that they result from known brain pathology, whether transient or not.

The origin of the distinction between organic and functional mental illnesses has been attributed to Stahl, a professor of medicine in Germany who wrote in the early years of the eighteenth century, but it did not come into prominence within psychiatry until the twentieth century.[52] According to Zilboorg the significance of the distinction lay in its implications for treatment, 'for the question of how to treat a patient cannot be answered unless the problem of whether a given mental disease is organic or functional is definitely and scientifically solved', a point that has been echoed more recently by both the sceptics and adherents of psychiatry.[53] However, the distinction raises numerous problems and is examined further in the next chapter. Certainly in practice mental illnesses identified as organic are viewed by psychiatrists almost exclusively in physical terms with respect both to causation and treatment, and there is little interest in the possible role psychological or social factors may play in their aetiology – a reflection of the primacy attributed to physical factors in medicine. The illnesses are usually treated with drugs, even if considered irreversible, with the aim either of slowing the disease process or of controlling certain neurological or psychotic symptoms. Beyond this, treatment is largely a matter of meeting the physical and practical needs of patients, many of whom are admitted to hospital.[54]

Psychoses and neuroses

Equally important to the diagnostic concerns of many psychiatrists has been a third distinction – that between psychoses and neuroses (although the latter term has been largely avoided in the nomenclature of the DSM–III).[55] The distinction between psychoses and neuroses is usually based on symptomatology, but often also involves aetiological implications (it is to circumvent the controversy surrounding aetiology that the DSM–III avoids the term where possible and argues for a descriptive, i.e. symptomatological, use of the phrase neurotic disorder, urging the use of the term neurotic process to refer to psychodynamic claims about aetiology). The contrast between psychoses and neuroses is a major distinction within the ICD–9 classification of mental disorders, and it is clear from the controversy surrounding its use in the DSM–III that there are many psychiatrists who are reluctant to abandon its use as a general label for a particular group of mental disorders. The difference between psychoses and neuroses has often been described, especially in day-to-day psychiatric practice, rather loosely in terms of the patient's 'contact with reality' – a formulation that owes much to Freudian ideas.[56] A psychotic condition is said to involve a loss of contact with reality – states of mind not structured and informed by the usual versions of reality – whereas a neurotic condition does not involve this loss; rather it involves what is sometimes referred to as an 'exaggerated' response to reality. The contrast is described by Stafford-Clark as follows:

the neuroses are those disorders of emotion or intellectual functioning which do not deprive the patient of contact with reality; the psychoses on the other hand, are characterized by a fundamental disturbance in the patient's appreciation of the nature of his environment and his response to it.[57]

In part the symptomatological contrast is a matter of the severity of the symptoms, a point that Karl Jaspers, an influential German psychiatrist of the early years of this century, suggests when he contrasts the two: 'Those psychic deviations which do not wholly involve the individual him-self are called neuroses and those which seize upon the individual as a whole are called psychoses.'[58] For him, as for many other psychiatrists, the two types should not be viewed as polar positions on a single continuum, but as qualitatively distinct. The significance of severity in contrasting the two types of illness is also shown in the frequent direct reference to the degree of 'grossness' or severity of the symptoms. For instance, the ICD-9 characterizes the psychoses, as 'Mental disorders in which impairment of mental function has developed to a degree that interferes grossly with insight, ability to meet some ordinary demands of life or to maintain adequate contact with reality', adding 'It is not an exact or well defined term.'[59]

When aetiological assumptions are involved in the distinction between psychoses and neuroses, the basic contrast is usually between 'biogenesis' and 'psychogenesis'.[60] Many psychiatrists, for instance, argue that all psychoses have organic causes, the British glossary of ICD-8 asserting 'To many psychiatrists the so-called psychoses have this in common that they are largely due, or supposed to be due, to an organic process', although other psychiatrists have argued for a psychodynamic or social aetiology of functional psychoses.[61] Neuroses, in contrast, are said to have 'no demonstrable organic aetiology' and are generally assumed to have psychological causes.[62] It is in relation to the neuroses that psychodynamic accounts following Freudian lines have been especially influential, although behaviourist accounts viewing neurotic symptoms as learned responses have provided an alternative psycho-logical account.[63]

The best known and most frequently diagnosed psychotic illness is schizophrenia. Though the term was first used by Bleuler in 1911 the condition had been identified in 1860.[64] Kraepelin called the illness dementia praecox and along with others initially considered it to be irreversible – an assumption that has been slow to disappear. Several types are usually distinguished; the main ones in the ICD–9, following

Kraepelin, are 'simple', 'hebephrenic', 'catatonic' and 'paranoid'. For many people schizophrenia epitomizes 'real' madness or insanity – terms which are generally restricted to psychotic conditions. It is characterized by disorders of thought, perception, emotion and motor behaviour, and the most well-known but by no means inevitable symptoms are hallucinations and delusions, though these may occur as symptoms of other illnesses.[65] An hallucination is described as 'a perception in the absence of an external stimulus', while a delusion is defined in standard text books as 'a false unshakeable belief which is out of keeping with the patient's cultural background'.[66] Believing oneself to be President Kennedy would be an example of a delusion. Delusions involve disorders of thought content; equally important as a symptom of schizophrenia is so-called 'formal thought disorder', which has been described in a number of different ways, but may involve thought blocking (sudden breaks in the flow of thought) and the inclusion of marginal and irrelevant features of a total concept.[67] It is such features that make the schizophrenic's thought and action seem incomprehensible and irrational, characteristics which Jaspers, for one, takes to be distinctive of schizophrenia:

The most profound distinction in psychic life seems to be that between
what is meaningful and *allows empathy* and what in its particular way is
ununderstandable, 'mad' in the literal sense, schizophrenic psychic life (even
though there may be no delusions). Pathological psychic life of the first
kind we can comprehend vividly enough as an exaggeration or diminution
of known phenomena without the usual causes or motives. Pathological
psychic life of the second kind we cannot adequately comprehend in this
way. Instead we find changes of the most general kind for which we have
no empathy but which in some way we try to make comprehensible from
an external point of view.[68]

Schizophrenia has been the most widely researched of all mental illnesses and there are numerous theories as to its causation, theorists variously emphasizing the role of genetic factors, biochemical processes, pathological family relationships, problems of ego development and so forth.[69] Much of this theoretical diversity exists within the confines of the liberal–scientific framework and reflects the capacity of that framework to incorporate and assimilate into a suitable mould a broad range of ideas as to the causes of illness. Generally the aetiological research on schizophrenia that has been carried out has been inconclusive – biochemical studies no less than the more controversial research on family processes.[70] However, the evidence that genetic factors play some part in its aetiology is seen as strong by many psychiatrists, although it is clear that environmental factors must play an important role.[71] As we would expect the range of treatments commonly used is more limited. Schizophrenia, like other psychotic conditions, is generally considered to require in-patient care in its acute phases, and treatment with drugs is common.[72] Indeed psychodynamically oriented psychotherapy and behaviour therapy are rarely used in the treatment of psychotic conditions, although there is some use of behaviour therapy in rehabilitation programmes for chronic schizophrenics.[73]

The so-called affective psychoses, the other main group of psychoses, are characterized primarily by disorders of mood or emotion rather than thought. The ICD–9 describes them like this:

Mental disorders, usually recurrent, in which there is a severe disturbance of mood (mostly compounded of depression and anxiety but also manifested as elation and excitement) which is accompanied by one or more of the following: delusions, perplexity, disturbed attitude to self, disorder of perception and behaviour; these are all in keeping with the patient's prevailing mood (as are hallucinations when they occur). There is a strong tendency to suicide.[74]

Under this general heading come various manic and depressive conditions including manic-depressive psychosis, mania and so-called endogenous depression. Whilst schizophrenia has been a more common diagnosis in the United States than in this country the reverse has been true for manic-depressive psychosis.[75] Endogenous or psychotic depression has been distinguished from 'reactive' or neurotic depression partly in terms of aetiology through the presence or absence of precipitating events, such as a death in the family, and partly in terms of symptoms. The symptomatological contrast has been described as follows:

hallucinations, delusions, agitation, retardation, weight loss, early morning waking, feeling worse in the morning (diurnal variation), and constipation seem generally to be judged as indicators of psychotic depression.
Indicators for neurotic depression have been feeling worse in the evening, crying a great deal, being a worrying type of a person, finding it hard to make decisions, as well as a variety of non-symptom features such as being younger. . . .[76]

However, many psychiatrists have been unhappy with the distinction between endogenous and reactive depression and the DSM–III has a single group of affective disorders divided, largely on grounds of severity, into 'major affective disorders' in which there is 'a full affective syndrome', 'other specific affective disorders' in which there is 'only a partial affective syndrome of at least two years duration', and 'atypical affective disorders', in effect a residual category for affective disorders that do not fit into the other two categories.[77]

Depression in its various forms has attracted increasing research attention in recent years and there have been a number of studies of possible psychosocial causes as well as of biochemical processes. One of the most interesting and significant of recent studies of the psychosocial aetiology of mental illness is George Brown and Tirril Harris's study of depression *Social Origins of Depression*.[78] This develops earlier work linking levels of stress with mental illness into a complex aetiological model in which socially generated vulnerability mediates the impact of severe events and long-term difficulties to affect the chances of becoming depressed. Brown and Harris also provide evidence which supports the work of other authors that events involving loss are especially conducive to depression. In line, however, with the organizational and ideological structure of clinical work, in practice depression is largely treated both on an in- and an out-patient basis by physical means, either with psychotropic drugs or with the more controversial electro-convulsive therapy (ECT).[79]

The term neurosis was first used by William Cullen, a Scottish physician of the second half of the eighteenth century, to refer to disordered nerve function.[80] Later the prefix 'psycho' was added for nervous disorders caused solely by psychological factors (Freud, for instance, made a distinction between neuroses proper and psycho-neuroses).[81] More recently the prefix has been largely abandoned and the term neurosis has come to refer to a more restricted group of disorders, generally assumed, following Freud, to be of psychogenic origin, although behaviourists have offered different accounts of their genesis. The ICD–9 glossary describes them as:

mental disorders without any demonstrable organic basis in which the patient may have considerable insight and has unimpaired reality testing, in that he usually does not confuse his morbid subjective experiences and fantasies with external reality. Behaviour may be greatly affected although usually remaining within socially acceptable limits, but personality is not disorganized. The principal manifestations include excessive anxiety, hysterial symptoms, phobias, obsessional and compulsive symptoms, and depression.[82]

The DSM–III offers the following description of a neurotic disorder:

a mental disorder in which the predominant disturbance is a symptom or group of symptoms that is distressing to the individual and is recognized by him or her as unacceptable or alien (ego-dystonic); reality testing is grossly intact; behavior does not actively violate gross social norms (although functioning may be markedly impaired); the disturbance is relatively enduring or recurrent without treatment and is not limited to a transitory reaction to stressors; and there is no demonstrable organic etiology or factor.[83]

Apart from neurotic depression which has been described above, the neurotic category usually includes disorders such as anxiety states, phobias, obsessive–compulsive states and hysteria. An anxiety state is described in the ICD–9 glossary as:

Various combinations of physical and mental manifestations of anxiety, not attributable to real danger and occurring either in attacks or as a persisting state. The anxiety is usually diffuse and may extend to panic. Other neurotic features such as obsessional or hysterial symptoms may be present but do not dominate the clinical picture.[84]

Phobic states are 'Neurotic states with abnormally intense dread of certain objects or specific situations which would not normally have that effect.'[85] The feared objects are quite often standard ones and common types include a fear of open spaces (agoraphobia); of closed spaces (claustrophobia), of snakes, spiders, dogs, and heights. Obsessive–compulsive disorders are familiar to us through the repetitive hand washing of Lady Macbeth: 'It is an accustomed action with her, to seem thus washing her hands. I have known her to continue in this a quarter of an hour' (Act V Sc. 1). The ICD-9 glossary describes the disorders like this:

States in which the outstanding symptom is a feeling of subjective compulsion – which must be resisted – to carry out some action, to dwell on an idea, to recall an experience, or to ruminate on an abstract topic. Unwanted thoughts which intrude, the insistency of words or ideas, ruminations or trains of thought are perceived by the patient to be inappropriate or nonsensical. The obsessional urge or idea is recognized as alien to the personality but as coming from within the self. Obsessional actions may be quasi-ritual performances designed to relieve anxiety e.g., washing the hands to cope with contamination. Attempts to dispel the unwelcome thoughts or urges may lead to a severe inner struggle, with intense anxiety.[86]

Hysteria, the subject of Freud's first major publication, has been one of the most controversial of the neurotic categories.[87] The ICD–9 retains the term and distinguishes two forms under the one heading. The disorder is characterized in the glossary as one in which 'motives, of which the patient seems unaware, produce either a restriction of the field of consciousness or disturbances or motor or sensory function which may seem to have psychological advantage or symbolic value', the latter symptoms representing the 'classic' conversion form, the former the dissociative form.[88] The DSM-III separates the two types; the conversion form being located as a subtype of the category somatoform disorders and the dissociative form constituting a group of dissociative disorders.[89]

The treatment of neurotic disorders varies.[90] Few are considered to require in-patient treatment and many do not receive specialist psychiatric care at all. General practitioners who deal with most of those with diagnosed neurotic conditions largely prescribe psychotropic drugs including the well-known Librium and Valium, though a few attempt some form of modified, brief psychotherapy or a more limited counselling. Patients who receive specialist care are more likely to be given some form of psychotherapy or behaviour therapy – the most common forms of psychological therapy – but many are treated with drugs.

Behaviour disorders

In addition to the organic mental illnesses, the psychoses and the neuroses, there are a number of other types of mental illnesses that have sometimes been grouped together under the general heading of behaviour disorders. More commonly in recent classifications they have not been given a general label but form a heterogeneous residue of non-organic, non-psychotic conditions, distinguished from neuroses on grounds of symptomatology – symptoms that seem to relate more to behavioural problems than to mental functioning. Consequently, for many commentators it is a particularly problematic group of mental illness that raises special problems of distinguishing wrongful from disturbed behaviour – madness from badness – problems that are considered in the following chapter.[91] This residue of mental disorders includes the so-called personality disorders, the DSM–III's substance use disorders, such as drug dependence and alcoholism, and a group of sexual deviations or disorders. Personality disorders are characterized in the ICD–9 glossary like this:

Deeply ingrained maladaptive patterns of behaviour generally recognizable by the time of adolescence or earlier and continuing throughout most of adult life, although often becoming less obvious in middle or old age. The personality is abnormal either in the balance of its components, their quality and expression or in its total aspect. Because of this deviation or psychopathy the patient suffers or others have to suffer and there is an adverse effect upon the individual or on society.[92]

Personality disorders, therefore, include what is sometimes called the psychopathic personality, a disorder that receives specific attention in current British mental health legislation where it is defined as 'a persistent disorder or disability of mind (whether or not including significant impairment of intelligence) which results in abnormally aggressive or seriously irresponsible conduct on the part of the person concerned'.[93]

Anorexia nervosa, a condition which has received widespread publicity over the past decade, is placed in the category of 'substance use disorders' in the DSM–III. In the ICD–9 it is located in the group of 'special symptoms or syndromes not elsewhere classified' and described as follows:

A disorder in which the main features are persistent active refusal to eat and marked loss of weight. The level of activity and alertness is characteristically high in relation to the degree of emaciation. Typically the disorder begins in teenage girls but it may sometimes begin before puberty and rarely it occurs in males. Amenorrhoea is usual and there may be a variety of other physiological changes. . . . Unusual eating habits and attitudes toward food are typical and sometimes starvation follows or alternates with periods of overeating.[94]

The group of sexual disorders includes paedophilia, fetishism and transvestism, and may include homosexuality. The latter provided one of the most striking examples of psychiatrists' own difficulties and uncertainties in defining the boundaries of mental illness and distinguishing the socially deviant from the mentally disordered, when in 1973 the American Psychiatric Association decided that homosexuality was not longer in itself 'necessarily' a mental illness.[95]

Explanations of personality disorders vary, with psychodynamic and behaviourist accounts having an important role as far as treatment is concerned, though generally behaviour and personality disorders are seen as more difficult to treat than neurotic conditions. In-patient admission is correspondingly more common than with neurotic conditions – though much treatment is given on an out-patient basis – and there has been a recent growth of special in-patient units for the treatment of alcoholism and drug addiction.[96]

Leaving aside mental retardation, the major groupings of mental illnesses and subtypes that I have outlined have often been treated as a hierarchy of disorders, with disorders higher up the list having diagnostic priority over those lower down. Kendell describes the hierarchy as follows:

First in the hierarchy come the organic psychoses. If there is evidence of organicity . . . this overrides all other considerations and no symptom, psychotic or neurotic is regarded as incompatible with that diagnosis. Next in the hierarchy comes schizophrenia. Certain symptoms are traditionally regarded as diagnostic of schizophrenia, regardless of what other symptoms may also be present, provided only that there is no question of organic cerebral disease . . .. The third position in the hierarchy is occupied by manic depressive illness. Even if its own characteristic features are present, organic or schizophrenic symptoms take precedence so that, for instance, patients with both schizophrenic and affective symptoms are classified as schizophrenics. On the other hand, neurotic symptoms of any kind may be present without disturbing the diagnosis, for neurotic illness comes at the bottom of the hierarchy . . .. In general, any given diagnosis *excludes* the presence of symptoms of all higher members of the hierarchy and *embraces* the symptoms of all lower members.[97]

The criteria involved seem to be twofold. On the one hand there is 'evidence of organicity' – a criterion that reflects medicine's concern with physical processes – organic mental illnesses coming at the top of the hierarchy. On the other hand there is a ranking in terms of symptomatological severity, with psychoses coming before neuroses, and disorders of thought coming before disorders of mood. The ICD–9 lists disorders according to this hierarchical ordering, and indicates that the classification schema may be used hierarchically in the way that Kendell outlines, although it makes provision for the use of more than one diagnosis.[98] The DSM–III has, however, to some extent moved away from the common hierarchical ordering, placing in particular the substance use disorders early in the listing, and it encourages multiple classification.[99]

The way in which psychiatric concepts of illness are used in practice can be examined in a number of ways. I want to consider two. First, I want to look at the social characteristics of those who do become patients, as well as of those persons who may have similar symptoms but do not have any contact with medical practitioners about them. Who are the people who are the recipients of these diagnostic labels? Second, I want to look at the evidence concerning psychiatrists' ability to distinguish different types of mental illness. How accurate is the diagnostic process?

The social characteristics of psychiatric patients

Social epidemiology – that is, the study of the social distribution of illnesses both within and between populations – has long been of interest to medical practitioners as well as to sociologists and policy makers.[100] On the one hand it provides clinicians with information about the likely social character of patients which may aid diagnosis, as well as about populations who may be 'at risk' of particular illnesses. On the other hand it serves as a useful starting point for the investigation of the aetiology of specific illnesses. Much of the data on the social epidemiology of psychiatric illness, as of other illnesses, is obtained from routine official statistics, especially those of hospital in-patients or from special surveys of patient populations, such as the occasional surveys of general practice. Unfortunately data collected routinely is usually limited in character and does not, for instance, always give the marital status of the person, or any clue as to their social or economic status.[101] For these items special surveys are required as they are for those areas, such as private psychiatric practice, where little or no information is collected on a routine basis. More important, for those concerned to obtain clues as to aetiology, patient data leave out people who may have the illness in question but for some reason or other have not sought medical help, perhaps because the illness is less serious, or because they have ignored its manifestations, or find it difficult to get to a doctor, or dislike seeking help, or whatever.[102] Consequently, some studies attempt to measure levels of illness in samples of people living in the community so that those who are ill but not in contact with a medical practitioner are also included. These so-called community surveys or field studies do not always attempt to identify cases of illness in the usual clinical manner.[103] It is quite common, for instance, to measure a more generalized psychiatric morbidity using a standard symptom check list so that although the results are less contaminated by the factors that influence the use of health services, the measures bear an uncertain relation to clinically diagnosed cases.

Epidemiologists produce two basic types of measure of the distribution of illness – measures of incidence and measures of prevalence.[104] Incidence refers to the number of new cases of an illness that arise over a particular period of time, prevalence to the number of cases that are current at a particular time (either at a single point in time – point prevalence – or at some time during a clearly defined period – period prevalence). As far as in-patient statistics are concerned incidence is likely, therefore, to be measured by the number of admissions that occur in a specific period, prevalence by the number of persons resident at a single point in time or over a specific period. The two types of measure often yield very different results particularly where, as in the case of psychiatric patients, illness is sometimes of lengthy duration, so that incidence may be low, but prevalence quite high.

Age and gender

Epidemiological data indicate significant differences in the social distribution of the varying types of mental illness. Overall, for instance, post-war patient statistics have shown higher rates of in-patient admission for women than for men at all ages over 15 with estimates suggesting that one in six women and one in nine men will at some time in their lives be psychiatric in-patients.[105] Data on in-patient admissions by age and gender are set out in Table 4 below, which also gives a breakdown into first and readmissions. The same table shows that although admission rates are highest among the over 75s and lowest among those under 15, they do not increase in a simple linear fashion with age. First admissions increase up to the 25 to 34 age group and then dip before increasing markedly from 65 onwards. With readmissions the initial increase with age continues up to the 25 to 44 age group for men and the 45 to 54 age group for women, and the decline in rates is then only small before the rates increase again from 65 onwards.

The variation in the gender differential in admission rates according

Table 4   Admissions to psychiatric beds in England, rates per 100,000 population for 1981

Age	ALL ADMISSIONS		FIRST ADMISSIONS		READMISSIONS	
	Male	Female	Male	Female	Male	Female
0–9	16	8	11	5	6	2
10–14	37	33	23	22	14	11
15–19	134	180	66	86	69	94
20–24	340	351	118	126	222	225
25–34	460	496	120	143	340	353
35–44	466	582	115	131	351	450
45–54	398	589	95	119	303	470
55–64	377	576	93	122	284	454
65–74	447	666	139	171	308	495
75 and over	882	1071	352	384	530	687
All ages	329	460	97	127	232	333

Source: In-patient statistics from the Mental Health Inquiry for England, 1981, Table A1.

Table 5   Ratio of female to male admission rates for 1981

Age	All admissions	First admissions	Readmissions
0–9	0.50	0.45	0.33
10–14	0.89	0.95	0.78
15–19	1.34	1.30	1.36
20–24	1.03	1.06	1.01
25–34	1.07	1.19	1.03
35–44	1.24	1.13	1.28
45–54	1.47	1.25	1.55
55–65	1.52	1.31	1.59
65–74	1.48	1.23	1.60
75 and over	1.21	1.09	1.29
All ages	1.39	1.30	1.43

to age can be seen more clearly in Table 5 which gives the ratio of female to male rates. The ratios are largest in the readmission figures for those aged 45 to 74. Some of the factors that may contribute to such gender differentials are discussion in Chapter 4.

Residence data show a rather different picture as can be seen in Table 6. On the one hand the rates increase steadily with age as a proportion of patients from earlier admissions remain to add to the prevalence rates for the older age groups. This increasing prevalence of psychiatric morbidity with age is also shown in community surveys.[106] On the other hand, despite their lower admission rates, male residence rates are higher than female up to the age of 65 (with the exception of the 15 to 19 age group). This is because men contribute somewhat disproportionately to the long-stay residents as Table 7 shows.

Table 6   Residents of psychiatric beds, average of estimated rates per 100,000 population for the years 1972-6, and female to male ratio of the average rates.

	Male	Female	F/M
0–9	4.8	1.8	0.38
10–14	12.2	8.8	0.72
15–19	32.8	38.0	1.16
20–24	71.8	65.2	0.91
25–34	103.4	80.4	0.78
35–44	157.4	119.2	0.76
45–54	278.0	201.6	0.73
55–64	364.6	303.6	0.83
65–74	448.8	541.2	1.21
75 and over	650.2	1100.0	1.69
All ages	173.8	218.2	1.26

Source: *In-patient statistics from the Mental Health Enquiry for England, 1976*, Table A5.

Table 7   Resident patients by set and duration of stay, 1976, percentage distribution

	Under 1 year	1–2 years	2–3 years	3–4 years	5 years and over
Persons	32.1	8.4	5.6	7.6	46.3
Male	29.5	7.3	4.6	6.8	51.8
Female	34.0	9.3	6.3	8.3	42.1

Source: Calculated from data in Table A6 of the *In-patient Statistics from the Mental Health Enquiry for England, 1976*, HMSO 1979.

As Table 8 shows the majority of all those admitted to a psychiatric bed now stay a relatively short time, over half leaving in under a month, and over 90 per cent leaving within a year. But the small proportion who stay for a longer period contribute disproportionately to the resident population at any point in time and produce the situation shown in Table 7, where nearly half the residents have been in-patients for five years or more.

In general practice it is the 25 to 64 year olds who have the highest episode and consultation rates for diagnosed mental disorders and the difference between male and female rates is greater than it is among psychiatric in-patients with women's rates being more than double those of men. The data are given in Table 9.

The size and nature of the gender differentials also varies according to the type of mental illness, with women showing especially high incidence rates for neuroses and affective disorders in both in-patient and general practice samples.[107] The gender differential is rather smaller for the psychotic conditions and for organic mental illnesses such as senile dementia, though female rates are still generally higher than male. The differential is, however, reversed for the substance use disorders such as alcoholism, drug dependence, and the alcohol and drug-induced psychoses, as well as for certain behavioural and personality disorders such as psychopathy and sexual deviation. The obvious exception in this group is anorexia nervosa, which as the description given earlier in the chapter shows, is regarded as a distinctively, though not exclusively, female condition.

Table 8   Discharges and deaths by duration of stay, 1972–6: percentage distribution

	Under 1 month	1–3 months	3 months –1 year	1–3 years	3–5 years	5–6 years	6 years and over
Persons	52.1	30.3	10.2	2.2	2.1	1.0	2.1

Source: *In-patient Statistics from the Mental Health Enquiry for England, 1976*, Table A4.1, HMSO, 1979.

Table 9 Episode and consultation rates for diagnosed mental disorders, and ratio of female to male rates

| | EPISODE RATES | | | CONSULTATION RATES | | |
Age	Male	Female	Ratio F/M	Male	Female	Ratio F/M
0–4	59.0	51.5	0.87	77.1	62.6	0.81
5–14	41.1	46.6	1.13	59.2	69.6	1.81
15–24	69.6	176.7	2.54	120.4	307.8	2.56
25–44	115.9	281.8	2.43	247.1	578.5	2.34
45–64	119.3	257.0	2.15	288.6	570.8	1.98
65–74	83.0	207.7	2.50	195.1	456.0	2.34
75 and over	92.8	162.7	1.75	197.8	366.8	1.85
All ages	89.1	195.2	2.19	186.2	400.5	2.15

Source: *Morbidity Statistics from General Practice, 1970–1*, Table 10.

One consequence of the strong association between gender and type of mental illness is that as the universe of conditions included in any study varies so does the size of the gender differential. This is one reason why the gender differential is greater in general practice samples than it is among psychiatric admissions, since neurotic conditions and affective disorders have a more important role in the former than the latter. For example, psychoses, both organic and functional, account for only some 6 per cent of the mental illness episodes diagnosed by general practitioners; they constitute some 43 per cent of the diagnoses of those admitted as in-patients.[108] The same association also helps to account for the fact that young boys generally show higher rates of mental illness than young girls, since among children it is a restricted group of behavioural deviations – bed-wetting, hyperactivity, violence and aggression – that receive much of the psychiatric attention.[109]

Marital status

Marital status, too, is clearly related to the rates of mental illness of patient populations, especially for in-patients, and the single have higher rates than the married. The data for psychiatric residents in England and Wales in 1971 are given in Table 10. A number of studies have suggested, however, that the differences in rates of mental illness in psychiatric in-patients by marital status are at least in part due to factors that affect whether someone who becomes ill is admitted to hospital and how quickly she or he is discharged – factors such as the existence of a family network to provide care and support.[110] Significantly community surveys produce less clear cut differences by marital status.[111] Further, as Table 10 shows, among psychiatric in-patients gender differentials also

Table 10   Patients resident in mental illness hospitals and units by sex and marital status, England and Wales, 31 December 1971 (rates per 100,000)

Marital status	Male	Female
Single	704	685
Married*	91	127
Widowed	535	647
Divorced	835	780
All	272	322

Notes: * Includes 1562 'separated' males, and 1898 'separated' females.
Source: *Census of Patients in Mental Illness Hospitals and Units in England and Wales at the end of 1971,* Table 3.

vary according to marital status with men having higher residence rates among the single, and women higher rates among the married. The American sociologist, Walter Gove, has used this finding, obtained across a range of patient statistics, to argue that the higher levels of mental illness observed in women are due to the deleterious consequences of marriage for women as compared with men.[112] However, not only is the theoretical basis of Gove's argument questionable, but recent work has suggested that at least in some community samples there is no relationship between the marital status of respondents and their psychological symptom levels.[113]

Social class

Data on the social class of patient populations and those with high symptom levels are less systematic. However a number of specially conducted surveys across a range of cultural settings have shown a consistent pattern of higher levels of mental illness among those of lower social status.[114] The classic study carried out in New Haven in the 1950s by Hollingshead, a sociologist, and Redlich, a psychiatrist, *Social Class and Mental Illness*, studied patients in all types of psychiatric treatment settings.[115] It showed that the percentage of patients from Class V, the lowest socio-economic group, was more than double the percentage of persons in that class in the population as a whole. The data are given in Table 11. Numerous subsequent studies have also produced a class gradient, and similar differences have been found in a number of community surveys.[116] One explanation offered for this type of distribution of mental illness is that individuals who become mentally ill are likely to drift down the social structure and so be over-represented in the lowest socio-economic groups, and there is some evidence that this does occur, especially in the case of more severe forms of mental illness.[117] Alternatively it has been suggested that class position is

Table 11   Class status and the distribution of patients and non-patients in the population

| Class | POPULATION (PER CENT) | |
	Patients	Non-patients
I	1.0	3.0
II	7.0	8.4
III	13.7	20.4
IV	40.1	49.8
V	38.2	18.4
	n = 1891	n = 236,940

Source: Hollingshead and Redlich, Social Class and Mental Illness, 1958, p. 199.

causally related to the development of mental illness and that persons towards the bottom of the social structure may have to cope with more difficult circumstances and events in their lives – more stresses – and so are more likely to become mentally ill.[118] Again, studies have provided some empirical support for such arguments.[119] One significant finding of the Hollingshead and Redlich study, however, was that there was a striking association between class position and the distribution of neuroses and psychoses in the patient population. Whereas in Classes I and II some 65 per cent of patients were diagnosed as neurotic, in Class V the figure was as low as 10 per cent.[120] Further analysis showed that whereas the prevalence of the psychoses increased with declining social position, the prevalence of neuroses was positively associated with socio-economic status.[121] Such findings raise questions both about differences between social classes in the perception of potential psychiatric problems and in the willingness to seek help for them, as well as in the evaluations made by psychiatrists – a matter we consider in the following section.[122]

Differences in the distribution of the patient population according to social characteristics are matched by differences in the treatment given to psychiatric patients of varying age, gender and social status. A number of studies have shown, for example, that among persons with diagnosed neurotic conditions, proportionately more women than men are prescribed psychotropic drugs.[123] However, proportionately more men with some diagnosed mental disorder are referred for specialist help.[124] The same holds for younger patients in comparison with older ones.[125] Similarly, there are differences in the type of treatment given according to the socio-economic status of the patient. In the United States, for instance, the Hollingshead and Redlich study showed not only that lower-class patients were treated in different psychiatric facilities (state rather than private), they were also given different forms of therapy (directive and physical therapies rather than psychodynamic therapies).[126] This again raises questions about the way in which psychiatrists evaluate their patients and whether their judgements may be biased in certain ways – questions which have been examined most thoroughly in connection with diagnosis. It is this matter that I now want to examine.

Psychiatric diagnosis and evaluation in practice

The importance attached to diagnosis within psychiatry varies as does the willingness to adhere to the national or international classifications, and the methods used in diagnostic assessment. Some psychiatrists, such as those concerned about the complex dynamics of personality functioning, may attach less importance to the nomenclature of diagnostic categories than to developing an initial formulation of personality dynamics.[127] For many psychiatrists, however, diagnosis is an important step in clinical work that provides guidance for subsequent action by the information that it offers about the likely course of the illness, suitable treatment, including the necessity for hospitalization and so forth.[128] Moreover, it is not considered an easy task, and for many it represents the centre point of clinical judgement, drawing upon all the skills and experience of the practitioner.[129] As in medicine the objective is to produce a diagnosis by examining a diverse range of information and making inferences from it. This information may include the individual's past illness history and illnesses among family members, the onset of symptoms, their development, the current signs and symptoms of illness and so forth. The intellectual process required is a form of hypothesis testing in which alternatives are considered and ruled out and the diagnosis sooner or later established (although there are clearly different styles of reasoning involved in making diagnoses).[130]

Within medicine an important distinction is made between the symptoms of illness – the patient's subjective experience of illness – and signs of illness, the doctor's measures of illness.[131] The patient's subjective experience of feeling hot and cold constitutes a symptom: the measurement of a raised bodily temperature with a thermometer a sign. The ready availability of many measures of bodily illness does not, however, make diagnosis straightforward, since the signs of illness are rarely specific and there is still considerable scope for interpretation, not only of what the combination of signs indicate, but also of the measures themselves. Lung X-rays, for instance, provide information about the state of the lungs, but deciding whether they indicate some pathology involves judgement and interpretation. Diagnosis is therefore subject to error, especially under the routine conditions of clinical practice that may require rapid decisions to be made.[132] Some indication of the extent of the diagnostic problem has been provided by a study comparing hospital diagnoses, the cause of death given on death certificates, and the clinical findings on autopsy.[133] The study showed that in 15 per cent of cases the main diagnosis (that is the principle condition for which the patients had been admitted) was not confirmed by the autopsy findings, and in 42 per cent of cases the cause of death given on the death certificate was not confirmed by the autopsy. And this was for a hospital sample, where a broad range of diagnostic testing would often have been involved.

In the case of psychiatric diagnosis there is the added problem of measuring psychological as opposed to physical functioning. The traditional psychiatric diagnostic examination places little reliance on measuring instruments and far more on directly eliciting the signs of the patient's mental state and on taking a case history that covers family background, previous morbidity, the onset of the illness, its development and current symptoms.[134] Kendell, a psychiatrist with a particular interest in the diagnostic process, describes the typical diagnostic situation as:

one in which a clinician, armed with a variable amount of background information, like the patient's age and occupation and source of referral, holds a free-ranging interview with the patient, lasting anything from twenty minutes to an hour or more. In this interview he seeks to establish a diagnosis by asking the patient first about his current symptoms and difficulties and then about an ever widening circle of other experiences and events, past and present.[135]

Hence many psychiatric assessments are made on the basis of what patients say about themselves without much support in the way of more formal measures. This is especially true of psychiatric assessments made by general practitioners, but also applies to many of the initial diagnostic assessments made by hospital psychiatrists.[136] Those who are admitted are, however, likely to be given further diagnostic tests, both physical and psychological. They may, if some organic mental disorder is suspected, be given an electro-encephalogram (EEG) and a brain scan which will themselves require skilled interpretation. They are likely, too, to be given various psychological tests for diagnostic purposes, including tests of intellectual functioning and personality.[137] The latter tests are usually given by psychologists with special training in the clinical field (clinical psychologists) rather than psychiatrists. Although some of the tests have a standardized format they usually require considerable interpretation when they are used for diagnostic purposes. Many of the intelligence and personality tests were developed in the 1920s and 1930s but the employment of clinical psychologists in psychiatric hospitals is largely a post-war phenomenon.[138] Various standardized diagnostic instruments have recently been developed, more often for research than for clinical purposes, though some are being used as an aid to diagnosis in clinical contexts, and most require patients to answer a fixed set of pre-coded questions which then yield scores on a range of dimensions of psychological functioning. They vary in the extent to which they involve clinical judgement in interpreting the results.[139] They also vary in the extent to which they try and measure pathology in terms of specific diagnostic categories or make a more general symptomatic assessment of mental pathology.[140]

Reliability

Given the difficulty of assessing symptoms of psychiatric pathology in any very precise way and of making diagnostic inferences it is not perhaps surprising to find that the reliability of psychiatric diagnosis has generally been poor.[141] However the implications and significance of this finding are more debatable. The evidence of the low reliability of psychiatric diagnosis began to accumulate in the 1930s and came from a range of studies of varying design.[142] First, from studies that have compared the independent diagnoses given to the same set of patients by different psychiatrists using the same set of diagnostic categories (the method of inter-observer agreement). Second, from studies that have compared the consistency of the diagnoses given to a particular group of patients over time (the consistency of diagnosis over time). And third, from studies that have compared the distribution of diagnostic categories assigned to comparable samples of patients (frequency of diagnostic categories for comparable samples).

A study using the inter-observer agreement method carried out by Kreitman and his colleagues, published in 1961, illustrates some of the findings of this type of research.[143] Kreitman compared the evaluation of ninety consecutive new referrals to the Chichester mental health service in England. Each case was independently examined by two psychiatrists: first by one of a group of three consultant psychiatrists, and then, three to four days later, by one of two psychiatrists from the Medical Research Council Unit. The interviews were unstructured and the two sets of psychiatrists were provided with the same background information about each case, and the assessment of the first group of psychiatrists was not made available to the second (an obvious restriction if the second is not to be biased, though it has not always been enforced). Each psychiatrist worked with an agreed list of eleven diagnostic categories (only one of which could be scored) and it was found that there was agreement in 63 per cent of cases. Agreement was highest on the affective psychoses, organic conditions and psychoses of old age, and lowest on schizophrenia, anxiety states and neurotic depression. Agreement on specific symptoms was generally lower. Each psychiatrist had a check list of twenty-eight common symptoms and was asked to mark for each patient which symptoms they considered important in deciding the diagnosis and disposition of the patients. Overall agreement (concordance) was 46 per cent. Agreement was, however, very variable. It ranged from 85 per cent for the symptom of depression to as low as 20 per cent for 'depersonalization', with symptoms such as anxiety, hallucinations, and sexual problems producing agreement in the region of 50 per cent. The findings from other studies using the method of inter-observer agreement are summarized in Table 12.

Although different studies have not produced exactly the same results (part of the difference is due to the different methods they use, the number of diagnostic categories offered, and so on) we can make a number of generalizations from them, which account for much of the variation and detail in the findings. First, as we would expect, psychiatrists are more likely to agree in their use of more general diagnostic categories than in their use of more specific ones. They may

Table 12 Levels of inter-agreement in studies of diagnostic reliability

Experimenter	*Average inter-observer agreement for specific categories of diagnosis (per cent)*	*Average inter-observer agreement for generic categories of diagnosis (per cent)*
Ash	20*; 31.4–43.5†	45.7*; 57.9–67.4†
Beck	54	70
Goldfarb		60
Kreitman	63.3	78.8
Sandifer	57	
Schmidt	55	84
Norris		57–60‡
Seeman	66	

Notes:
* In cases diagnosed by three psychiatrists
† In cases diagnosed by pairs of psychiatrists
‡ Some specific diagnoses were included.
Source: Gostin, 1975, p. 50

well agree that a patient is psychotic but not whether he or she is schizophrenic. Second, there is more agreement over some diagnoses than others. There tends to be most agreement over organic diagnoses, and more agreement over psychotic than neurotic diagnoses – an ordering of agreement that interestingly matches the hierarchical ordering of illnesses that is adopted by some classification schemes. However, there is variation within major groupings: agreement for schizophrenia tends to be lower than that for affective psychoses, for example.

Third, agreement is affected by the level of standardization built into the study. Agreement is greater if psychiatrists use the same classification scheme, draw on the same information about the cases in making their judgement or use a standardized diagnostic instrument, are trained to attach similar importance to specific symptoms and have similar theoretical orientations, levels of clinical experience, and so on. It is relatively easy, therefore, to increase the concordance achieved within studies by standardizing procedures. The way in which agreement can be enhanced is clearly illustrated by a study carried out by the British Medical Research Council's Social Psychiatry Research Unit.[144] The psychiatrists were trained in the use of a version of an elaborated semi-structured diagnostic interviews known as the Present State Examination.[145] 172 patients were then evaluated through a joint interview by two psychiatrists. The two independently agreed on the diagnosis in 84 per cent of cases and partially agreed in a further 7 per cent. Agreement in this study was highest for schizophrenia (92 per cent) and other psychoses (87 per cent), but agreement on neuroses was considerably higher than in previous studies (80 per cent for neurotic depression; 77 per cent for anxiety states).

But how do we interpret such findings? Do they tell us what can and will be achieved in clinical diagnosis in the future or do they highlight the fact that to achieve relatively high concordance conditions very different from those operating in normal clinical practice have to be introduced. There can be no doubt that diagnostic reliability can be improved by further standardization, and this can and will undoubtedly be introduced in many research contexts. The extent to which standardization will be introduced in clinical contexts is more doubtful. Certainly there are definite moves towards standardization at present – the work and development of the International Classification of Diseases is an obvious example. Another is the effort that is put into the development of standardized diagnostic instruments such as the Present State Examination, which can be used in clinical as well as research contexts.

Yet another is the introduction and use of computers as an aid to diagnosis.[146] However, while the need for standardization is clearly recognized in research contexts, it seems likely that in clinical practice psychiatrists will not only want to retain some element of discretion in their use of diagnostic categories (they will continue to argue that particular categorizations should be abandoned and new ones introduced), but they will also want to retain an element of clinical judgement in making their diagnosis. Overall the pressure for consensus and the need for standardization is far weaker in the clinical context, given the commitment to the needs and interests of the individual patient. Consequently, it seems likely that although reliability in clinical contexts may increase, it will never reach the high levels shown in research contexts.

The Temerlin and Rosenhan studies

The limitations and difficulties of psychiatric evaluation have been highlighted by other studies. One study by Temerlin, published in 1968, produced experimental evidence of psychiatrists' suggestibility.[147] A group of ninety-five psychiatrists, clinical psychologists and graduate students in clinical psychology were asked to give their diagnosis of a man after hearing a recording of an interview with him, in which an actor was trained to portray a mentally healthy man. Their diagnosis had to be selected from a list containing ten psychotic diagnoses, ten neuroses, and ten miscellaneous personality types of which one was 'normal or healthy personality'. But before hearing the interview a prestige figure (a high status psychologist) commented that the case was very interesting because 'the patient looked neurotic but actually was quite psychotic'. Only eight out of the ninety-five subjects subsequently diagnosed mental health, with twenty-seven diagnosing some type of psychosis, and the rest some type of neurosis or personality disorder. In contrast twelve out of a control group of twenty-one who did not hear the comment of the prestige figure assessed the man as mentally healthy, and nine assigned him to one of the neurotic or personality disorder categories. Of the three groups the psychiatrists turned out to be the most suggestible and the graduate students the least.

In many respects the findings of this study are relatively easy to explain. The power of suggestion effects has been subject to considerable experimental examination and is not in doubt, and there is no reason to believe that clinicians would be exempt from such effects, although the scientific aura surrounding medicine might lead us to expect more objective assessments.[148] Moreover, the fact that the psychiatrists are so ready to diagnose illness follows from their clinical training with its voluntaristic assumptions that focus, as we have seen, far less on detecting the boundaries of sickness, than on specifying the type of sickness. Psychiatrists also tend to operate with the rule 'when in doubt, diagnose illness' since diagnosing sickness when a person is healthy is regarded as a less dangerous error than asserting someone is healthy when in fact there is something wrong.[149] And this applies to the hierarchy of illnesses too, so that missing serious illness is considered a greater mistake than diagnosing a more serious illness when in fact the person has a less serious one. Clinical values like this arguably play a less important part in the psychologists' role, since they do not have overall clinical responsibility. However, the fact that we can explain the findings does not make them any more reassuring. On the one hand psychiatrists may at times have to rely on the comments and perceptions of family members or nursing staff in making their psychiatric evaluations. They will also often receive comments from general practitioners or previous psychiatrists.[150] On the other hand, even if the judgements of others play little part in their own assessments, the research points clearly to the subjectivity involved in psychiatric, as in many other medical assessments.

The tendency to diagnose illness that is apparently encouraged by clinical training is also clearly illustrated by another study that has provoked even more concern about psychiatric evaluation than Temerlin's work. This is a study by Rosenhan in 1973. [151] Eight 'pseudopatients' had themselves admitted to twelve different mental hospitals in the United States by telephoning the admissions office and complaining that they had been hearing voices. Upon admission, however, the pseudopatients acted normally and made no further complaint of symptoms. Nevertheless in eleven out of twelve instances they were diagnosed as schizophrenic, their normality was never detected by staff and when they were eventually discharged, after an average of some seventeen days in hospital, they were given the label 'schizophrenia in remission'. Again this shows the clinicians' assumption of sickness, as Rosenhan points out. He argues, however, as others have before him, that the balance of dangers is reversed in psychiatry, with the consequences of wrongly identifying sickness outweighing the consequences of claiming a sick person is healthy.

In addition to the predisposition to define sickness, other routine features of clinical practice militated against the detection of the pseudopatients. It tends to be assumed, for instance, that patients do not normally feign sickness, although such a possibility may be considered under certain circumstances, for instance, if extended contact with a particular patient fails to reveal any signs of illness.[152] When clinicians are sensitized to detecting pseudopatients the results may be very different. When staff in one hospital claimed that they would have detected the pseudopatients they were told that in the following three months one or more pseudopatients would attempt to be admitted. During this period some twenty-three out of the 195 patients admitted to the hospital were alleged to be pseudopatients by at least one psychiatrist, although none had tried to gain admission.[153] Despite this ready reversal in the psychiatrists' willingness to detect mental health the findings hardly provide prima facie encouragement as to the psychiatrists' capacity to distinguish the mentally ill from the mentally healthy.

The problems highlighted by Temerlin's and Rosenhan's studies as to the accuracy of psychiatric evaluation in clinical contexts have also been raised by some rather different studies which suggest there may be certain more or less systematic biases in psychiatric evaluation. More specifically it has been suggested that psychiatrists' judgements may be affected by the social class, gender and race as well as the marital status and age of those whose symptoms they are evaluating, so that the same behaviour manifested by two people who differ according to one of these salient social characteristics may not be given the same significance, thereby contributing to the associations between social characteristics and mental illness that have been described. This is a complex question since psychiatric judgements must often take account of the social contexts in which possible symptoms occur, and the cultural expectations for people of different classes, races or genders.[154] However, a number of studies provide evidence of biases in clinical evaluation.[155] Consider, for instance, an early study carried out by William Haase of the interpretation of data obtained from a projective personality test, the Rorscharch, by psychologists.[156] Four pairs of Rorschach protocols were constructed with accompanying case histories distinguished only in terms of socio-economic variables and given to the psychologists for interpretation. Their evaluations systematically favoured those with middle-class histories, who were less likely to be judged 'sicker'. The bias occurred in those parts of the test assessment where more speculation on the part of the psychologist was required in the interpretation of the data and the author argues for the development of more quantitatively verifiable signs of pathology in order to avoid the possibility of projection of bias. However, as we have seen the exercise of clinical judgement, including the interpretation of test results, is likely to remain an important feature of clinical work.

A more recent study by Broverman and colleagues published in 1970 has aroused considerable interest in the issue of psychiatric bias.[157] It found that the stereotypes of the mentally healthy male and the mentally healthy female produced by clinicians were markedly different. According to those stereotypes mentally healthy women differ from healthy men in being

more submissive, less independent, less adventurous, more easily influenced, less aggressive, less competitive, more excitable in minor crises, having their feelings more easily hurt, being more emotional, more conceited about their appearance, less objective, and disliking maths and science.[158]

The authors comment 'This constellation seems a most unusual way of describing any mature, healthy individual', and went on to show that the male stereotype was far closer to that for a mentally healthy adult (sex unspecified) than the female stereotype. The problem with this study from the point of view of psychiatric evaluation is not only that it focuses on stereotypes of mental health rather than mental illness, but also that it provides no direct evidence about their actual use in psychiatric evaluations. We do not know which, if any, of the different stereotypes of mental health would come into play in evaluating the symptomatic behaviour of particular gendered individuals. Are women, for instance, judged by the standard of the general adult stereotype or the female stereotype?[159] Nevertheless, the study indicates that one ground for concern about psychiatric evaluation is the extent to which different standards of health and illness are applied to different categories of people – to men and women, the upper and lower classes, black and whites. And it suggests that the criteria for mental health may be largely a matter of social adjustment – of adjustment to social expectations about differing roles within society. If this is so, then the medical assumption of clear, universal criteria for distinct mental pathologies is called into doubt.

The Broverman study, therefore, raises more questions about what precisely is being measured and assessed by psychiatrists than about the reliability of their assessments. It is validity rather than reliability that is at issue, and reliability (which as we have seen can reach high levels in research contexts) is no guarantee of validity.[160] In looking at the question of validity in the psychiatric field, one area for study is the validity of the specific diagnostic categories of the psychiatric schema – an exercise that Kendell points out has rarely been attempted, though he argues that there is supporting evidence for some of the categories.[161]

More fundamental is the question which concerned the critics of the 1960s, of the basic validity of the concept of mental illness itself. Or in other words the question is 'what is it that psychiatrists are measuring when they identify someone as mentally ill?' It is to the controversies and debates raised by the critics of the 1960s that I now turn.

Notes and references

1 Freidson, 1970a, p. 251.
2 Scull, 1975, p. 221.
3 See Section 2 of the Mental Health Act, 1983.
4 See Mishler *et al.*, 1981, pp. 3–6.
5 ibid., p. 4.
6 Eysenck, 1975, p. 8.
7 Kendell, 1975b. This book uses the terms illness and disease interchangeably although they have rather different connotations. See Boorse, 1975; Brown, 1977.
8 Mishler *et al.*, 1981, p. 4.
9 Kraupl Taylor, 1979, p. 63.
10 See Scadding, 1967; Kendell, 1975a.
11 King, 1954.
12 Scadding, 1967; Kendell, 1975a.
13 See Shryock, 1947; Mishler *et al.*, 1981, pp. 6–9.
14 ibid., Dubos, 1959; Armstrong, unpublished.
15 Dubos, 1959, p. 85.
16 See Kendell, 1975b, Chapter 9.
17 For a discussion of the use of typological models in the psychiatric field, see Strauss 1973, and 1975.
18 Engel, 1977, p. 131.
19 McKeown, 1976b, p. 129.
20 McKeown, 1976a, *passim*.
21 See Hart and Honoré, 1959, especially Chapter 2.
22 The importance of some of these factors in accounting for the historical changes in patterns of infectious illnesses is discussed by McKeown, 1976a.
23 See, for instance, Cairns, 1978, Chapter 8; Creasey, 1981, Chapter 6.
24 Dubos, 1959, p. 129.
25 Foucault, 1973, *passim*.
26 Some of the research is described in Mechanic, 1978, part 3.
27 The Glossary for the ninth revision of the International Classification of Diseases comments 'As far as the terms in the ICD–9 permit, the glossary consists merely of descriptions of symptoms or syndromes. Etiological statements and assumptions have been avoided except where a widespread demand for their inclusion became apparent' (World Health Organisation, 1978, p. 11). See also Kendell, 1975a, p. 93.

28 On the concept of typification, see Schutz, 1964. See also Sudnow, 1965.
29 The changing meaning of the concept of hysteria provides an obvious example, see Veith, 1965.
30 Early categorizations of mental diseases are outlined by Menninger in the Appendix of *The Vital Balance* (1963).
31 Zilboorg, 1941, p. 47.
32 ibid., Chapter 10; Menninger, 1963, pp. 457–64.
33 ibid.
34 World Health Organisation, 1978.
35 Kendell, 1975a, p. 96.
36 The history of the International Classification of Diseases, including the introduction of a classification of mental disorders is briefly outlined by Kendell (1975a, Chapter 7).
37 General Register Office, 1968.
38 Kendell presents a number of reasons why uniformity is unlikely to be achieved in the near future (1975, pp. 84–5).
39 American Psychiatric Association, 1980.
40 See Kendell, 1975a, pp. 100–1.
41 Kendell (ibid.) points out that it is important to distinguish an axis from a dimension.
42 The first separate institution for idiots was opened at Highgate in 1848.
43 Mental Health Act, 1953; Mental Health Act, 1983.
44 Mental Health Act, 1983, Section 1.
45 Some have argued that it should not be included within the scope of the Mental Health Act; see Department of Health and Social Security, 1978b, pp. 6–8.
46 General Register Office, 1968.
47 Stafford-Clark, 1963, p. 83.
48 See, for instance, Cobb, 1958, Chapter 6.
49 Stafford-Clark defines dementia as 'a true loss of previously existent intellectual power' (1963, p. 84). Senile dementias are those usually occurring after the age of 65 'in which any cerebral pathology other than that of senile atrophic change can be reasonably excluded'; pre-senile dementias are those occurring 'usually before the age of 65 in patients with the relatively rare forms of diffuse or lobar cerebral atrophy' (World Health Organisation, 1978, p. 22).
50 Delirium is 'a temporary state of extreme excitement with restlessness, confused speech, and hallucinations' (Zax and Cowen, 1976, p. 626).
51 World Health Organisation, 1978, p. 21.
52 Zilboorg, 1941, pp. 279–80.
53 ibid., p. 294.
54 See, for instance, the comments on the treatment of senile dementia in Slater and Roth, 1968, p. 610.

55 Neurotic disorders in the DSM–III are included in 'affective, anxiety, somatoform, dissociative and psychosexual disorders', and are not placed together in a separate group (American Psychiatric Association, 1980, p. 17).

56 Freud comments, for instance, 'In a psychosis a loss of reality would necessarily be present, whereas in a neurosis it would seem, this loss would be avoided' (1979, p. 221).

57 Stafford-Clark, 1963, p. 92.

58 Jaspers, 1963, p. 575.

59 World Health Organisation, 1978, p. 21.

60 That is, between explanations that account for the development (genesis) of mental illness in terms of biological factors and those that account for its development in psychological terms.

61 General Register Office, 1968, p. 2.

62 American Psychiatric Association, 1980, p. 10.

63 Freudian ideas are discussed further in Chapters 3 and 9. On behaviourist accounts of the neuroses, see Wolpe, 1958; Eysenck, 1960. A useful evaluation of such behaviourist ideas is provided by Erwin, 1978.

64 The development of the concept of schizophrenia and its more recent use are outlined by Fish, 1962. For a more critical discussion, see Szasz, 1979.

65 ICD-9 Glossary begins its description of schizophrenic psychoses as follows: 'A group of psychoses in which there is a fundamental disturbance of personality, a characteristic distortion of thinking, often a sense of being controlled by alien forces, delusions which may be bizarre, disturbed perception, abnormal affect out of keeping with the real situation, and autism. . . . (World Health Organisation, 1978, pp. 26–7).

66 Fish, 1962, p. 35 and p. 29.

67 ibid., pp. 18–28.

68 Jaspers, 1963, p. 577.

69 Some of the different explanations of schizophrenia are discussed by Clare, 1976, Chapter 5. See also Shields, 1978; Iverson, 1978; and Leff, 1978.

70 ibid.

71 Rosenthal and Kety, 1968; Shields, 1978.

72 Freeman, 1978; Cawley, 1967.

73 Azrin and Ayllon (1978) describe a 'token economy' system which has been used in the rehabilitation of schizophrenic patients. The rehabilitation of such patients is discussed more generally by Bennett, 1978.

74 World Health Organisation, 1978, pp. 29–30.

75 Kendell, 1975, pp. 71–5.

76 Brown and Harris, 1978, p. 24.
77 American Psychiatric Association, 1980.
78 Brown and Harris, 1978.
79 Clare, 1976, pp. 241–4; Davis, 1971; Silverstone and Turner, 1974, Chapter 6.
80 W. Cullen, *First Lines in the Practice of Physic*, Vols. I–IV, 1777–84 (See Hunter and MacAlpine, 1963, pp. 473–8).
81 Freud, 1974, pp. 435–6.
82 World Health Organisation, 1978, p. 35.
83 American Psychiatric Association, 1980, pp. 9–10.
84 World Health Organisation, 1978, p. 35.
85 ibid., p. 36.
86 ibid., p. 36.
87 Breuer and Freud, *Studies on Hysteria*, 1974.
88 World Health Organisation, 1978, p. 35.
89 American Psychiatric Association, 1980, p. 18.
90 See Lader, 1979; Silverstone and Turner, 1974, Chapter 7; Slater and Roth, 1969, Chapter III.
91 See pp. 94–111.
92 World Health Organisation, 1978, p. 38.
93 Mental Health Act, 1983, Section 1.
94 World Health Organisation, 1978, p. 46.
95 See Spector, 1977.
96 Between 1970 and 1981 the number of first admissions for alcohol dependence doubled (Department of Health and Social Security, 1984, Table A3.1).
97 Kendell, 1975, pp. 102–3.
98 World Health Organisation, 1978, p. 13.
99 American Psychiatric Association, 1980.
100 See Reid, 1960; Morris, 1964.
101 Kathleen Jones discusses official mental health statistics in Halsey, 1972, Chapter 11. On the general limitations of health statistics, see Doyal, 1979.
102 See, for instance, Mechanic, 1978, Chapter 9.
103 Some of the problems of case identification are discussed by Mechanic, 1970.
104 Reid, 1960, pp. 26–7.
105 Ennals, 1973, p. 11.
106 Srole *et al.*, 1975, p. 224.
107 See Busfield, 1983; Smith, 1975.
108 Royal College of General Practitioners, 1974, Table 16; Department of Health and Social Security, 1984, Table A2.2.
109 However, see Gove and Herb, 1974.
110 Kreisman and Joy, 1981, summarize some of the literature.
111 See, for instance, Srole *et al.*, 1975, Chapter 12.

112 Gove, 1972.

113 Cochrane, 1983, pp. 52–7.

114 Dohrenwend and Dohrenwend, 1969.

115 Hollingshead and Redlich, 1958.

116 See Dohrenwend and Dohrenwend, 1969; Cochrane, 1983, Chapter 2.

117 Lapouse, Monk and Terris, 1956; Goldberg and Morrison, 1963; Turner and Wagenfeld, 1967; Birtchnell, 1971.

118 Dohrenwend and Dohrenwend, 1969; Turner and Wagenfeld, 1967; Phillips, 1968.

119 ibid.

120 Hollingshead and Redlich, 1958, p. 222.

121 ibid., pp. 229–33.

122 Hollingshead and Redlich (ibid.) provide some data on these issues.

123 Shepherd *et al.*, 1966; Cooperstock, 1971.

124 Goldberg and Huxley, 1980, p. 111.

125 ibid.

126 Hollingshead and Redlich, 1958, Chapter 9.

127 Menninger, 1963.

128 Kendell, 1975, Chapter 1.

129 Slater and Roth, 1969, Chapter 2.

130 Some empirical studies of psychiatric diagnosis as a decision making process are discussed by Kendell, 1975, Chapter 4.

131 MacBryde, 1964.

132 Mechanic, 1978, pp. 105–11.

133 Bussutic, Kemp and Heasman, 1981.

134 See Kendell, 1975, Chapter 4; Slater and Roth, 1969, Chapter 2.

135 Kendell, 1975, pp. 49–50.

136 The assessment of psychiatric morbidity in primary care settings is discussed in detail by Goldberg and Huxley, 1980, Chapter 4.

137 Slater and Roth, 1969, Chapter 2 and *passim*.

138 Department of Health and Social Security, 1975, pp. 76–7.

139 The Present State Examination developed by Wing, Cooper and Sartorius (1974) is one of the best known.

140 Some of the instruments are described by Kendell, 1975, Chapter 10.

141 Reliability in the context of psychiatric diagnoses means 'the ability of psychiatrists to agree upon a diagnosis when viewing the same person or an identical set of symptoms' (Gostin, 1975, p. 37).

142 See Kendell, 1975, Chapter 3; Gostin, 1975, pp. 37–8; Zigler and Phillips, 1961; Mechanic, 1978, pp. 105–11 for discussions of the findings of the studies and the methods used.

143 Kreitman *et al.*, 1961.

144 Wing *et al.*, 1967.

145 Wing, Cooper and Sartorius, 1974.

146 Kendell, 1975, Chapter 11; Scadding, 1967; Duckworth and Kedward, 1978.

147   Temerlin, 1968.
148   The classic studies are those by Asch (1951) and Sherif (1936).
149   Scheff, 1963.
150   This is more true in Britain than in the United States since in Britain a referral from a general practitioner is the usual method of entering psychiatric treatment.
151   Rosenhan, 1973.
152   The notion of malingering may be invoked in this context. On the relationship between hysteria and malingering see Szasz, 1961, pp. 25–30.
153   Rosenhan, 1973.
154   See the points made by Aubrey Lewis, 1955.
155   Goldberg and Huxley (1980, Chapter 4) distinguish between bias and accuracy in psychiatric evaluation. Bias they suggest is a measure of the relation between a doctor's tendency to diagnose psychiatric illness in a patient population and the level of illness in the population as assessed by some psychiatric screening instrument. Doctors with a high bias diagnose more illness than the level predicted by the screening instrument; doctors with a low bias far less. Accuracy is a measure not of the general tendency to diagnose psychiatric illness, but of the match between a doctor's evaluation of cases and the assessment of the same individuals made either by an experienced clinician or a screening instrument. In both cases, however, they focus on characteristics of the doctors that affect bias and accuracy: factors such as age, experience, interest in psychiatry. The authors pay much less attention to the issue of the extent to which social characteristics of the patient affect diagnosis – the issue which concerns me here. From this point of view the interest is in systematic biases in evaluation stemming from patient characteristics rather than variations in levels or bias between individual doctors.
156   Haase, 1964.
157   Broverman *et al.*, 1970.
158   Ibid., pp. 4–5.
159   Gove and his colleagues (Tudor, Tudor and Gove, 1977) argue that different standards are applied in assessing the mental health of men and women, and that the standards for men, since they are closer to the overall ideal of mental health, are more stringent than those for women. However, it may well be that the general adult standard is applied to both men and women, in which case women are more likely to fall short and be judged mentally disturbed, since social expectations encourage conformity to patterns of behaviour that by this standard are not indicative of good mental health.
160   The validity of a measure or assessment refers to 'the extent to which it measures what it is supposed to measure' (Cattell, 1965, p. 84).

Psychologists have developed a number of different procedures for assessing validity. Of particular importance as far as psychiatric categories are concerned is so-called predictive validity, which involves checking initial assessments against subsequent outcomes (Anastasi, 1961, pp. 138–41; Kendell, 1975, pp. 39–48).

161 Kendell, 1975, pp. 39–48.

3 Deviance, social control and mental illness

One alternative to the liberal–scientific conception of psychiatry is provided by the ideas of a number of critics of psychiatry whose work attracted considerable attention in the 1960s. Despite their theoretical and political diversity and their sometimes overt antipathy to one another, these critics earned themselves the common label 'anti-psychiatrists' for their forceful and widely publicized attacks on psychiatry and the concept of mental illness.[1] The best known of the critics, Thomas Szasz in the United States (who explicitly rejects the label anti-psychiatrist) and R. D. Laing in Britain, both psychiatrists and trained psychoanalysts, attacked psychiatry from within the profession; but similar arguments were also developed in a more academic context by sociologists such as T. J. Scheff and the labelling theorists of deviance. United in time and in their attack on psychiatry, these commentators developed ways of thinking about psychiatry that have sufficient similarities to justify treating them together. All share a conception of psychiatry in which mental illness is viewed as a form of socially unacceptable, rule-breaking behaviour, are critical of the medical focus on organic processes in the conceptualization and treatment of mental illness, and consider psychiatry to be an institution of social control.

Some of the precursors of this conception of psychiatry and mental illness are to be found both in the ideas of psychologists of opposing theoretical persuasion who pointed to the limitations of psychiatric understanding and methods, and in the work of a number of sociologists and anthropologists who have examined the nature of concepts of mental health and illness in some detail. I shall begin by considering the ideas of these writers and then describe the critique of psychiatry that developed in the 1960s, before concluding with an evaluation of their central arguments.

Twentieth-century precursors

The increasing reliance of medicine during the nineteenth century on the natural sciences led a number of twentieth-century writers to question the impact of medical ideas on psychiatric work, and to assert the need for a distinctively psychological approach to some (though not usually all) mental illnesses and for a reassessment of the nature of psychiatric knowledge.[2] Such ideas have constituted an important underpinning of other, more radical critiques of psychiatry.

In his development and advocacy of psychoanalysis Freud, whose impact on psychiatric thought and practice will be considered in a later chapter, explicitly concerned himself with the issue of the direction and nature of psychiatry.[3] He believed that science did and should provide the basis of psychiatry, and he believed, moreover, that science could and should be modelled on the principles of positive science – though whether he actually followed these principles is more debatable.[4] Nevertheless, he contended, the scientific base of psychiatry was too narrow. This was particularly apparent in the case of disorders such as the neuroses, which had, he asserted, no ascertainable physical cause. The explanation and treatment of these disorders required an examination of the individual's psychological experiences – especially unconscious wishes, feelings and inner conflicts and the whole realm of unconscious meaning.[5] This could and should be provided by what he regarded as the new science of psychoanalysis, not by subjects like anatomy and physiology. Medical training, he argued, paid too much attention to the physical origins and treatment of mental illness and too little to the psychological:

in his medical school a doctor receives a training which is more or less the opposite of what he would need as a preparation for psycho-analysis. His attention has been directed to objectively ascertainable facts of anatomy, physics and chemistry . . . . His interest is not aroused in the mental side of vital phenomena . . . . Only psychiatry is supposed to deal with the disturbances of mental functions; but we know in what manner and with what aims it does so. It looks for the somatic determinants of mental disorders and treats them like the other causes of illness.[6]

Freud did not contend, however, that the science of psychoanalysis should simply be incorporated into psychiatry. Indeed, he thought that this would diminish its stature and it would be treated merely as another method of treatment and not as a distinctive science.

For we do not consider it at all desirable for psycho-analysis to be swallowed up by medicine and to find its last resting-place in a textbook of psychiatry under the heading 'Methods of Treatment', alongside of

procedures such as hypnotic suggestion, autosuggestion and persuasion . . . .
It deserves a better fate and it may be hoped, will meet with one. As a
'depth-psychology', a theory of the mental unconscious, it can become
indispensible to all the sciences which are concerned with the evolution of
human civilization and its major institutions such as art, religion, and the
social order.[7]

Consequently, he did not feel it was either necessary or desirable for all
doctors to be trained in psychoanalysis or for all analysts to be medically
qualified.[8] In effect he argued that there should be some division of
labour between psychiatrists and psychoanalysts in the treatment of
mental disorders, both drawing on their respective body of scientific
knowledge.

A similar division of specialists between the physical and psychological
aspects of mental illness (with the latter also located outside the medical
umbrella) has also been advocated by the opposing group of behaviourist
psychologists. Eysenck, one of Freud's most severe detractors, recommends a psychological training for those responsible for the care and
treatment of neuroses and personality disorders.[9] And since cost and
efficiency prohibit the full training of doctors in both physical and
psychological science, each should have their own sphere of competence,
with a divorce in psychiatry between its organic and psychological parts.
Eysenck, moreover, takes the argument further than Freud; if psychology
can provide the explanations and treatment of some mental disorders
then certain medical ideas and concepts are misguided and unhelpful
and should be abandoned. He objects to the language of sickness, illness
and pathology, to the idea of disease entities, and to the psychiatric
classifications of mental illnesses. He prefers instead to talk of abnormal
behaviour or deviance and to characterize patients along a series of
personality dimensions.[10] In this respect Eysenck gives voice to some of
the ideas more commonly associated with Szasz, Laing and the labelling
theories of deviance. However, one crucial concern of these authors is
missing: their deep-seated wish to examine the ideological role played
by psychiatry and to question both the supposed objectivity and value
neutrality of its science and the benign and beneficial nature of its
practice. These concerns follow from their belief that mental illness as
human action must be conceptualized and understood in very different
ways from those adopted by positive scientists. For Eysenck the notion of
mental illness is inappropriate because it suggests some underlying
physical pathology generating the behavioural symptoms of mental
disorder. For Szasz and Laing it is inappropriate above all because it

makes a moral judgement under the guise of a scientific one.

However, the argument that notions of mental health and illness incorporate value judgements does not originate from either Szasz or Laing; earlier commentators developed the theme in a variety of ways. Some pointed to the way in which conceptions of mental health and illness are based on personal conceptions of what is ideal or desirable human behaviour; some to the lack of consensus in conceptions of mental health and illness; others to the difficulty of distinguishing mental health and illness from social conformity and nonconformity; yet others to the cultural relativity of notions of mental health and illness. All concerned themselves not so much with the problems of measuring mental health and illness but with the prior problem of definition.

Anthropologists were among the first to express concern about the concepts of mental health and illness. In the early 1930s a number of them began to argue, on the basis of their fieldwork observations, that what constituted mental illness varied from society to society; what was normal in one culture might well be regarded as abnormal in another, and mental health or illness was a matter of cultural adaptation.[11] Hallucinations, for instance, among Plains Indians in Mexico would be considered normal, whereas in our own society they would be regarded as symptomatic of mental illness. We need to start, therefore, by looking at what is considered desirable within a particular society, not by specifying certain patterns of behaviour as pathological for all societies. Ruth Benedict, writing in 1934, put the argument in this way:

Obviously, adequate personal adjustment does not depend upon following certain motivations and eschewing others. The correlation is in a different direction. Just as those are favoured whose congenial responses are closest to that behaviour which characterizes their society, so those are disoriented whose responses fall in that arc of behaviour which is not capitalized by their culture. These abnormals are those who are not supported by the institutions of their civilization. They are the exceptions who have not easily taken the traditional forms of their culture.

For a valid comparative psychiatry, these disoriented persons who have failed to adapt themselves adequately to their cultures are of first importance. The issue in psychiatry has been too often confused by starting from a fixed list of symptoms instead of from the study of those whose characteristic reactions are denied validity in their society.[12]

Such arguments did not, of course, go unchallenged. Wegrocki in 1939 produced one well-known reply in which he tried to refine the argument about cultural relativism and mental health.[13] It was true, he argued, that abnormal behaviour is called abnormal because it deviates from the behaviour of the general group. But it is not the fact of deviation that makes it abnormal but its causal background. Thus hallucinations among Plains Indians are not abnormal while those of schizophrenics are. For it is not the fact of the social sanction that makes the former normal, but the fact that it does not have the background of a symptomatic resolution of inner conflict as in schizophrenia. The one may be analogous to the other but it is not homologous.

The claim that definitions of mental health and illness involve assessments of the normality of the psychological processes underlying behaviour is a theme to which other authors return.[14] It leaves untouched, however, the question of whether judgements of the psychological background of behaviour are themselves impregnated with values relative to the culture or the personal beliefs of the observer. Direct claims that moral and ethical judgements are involved in notions of health and illness were, however, made by a number of sociologists and social scientists. The sociologist Kingsley Davis, for instance, in an influential paper published in 1938 analysed the premises of the 'mental hygiene' movement that developed in the United States in the early decades of the twentieth century.[15] This movement had, he argued, taken over the values of the Protestant Ethic which had been accepted in American society 'not simply as the basis for conscious preachment but also as the unconscious system of premises upon which its "scientific" analysis and its conception of mental health are based'.[16] Normality, he contended, has an ethical meaning of which the mental hygienist is unaware. Hence

when specific advice is given concerning life problems, the conduct prescribed is ordinarily such as would conform to our ideals, not to the statistical average. The mental hygienist tends to justify such advice, however, not on moral but on rational or 'scientific' grounds.[17]

What Kingsley Davis emphasizes is not only the ethical, and, thereby, ideological nature of ideas about what constitutes mental health, but also the failure of those who hold them to recognize this – an observation that is also central to Szasz's concern about the concept of mental health. Both point to the way in which ethical judgements are presented as scientific ones, though the implication for Szasz, that they should be withdrawn from the arena of medicine because it legitimates their scientific guise, is not developed by Davis.[18]

While Kingsley Davis drew attention to the ideological nature of the ideas of a particular mental health movement, Marie Jahoda argued two decades later that there was little consensus amongst professionals in their attempts to formulate positive conceptions of mental health.[19] She identified four distinct strands in positive definitions of mental health: normality of behaviour; adjustment to the environment; unity of personality; and correct perception of reality. All, she contended, involve value judgements, a point reiterated by Barbara Wootton writing in the same period, who had this to say about conceptions of mental health:

Most of them with their visions of 'inner harmonious adjustment', of 'trustfulness' and of 'socially considerate behaviour' – not to mention happy family life, successful sex adjustment, training for citizenship, economic independence and freedom from industrial unrest – most of them are clearly attempts to formulate conceptions of the ideal, under the guise of the healthy, man. They express the personal value-judgements of their authors, rather than scientifically established facts.[20]

The difficulties of formualting positive conceptions of health, whether mental or physical, have, however, often been recognized. More important are claims about the ideological nature of concepts of mental illness. Wootton makes the case for the involvement of value judgements by arguing for the impossibility of drawing clear boundaries between behaviour that is symptomatic of mental illness and anti-social conduct. Mental illness, she argues, is supposed to be an objectively identifiable phenomenon like physical illness, independent of antisocial conduct and, indeed, a potential excuse for the latter.[21] In practice, however, it is all too often the failure to conform to social norms that constitutes the main evidence of mental illness. An attempt at suicide is taken as evidence, sometimes in itself, of mental illness, or frequent divorce and remarriage as evidence of psychological instability, with the result that moral and medical judgements become inextricably confused. The conclusion for Wootton is that the attempt to assimilate mental and physical disorders and to treat both alike breaks down.[22] This is the case reiterated, reinforced and reformulated in the critiques of the 1960s.

The 1960s critiques

The focal point of Szasz's critique is the notion of mental illness, and, like earlier commentators, he asserts the value-laden nature of concepts of mental health and illness. As he puts it 'we call people physically ill when their bodily functioning violates certain norms; similarly we call people mentally ill when their personal conduct violates certain ethical, political and social norms'.[23] Elsewhere he elaborates the point in this way:

The concept of illness, whether bodily or mental, implies deviation from some clearly defined norm. In the case of physical illness, the norm is the structural and functional integrity of the human body. Thus, although the desirability of physical health, as such, is an ethical value, what health is can be stated in anatomical and physiological terms. What is the norm, deviation from which is regarded as mental illness? This question cannot be easily answered. But whatever this norm may be, we can be certain of only one thing: namely, that it must be stated in terms of psychosocial, ethical, and legal concepts.[24]

The notion of mental illness is, Szasz claims, but a metaphor for what should, more accurately, be called 'problems in living', for except for the obvious organic mental illnesses (those with identifiable physical causes) which would be better thought of as brain diseases, what is termed mental illness is actually behaviour that breaks social rules. Consequently to talk of illness mystifies what is in fact a moral judgement, for the term illness suggests a scientific and objective assessment of sickness based on identifiable physical pathology. On the contrary it is a moral judgement and should be recognized as such.

Szasz's claim that to define a person as mentally ill is to make a moral judgement is not based, like the claims of Kingsley Davis and Barbara Wootton, on consideration of the way in which concepts of mental health and illness are used in practice. His is an analytical point, derived from the fact that it is human thought and action that is being judged, not physical functioning. Hence, by definition, the standards must be ethical, social and political, since, he asserts, human behaviour can only be properly understood by reference to social rules and cannot be analysed in terms of scientific, causal laws. The claim that mental illness involves rule violation stems from his underlying philosophy of social science.

Szasz goes on to argue that what we regard as the symptoms of mental illness should not be viewed as outside the individual's responsibility, as the term illness implies, though the individual may have problems and benefit from help in solving them. To talk of sickness is inappropriate as far as human behaviour is concerned; it exempts the individual from responsibility, and individual liberty and autonomy are thereby reduced. Szasz is an eighteenth-century libertarian who objects to the paternalistic control that psychiatry exercises.[25] For him the autonomy and liberty of the individual are crucial and in his ideal society they would be at a maximum: control by others would be replaced by self-control. While Szasz points to the social control that psychiatry effects in the name of care and cure, his objection is not to the control of behaviour as such, but to the fact that the control is hidden and unacknowledged, and is exercised by others rather than the individual. If there is to be social control (that is control by other people in their own or society's interests) – and he believes in the need for some social control – then its real nature should be visible. This is one reason why he objects so strongly to the compulsory commitment of the mentally ill, which he calls 'a crime against humanity', for he believes this type of repressive social control is alien to the domain of humanistic, scientific medicine.[26] The end result of this distortion is that psychiatry, far from being beneficial and humane, results in 'dehumanization, oppression and persecution of the citizen branded "mentally ill" '.[27]

Szasz has developed his critique in a number of different directions: historically through comparisons of the present-day treatment of the mentally ill with the earlier persecution of witches; substantively into other areas of deviant behaviour now dealt with by the medical profession such as alcoholism, obesity and drug addiction; and institutionally into studies of the legal procedures governing commit-ment of the mentally ill, patient rights, and so on.[28] He contends that medicine has become the new religion of our society and that those labelled mentally ill, alcoholics or drug addicts are the scapegoats of society, just as witches formerly were. Szasz does not, however, provide us with any clear theoretical account of why medicine should be the new religion, why the mentally ill should be the new scapegoats, or indeed why there need to be any scapegoats at all; we are simply asked to accept his assertions that any society has its scapegoats, its religious beliefs and its false gods.[29]

R. D. Laing has been equally concerned with the evaluative content of judgements of mental illness; however, his theoretical orientation differs markedly from Szasz's and his ideas have altered more over time.[30] His dominant and continuing theme has been the need to understand and make intelligible the thoughts, feelings and behaviour of the person who is said to be disturbed, an injunction very much in line with the psychoanalytic assumption of the meaningfulness of all human behaviour, but also founded in Laing's case on the philosophical base of existentialism.[31] Initially his emphasis was on understanding the subjective (and mainly conscious) experience of the schizophrenic; later it was on understanding the behaviour within its social context, in particular the context of the family. Here Laing incorporated the ideas of a number of American social scientists that schizophrenia is a response to disturbed relationships within the family, though he rejected the scientific, causal language of their analyses.[32] Laing's stress on the intelligibility of supposedly pathological behaviour led him like others to question the value neutrality of judgements of sanity and insanity. He uses, for example, an account of a clinical examination provided by Kraepelin, whose influence on psychiatric classifications I have already mentioned, to argue that unintelligibility and irrationality – and hence our judgements of sanity and insanity depend on looking at a situation without taking the individual's experience into account:

Here are a man and a young girl. If we see the situation purely in terms of Kraepelin's point of view, it all immediately falls into place. He is sane, she is insane: he is rational, she is irrational. This entails looking at the patient's actions out of context of the situation as she experienced it. But if we take Kraepelin's actions . . . he tries to stop her movements, stands in front of her with arms outspread, tries to force a piece of bread out of her hand, sticks a needle in her forehead, and so on – out of the context of the situation as experienced and defined by him, how extraordinary *they* are![33]

What counts as sanity and insanity, Laing contends, is a matter of normative consensus, and the statistically normal may be regarded as sane and rational regardless of its characteristics (i.e. whether it is more sensible, morally desirable, beneficial and so on).

From an ideal vantage point on the ground, a formation of planes may be observed in the air. One plane may be out of formation. But the whole formation may be off course. The plane that is 'out of formation' may be abnormal, bad or 'mad' from the point of view of the formation. But the formation itself may be bad or mad from the point of view of the ideal observer. The plane that is out of formation may be also more or less off course than the formation itself is.[34]

All too often the 'sane' person is simply someone who adjusts to the world as it is without question. Building, therefore, on the view that in practice what counts as mental illness is a matter of adaptation to cultural norms, Laing recommends that we question the society's values. Schizophrenia, he then goes on to claim, should be viewed as a voyage of discovery in which individuals find themselves through a natural process of healing.[35] Laing's ideas came, therefore, to involve not only a commitment to the rationality of the 'mad' person, with the consequential rejection of the twin assumptions of value neutrality and humanism of the liberal–scientific conception of psychiatry, but also a rejection of the particular values that judge people insane and the institutions such as the family which constrain them. Hence his alignment with left-wing radicals and his association with a politics far removed from Szasz's strongly conservative sympathies.[36]

Nevertheless, despite the theoretical and political divergence of Szasz and Laing, they develop common and interrelated themes and concerns. In the first place their critiques of psychiatry are, as I have indicated, founded on a common premise, that in studying the phenomena of mental disorder we are studying human thought and action. The failings of psychiatry, they suggest, follow from its failure to recognize this fundamental point. For Szasz it means that in any explanation of functional, that is, non-organic mental illnesses, the ideas and ways of thinking of the natural sciences are inappropriate, While physical processes can be explained in terms of cause and effect (the type of explanation favoured by the natural sciences) human action can only be explained and dealt with in terms of rule following, role playing and an analysis of meaning and communicative languages.[37] For Laing the implication is that the behaviour must have meaning and be intelligible, if only we bother to listen and to understand, and he, too, explicitly rejects any causal explanation of human behaviour emphasizing instead experience and subjectivity.[38] Both, consequently, depart from the approach of many social scientists who believe that causal explanations of human behaviour are possible, and do not want to assert such a radical disjunction between the study of bodily processes and human action. Both reject the assumption of the unity of science that is integral to positivism.[39]

Second, both, by virtue of this basic assumption, emphasize the role of values in our concepts and definitions of mental illness. In Szasz's case this is an inevitable consequence of locating mental disorder within the realm of human action, since action, he contends, can only be properly understood by reference to social rules. Laing, in contrast, is less concerned to assert that value judgements must be involved, than to display their relativity and partiality, and the failure of understanding they involve.

Third, both stress the social nature of human action. Not only is it social rules – what is considered appropriate and acceptable – that define people as mentally ill, but an individual's action is only explicable in relation to the social environment. As a result they are critical of the individual frame of reference usually embodied in psychoanalytic and psychiatric ideas and advocate a more social framework. For Szasz 'problems of living' are essentially social problems, problems of social and interpersonal relationships that have a social rather than a biological origin. For Laing the schizophrenic experience is a response to family stresses and strains. Therefore, while neither has a clearly formulated theory of society both transpose the locus of the problem from the individual to the society. It is society and social groups such as the family that have their deficiencies and pathologies, not the individual.[40]

Szasz's and Laing's rejection of causal analysis relates to a fourth common feature of their ideas, the emphasis they give to individual autonomy. In Szasz's case this is, as we have seen, part of a libertarian view of the world, for Laing it is part of an existential one. Both want us to view human beings as determining rather than determined, and as playing an active role in their lives.[41] They assume a voluntaristic rather than a deterministic stance. This is one reason for their rejection of the term mental illness, for they feel that to view behaviour as symptomatic of sickness is to deny human agency – to see individuals as not responsible for what they do.[42]

Fifth, both consequently emphasize the role of psychiatry in controlling the behaviour of individuals, through its judgements, conceptualizations and modes of treating the mentally disordered. But there is a difference here. For Szasz the force and the odiousness of the control inheres in its ideological and institutional nature, which should be made apparent. Laing, however, by throwing doubt on the validity of the judgements themselves, rejects not just the form of the control but its very existence.

Sixth, and finally, both cast doubt on the existing medical control of the care and treatment of the mentally ill. Help should be available if the individual wants it, and neither deny that some people termed mentally ill suffer and could benefit from help, but medicine should not provide it.[43] Szasz makes this point more forcefully than Laing and is hostile to the medical hegemony for a number of reasons. He objects, as we have seen, to the scientific camouflage it provides for social and ethical rules; he objects, as did Freud, to its concentration on bodily processes, and he objects to what he sees as its institutional bias – the fact that it serves the interests of some group – the family or the state – rather than the interests of the individual. His ideal is a 'contractual' psychiatry in which the individual as a client freely enters into a relationship with a therapist – a private entrepreneur who is directly paid by the client – and as a result, Szasz argues, has some control over what goes on.[44]

Many of Szasz's and Laing's predominant assumptions are shared by certain sociologists of deviance, especially those who developed the labelling theory of deviance in the United States in the 1960s. This theory – or sensitizing perspective – has its origins in the Symbolic Interactionism that thinkers such as G. H. Mead and Thomas Cooley developed in the 1920s and 1930s.[45] They analysed the way in which meanings are acquired and generated through social interaction, and in particular the way in which the individual's own self is built up through taking over the ideas and attitudes of others. Applied to the field of deviance the orientation led to an especial concern both with the way in which behaviour comes to be defined as deviant, and more generally with the societal reaction to deviant behaviour and its impact on the person who is thought to have transgressed. Lemert, in his book *Social Pathology*, published in 1951, indicated the questions generated by a focus on societal reaction when applied to mental illness:

One of the more important sociological questions here is not what causes human beings to develop such symptoms as hallucinations and delusions but, instead, what is it about their behaviour which leads the community to reject them, segregate them, and otherwise treat them as irresponsibles, i.e. as insane.[46]

He continued 'A second important question, corollary to this, revolves about the function of such rejections and concomitant societal definitions in the dynamics of mental deviation itself.'[47]

One application of symbolic interactionist ideas to mental illness can be found in the work of Goffman. In his convincing study *Asylums* he analysed the way in which the mentally ill are controlled and manipulated within the asylum in the interests of the maintenance of staff power and convenience and patient compliance and conformity by use of techniques of degradation, discrediting and so on.[48] The central concepts used by Goffman, following other interactionists, are those of 'career' and 'self'. He describes what he calls 'the moral career of the mental patient', distinguishing the pre-patient, in-patient and ex-patient (or post-patient) phases of this career, defining the moral aspects of a career as 'the regular sequence of changes that career entails in the person's self and in his framework of imagery for judging himself and others'.[49] The notion of career, and the focus on the pre-patient phase draw attention to the process of becoming a patient, and symbolic interactionists have illuminated many aspects of this process, looking in particular at the way in which individuals themselves and those around them come to define themselves as mentally ill.

Labelling theories of deviance provide a rather different application of symbolic interactionist ideas. Labelling theorists defined deviance not as the breaking of some social rule but as an action to which a label of deviance had successfully been applied. In his influential book *Outsiders*, published in 1963, Becker extended Durkheim's discussion of deviance, contending that the central point about deviance is:

that *social groups create deviance by making rules whose infraction constitutes deviance*, and by applying those rules to particular people and labelling them as outsiders. From this point of view deviance is *not* a quality of the act the person commits, but rather a consequence of the application by others of rules and sanctions to an 'offender'. The deviant is one to whom that label has successfully been applied, deviant behaviour is behaviour that people so label.[50]

Applied to mental illness in the work of Scheff, psychiatric symptoms are defined as 'labeled violations of social norms' and chronic or stable mental illness (to which his analysis is directed) is viewed as a social role.[51] The rules in question are what Scheff calls residual (that is taken-for-granted) rules and it is societal reaction that transforms the normal (meaning here common) occurrence of residual rule breaking into the social role of the chronically mentally ill person.[52] And though other contingencies are involved 'Among residual rule breakers, labelling is the single most important cause of careers of residual deviance.'[53]

Scheff's work, although presented as a complementary to organic or psychological accounts of mental illness, in fact provides an alternative model that raises serious doubts about some of the basic assumptions of the liberal–scientific conception of psychiatry, many of which echo the ideas of Szasz and Laing.[54] First, and most obviously, that notions of mental illness are absolute and objective; labelling theory stresses instead their social and cultural relativity.[55] According to the premises of symbolic interactionism illness must, like any other concept, be a social construct. Second, that psychiatry serves the interests of the patient and is humane and beneficial. By emphasizing the role of societal reaction Scheff, like Szasz and Laing, points to the social control involved in psychiatry, as the institution which gives official legitimacy to labels of mental illness. Indeed, and here he differs from Szasz and Laing, there is little suggestion that the individual (at least before being moulded and shaped by the societal reaction) experiences pain or suffering or is in any need of help. Moreover, unlike Durkheim, Scheff suggests that though rule breaking is inevitable, deviance is not. Psychiatry, rather than trying to help and cure sickness, becomes its creator.

Szasz, Laing, and Scheff, therefore, through their criticisms of the concept of mental illness, directly call into question certain fundamental features of the liberal–scientific conception of psychiatry; in particular they cast doubt on the assumption that mental health and sickness are defined in an ethically neutral way and on the belief that psychiatry is essentially beneficial and humane. They do so, however, without directly attacking or calling into question the appropriateness of that framework for the analysis and evaluation of medical practice as a whole. Psychiatry (because it deals with human action) is treated as a special case, with the implication that the criticisms do not extend to the main body of medicine. Even Szasz, who has considered a far broader range of phenomena than Laing, and in so doing has had a great deal to say about modern medicine, nevertheless directs most of his attention to conditions that do not obviously fall under the heading of physical illnesses. The contrast between physical and mental illness implicit in much of the argument is set out in Table 13. How appropriate is such a contrast? Would it be better to abandon the notion of mental illness, at least as far as the so-called functional mental illnesses are concerned? Is the concept of physical illness any more objective than that of mental illness? Is psychiatry an essentially repressive force serving to control and regulate socially undesirable behaviour rather than to provide help for those who are sick in mind? Let us consider some of the issues raised by these arguments in a more critical vein.

Table 13   Contrasting conceptions of physical illness and functional mental illness

Characteristic of the conception	Physical illness	Functional mental illness
Appropriate label	Illness	Problem in living/deviance
Refers to	Bodily functioning	Human action
Type of norms	Norms of bodily functioning	Social, ethical and legal rules
Nature of judgement	Objective, value-free, scientific	Subjective, value-laden, ideological
The individual's relation to the deviation	Passive, victim	Active, agent
Type of explanatory factors	Organic	Social and psychological
Type of explanation	Causal	Non-causal, rule-following, understanding
Role of medicine	Care and cure	Social control

Evaluating the arguments
Value judgements and mental illness

Central to the arguments of Szasz and Laing is the claim that value judgements intrude into concepts of mental health and illness. It is this claim that provides an important basis for arguments that psychiatry serves as a force of social control, since it is generally assumed that definitions of mental health and illness, like those of physical health and illness, are scientific and objective, and do not involve any moral evaluation of behaviour. Attacks on this position can assert the value-free nature of notions of mental health and illness and their independence from notions of deviance; equally they can assert the value-laden nature of all notions of health and illness, whether mental or physical.

There have been a number of attempts to defend the objectivity of concepts of mental health and illness. The British psychiatrist, Aubrey Lewis, writing in 1959, framed the issue in terms of whether conceptions of mental health and illness have a social content, that is, whether they depend on the social approval of the behaviour in question.[56] The social realm, he concluded, provides an essential context to our judgements of mental health and illness, but does not define their content. Concepts of mental health and mental illness are often, he admits, ambiguous and some, like the notion of psychopathic personality, raise especial problems.[57] Nevertheless, if we concentrate on disturbance of 'part functions' as well as general efficiency we can distinguish mental illness from social deviation:

in mental disorders it is shown by the occurrence of say, disturbed thinking as in delusions, or disturbed perceptions, as in hallucinations, or disturbed emotional state, as in anxiety neurosis or melancholia. Deviant, maladapted, nonconformist behaviour is pathological if it is accompanied by a manifest disturbance of some such functions.[58]

The key to the distinction is a double one – to concentrate on part functions – that is to look at separate spheres of functioning rather than total functioning – and to focus on psychological functioning rather than social behaviour itself. Hence, 'Though our estimate of the efficiency with which functions work must take account of the social environment which supplies stimuli and satisfies needs, the criteria of health are not primarily social'.[59] For him, therefore, physical and mental illness can be grouped together and contrasted with anti-social conduct since neither has an essentially social content. This contrasts with Szasz's analysis that groups mental illness and anti-social conduct together and juxtaposes both to physical illness.

But what does Lewis' argument amount to? His most important claim is the obvious point that concepts of health and illness refer to aspects of physiological and psychological functioning and not to social behaviour as such. This suggests a distinction between mental illness and deviance, the former involving a pathology of mental processes that underlie behaviour whereas the latter is defined in terms of the breaking of social rules governing behaviour. Physical illness, mental illness, and deviance then differ in their referents: body, mind and behaviour respectively (though Lewis does not like the dualism of emphasizing the distinction between mental and physical illness). This is an important analytical point, though it is not without its problems as far as the group of personality or behaviour disorders is concerned, and, more generally, since assessments of mental processes depend on assessments of behaviour. Moreover it does not establish that the criteria whereby we judge psychological processes to be pathological are any less value-laden or any less social in origin (i.e. the referent may not be social behaviour but the evaluative criteria may be social). Lewis's argument is that we can potentially assess the normality of separate psychological functions on a factual, statistical basis in the way that we do for physiological functioning, although he recognizes that our knowledge of psychological functioning is far more limited. However, precisely what assessments of normal functioning of parts of the body or mind involve is little explored by him and we need to turn elsewhere for further elaboration of this matter.

Christopher Boorse, a philosopher writing in the 1970s, exemplifies the attempt, implicit in Lewis' argument, to root the objectivity of all notions of health and illness in biology.[60] Like Lewis he admits that concepts of health and illness, especially in the mental sphere, are usually vague, and he also admits that in practice they often incorporate value judgements. Nevertheless, he contends that this is not inevitable. His argument is based on a particular view of notions of health and illness, which he sets out as follows:

an organism is *healthy* at any moment in proportion as it is not diseased; and a *disease* is a type of internal state of the organism which: *i* interferes with the performance of some natural function – i.e. some species-typical contribution to survival and reproduction – characteristic of the organism's age; and *ii* is not simply in the nature of the species, i.e. is either atypical of the species or, if typical, mainly due to environmental causes.[61]

It follows from this, he argues, that concepts of illness are value-free since disease is defined as an interference with natural functions and the functional organization typical of a species is a biological fact. Hence 'Whether or not an organism is diseased can be settled in principle by the methods of natural science'.[62] And this applies to mental as well as bodily functioning:

> Only empirical inquiry can shown whether normal human beings have an even temper, engage in socially considerate behaviour, and advance the species – or make love with 'dignity and decency'. Some animals are naturally irascible and treat their peers with unbroken hostility. Most copulate with utter abandon. Perhaps we are not so constituted; perhaps we are. The point is that a theory of health should be a description of how we are constituted and not how we would like to be.[63]

Boorse's faith in the possibility of factual definitions of mental health and illness raises a number of problems. Central to them is not so much his particular delineation of the notions of health and illness in general terms – though it could be questioned – as his belief that this delineation extracts the criteria of mental health from the realm of values and puts them squarely into the domain of pure description. First, there is the problem of identifying 'natural' psychological functions and inter-ferences with them. Even if we concern ourselves only with what people do do and can do rather than what they should do (with statistical norms and capacities rather than ideal norms) it is difficult to see how value judgements can be avoided in making decisions about what constitutes a natural function or an interference with it. Is it reasonable to identify as natural functions, as Boorse suggests, those functions that contribute to the survival and reproduction of the species? Moreover how do we decide what contributes to an interference with a particular function? (There is little agreement about the best way to avoid war and advance peace, for instance.) And even if we can assess the contribution of particular processes to the survival and reproduction of the species are we to be forced to define decisions such as those to remain childless as pathological? The problem is not that there can be no facts, but that when it comes to questions of 'how we are constituted' psychologically there can be no merely descriptive, statistical answers. Human psycho-logical functioning is too responsive to the social and cultural context to decide what is 'normal' or 'natural' without making some value judgements.

Is the same true of bodily functioning? Can we make a clear contrast between mental and physical illness as writers like Wootton and Szasz contend? Sedgwick, a political theorist, in a paper published in 1973 argued that we cannot. Both, he contended, are value-laden concepts. As he put it: '*All sickness is essentially deviancy.* That is to say, no attribution of sickness to any being can be made without the expectation of some alternative state of affairs which is considered more desirable.'[64] And elsewhere 'Outside the significances that man voluntarily attaches to certain conditions, *there are no illnesses or diseases in nature.*'[65] This point is then elaborated more graphically:

The fracture of a septuagenarian's femur has, within the world of nature, no more significance than the snapping of an autumn leaf from its twig: and the invasion of the human organism by cholera-germs carries with it no more the stamp of 'illness' than does the souring of milk by other forms of bacteria.[66]

And he adds 'The existence of common or even universal illnesses testifies, not to the absence of a normative framework for judging pathology, but to the presence of very widespread norms.'[67]

Sedgwick's proposition that all concepts of illness involve some value judgement is a dual one, as these quotations make clear. On the one hand he develops the argument, familiar to sociologists, that all concepts are social constructs – that is, it is people who give conditions, events, processes, all phenomena, meaning – the concepts of health and illness no less than any other.[68] In that sense they are both interpretive and selective. This is an extremely important point that directs our attention to the way in which the concepts have been constructed historically, and gives full recognition to their cultural relativity. On the other hand, Sedgwick claims that concepts of health and illness not only select out certain phenomena and categorize them as illnesses, but that in so doing they evaluate them: that an attribution of sickness is an attribution of the undesirability of the state in question. This is a point made forcefully by Lester King in a paper published in 1954:

Now, when we speak of health or disease, we use certain implicit values. Health is something good and desirable, while disease, whatever else it means, implies something bad. These values of 'good' and 'bad' indicate attraction towards or repulsion from something. There is a very definite sphere of relevance, within which the values apply. The sphere of disease is the realm of pain, disability and death, for its major groupings, while the minor stages we can call (subject to quibbling) 'unpleasant' or 'disagreeable', or some such term. Health deals with the opposite, with the conditions which give rise to the subjective report, 'I feel fine'. This state of awareness is subjectively recognized, although indescribable.[69]

This is also a key argument and we can readily agree with Sedgwick and King that concepts of health are intrinsically evaluative. But what are its implications? Does it mean that the anxieties expressed by so many writers about the evaluative, ideological nature of concepts of mental health and illness must be set aside since there appears to be no difference between concepts of mental health and illness in this respect, and that both should be embraced as forms of social deviance? Or should we encompass physical as well as mental illness in our concern about the role of values? Or is there some extra ground for concern about the operation of values in notions of mental health? The theorists whose work we consider in the following chapter make the case for widespread concern about the operation of values throughout medicine; but we still need to consider whether there are especial grounds for concern in the mental health field.

What Sedgwick's analysis ignores is that by virtue of their different referents – mental as opposed to physical functioning – there are important differences in the place values occupy in concepts of physical and mental illness. On the one hand, there is not the same degree of consensus about what constitutes undesirable, pathological mental functioning as there is about pathological physical functioning (cultural variations in concepts of physical illness notwithstanding). On the other hand, there is the difficult problem of distinguishing mental illness from behaviour that is considered social and morally unacceptable but not psychologically disturbed – badness from madness. The problem is that the intended distinction of referent – mental processes rather than behaviour – is one that is in practice is hard to make, since very often mental processes have to be inferred from behaviour. And in the case of so-called personality or behaviour disorders there is little real attempt to make it at all.

We do not need, therefore, to commit ourselves to the view that there is no scope for the intrusion of personal or cultural values in definitions of physical functioning as pathological to accept that there are in practice important differences in the place values occupy in the mental health field. This is partly because of the difficulty of achieving consensus about what counts as mental health and illness, especially in the case of less severe pathology; it is partly because of the difficulties of measuring and evaluating an individual's psychological functioning that were outlined in the previous chapter; and it is partly because the putative patient may not share the medical view that something is wrong, so that the voluntarism that legitimates much medical intervention is undermined.

To recognize these differences does not necessarily commit us to

Szasz's position that we should abandon the concepts of mental illness and talk instead of problems of living or of deviance, although it does indicate that we should not ignore Szasz's concern about the way in which the values involved are hidden under the scientific gloss of psychiatry. To identify behaviour as symptomatic of mental illness is to construct a set of phenomena in a particular way – in a way that legitimates a particular response – that is, some form of medical intervention. Szasz's concern is that the values should be revealed and laid bare from the encrustations and distortions of scientific objectivity. This, for him, is the major problem of social control. Once we reveal the values, however, there is still room for a debate about the sort of response, if any, that is appropriate, including the desirability of some form of medical intervention. The issue of medical intervention cannot be reduced to that of mystifying values under the guise of objectivity alone. There is also the question of whether the putative problem should be considered a physical, psychological or social one. Before considering this issue further, there is another argument about the nature of concepts of mental health and illness that needs to be considered. This relates to the content of the criteria for defining mental illness.

Rationality, intelligibility and intentionality

Laing's main objection to notions of mental disorder is that they involve defining a person's thought and behaviour as meaningless, irrational or unintelligible. This, Laing claims, results from a failure to understand the thoughts, feelings or actions in question – something that can and should be overcome. All action is, he suggests, intelligible – if only we take the pains to understand it. This argument is founded on the belief that all human thought and action is meaningfully related to the person's situation – a view developed and elaborated by Freud.[70] Like Freud he asserts that this is as true of supposedly pathological as of normal thought and action. But he goes on to argue that to define it as pathological on the grounds of its lack of intelligibility is, therefore, mistaken. The point is elaborated by Laing when he suggests that the actions of 'schizophrenic' offspring are intelligible if set in the context of what is going on within their families, and when he suggests that the behaviour of Kraepelin in the clinical examination would, if we adopted a different perspective, readily seem irrational.[71]

There are two issues here. First, to what extent is the attribution of mental sickness based on judgements of the meaningfulness, rationality and intelligibility of thought and action as the argument presupposes. Is intelligibility the main criterion for judging mental pathology? Second, does the behaviour of the mentally ill lack this quality? Undoubtedly in societal perceptions of mental illness, which play a crucial role in determining who seeks professional help, assessments of the intelligibility of what the person in question says and does are an important feature of judgements of psychological disorder. As Dorothy Smith comments:

When people describe the behaviour of people defined as mentally ill or who are later judged to be so, they make such remarks as 'she acted funny', 'he was a changed person', 'I felt he might do anything', 'he was out of his mind', 'I couldn't understand what he was up to', 'he didn't seem to know who I was'. The behaviour of persons who are defined as mentally ill may be seen as odd, bizarre, inexplicable, wild or excessive.[72]

And she goes on to argue about the use of the notion of mental illness more generally:

I suggest then that the behaviour of persons who come to be labelled as mentally ill fails to confirm that they share the same version of reality as does the observer. What they do and say indicates that they do not construct reality in a way that the observer can understand and which he also believes to be how it is understood by other members of the cultural community of which they are both members. Mental illness thus bears an analogous relation to social reality as that which nonsense has to sense in language. Behaviour is recognized as odd, funny, bizarre, etc. because it does not make sense in terms of the rule for producing intelligible behaviour in a given cultural community.[73]

Such views are echoed by Ingleby:

If we go back to first principles, what the 'mentally ill' have lost is not their bodily health, nor their virtue, but their *reason*: their conduct simply does not 'make sense'. Insanity ascriptions, on this view, are made when behaviour does not seem accountable by any plausible motive, or when belief seems to be quite unfounded: they may be ruled out simply by providing a credible motive for action, or a reasonable ground for belief.[74]

But, as Ingleby argues, the criterion of intelligibility, though important, does not take us far enough. It is not clear that intelligibility is an issue in all attributions of mental illness. Lack of intelligibility is more obviously in question in the case of psychotic disorders – real insanity – than it is with the neuroses, behaviour disorders or organic conditions like senile dementia. We can argue that the behaviour of someone with a severe phobia does not 'make sense' (there seem no reasonable grounds for the strength of their fear), but if we do see this as a matter of intelligibility the problem of comprehension is rather different from that involved in comprehending say psychotic delusions. In the one case what we view as pathological is the extent and severity of the fear, in the other it is the substance of the belief. Ingleby tries to clarify this difference by talking of gradations of intelligibility, and of different types of rules involved in governing conduct. Some rules are what he calls constitutive rules – they are rules that constitute the activity in question, which must be followed if the activity is to be of a particular type; psychotic and sometimes neurotic behaviour may involve infractions of these rules.[75] But mental illness does not always raise such fundamental issues of intelligibility; it may make obvious sense but be considered perverse, inadequate, unrealistic, or 'uncalled for'. We could here introduce the concept of strategic rules – rules that define more or less competent play – to cover such infractions (though Ingleby does not do this), but this would stretch the concept of intelligibility very considerably.[76]

It seems more likely, however, that the search for a single criterion for the diverse behaviours – thought and action – that can be regarded as symptomatic of mental illness is mistaken. And this applies as much to Scheff's attempt to typify the 'rule breaking' involved as 'residual' rule breaking as it does to the criterion of intelligibility.[77] Calling the rules in question 'residual', though it allows for some diversity in the rules at issue, does not produce any clear criterion of what is considered symptomatic of mental illness. In one sense, as the term implies, residual rule breaking is simply that rule breaking which remains when all other types have been specified:

The culture of the group provides a vocabulary of terms for categorizing many norm violations: crime, perversion, drunkenness, and bad manners are familiar examples. Each of these terms is derived from the type of norm broken, and ultimately, from the type of behaviour involved. After exhausting these categories, however, there is always a residue of the most diverse kinds of violations, for which the culture provides no explicit label . . . . In this discussion the diverse kinds of rule-breaking for which our society provides no explicit label, and which, therefore, sometimes lead to the labelling of the violator as mentally ill, will be considered to be technically *residual rule breaking*.[78]

However, the label 'mentally ill' is not merely a residual category of this sort, for a person may, for instance, break legal rules and yet be called mentally ill. Moreover there is an overtone of circularity in this definition of residual rules and residual deviance by virtue of the suggestion that the easiest way to identify a residual rule is to observe which violations cause the label of mental illness to be applied.

A similar circularity is also apparent in his second, more positive definition of residual rules:

There are innumerable norms, however, over which consensus is so complete that the members of a group appear to take them for granted. A host of such norms surround even the simplest conversation: a person engaged in conversation is expected to face toward his partner, rather than directly away from him; if his gaze is toward the partner he is expected to look toward the other's eyes, rather than, say, toward his forehead; to stand at a proper conversational distance, neither one inch away nor across the room, and so on. A person who regularly violated these expectations probably would not be thought to be merely ill-bred, but as strange, bizarre, and frightening, because his behaviour violates the assumptive world of the group, the world that is construed to be the only one that is natural, decent, and possible.[79]

Calling the rules 'taken for granted' does not help us very much with the problems of identification.[80] How do we decide whether a rule is taken for granted or not? Not only does taken-for-grantedness depend on the individuals involved as well as on the nature of the society, but once again identification of taken for granted rules appears to be possible only when someone is called mentally ill; there is no independent criterion for identifying such rules.

Let us accept, however, for the moment, that some aspect of the intelligibility of a person's behaviour may often be at issue in defining mental illness. Is any judgement of irrationality simply due to a failure to properly comprehend the thought and action in question? Laing offers two rather different grounds for his claim about the necessary intelligibility of the thought and action of the supposedly mentally ill person. First, that people's behaviour is a reasonable response to the situations they have experienced. Psychotherapists, he asserts, have been led to 'the impression that, if their patients were *disturbed*, their families were often very *disturbing*'.[81] Any individual faced with a similar situation would act in a similar manner, and this makes the response both normal and intelligible. Here Laing is using the word intelligible in the sense of explicable, pointing to the fact that we can give an account of how individuals who have been labelled mentally ill have come to act as they do. But even if we accept that some families are 'pathogenic' (and the evidence on this matter is not clear cut), the fact that actions may be accounted for in terms of family pressures and that they may be typical responses to such pressures, does not in itself mean that we should not regard the behaviour in question as abnormal or pathological. Consider physical illness: the fact that it may be generated by environmental factors and that it may be typical for that illness to result from these environmental factors, does not mean that we want to change our ideas about whether the condition is pathological. It is the nature and the consequences, not the causes of the condition that lead to the designation illness. Moreover, the fact that an action may be explicable does not necessarily make it readily intelligible or comprehensible in the immediate context; it can still seem strange, bizarre or abnormal.

Laing's second argument relates to intelligibility in the immediate context: the apparent lack of intelligibility arises, he suggests, through our failure to adopt the person's perspective on the situation: to see the situation as the person sees it.[82] The result is that, devoid of its experiential context, the behaviour appears irrational; place it in its full experiential context and it does not. The difficulty with this argument is that it is often not simply a matter of choice whose perspective we take. In his example of Kraepelin's clinical examination both the actions of psychiatrist and of the patient may be made intelligible and meaningful, but we must adopt rather different procedures in each case. Kraepelin's behaviour is part of a routine programme of action whose content is immediately comprehensible because it is in tune with the norms that govern his activities as a psychiatrist; his behaviour fits our socially structured expectations. In contrast, the content of the patient's behaviour cannot be understood so readily. To make much of the content of her behaviour comprehensible we need to have more information about her personal experience, her way of thinking, her meanings: a personal rather than a socially constructed reality. The intelligibility of her actions remains idiosyncratic and personal rather than conventional and social, restricted to those who gain more knowledge of her private world than is usually necessary for the routine interpretation of action.

It has been argued, moreover, that relating the patient's actions to her experience in this way only makes her actions rational in the limited sense that we can posit some set of beliefs or objective that can explain the action.[83] It does not make the action rational in the sense that the beliefs on which the action is predicated are themselves rational. But to assert that certain beliefs are in themselves irrational is itself contentious. What are our criteria for judging them irrational? Judging the rationality of a belief in terms of its content is likely to lead to the problem of confounding rationality with social acceptability. One possibility is to focus not on the content of the beliefs but on the rigidity with which they are held and the unwillingness to modify them in the face of evidence. As one author puts it:

While the topic of rational belief is a difficult one, prima facie the most obvious way to differentiate beliefs that are irrational from those that are merely false is by looking at the influence relevant evidence would have on the holder of the belief. It is characteristic of irrational beliefs that their holder maintains them despite countervailing evidence or despite inconsistencies with other beliefs he has. There is a 'fixed' or 'frozen' nature about such beliefs, in the sense that they are not corrigible by relevant evidence. Irrational beliefs are held with a strength (relative to other beliefs the actor has) disproportionate to the evidence known to the actor.[84]

We do not, however, have to commit ourselves to the assertion that the beliefs on which the action is based are themselves irrational, either in terms of content or in terms of the manner in which they are held, to sustain the claim that the content of the actions is not readily intelligible in the light of routine knowledge of the situation.

There is, however, an additional point implicit in Laing's arguments about the intelligibility and meaningfulness of supposedly pathological behaviour. Attributions of pathology deny not only intelligibility but also intentionality to the behaviour, since contained within the idea of illness is the assumption that the phenomena in question are essentially outside the individual's control – the individual is seen as acted upon rather than as actor.[85] Such a denial of intentionality and agency would not be consistent with Laing's stress on the rationality and meaningfulness of all human behaviour, nor with his existentialism, given the importance that is attached to individual autonomy.[86] Szasz, because of his commitment to an analysis of human behaviour in terms of its rule-guided, meaningful nature and his assumptions about individual autonomy, also objects to the language of sickness on these grounds.

The issue is significant since assertions of intentionality are involved in the everyday distinction between madness and badness – between *having* something wrong and *doing* something wrong. It is the difference between saying something happens to a person and saying a person does something and involves therefore, attributions of responsibility. These attributions of responsibility are themselves based on different ways of thinking. When we talk of people *having* something wrong our model is mechanistic and deterministic, and when applied to behaviour it assumes this is outside the individual's control, and the individual cannot be blamed for what she or he does. On the other hand when we talk of people *doing* something wrong, our model is more humanistic and voluntaristic. People are viewed as conscious agents whose actions are intentional, and for which they can and should be held responsible. Laing and Szasz clearly prefer the latter model. However, where we draw the boundary between behaviour that can be controlled and behaviour that cannot is a matter of convention and political preference, not of fact. The label of illness suggests the person needs help, but seems to deny the validity of their actions. The label of deviance attributes full agency to the person, but in so doing holds them responsible, thereby legitimating blame, punishment and demands for individual self-control. The debate about attributions of intentionality raises, therefore, questions about how we can best explain behaviour considered symptomatic of mental illness, as well as about how we should treat it.

Physical causes, social processes and mental illness

An underlying assumption of those who suggest a marked contrast between mental and physical illness and in turn advocate a reconceptualization of mental illness in terms such as deviance or 'problems in living', is the absence of any physical pathology or physical aetiology that could account for the behaviour that is considered symptomatic of mental illness. Where such pathology is known to exist, as in the case of the organic mental illnesses, then the term illness is considered appropriate, as is the active involvement of the medical profession. Where it is not, the argument is that there should be a distinctive psychological or social analysis – a view that unites Szasz and Laing as well as Eysenck and Freud, though they differ in the nature of the analysis they recommend, as well as in their commitment to the need for a new label for the phenomena in question.[86]

Precisely where and how the boundary is drawn between the organic and the 'functional' mental illnesses varies and, as we have seen, the conventions of psychiatric classifications are by no means straightforward.[87] Szasz sets the boundaries at already established physical pathology and excludes the organic mental illnesses from his strictures.[88] Eysenck, in contrast, sets the boundaries in terms of what he considers to be the likely outcome of scientific studies. He is convinced that 'psychotic disorders have definite biological roots' and includes the functional psychoses in the organic group, leaving the neuroses and the behaviour disorders specifically for psychology.[89]

But can a clear distinction be drawn between organic and functional mental illnesses? Is there a residue, however large or small, of mental illnesses where no physical pathology is implicated? The case for the involvement of physical factors in all mental illnesses is strong. On the one hand there is the general point that all mental states – all our thoughts, feelings and emotions – are dependent on bodily processes such as biochemical changes, though the precise mechanisms involved have not always been established. Anxiety, for instance, involves bodily changes such as increased levels of sweating, raised heart beat, and so forth.[90] On the other hand, there is considerable evidence of the way in which mental states can be modified by physical means. Though psychotropic drugs may not cure mental illnesses, there can be little doubt that most have some effect on mental states, and this is true of other physical methods of treatment for mental illnesses, whatever their ethics and precise efficacy.[91]

For some psychiatrists, particularly those who are inclined to contrast biological and psychological explanations of mental illness and treat them as mutually incompatible – to oppose biogenesis with psychogenesis – this is enough to establish the ultimate biological aetiology of all mental illnesses, and, by implication, to undermine the distinction between organic and functional illnesses.[92] However, such conclusions involve a number of assumptions that need to be examined. One is that any bodily correlate of mental process should be regarded as a cause of that process: that identifying physical correlates is the same as establishing physical causes and, by implication, physical pathology. Second, that physical causes have priority over any psychological ones – the hierarchy of causes that has usually been built into psychiatric classifications of mental illness. However, to take the second point first, even if we establish the role of biological factors in the aetiology of a particular mental illness, this does not exclude the role of psychological or social factors, which could be treated as just as, if not more, important. The case for the importance of psychological factors in many, though probably not all mental illnesses, is as strong as that for the involvement of organic factors and there is no logical reason for giving the latter priority.[93] The establishment of the organic base of senile dementia does not rule out the possibility that psychological factors may precipitate or generate such biological changes. Mind affects body just as body affects mind and the treatment of biological processes as somehow primary ignores this interrelation. Moreover, even where there is no psychological mediation of the illness in question, social factors will be involved in its causation, just as they are in all physical illnesses, if we take a broad rather than narrow view of causation. As in the case of psychological factors there is no a priori reason why they should be ignored. Their exclusion is a matter of clinical values rather than of empirical fact.

The issue of whether physical factors are implicated in the aetiology of all mental illnesses is more difficult. Szasz clearly rejects their importance in the aetiology of functional mental illnesses though not of organic conditions (thereby accepting a clear mind-body dualism as far as explanations of mental illnesses are concerned).[94] He contrasts the explanation of physical pathology with the explanation of any belief, whether it is considered pathological or not, like this:

a disease of the brain, analogous to a disease of the skin or bone, is a neurological defect, not a problem in living. For example, a *defect* in a person's visual field may be explained by correlating it with certain lesions in the nervous system. On the other hand, a person's *belief* – whether it be in Christianity, in Communism, or in the idea that his internal organs are rotting and that his body is already dead – cannot be explained by a defect or disease of the nervous system. Explanations of this sort of occurrence – assuming that one is interested in the belief itself and does not regard it simply as a symptom or expression of something else that is more interesting – must be sought along different lines.[95]

In part Szasz's argument follows from the radical disjunction he asserts between the natural and the human sciences – the former producing causal explanations, the latter an understanding in terms of roles, rules and game playing. This commits him to the view that if the object of concern is human behaviour, as it is in functional mental illnesses, then they must be analysed in the latter terms. He asserts *'psychiatry, as a theoretical science consists of the study of personal conduct* – of clarifying and "explaining" the kinds of games that people play with each other; how they learned these games; why they like to play them; and so forth'.[96]

We need not, however, share Szasz's view of the nature of human sciences to accept the force of the anti-reductionist argument – that an explanation of a person's belief cannot be reduced to some statement of physical conditions or processes or that anxiety cannot be reduced to the physical changes with which it is associated, and in that respect physical factors cannot provide a complete explanation of mental events.[97] But what are the implications of this argument for claims about physical aetiology? According to one commentator there is a confusion between identifying mental events in terms of physical factors and correlating the two.

What the irreducibility of these entails is that one cannot *identify* mental entities such as beliefs, desires, pains, etc., with physical events, either behaviouristic or physiological. It does not entail that one may not *correlate*, e.g., the mental experience of pain with certain physiological events (the stimulation of c-fibers in the brain). Nor does it entail that, e.g., schizophrenia may not be correlated with some sort of events in the brain.[98]

Claims about correlation do not necessarily involve claims of identity. However even if we accept this point there is still the problem of whether physical correlates should be viewed as explanatory factors. Certainly we can reject biological reductionism and still claim that physical correlates should count as causes of functional mental illnesses since they are necessary to their occurrence. Szasz himself accepts this in the case of organic mental illnesses, where the mental symptoms, which may include delusions and hallucinations as well as deterioration of memory, depression and so on, are held to result from physical causes. He does not allow it in the case of the functional mental illnesses, presumably because he regards the psychological experiences as all important – as he puts it in the extract above, he 'is interested in the belief itself and does not regard it simply as a symptom or expression of something else that is more interesting'. Yet this begs the question. Under what circumstances should we regard the belief as interesting in itself, and under what circumstances as 'a symptom or expression of something else that is more interesting'. Szasz, unfortunately, seems to rely in practice on psychiatric conventions in making the decision, accepting the legitimacy of the distinction between organic and functional mental illnesses with the primacy that it gives to identifiable physical processes.

Eysenck's approach is rather different. While he accepts the importance of the biological substratum that makes human behaviour possible, he contends that in the case of neuroses and personality disorders 'the body only enters the picture as it does in relation to healthy psychological development'.[99] Bodily processes do not explain the occurrence of these disorders. For that we have to turn to psychology. Again the issue is one of explanatory adequacy, but the argument is not about the inadequacies of biological reductionism as such; it is rather an empirical claim about the key factors involved in explaining the disorders in question. In this Eysenck is apparently working with the view of causality discussed in the previous chapter in which a factor only counts as a cause of an event or phenomenon, if it is the factor that 'makes a difference'.[100] Other factors that may be necessary to the occurrence in question are 'mere conditions'. This is the sense of cause used when infectious illnesses are classified according to specific aetiology. However if we apply a rather different convention about the use of the notion of cause all the conditions necessary to the occurrence of an event become causes of that event. By this token the 'normal' physical processes involved in neurotic behaviour which are 'necessary conditions' of that behaviour are also causes.

Clearly the way in which we use the word cause affects the outcome of this debate. At first sight it might seem that in the case of any illness it is the factor that 'makes a difference' which should be regarded as the cause of the illness and any other factors involved should be treated as necessary conditions. By this token the question of which correlates merit the status of causes then becomes an empirical one. Hence we could argue that though the occurrence of depression may involve biochemical changes (accepting that the precise nature of these has not yet been identified), nevertheless, if we can establish it is the individual's experience – the loss of a child, for instance – that is the factor that made the difference in this instance, (if it had not happened he or she would not have become depressed) then the latter, rather than any biochemical changes should be viewed as the cause of the depression.[101] This claim could be further justified by adding another common criterion for assigning causal status: that a cause of a particular event must precede it in time.[102] We then additionally argue that the loss of the child is the cause of the depression not the biochemical changes, because the one is temporarily prior to the depression, whereas the latter are coincident in time.

It is important to recognize, however, that what we define or treat for practical purposes as *the* cause of an event or phenomenon – the factor that makes a difference – depends on our interests and objectives as well as a particular use of the notion of cause. It is not, therefore, solely an empirical question. And this applies to the contrast between individual and social causes as well as to that between psychological and physical causes. If a doctor's concern is to treat the individual's depressed mental state, attempts directly to modify the biochemical changes involved may seem the most feasible thing to do, given his or her knowledge, interests and values, and is likely to encourage the practitioner to view the biochemical changes as the cause of the depression. On the other hand, a psychologist with a similar concern may well seek to transform the individual's feelings by psychological means, and treat them as the cause of the depression. Yet again, someone seeking to prevent depression might well focus on the reasons for the child's death, and the causal account s/he offers might well locate the particular event of the child's death in a broader analysis of social and economic factors. The point is that what we count as the cause of an occurrence partly depends on what we are trying to do. This makes it as much a political as a scientific matter – a question of values as well as of facts. The same is true of assigning the label pathological to particular processes. Processes come to be defined as pathological if they are the ones in which the researcher, clinician, or policy maker is interested and hopes to change. Within psychiatry, for instance, once organic correlates of particular mental illnesses have been identified, given the existing physical orientation of medicine, the organic processes in question tend to be regarded as pathological and attention focuses on them. If, on the other hand, you focus, as Brown and Harris have done, on locating the roots of depression within the social environment and successfully show that social events and conditions 'make a difference', then you may come to regard certain features of society as problematic, even pathological, rather than the particular individual's mind or body.[103]

There are a number of implications of this discussion of the organic correlates of mental illness, as well as of the earlier discussion of the issues of value judgements and of rationality and intentionality in concepts of mental illness. First, the distinction between organic and mental illness is a matter of convention rather than fact which tends to reflect the actual or expected success of medicine in identifying physical correlates of mental illness, and the priority psychiatry gives to organic processes. Second, concepts of mental health and illness, because they involve evaluations of thought and action, do not permit any precise or exact division between mental illness and social nonconformity. In theory there is a distinction of referent – mind rather than behaviour – and a differential assumption of intentionality and responsibility; but in practice these distinctions are not based on any clear, consistent principles. Third, the question of whether it is preferable to abandon the language of illness for certain mental disorders is ultimately a political matter. It is a question of where we want to intervene in the complex interplay of factors that produce the end result that we now define as mental illness; of the changes that we want to achieve; and of the persons or groups to whom we want to assign responsibility for making the relevant changes. There are, for instance, a number of arguments against the involvement of the medical profession in much of what now falls within the category of mental illness – apart from the gloss of science and objectivity medicine gives to definitions of mental health and illness. Not the least is the lack of interest many medical practitioners show in mental illness, especially in its milder forms where there is more agreement as to the importance of psychological and social factors in its genesis. Fourth, when we talk of psychiatry acting as an agent of social control we need to be more precise about the exact process to which we are referring. Social control is a loose term that labels some aspect of social interaction as undesirable and suggests there is a manipulation of one individual by another (the more powerful) or one individual by some institutional arrangement or practice. In the case of psychiatry we need, for example, to distinguish the 'social control' that stems from denial of the value-laden nature of notions of mental health and illness from the social control involved in treating problems as individual rather than social in character. Some of the different ideas about the ways medicine, not just psychiatry, may operate as a force of social control are considered in the following chapter; they throw further light on the question of the nature and appropriateness of the medical response to mental illness.

Notes and references

1 Szasz rejects the term anti-psychiatry on the grounds that it is 'imprecise, misleading, and cheaply self-aggrandising'. He argues in particular that the term 'implicitly commits one to opposing everything that psychiatrists do – which is patently absurd' (Szasz, 1981, p. 335).

2 On nineteenth-century changes in medicine see Shryock, 1947; see also Chapters 6 and 8 below.

3 See especially his *The Question of Lay Analysis* (Freud, 1962).

4 Hughes, 1958, Chapter 4; Kline, 1972; MacIntyre, 1958.

5 For interesting accounts of Freud's ideas see Wollheim, 1971; Mannoni, 1971.

6 Freud, 1962, pp. 146–7.

7 ibid., pp. 167–8.

8 Internationally an agreement was reached that each national society of analysts should decide whether a medical qualification was necessary or not (Mannoni, 1971, p. 169).

9 His ideas about psychiatry are set out most clearly and simply in his pamphlet *The Future of Psychiatry*, 1975, though many of them had been expounded much earlier. See, for instance, his *Handbook of Abnormal Psychology*, 1960.

10 ibid., Chapter 1.

11 Benedict, 1934, and 1935; Fortune, 1932.

12 Benedict, 1935, p. 258.

13 Wegrocki, 1939.

14 See, for instance, Aubrey Lewis's arguments discussed below.

15 Davis, 1938.

16 ibid., p. 56.

17 ibid., p. 59.

18 ibid., *passim*.

19 Jahoda, 1956.
20 Wootton, 1959, p. 216.
21 ibid., especially Chapter VIII.
22 ibid., p. 224.
23 Szasz, 1970a, p. 23.
24 ibid., p. 15.
25 Sedgwick, 1982, Chapter 6.
26 Szasz, 1970b.
27 Szasz, 1971, p. xvii.
28 Szasz, 1963; 1965; 1971; 1974; 1977; 1979.
29 See, for instance, Szasz, 1974, Chapter 2.
30 For an account of his changing ideas see Sedgwick 1972 and 1982. See also Friedenberg, 1973; Howarth-Williams, 1977; Collier, 1977.
31 Together with David Cooper he produced a study of Sartre's philosophy in 1964, published as *Reason and Violence*.
32 The three key books are *The Divided Self*, 1960; *Self and Others*, 1961; and *Sanity, Madness and the Family*, 1964. The best-known of the American work is Gregory Bateson and his co-workers' paper published in 1956 on the concept of the 'double-bind'. But see also the work of Lyman Wynne (Wynne *et al.*, 1958) and Theodore Lidz (Lidz, 1958, Lidz and Fleck, 1960). The range of work is reviewed by Mishler and Waxler, 1968.
33 Laing, 1967, p. 89.
34 ibid., p. 98.
35 In Laing's words 'Instead of the mental hospital, a sort of re-servicing factory for human breakdowns, we need a place where people who have travelled further and, consequently, may be more lost than psychiatrists and other sane people, can find their way *further* into inner space and time, and back again' (1967, pp. 105–6).
36 Manifest most obviously in his involvement in the Congress of the Dialectics of Liberation held in London in 1967 (Cooper, 1968). Szasz in dissociating himself from anti-psychiatrists such as Laing and Cooper claims 'the anti-psychiatrists are all self-declared socialists, communists, or at least anti-capitalists and collectivists' (Szasz, 1981, p. 335).
37 Szasz, 1961, *passim*.
38 See for instance Chapter 1 of *The Divided Self*, 1960.
39 Benton, 1977, p. 12.
40 Laing rejects, however, the notion of family as opposed to individual pathology arguing that 'Its initial impact is seductive, but it creates ultimately even greater difficulties than the biological analogy as applied to the one person' (1964, p. 9).
41 In this context Laing uses the distinction between praxis and process (1962, p. 7).

42   The significance of this dimension to notions of disease and illness is discussed by Flew (1973).
43   Laing talks of natural healing, with the person assisted on his or her journey by those 'who have been there and back again', adding 'Psychiatrically, this would appear as ex-patients helping future patients to go mad' (1967, pp. 106–7).
44   Szasz, 1971, Introduction; Sedgwick (1982, Chapter 6), provides a useful critical appraisal of this aspect of his ideas.
45   For general discussions of symbolic interactionism see Blumer, 1969, Meltzer, Petras and Reynolds, 1975; Rose, 1962.
46   Lemert, 1951, pp. 387–8.
47   ibid., p. 388.
48   Goffman, 1968. Goffman specifically dissociates himself from the labelling theory of writers such as Scheff (1971, p. 356).
49   Goffman, 1968, pp. 119–55.
50   Becker, 1963, p. 9.
51   Scheff, 1966, p. 25.
52   ibid., Chapter 2.
53   ibid., pp. 92–3.
54   Assessments of certain theoretical and empirical aspects of labelling theory are to be found in Schur, 1971, Gove and Howell, 1974; Gove, 1975; Gove, 1982; Cockerham, 1979; Plummer, 1979; Coulter, 1973.
55   Scheff, 1966, p. 22.
56   Lewis, 1953.
57   ibid., p. 119.
58   ibid., p. 118.
59   ibid., p. 124.
60   Boorse, 1976.
61   ibid., pp. 62–3.
62   ibid., p. 63.
63   ibid., p. 70.
64   Sedgwick, 1972, p. 213; see also Chapter 1 of his *Psycho Politics*, 1982.
65   Sedgwick, 1972, p. 211.
66   ibid., p. 211.
67   ibid., pp. 214–5.
68   This is a point emphasized more by some social theories (for instance, symbolic interactionism) than others.
69   King, 1954, p. 195.
70   See Wollheim, 1971; Mannoni, 1971.
71   Laing, 1964, *passim*; Laing, 1967, pp. 88–90.
72   Smith, 1967, p. 6. See also her later article ' "K is mentally ill": the anatomy of a factual account' (Smith, 1978).
73   Smith, 1967, p. 11.
74   Ingleby, 1982, p. 128.

75   ibid., p. 132.
76   Aubert, 1967, p. 54.
77   Scheff, 1966, Chapter 2.
78   ibid., pp. 33–4.
79   ibid., p. 32.
80   ibid., p. 32. The notion of taken-for-granted rules is developed more fully by Garfinkel in his *Studies in Ethnomethodology* (1967).
81   Laing, 1967, p. 93.
82   ibid., pp. 88 90.
83   Moore, 1975, p. 239.
84   ibid., pp. 242–3. Moore's characterization of irrational beliefs has affinities with Rokeach's definition of dogmatism (1960).
85   Flew, 1973.
86   ibid., Chapter 3.
87   See above pp. 47–8.
88   Szasz, 1970a.
89   Eysenck, 1975, p. 16. However, he adds that 'these are not sufficient to produce the final breakdown' and argues that there is a place for 'psychological advice' on their treatment.
90   This is, of course, the basis for physiological methods of lie detection using polygraph techniques.
91   The way in which psychiatrists use such observations to make inferences about biochemical explanations of mental disorders is discussed by Bignami (1982) and by Rose (1983).
92   This is the logic of the argument in Rimland's paper 'Psychogenesis versus Biogenesis: the Issues and the Evidence' (1969).
93   As the notion of psychosomatic illness reflects.
94   On mind-body dualism see Campbell, 1971, Chapter 3.
95   Szasz, 1970a, p. 13.
96   Szasz, 1961, p. 7.
97   See Taylor, 1964.
98   Moore, 1975, pp. 253–4.
99   Eysenck, 1975, p. 5.
100   Hart and Honoré, 1959, pp. 26–30.
101   See Rose, 1983.
102   This was David Hume's second criterion for attributing causal status; see Keat and Urry, 1975, pp. 27–88; Hart and Honoré, 1959, pp. 12–20.
103   Brown and Harris, 1978.

4 Medicine and power

It is convenient to contrast two ways of thinking about medicine in general and psychiatry in particular, which were developed and amplified in the 1970s. Both identify little difference in the problems surrounding psychiatry from those of medicine as a whole, and both locate medicine within the context of a broader analysis of society. The first emphasizes the power of medical practitioners as a professional group situated within a bureaucratically organized and technological society increasingly dependent on experts. It points to the success of medical practitioners in appropriating the knowledge and mystique of science as the foundation of their professional power and to their use of science in the service of their professional interests. The second stresses the importance of other more powerful groups, in particular the capitalist class, in shaping and moulding the development of medical practice and it views medical practitioners as agents of social control operating not so much in their own specific interests as in the interests of capital. In sociological terms the first approach works within a largely Weberian tradition; power is viewed as arising from a number of different sources and as being acquired by various separate, though often overlapping, elite groups.[1] The second adopts a Marxist approach; it conceptualizes power as essentially economic in origin and sees it as concentrated in the hands of those who own the means of production and constitute the ruling class.[2]

The power of the medical profession
Illich

Illich's ideas about medicine provide one example, albeit with some rather special characteristics, of the first way of thinking. Illich's main publication on medicine is his book *Limits to Medicine* published in 1976 – an earlier version of which had appeared as *Medical Nemesis* the previous year.[3] The starting point of his highly polemical analysis is a broad attack on the beneficial nature of medicine and its ability to serve the patient's interests. He contends that far from providing help and curing sickness medicine 'has become a major threat to health'.[4] It is producing what he calls iatrogenic sickness, that is, damage resulting from medical intervention itself.[5] He distinguishes three types of iatrogenesis; first, clinical iatrogenesis which exists 'when pain, sickness and death result from medical care'.[6] This is a generally recognized consequence of medical activity, though its extent is a matter of dispute. For his part Illich aims to show that the negative effects of clinical intervention outweigh the positive ones. He attempts to do this, first, by listing some of the dangers of modern medicine – the poisoning effects of drugs, the infections picked up in hospital, and the medical misadventures and errors – and making some assessment of their scale (the analysis here is not especially thorough or systematic); and second, by asserting (as certain other writers such as McKeown have done), that medicine has had little impact on mortality.[7] The argument is that the sweeping declines in mortality over the past two hundred years have largely occurred without the assistance of medicine; they have resulted from improvements in nutrition, sanitation, housing and so on, which have improved health by increasing the resistance to sickness. The support provided by other studies for this claim is good. It does not, of course, show that there has been no improvement over time in doctors' ability to provide more effective treatment for those who do become sick, or to ameliorate pain and suffering, or to provide useful treatments for non life-threatening conditions.[8] However, systematic studies of the efficacy of medical treatments are relatively rare and the problems of historical comparisons of efficacy even greater.[9]

Second, there is social iatrogenesis. Medicine, Illich asserts, also undermines health indirectly by the 'impact of its social organization on the total milieu'.[10] Social iatrogenesis arises:

When medical bureaucracy creates ill-health by increasing stress, by multiplying disabling dependence, by generating new painful needs, by lowering the levels of tolerance for discomfort or pain, by reducing the leeway people are wont to concede to an individual when he suffers, and by abolishing even the right to self care . . . when health care is turned into a standardized item, a staple; when all suffering is 'hospitalized' and homes become inhospitable to birth, sickness, and death; when the language in which people could experience their bodies is turned into bureaucratic gobbledegook; or when suffering, mourning, and healing outside the patient role are labelled a form of deviance.[11]

Illich introduces the term medicalization to refer to the changes that characterize social iatrogenesis, arguing that the most obvious measure of social iatrogenesis is the increasing amount spent on health care – a sum that he argues has increased not only in absolute terms but relative to GNP.[12]

The United States now spends about $95 billion a year for health care, about 8.4 per cent of the gross national product in 1975, up from 4.5 per cent in 1962. During the past twenty years, while the price index in the United States has risen by about 74 per cent, the cost of medical care has escalated by 330 per cent. Between 1950 and 1971 public expenditure for health insurance increased tenfold, private insurance benefits increased eightfold, and direct out-of-pocket payments about threefold. In overall expenditures other countries such as France and Germany kept abreast of the United States. In all industrial nations – Atlantic, Scandinavian, or East European – the growth rate of the health sector has advanced faster than that of the GNP. Even discounting inflation, federal health outlays increased by more than 40 per cent between 1969 and 1974. The medicalization of the national budget, moreover, is not a privilege of the rich: in Colombia, a poor country that notoriously favours its rich, the proportion, as in England, is more than 10 per cent.[13]

He then goes on to provide evidence of the way in which doctors are increasingly involved in assigning people to medical categories for different purposes and telling them how to run their lives – which he calls diagnostic and preventive imperialism respectively – as well as describing other facets of medicalization.

Medicalization, Illich argues, creates a culture of dependence which constitutes the third and final form of iatrogenesis – cultural iatrogenesis. It differs from social iatrogenesis primarily in its focus on the level of ideas and beliefs, although it was initially termed structural iatrogenesis.[14] It is the iatrogenesis which arises 'when medically sponsored behaviour and delusions restrict the vital autonomy of people by undermining their competence in growing up, caring for each other, and ageing, or when medical intervention cripples personal responses to pain, disability, impairment, anguish and death'.[15] The result is dependence – a situation in which individuals, families and neighbours no longer control their own feelings and milieu, but rely instead on bureaucrats and professionals. And here Illich's values are especially apparent; like Szasz he shares a strong belief in the importance of self-control and autonomy. Self-help is his ideal for the handling of any problems.

According to Illich it is industrialization and economic growth, and the technological developments integral to them, that have given rise to iatrogenesis in its various forms. Iatrogenesis is but one aspect of 'the destructive dominance of industry over society'; it is an instance of 'that paradoxical counterproductivity which is now surfacing in all major industrial societies'.[16] And he adds 'Like time-consuming acceleration, stupefying education, self-destructive military defence, disorienting information, or unsettling housing projects, pathogenic medicine is the result of industrial overproduction that paralyses autonomous action.'[17] The problem, as he sees it, is that industrialization directs human activity towards intensive commodity production and this means that 'people are trained for consumption rather than for action' and 'their range of action is narrowed'.[18] Professionals play a key role in this process because they form an important part of the bureaucracies that develop with industrialization and intervene in the relation between individuals and their environment. On the one hand it is the professionals who make use of science and in so doing lose any concern for the individual, as in the case of physicians.

By turning from art to science, the body of physicians has lost the traits of a guild of craftsmen applying rules established to guide the masters of a practical art for the benefit of actual sick persons. It has become an orthodox apparatus of bureaucratic administrators who apply scientific principles to whole categories of medical cases. In other words, the clinic has turned into a laboratory.[19]

On the other hand professionals 'gain legal power to create the need that, by law, they alone will be allowed to satisfy'.[20] Illich suggests, therefore, that power, rather than being diffused throughout the society and belonging to the individual members of the society, belongs to certain elite groups, who may use it to enhance their own interests and perpetuate their power.[21] And this applies to the medical profession no less than to other professions. Consequently, medicine as a whole, not psychiatry alone, acts as a moral force in society (Illich here specifically dissociates himself from Szasz and Laing).[22] Medicine is

a moral enterprise and therefore inevitably gives content to good and evil. In every society, medicine, like law and religion, defines what is normal, proper, or desirable . . . . Morality is as implicit in sickness as it is in crime or in sin.[23]

Illich's account of the role of medicine raises a number of problems, many of which can be highlighted by an examination of the notion of medicalization, an important concept which could be regarded as a shorthand summary for his overall thesis. In Illich's work the concept seems to embrace a number of phenomena that he sees as closely interrelated. First, it denotes the increasing pervasiveness of medicine in the spheres and activities of everyday life – the doctor's presence at birth and death as well as on so many other occasions throughout life; a pervasiveness which he contends can be most obviously measured by the increasing proportion of national wealth spent on medical care. Second, it refers to the increasing commitment of medicine to science and the technologization of its practice, which Illich sees as undermining its ability to help patients and also helping to generate and legitimate its increased role in the events of daily life. And third, it indicates an increasing abrogation of power by medicine away from the individual and the community – a medical imperialism aided by the use of science and technology.

> The technocrats of medicine tend to promote the interests of science rather than the needs of society. The practitioners corporately constitute a research bureaucracy. Their primary responsibility is to science in the abstract or, in a nebulous way, to their profession. Their personal responsibility for the particular client has been resorbed into a vague sense of power extending over all tasks and clients of all colleagues.[24]

An initial problem with Illich's analysis of medicine's changing position within society is his lack of historical specificity. For someone with a historical training this is surprising. His argument that industrialization underlies the various forms of iatrogenesis he describes would seem to indicate that his overall concern is with the whole period since the middle of the eighteenth century. Yet much of the specific data he considers relates to the twentieth century, especially recent decades. When he suggests, for example, that health budgets constitute a 'handy measure' of the medicalization of life, he considers post-war health budgets.[25] It is hard to sustain a general thesis of medicalization over the whole period of industrialization by reference to health budgets for such a limited and recent time span. In defence of Illich, it could be said that post-war growth in health care expenditure is merely the most recent evidence of long sustained expansion, and that the data for this period is simply more exact, precise and readily available. But can we assume that there has been a steady linear expansion over a longer period of time? What are we to make of periods of slower growth or even decline in medical expenditure?

A more convincing defence might be to suggest that the phenomena which interest Illich are in fact largely post-war occurrences. Two of the three aspects of medicalization – medicine's spread to a wider range of aspects of our daily lives, and its reliance on technology – have arguably occurred largely in the post-war period, certainly in the twentieth century. The shift to hospital births, the widespread medical involvement in contraception, the increasing part medicine plays in the lives of the elderly from hip replacements to open heart surgery, the shift of death from home to hospital, all these are largely, though not entirely, post-war phenomena.[26] Hence Illich's reliance on post-war data, including that of medical budgets, could be justified. However, if we adopt this interpretation there is a problem with his explanation of medicalization in terms of a loosely specified industrialization. If many of the phenomena he describes belong to the twentieth century, especially the last four decades, then vague references to industrialization can hardly provide a satisfactory explanatory account. There are of course occasional allusions to 'advanced' industrial societies, but Illich is no more specific than this about the stage of industrialization with which he is concerned. Indeed, at times he is at pains to suggest that medicalization is a near universal contemporary phenomenon and does not depend on the type of society, the stage of development or the precise level of industrialization.[27]

Given the broad historical sweep of many of Illich's generalizations (if not of his specific supporting data) there is, too, a surprising omission in his analysis of the changing role of medicine. This is his failure to direct attention to what could, in policy terms, be described as the increased access of the population to official medical practitioners and, in sociological terms, as the changing class composition of medicine's patient population.[28] Illich suggests that the major historical change in the place medicine occupies within society lies in the range of events with which it deals. Equally, if not more important has been the change in the number and composition of people who make use of professional medical services. Illich suggests that the medical involvement with birth, death and ageing is new. What is new is for medical professionals to be involved with these events not just in the case of the aristocracy and the upper classes, but also for the majority of the population.[29] Members of the lower classes have long called upon some type of healer for help and care in times of sickness and in childbirth, but the limitations of their resources and the relative scarcity of licensed, professional healers ensured that their contact with official medicine was kept to a minimum. Only with changes, such as the growth of the middle classes, improvements in the standard of living of the lower as well as the upper classes, and the involvement of the state in the financing of medicine, has what was once the prerogative of the rich come within reach of the poor. In that respect it might be better to talk of the proletarianization of access to official medicine rather than of the medicalization of life. This is not to say that we should ignore or underestimate the importance of the changes in medicine Illich discusses. But it is surprising that he pays so little attention to changes in the social character of the recipients of professional medical intervention. This has been an important factor in the growth of spending on health services and must be taken into account if there is to be an adequate social or political analysis of health care.

Against this it might be argued that in recent decades any proletarianization is of little importance and it is the medicalization of life that accounts for all the increase in medical expenditure. However, there is ample evidence that some proportion of the post-war increase in expenditure does stem from better access to and take-up of medical services and not just from new forms of medical intervention. In England the legalization of abortion and its availability on the National Health Service provides one example,[30] the spread of publicly funded psychiatric outpatient clinics another.[51] Illich, unfortunately, not only concentrates on post-war budgets, he also fails to offer any breakdown of their components.

In fact four main factors have contributed to the recent increase in medical expenditure.[32] First, there have been the technological developments which so concern Illich. These have increased medical expenditure, both because they lead to new forms of intervention (foetal monitoring, kidney dialysis, hip replacements) and because many of the new forms of intervention are extremely expensive.[33] They involve capital in the form of machinery; they are labour intensive (requiring more nurses per hospital bed, for instance), and demand higher levels of skill and training for both doctors and nurses.[34] Second, services have been extended to new groups and made more accessible to others; the proletarianization that I have already mentioned. Third, the demographic composition of the population has changed. In particular there has been an increase in the proportion of the elderly in the population, who have higher levels of morbidity and make greater use of medical services.[35] And fourth, the unit costs of labour have increased as a result of higher wages, reduced working hours, better pensions and so forth – improvements that the union and professional activities of the workers in question have helped to secure.[36] All four factors, not just the first, have contributed to the increase in medical expenditure over the post-war period.

A further problem with Illich's account of the iatrogenic effects of medicine, to which Navarro has drawn special attention, relates to the issue of medical power.[37] Illich's analysis implies that the medical profession has become an increasingly powerful group (again the period in question is not specified) and that this power is exercised largely in its own interest. For him, pervasiveness and power go hand in hand. Navarro contends, however, that power and authority are delegated to the medical profession and the profession's power is but one facet of the power of a ruling class in whose general interests the health services operate. It is the ruling class's interests which determine the shape and form of the health services and the place of medicine within them. It is capital not the medical profession which generates the needs and dependencies that medicine satisfies.[38] Navarro comments:

Illich's bureaucracies, including the medical bureaucracies, are not the generators, but the administrators of those dependencies, consumptions and dissatisfactions. Indeed, those bureaucracies are not the owners nor the controllers, but the administrators of that system.[39]

Illich and Navarro agree, therefore, in seeing a marked expansion in medical activities and an increased public dependence on the medical profession, but they differ both in their account of the origin of that expansion and also on the independence of medicine. Navarro counterposes capitalism to Illich's industrialization, and the power of the capitalist class as a whole to the separate power of the medical profession and other professionals. The extent to which the medical profession can and does wield independent power is an issue that has concerned other authors who work within a largely Weberian framework and their arguments help to clarify the debate between Illich and Navarro.

Freidson

Freidson is a sociologist who shares some of Illich's concerns about the extent of the medical profession's power and the way in which it can be used to serve the practitioner's own interests rather than those of the client. However, his analysis is less polemical than Illich's and is more informed by sociological thought. Two books published in 1970, *Profession of Medicine* and *Professional Dominance*, set out the basic parameters of his argument.[40]

Freidson deals with three major aspects of medical power: its origins, its nature and its extent. Central to his analysis is his claim that the defining characteristic of a profession is its autonomy – its freedom from the control of outsiders.[41] This autonomy is evidenced by its right to determine the content of its work, to control recruitment and training, and to police its own activities.[42] Autonomy is however, conditional on the backing of the state which grants a profession autonomy:

The most strategic and treasured characteristic of the profession – its autonomy – is therefore owed to its relationship to the sovereign state from which it is not ultimately autonomous. . . . Clearly, professional autonomy is not absolute: the state has ultimate sovereignty over all and grants conditional autonomy to some.[43]

The first issue, therefore, is how this professional autonomy, granted by the state, has been acquired.

It has been gained, Freidson contends, over a lengthy period of time.[44] What was crucial, initially, was the medical practitioners' ability to provide adequate solutions to practical problems. 'Choice to consult cannot be forced; it must be attracted. The "good results" of medical practice with a sound foundation of knowledge, I believe, is one important source of attraction.'[45] But though good results may have attracted clients initially they did not give medical practitioners the degree of power and autonomy that, in Freidson's view, they now have. Another key factor was their ability to secure the support of the elite of the society.

A profession attains and maintains its position by virtue of the protection and patronage of some elite segment of society which has been persuaded that there is some special value in its work. Its position is thus secured by the political and economic influence of the elite which sponsors it. . . .[46]

In this process, however, it is not the objectively determinable attributes of the occupational group that are crucial but the ability of the group to persuade the state to grant professional status.[47] This ability will depend on the group's social characteristics – the social standing of its members and their access to ruling elites – as well as on its competence and skill in persuading others of the social need for the service it provides and its special expertise in meeting that need.[48] It is these factors that determine its ultimate success in the exclusionary practices which are involved in successful professionalization.[49]

Consequently, though medical practitioners may have initially attracted clients because they could satisfy clients' needs, their ability to establish themselves as a profession, to develop autonomy and power as an occupational group, did not depend by any means exclusively on their ability to satisfy these needs. Moreover, the development of professional status provides no guarantee, in itself, that clients' interests are being served. Freidson points, in particular, to the limited control the medical profession attempts to exercise over the quality of its work and to the moral and political nature of the role it plays in defining the boundaries of illness, in determining the desirable forms of treatment, advising patients and so forth. There should, he therefore argues, be a general restriction of medicine's professional autonomy.[50] Like Illich he contends that medicine inevitably involves moral judgements, for it has to make decisions about the application of scientific knowledge:

Medicine is not merely neutral, like theoretical physics. As applied work it is either deliberately amoral – which is to say, guided by someone else's morality – or it is itself actively moral by its selective intervention. As a moral enterprise it is an instrument of social control which should be scrutinized as such without confusing the 'objectivity' of its basic knowledge with the subjectivity of its application.[51]

And there is, Freidson argues, no particular reason for believing that medical practitioners are the best qualified to make the moral judgements involved in decisions about the proper use of scientific knowledge.[52] Hence, it is not that science dictates the form and content of medicine or psychiatry as the liberal–scientific conception of medicine assumes, but that medicine makes moral judgements about the use of science, and in so doing science often becomes an instrument that serves the interests of medicine rather than the patient.

Freidson's analysis of the origins of medicine's professional status also throws light on the second related issue with which he is concerned, that of the source of the medical profession's power over its patients. Freidson follows Weber in differentiating between power and authority. For Weber power is 'the chance of a man or of a number of men to realize their own will in a communal action even against the resistance of others who are participating in the action', while authority exists where power is socially legitimized and there is voluntary obedience.[53] It is authority that Freidson regards as important in the doctor–patient relationship.[54] He argues that practitioners' authority over their patients stems from two main sources. On the one hand, as doctors themselves believe, it derives from the expertise, real and perceived, that is monopolized more or less completely by the members of the profession.[55] In this respect doctors have authority over their patients because of their assumed technical competence – an authority that is backed up by the potential threat that access to this knowledge can be denied if the patient does not comply. For this reason it is in the profession's interests to maintain an aura of expertise, and to emphasize the disparity in knowledge between doctor and patient. Hence, the typical reluctance to reveal precise details of what is wrong, the treatment that is to be given, and the tendency to use technical jargon.[56]

On the other hand practitioners' authority over their patients stems from their office, and from the fact that they have a formal position within some institution which gives them certain legal powers exclusive to that office.[57] Freidson comments:

In a strictly logical sense, the capacity of the officeholder to influence the behaviour of others (that is, to exert authority) is a function of the office he holds, with no necessary relation to how much he may have to know to do his official job. 'Thus the treasurer of a corporation is empowered to sign checks disbursing large funds. There is no implication in the "power" that he is a more competent signer of checks than the bank clerks or tellers who cash or deposit them for the recipient. Legal "competence" is a question of "powers" in this sense; technical competence is of a different order'.[58]

In the case of the medical profession its historically gained powers are extensive: in this country in addition to the right to prescribe certain drugs, to sign death certificates, and to provide treatment within the state medical service, practitioners also have the right to admit patients to hospitals, to sign sickness certificates, to carry out certain operations, including legal abortions, and so on.[59] Consequently, it is in many respects the range of specific powers that doctors have by virtue of their office, rather than their knowledge and expertise, that is the basic source of their authority over their patients. However, the two types of authority are interrelated, for the presumption of technical competence is the legitimation of office, and the acquisition of office gives rise to the presumption of technical competence. In addition the authority of the professional may be further reinforced by traditional authority as a result of status discrepancies between professional and client.[60] The selection of medical practitioners from higher status groups allows the medical profession to draw on the traditional authority of one class over another when dealing with many patients, and is consequently advantageous to the profession. Certainly doctors have been anxious to maintain the high status of their recruits, even though historically their status as practitioners has varied. As recently as 1958 the Royal College of Surgeons commented:

there has always been a nucleus in medical schools of students from cultured homes. . . . This nucleus has been responsible for the continued high social prestige of the profession as a whole and for the maintenance of medicine as a learned profession. Medicine would lose immeasurably if the proportion of such students in the future were to be reduced in favour of the precocious children who qualify for subsidies from the Local Authorities and the State purely on examination results.[61]

Even allowing for qualifications and measured ability, medical students are drawn disproportionately from the middle and upper middle classes. In 1966 the proportion of first year medical students from classes 1 and 2 was 75.7 per cent, and proportionately fewer applicants from these groups were rejected than from classes 3, 4 and 5.[62]

Analysis of the source of medical practitioners' authority and power over their patients is of some interest; nevertheless it leaves open the matter about which Illich and Navarro disagree – that of the extent to which the medical profession has acquired independent power as a professional group. How far reaching is doctors' autonomy? Do other groups within the society exercise power over them? Freidson puts two important qualifications on the extent of medicine's autonomy. First, as we have seen, it is conditional on the authority of the state, which grants the profession autonomy in the first place. Second, the increasing involvement of the state in the provision of medical care diminishes the profession's power to control the social and economic organization of its work; it does not, however, infringe its clinical autonomy: 'while the profession may not everywhere be free to control the *terms* of its work, it is free to control the *content* of its work. Similarly, it is free to control the technical instruction of its recruits.'[63]

What Freidson's formulation ignores, however, is the extent to which the social and economic aspects of medical work and its content are closely interwoven. While he is right to claim that any diminution in medical practitioners' freedom to control the terms of their work does not reduce their freedom to control the content, if by that we mean the legal powers to make clinical judgements as to what is wrong with the patient, to make recommendations as to treatments and so forth without interference from outsiders; none the less the terms of medical work do affect its content since they set the constraints within which clinical judgements are made. Consequently, if doctors do not control the social and economic organization of their work their clinical autonomy, in this second sense, is limited.

The impact of the social and economic organization of medical work can be seen most clearly in situations where the relationship between practitioners and patients is mediated by some third party involved in the financing of medicine, whether it be the state or some providential or profit making insurance company, for the financial policies of this third party will reduce clinical autonomy.[64] In the case of state medicine, for instance, financial controls may make it impossible to offer certain forms of treatment that doctors consider clinically desirable such as heart transplants or kidney dialysis – to name the most obvious examples.[65] It is true that within the British National Health Service, for instance, the nature and extent of the financial controls vary.[66] Moreover medical practitioners play an important role in policy making bodies within the NHS: 'this was the price that had to be paid for such co-operation as was given in inaugurating the service'.[67] Even so there are important financial limits on what can be done within the NHS which do reduce clinical autonomy – limits that seem greater as the pace of technology and demands for cuts to public expenditure increase. These limits are imposed by government, not by doctors themselves, although by contributing to a climate of health consciousness, medical practitioners help to create an ideological framework that influences government decision making.

Within a private system of medicine financed by insurance companies, the financial policies of the insurance companies affect clinical judgements not so much by introducing limits on what doctors can spend (though there are increasing signs that even the insurance companies are worried at the escalation of medical costs), but by the precise form of the coverage that they offer under their insurance policies.[68] One critic of the system describes the effects like this:

Insurance companies have helped to grossly distort medical practice, with expensive and dangerous effects. The best known distortion is the push of health insurance towards hospitalization. Many more people have hospital insurance than insurance for ambulatory care. Therefore patients are hospitalized for minor diagnostic tests and treatment which could be done outside the hospital. It is estimated that 30 per cent of days spent in hospital are unnecessary. A more significant distortion has been the push towards surgery. Many more people have surgical insurance than insurance for non-surgical physician services. Thus the tendency of surgeons to over-operate is reinforced by the insurance structure. 2 million unnecessary operations are performed in the US each year resulting in at least 10,000 needless deaths.[69]

In other words, while the decision to hospitalize a patient for minor diagnostic tests is made by the medical practitioner, and is in that respect a medical judgement, it is not a judgement made primarily in terms of what is clinically necessary or desirable, but rather in terms of the economic aspects of benefit coverage. Again, however, medical practitioners themselves may have an impact on the terms of their work in this type of system as consultants, managers or owners of the insurance companies.[70]

Nor does the paradigmatic fee-for-service medicine escape the impact of economic factors on clinical decisions, whether they come from concerns about the patient's ability to pay for some costly procedure, or from the practitioner's desire to make a more or less profitable living from medical work. In the one case the 'best' treatment may be impossible because of its cost; in the other the treatment that allows the practitioner to make a living – or even a considerable profit – will be chosen even if it is not necessarily clinically the 'best'.[71] A disarming comment in Freud's autobiography describing his initial attempts to establish a private practice illuminates how clinical and economic considerations can become inextricably confused in fee-for-service medicine:

Anyone who wanted to make a living from the treatment of nervous patients must clearly be able to do something to help them. My therapeutic arsenal contained only two weapons, electro-therapy and hypnotism, for prescribing a visit to a hydropathic establishment after a single consultation was an inadequate source of income.[72]

In no system, therefore, is there complete, clinical autonomy, in the sense of medical decision making that is routinely based solely on assessments of the individual's clinical condition and the most suitable form of treatment, although practitioners usually have the power to weigh the economic considerations as they think fit. What varies is the source and nature of the social and economic factors that intrude on clinical judgements, as well as the influence medical practitioners have over these aspects of their work. Before looking at some of the Marxist approaches to these issues, I want to consider the work of one more author who does not fit very well into the alternative perspectives that I have delineated in this chapter – Michel Foucault.

Foucault

Foucault is a French historian of ideas whose work is of considerable interest to anyone seeking to examine the different ways of trying to understand mental illness and psychiatric practice, both because of his detailed focus on psychiatric and medical ideas, and because of his far-reaching impact on historians and sociologists of medicine in recent years.[73] He offers a way of thinking about medical ideas and medical knowledge as a whole, that is concerned not so much to question its values – i.e. Does medicine actually help people? – but to examine its changing nature and influence. Like the symbolic interactionists, one of Foucault's fundamental assumptions is that ideas and meanings structure social reality and are a product of society. However, Foucault moves beyond this assumption to emphasize two things. First, for him the ideas and meanings, which the symbolic interactionist sees as grouped in relatively discrete clusters, form holistic structures, which in his later work he terms discourses.[74] These structures, rather like the paradigms described by Kuhn, constitute social reality and define what counts as knowledge.[75] Second, the discourses, since they define knowledge, are the form in which the power of a particular group exists and operates, and for Foucault knowledge and power are inextricably linked.[76] It is not just that knowledge is a form of power so that those who have power can control others by denying access to knowledge (as, for instance, when doctors are reluctant to tell their patients much about their illnesses in order to maintain their authority), but that discourses define what knowledge is. Hence the power of the medical profession exists in its ideas. In this context Foucault, like Illich, uses the notion of medicalization, but Foucault uses it largely to refer to the spread of medical ways of thinking.[77]

Foucault's book, *Madness and Civilization*, published in France in 1961 and in Britain in 1967, dealt specifically with ideas about insanity.[78] At this stage his ideas about discourses and power had not been formulated in abstract terms; nevertheless the book offers a forceful analysis of the changing structure of ideas anout insanity, from the meanings embodied in the 'ships of fools' at the end of the middle ages to those represented in the 'birth of the asylum' at the end of the eighteenth century. His objective throughout is to tease out and illuminate the meanings that surround insanity. Discussing, for example, 'the ships of fools' sailing in the 'imaginary landscape of the Renaissance' he comments:

Thus we better understand the curious implication assigned to the navigation of madmen and the prestige attending it. On the one hand, we must not minimize its incontestable practical effectiveness: to hand a madman over to sailors was to be permanently sure he would not be prowling beneath the city walls; it made sure that he would go far away; it made him a prisoner of his own departure. But water adds to this the dark mass of its own values; it carries off, but it does more: it purifies. Navigation delivers man to the uncertainty of fate; on water, each of us is in the hands of his own destiny; every embarkation is, potentially, the last. It is for the other world that the madman sets sail in his fools' boat: it is from the other world that he comes when he disembarks.[79]

His focus is far more on the symbolism of insanity, which is held to change radically over time, than in the changing institutions and practices. For him the changing institutions and practices are of interest as sources of data, sources like the art and literature of the particular period. They are to be mined in depth for what they can yield of ideas about insanity, rather than to be studied for their own intrinsic importance, or as something to be explained. Indeed, Foucault, like other French contemporaries such as Levi-Strauss, offers a structural analysis of ideas in which the object is to analyse and specify the interrelated structures of ideas, not to explain them in any causal terms.[80] The context for ideas about insanity is a broader range of ideas of the historical period, not the material conditions of the society or the antagonism between classes. It is in this respect above all that discourses differ from the ideologies of Marxist thought.[81] Ideologies not only represent the ideas of particular groups in society, as may discourses, but they are also weapons in the struggle between classes and are, in the last analysis, economically determined. Foucault's lack of direct interest in the extent and nature of the institutions and practices that have arisen to deal with the insane is, therefore, matched by his lack of interest in attempting to link ideas to specific social and economic conditions. His is an idealist not a materialistic conception of history, in the tradition of the historians of *mentalités*.[82]

For all that, the analysis of ideas in *Madness and Civilization*, though thematic, is invaluable, and later books such as *The Birth of the Clinic*, published in France in 1963 and in Britain in 1973, and *The History of Sexuality*, published in France in 1976 and in Britain in 1979, provide further important insights into medical and psychiatric ideas.[83]

Class struggle, the state and psychiatry

Vincente Navarro is the most prominent of those Marxists who assert that the medical profession, rather than having independent power, is itself subject to powerful external forces which guide and mould its activities; it is but part of the apparatus that has been developed by the ruling class to control and constrain the individual.[84] Consequently, rather than primarily serving its own specific professional interests, medicine serves those of the major locus of power within the society – the ruling or capitalist class – of which it is but one component part.

According to Navarro, medicine and our existing health care institutions can only be understood by a proper analysis of contemporary society as a whole – a capitalist society characterized by class stratification in which power is concentrated in the hands of the ruling class.

In *Medicine Under Capitalism*, a collection of his most important papers, Navarro's basic assumption is that 'social class influences on the institutions of production, reproduction and legitimization determine the composition, nature and functions of the health sector.'[85] His claim is, in other words, that the form and content of the health services can be accounted for in terms of the role they play in supporting and sustaining what he views as the three major tasks of capitalist society: the production of commodities, the reproduction of the labour force, and the legitimation of the capitalist order.[86] Navarro's analysis of class stratification follows Miliband, and he distinguishes an upper or corporate class consisting of the owners and controllers of wealth – the ruling class; a working class consisting of blue collar workers, service workers and agricultural wage earners with an upper middle and a lower middle class between the two. This hierarchy is reflected both in the control of the health services, where the corporate class are disproportionately represented, and in the inequalities in power, status and income within the health service labour force.[87] Navarro, therefore, unlike any of the theorists we have considered so far, draws attention to the role and position of other health service workers besides doctors, pointing to the marked stratification within the health care system and to the social backgrounds of those who make up the medical hierarchy.[88] But the impact of the class stratification of capitalism is not just on the medical hierarchy. More importantly, the health care system itself has, he argues, developed its particular form and content so that it can deal with the contradictions and difficulties that capitalism itself generates – with the problems created by the exploitation of the working class, problems that increasingly find expression in sickness and ill-health.[89] Hence the sickness with which medicine largely deals is sickness arising from the misery, alienation and stress of capitalist society. And clinical medicine acts as an ideological and practical panacea controlling and minimizing potential dissatisfaction and discontent, transforming structural exploitation into individual sickness.

Navarro's analysis, therefore, provides a theoretical foundation for the widely observed inequalities in health between those of different social classes which, despite the overall decline in mortality over the past two centuries, are still considerable. Mortality data for England and Wales in 1971, for example, showed that the death rate of the 15 to 64 age group was two and a half times higher for men and women of occupational Class V than of occupational Class I.[90] There is evidence, too, of significant class differences in mortality in the United States, although because of the character of the official statistics the data are more fragmentary.[91] Morbidity data equally show marked class differences, paralleling those already described in the previous chapter for the psychiatric sphere.[92]

In his analysis of the way in which medicine plays an ideological role Navarro develops and modifies Parsons' ideas concerning illness and social control and echoes his functionalism. In his book *The Social System* Parsons put forward the view we have already encountered that any illness can be viewed as a form of deviant behaviour, though the grounds on which he makes this claim are distinctively his own.[93] No illness, he argues, is purely a bodily phenomenon, for there are always certain elements of motivation to deviance involved (it is not just that the term involves an assertion of the undesirability of the state in question).[94] This is because illness is also a social role that provides a way of departing from normal social obligations, and is itself governed by its own specific social expectations. Parsons lists four main expectations. The first is that sickness provides an 'exemption from normal social responsibilities, which of course is relative to the nature and severity of illness. This exemption requires legitimation by and to the various alters involved and the physician often serves as a court of appeal as well as a direct legitimatizing agent'. Second he suggests that 'the sick person cannot be expected by "pulling himself together", to get well by an act of decision or will'. Third, there is a 'definition of the state of being ill as itself undesirable with its obligation to want to get well'. And fourth there is an 'obligation – in proportion to the severity of the condition, of course – to seek technically *competent* help, namely, in the most usual case, that of a physician and to co-operate with him in the process of trying to get well.'[95]

Illness can consequently be regarded as an alternative channel for acting out certain deviant motivations: 'Illness may be treated as one mode of response to social pressures, among other things as one way of evading responsibilities'. The sick role serves, therefore, according to Parsons, as a mechanism of social control.[96] As such it has rather special and important characteristics:

The sick role is, as we have seen, in these terms a mechanism which in the first instance channels deviance so that the two most dangerous potentialities, namely, group formation and successful establishment of the claim to legitimacy, are avoided. The sick are tied up, not with other deviants to form a 'sub-culture' of the sick, but each with a group of non-sick, his personal circle and, above all physicians. The sick thus become a statistical status class and are deprived of the possibility of forming a solidary collectivity. Furthermore, to be sick is by definition to be in an undesirable state, so that it simply does not 'make sense' to assert a claim that the way to deal with the frustrating aspects of the social system is 'for everybody to get sick'.[97]

Social control operates even if there is no intervention by a medical practitioner. In addition, however, medical practitioners themselves serve as a further mechanism for social control by attempting to reintegrate the sick individual into society through the use of therapeutic procedures. Parsons differs, therefore, in his analysis of the social control aspect of medicine from the writers I have so far considered. They tend to emphasize the way in which medicine controls people by its use of science and scientific language and ideas, and to argue that, as a result, the political and moral judgements it makes are covert. According to Parsons the very existence of the two social roles of patient and healer provides mechanisms for social control, whatever methods adopted by the healer, for control is an integral part of that role's objective. It is, in Merton's terms, a 'latent' function.[98]

In Parsons' view, by serving as mechanisms of social control the sick role and the medical practitioner are functional for the social system. For Navarro the social system is a capitalist system and it is the interests of one component of that system – the ruling class – which are being served. Hence we have to focus on the sphere of production if we are to understand the health services, and it is the productive system that generates the high levels of consumption of health care: 'To understand the sphere of consumption we have to understand the world of production, or who does what, who controls that work, and how that control takes places.'[99] The health care system provides a way of containing the alienation and stresses of the existing social order, a way which individualizes and depoliticizes exploitation and so prevents it from finding more active political expression. In this process science and technology are themselves controlled by and serve the interests of the ruling class:

Within that process of production, technology and its requirements do not determine the hierarchical division of labour, but the hierarchical division of labour determines the type of technology used on that process. Technology then reinforces the already existing hierarchical and fragmentary division of labour. Indeed that hierarchicalization is already there and is determined primarily by the class and sex roles existent in our societies.[100]

In developing his analysis of health care institutions Navarro pays especial attention to the role of the state in the provision of health services.[101] He considers, for instance, why there has been an increased involvement by the state in the funding and administration of health services. Here as elsewhere his theoretical orientation is both functionalist and Marxist. He views the state as 'the configuration of public institutions and their relationship whose primary role is the reproduction of an economic system based on private ownership of the means of production, i.e. the capitalist economy'.[102] He consequently accounts for any increased state intervention in health care provision in terms of the functions it serves for capitalism. More specifically, he contends that the increased economic concentration of the present stage of capitalism, which like others he describes as monopoly capitalism, requires 'increased state intervention to stimulate that concentration, as well as to rectify the dislocation of well being created by that concentration'.[103]

Before considering some of the problems of this type of Marxist–functionalist account of the health services, two examples of its application to the psychiatric field should be mentioned. The most faithful is provided by a recent paper by Kovel entitled 'The American Mental Health Industry' dealing with the enormous expansion in mental health services in the United States during the twentieth century.[104] The author uses the term 'psychologization' to refer to this growth – a growth that includes not only the increase in the numbers of psychiatrists, but also of psychoanalysts, psychotherapists, psychologists, social workers and others working in the mental health field.[105] He argues that what he calls a 'fetish of psychology' is a particular manifestation of late – or monopoly – capitalism in whose working it plays a direct role.[106] The role is one of social control, not a repressive but an ideological control, through 'an alteration of the structures of experience' which represents an invasion of private life.[107] This control is necessary in order to satisfy the capitalist imperatives of consumption and work which he holds to be contrary to human inclinations and potentialities. Otherwise the continued accumulation of capital would be undermined and there might be organized resistance to the system. Kovel then elaborates and illustrates this analysis with a detailed discussion of the growth of the mental hygiene movement in the United States in the early decades of this century (the mental hygiene movement that was the source of the conceptions of mental health Kinglsey Davis had analysed so effectively in the late 1930s.[108]

A further example of Marxist functionalism applied to the psychiatric field has been provided by Andrew Scull in two books *Decarceration*, published in 1977, and *Museums of Madness*, published in 1979.[109] In the first book he looks at the post-war movement towards the deinstitutionalization of delinquents and the mentally ill (mostly in the United States, though he identifies a more limited decarceration in Britain). He explains the shift in terms of the economics of capitalism, arguing that with the growth of what he calls welfare capitalism the increasing costs of institutional care relative to other forms of welfare provision, in addition to the fiscal crisis of the state, have led to an abandonment of the segregative forms of social control which characterized the nineteenth century.[110] For him the welfare provisions of the twentieth century serve to strengthen capitalism by modifying its self-destructive tendencies and ensuring the reproduction and maintenance of labour power; the precise form they take depending on their cost and what the state can afford.

In *Museums of Madness* Scull turns back to the nineteenth century and attempts to account for the growth of separate asylums for the insane controlled by medical men – a movement both of segregation and professionalization. Again, he proposes that changes internal to capitalism are the moving force underlying the new developments. Rejecting the idea that the rise of the asylums should be related either to industrialization or to urbanization, he argues that:

The main driving force behind the rise of a segregative response to madness (and to other forms of deviance) can much more plausibly be asserted to lie in the effects of the advent of a mature capitalist market economy and the associated and even more thorough-going commercialization of existence. While the urban conditions produced by industrialization had a direct impact which was originally limited in geographical scope, the market system observed few such restrictions, and had increasingly subversive effects on the whole traditional rural and urban social structure. These changes in turn prompted the abandonment of long-established techniques for coping with the poor and troublesome.[111]

This book, unlike its predecessor, pays particular attention to the role of the medical profession, seeing the increasing involvement and power of the medical profession as part of the new response to insanity. However, the precise location of the activities of the medical profession within the overall analytic framework is none too clear. In part this is because there is little specific discussion of the nature of class stratification within capitalist society and the place of professional groups within it. At times the medical profession seems to be viewed more from the perspective of Freidson and Illich than from a Marxist stance, and defined as an independent force. Nevertheless, in his attention to the detailed activities of the medical profession and in his occasional reference to the dynamic of class struggle it could be argued that in *Museums of Madness* Scull does try to offer a more complex framework than the simple economic determinism and Marxist functionalism of *Decarceration*.

The problems of simple variants of Marxist economic determinism and Marxist functionalism have been widely discussed.[112] The idea that social relations have a direct, simple relation to economic conditions is one that many Marxists, let alone other social theorists, now eschew, and concepts such as 'relative autonomy' have been introduced in an attempt to pinpoint that independence, while accepting the ultimately determining role of economic conditions.[113] Similarly, the assumption that any social development must be functional for capital and can be explained in those terms has also been questioned. The general problems of functionalist explanations were widely discussed in sociology in the 1950s and 1960s since they were integral to the structural functionalism of Parsons and Merton, and such criticisms equally apply to Marxist functionalism.[114] But this does not mean that we can or should ignore the needs or interests of capital altogether. What is needed is a more complex analytical framework in which they feature as one component of the analysis. One critic of Scull's account of decarceration describes the deficiencies of the approach and the way it can be improved like this:

By concentrating entirely on the level of the state (political) the changing control practices appear to be determined either by the 'desires' of the state agencies (politicism), or the 'needs' of capital (functionalism). The crisis of capital accumulation since the end of the 1960s has had an important influence on control practices (as well, of course, as in most other areas, for example, education) through a reorganization and re-evaluation of the 'law and order' industry. There have been massive cuts in public spending, but they have been differently distributed and subject to a complex set of pressures of a political and ideological, as well as an economic nature.[115]

A number of Marxists have, therefore, tried to develop models giving more place to the 'complex set of pressures of a political and ideological' nature. Significantly, Navarro is one. In his later book *Class Struggle, the*

State and Medicine, published in 1978, he offers an analysis of the development of the National Health Service in Britain that tries to include both the politics of class struggle and the ideologies of a range of groups in this society.[116] Class struggle becomes the main motive of history. The introduction of the NHS was, he argues, the result on the one hand of specific demands by classes and groups outside the ruling class, and on the other hand of the endeavour of the capitalist class to ensure that their interests continue to be served. And in these struggles ideas as well as economics played a part:

To sum up, a process occurred in this period that has repeated itself in many Western capitalist countries since then. That is, there emerges a popular demand for assuring the availability of services on the one hand, and the capacity to pay for them on the other. And that demand eventually determines a response from the dominant class, a response based on the necessity for that class to legitimate the social order in which it holds dominance. And that dominance further reflects itself in the nature of the response, i.e. it primarily mirrors and reproduces the class interests and ideology of that dominant class. But this is not a sufficient explanation for the final shape of the response. Indeed, once the response has been triggered and its class character established, the specific interest groups, including, among others, professional interests, creep in and substantially shape its final form.[117]

A similar approach has also been adopted by Ian Gough in his account of the development of the welfare state.[118] He argues that the welfare state can only be explained as the outcome both of the degree of class struggle and of 'the ability of the capitalist state to secure the long-term reproduction of capitalist social relations', two factors whose relative importance varies depending on the policy at issue.[119] What is required, Gough argues, is a thorough, comparative, historical analysis of the 'unique configuration of circumstances' for each policy in each period.[120] In this formulation Gough does not specifically mention the role of ideas and in practice neither Gough nor Navarro pay them much attention in their historical accounts.

Figlio, and a number of other historians of medicine, have attempted to develop the ideas of Marxist historians of science in a way that combines elements of Marxist materialism and of Foucault's structural analysis of ideas.[121] Like Foucault they focus on ideas, but on ideas understood in relation to social forces. Medical concepts are treated 'as symbolic systems whose political function is to reinforce social relations necessary to the capitalist mode of production'.[122] Ideas, it is suggested, play a mediating, dynamic role in social relations. Hence as Figlio puts it 'medicine mediates social relations, and is itself constructed in the process'.[123] Elsewhere he elaborates the part played by ideas:

The symbolic systems will make those relations appear natural, and this naturalness will both reinforce those relations and render the symbolic system apparently autonomous from its social roots. Finally they will conceal the origins of social relations in the mode of production, and thus hide the roots of structural domination and hierarchy in society.[124]

In many respects this seems at first sight little different from Navarro's approach in his later work or that of Gough. However, social forces and ideas, rather than being viewed as essentially autonomous sets of phenomena whose relation, where it exists, is of a causal nature, are viewed as mutually constitutive of each other and the stress is on a processual, non-causal analysis, and on the way in which practices take on a reified character. 'Knowledge, like machinery, is accumulated "dead labour" from previous practices, which now confronts "living labour" as if it were alien to it.'[125] Theoretically there are distinct echoes here of Berger and Luckmann's attempt to combine Marxist and phenomenological approaches in their book *The Social Construction of Reality*.[126] But that book did not attempt to apply or develop its approach in relation to particular socio-historical situations. The merit of the work of Figlio and other recent historians of medicine and science is to grapple with, and to help to illuminate the complex interplay of ideas, practices and material conditions in relation to concrete historical situations. And in so doing their work pays far more attention both to historical detail and to the complexity of ideas than that of Navarro.

There are, of course, problems with the approach. To talk about knowledge and social forces as mutually constitutive may point us in the right direction (and have more potential than, for instance, a conceptualization in terms of the relative autonomy of ideology) but it is only a first step towards the production of a satisfactory sociology of knowledge. Moreover, it is far from clear that it is necessary to throw out the notion of causality; existing causal models tend to be over simple, but this does not mean that the notion of cause has no analytic value.[127] And if we do abandon the language of causality the problem of choosing between alternative accounts of the same phenomena becomes highly problematic.[128] However, these problems aside, the approach provides a valuable model for theoretically and historically sensitive work on the development of medical and psychiatric ideas and practice that avoids many of the problems of Marxist functionalism and over simple economic determinism.

The issue of gender

The theorists that we have considered so far pay little or no attention to gender in their theorizing about medicine and society (though some of the Marxist writers, such as Navarro, do not ignore it entirely).[129] Yet, like class, gender must be brought into any analysis of psychiatry, medicine and the health services. On the one hand, issues are raised by the nature of women's participation in the health care labour force. Why is it that women are so heavily represented throughout much of the health care labour force – as nurses, technicians, therapists, cleaners and so forth, yet so poorly represented at the top of the health service hierarchy?[130] The proportion of women doctors is far lower than the proportion of women nurses, and within the medical profession itself there are proportionately far fewer women consultants than women general practitioners.[131] On the other hand, gender differences in the observed patterns of health and sickness and in the use of the health services need to be analysed and explained. For example, although women's life expectancy is now considerably higher than men's, they make much more use of the health services, and generally report higher levels of morbidity.[132] Moreover, as we saw in Chapter 2, women have higher levels of admission to psychiatric beds, constitute a higher proportion of residents, make more use of psychiatric outpatient clinics, and have far more contact with general practitioners for conditions medically defined as mental illnesses.

Issues such as these have been explored in a number of feminist studies of medicine. One of the most influential and most controversial is to be found in the work of Ehrenreich and English whose initial pamphlets *Witches, Midwives and Nurses* and *Complaints and Disorders*, both first published in 1973, were developed into a book *For Her Own Good: 150 years of the Experts' Advice to Women* that appeared in 1978.[133] Ehrenreich and English bring together the two issues of male control of the medical profession and the female predominance among patients, seeing the latter as the corollary of the former. Historically they identify a struggle between unlicensed healers, commonly women – the wise women who offered help with childbirth, abortion and sickness – and licensed healers, increasingly men, who sought to exclude women from the newly emergent profession of medicine.[134] In this struggle it was not, they suggest, the knowledge and competence of the licensed male healers that brought success, for in the fourteenth, fifteenth and sixteenth centuries, when much of the suppression of female healers occurred, the medical men's learning was often religious and classical rather than scientific.[135] Female healers, in contrast, had an empirically based knowledge that was likely to have a beneficial effect:

She relied on her senses rather than on faith or doctrine, she believed in trial and error, cause and effect. Her attitude was not religiously passive, but actively enquiring. She trusted her ability to find ways to deal with disease, pregnancy and childbirth – whether through medication or charms. In short, her magic was the science of her time.[136]

It was, rather, the development of a partnership between church, state and the emerging medical profession and their efforts to discredit and denounce the unlicensed healers on grounds of ignorance which led to the success of the licensed healers. Some of the unlicensed healers were persecuted as witches for their use of magic and they were excluded as women from the formal centres of learning, the universities. The latter was important since membership of the official medical associations increasingly demanded formal qualifications, and the necessity for official recognition was backed by state legislation. Later with a shift to a more scientific orientation in official medicine, science became the new weapon of the licensed healers in the competition to attract clients.[137] By the middle of the nineteenth century these male medical experts in turn set the parameters of female dependence and frailty, encouraging a cult of invalidism among upper- and middle-class women:

The medical profession was consolidating its monopoly over healing, and now the woman who felt sick, or tired or simply depressed would no longer seek help from a friend or female healer, but from a male physician. The general theory which guided the doctors' practice as well as their public pronouncements was that women were, by nature, weak, dependent and diseased. Thus would the doctors attempt to secure their victory over the female healer: with the 'scientific' evidence that women's essential nature was not to be a strong, competent help-giver but to be a patient.[138]

For female dependence directly served the interests of medical men:

As a businessman, the doctor had a direct interest in a social role for women that encouraged them to be sick: as a doctor, he had an obligation to find the causes of female complaints. The result was that, as a 'scientist', he ended up proposing medical theories that were actually justifications of women's social role.[139]

Ehrenreich and English's account of women's place within the health services could be said to add the dimension of patriarchy (which they interpret as the rule of the father) to Illich's version of medicalization (though there is no explicit reference to Illich's work). However, although they appear to attribute considerable independent power to the medical profession in the spirit of Illich, they cast their ideas into a loose Marxist framework. It is not industrialization but the development of the market economy of capitalism that is held to have produced the extension of medical power they identify and to have made science the new ideology replacing philosophy and religion. Nevertheless, overall they seem to suggest it is not so much the general needs of capital as the specific needs of the medical profession that structure and determine developments within medicine.

Apart from the accuracy of the historical detail, which has been seriously questioned, there are other problems with the thesis.[140] Jordanova argues, for example, that in dealing with the issue of gender Ehrenreich and English tend to construct stereotypical categories:

The authors are acutely sensitive to how the experts construct a category 'woman', but they, covertly, do the same. They construct two categories – 'women' and 'expert'. Both these are stereotypes, with the status of myths in that they appear to transcend any specific case without respecting real human complexity and variety.[141]

And she adds:

There is here a danger of a new biologism emerging which assumes certain shared characteristics among a group because of a shared biological character. 'Woman' is now a transcendental category. This time it is constructed in the service of feminism but its implications remain unexplored.[142]

To criticize the details of the account offered by Ehrenreich and English is not to suggest that we should ignore the dimension of gender in examining psychiatry and medicine. There have been a number of other historical accounts of the exclusion of women healers and theoretical attempts to explain the male domination of the medical profession.[143] The general predominance of women within the 'caring' professions, such as nursing, is a matter that has received some attention and has been tied to the overall sexual division of labour within society. Gamarnikow, for instance, in a discussion of nursing argues from a

Marxist–feminist stance that it is the ideological construction of biological categories that is crucial to understanding the sexual division of labour:

The sexual division of labour treats all women as potential wives – mothers – that is, as dependent on men – precisely because they are biological females. The ideologically implicated nature of this mode of work and task allocation lies in its emphasis on sex differences rather than on, say, human similarities; and the priority granted to biological differences rather than human similarities provides a focus and a legitimation for hierarchical differentiation between men and women. The sexual division of labour as ideology is articulated at the point of differentiation and hierarchisation in the patriarchal labour process.[144]

This ideologically constructed sexual division can in turn be explained (though Gamarnikow does not seek to do this) in terms of what is functional for capital. A common, though recently contested, argument is that the capitalist division of labour which assigns women to the home and men to the labour market provides for the reproduction of labour power in an economically effective way.[145]

Medical control over childbirth, contraception and abortion, which has been examined in numerous studies, plays an essential part in any understanding of women's use of the health services since it is the 'medicalization' of these events (i.e. the fact that they are in the hands of the medical profession) that accounts to a considerable extent for women's greater use of the health services.[146] But it does not fully account for the high levels of consultation. In particular, it does not readily account for the disproportionate use of the health services by women for problems identified as psychiatric. The pattern as we have seen is complex. Women's over-representation is especially marked amongst the over-65s, among the married (men tend to be over-represented among the single), among the milder forms of mental disorder (anxiety disorders, depression) and at the non-specialist and out-patient, rather than in-patient sectors.[147] Above all it is at the level of the general practitioner, where the typical treatment is the prescription of some psychotropic drug, that women are over-represented.[148]

The observed gender differences in current patterns of use of the psychiatric services arise from a complex interplay of medical and psychiatric provision and of social expectation and definition of male and female behaviour that have developed historically.[149] Of especial importance is the way in which the boundaries of mental illness have been established both conceptually and practically. To the extent that specific types of mental illness have been defined as pathologies of thoughts, feelings and actions which are governed by gender specific expectations, then rates of mental illness will differ between men and women. In as far, for example, as women are expected and encouraged to be sensitive to the feelings of others, to be more dependent and to show certain types of feelings, such as sadness, fear and anxiety, then categories of mental illness that focus on the pathological expression of these feelings have a tendency to be gender specific and to produce gender differences in the observed levels of that disorder. Furthermore, changes in the provision of medical services seeming to offer help for such problems also facilitate the emergence of a gender difference.[150] A further factor which contributes to gender differences in observed psychiatric morbidity is the diverse evaluation and assessment of men's and women's experiences and behaviours, whether by the individual or others both professional and non-professional. Judgements as to whether the experiences are problematic, merit medical attention, are of a psychological nature and so forth depend in part on the sex of the person whose actions are under consideration.[151]

Since the expectations governing male and female behaviour vary historically, as do the nature and content of medical and psychiatric services, gender differences in the use of psychiatric services and in the observed levels of mental illness are not constant over time. The over-representation of women as users of public mental health services is largely a post-war phenomenon tied to the expansion of publicly funded medical and psychiatric services with the attendant broadening and change in the range and distribution of phenomena brought within the purview of such services.[152] These changes are considered in the following chapters.

Understanding psychiatry

No single perspective presently provides an adequate understanding of psychiatry. The liberal–scientific approach favoured by medical practitioners themselves, by many policy makers and by much of the general public, has major deficiencies. Locating contemporary psychiatry within its medical context, it idealizes medical practice, seeing it as the best solution to the problems of sickness and ill-health which are viewed as natural and inevitable occurrences in any society. The medical profession is assumed to assemble the best of the available scientifically based knowledge, skills and expertise; to inculcate, require, and ensure dedication and commitment from its practitioners, and consequently to act in the best interests of patients. Inefficiencies and inadequacies, when they do occur, are merely the result of individual wickedness and incompetence, or deficiencies in scientific knowledge, or the lack of financial and social support for the health services which offer the public their means of access to medical practitioners. The possibility that a curatively oriented medical system, in which the application of science and technology are the source of status and prestige within the profession and the focus of the bulk of medical resources, may not be the best way of maintaining the overall health of the population or even of maximizing the health of sick individuals is largely ignored.

The conception of psychiatry propounded by the 1960s critics stands opposed to the liberal–scientific perspective and casts doubt on many of its basic assumptions when applied to the sphere of psychiatry and mental illness. Taking as its starting point the idea that the phenomena considered symptomatic of mental illness are those forms of human behaviour which break social rules, it suggests that medical practice – at least as it is currently structured – is deficient and defective because it ignores the social processes and values involved in definitions of mental health and sickness, and in the genesis of the behaviour in question. Interpersonal communications, values, subjective experiences, and meanings are all largely left out of the analysis. Yet the critics' theorizing about psychiatry and mental illness has its own deficiencies, most obviously that the focus is primarily on mental illness itself. The typical questions are: Is mental illness really an illness? Do definitions of mental illness involve value judgements? How can we best understand the behaviour of people who are identified as mentally ill? The contemporary character of psychiatric practice and its medical context are largely taken as given. There is no attempt to understand how and why medical practice has come to take on its narrow, natural scientific mould, to understand why there is so little attention given to the social processes and subjective experiences in psychiatry, or to understand how medicine functions as a profession.

It is questions like these which theorists such as Illich, Freidson and Navarro consider: they all attempt to offer an understanding of the power of the medical profession, its place in society and of the character of medical practice. As my detailed comments on the different theorists in this group indicate, in my view the Marxist accounts, except those in a narrowly functionalist mould, currently provide the most useful understanding of the character of contemporary health services. including the mental health services. One reason, however, why the strongly functionalist accounts which focus on the needs of capitalism are unsatisfactory is that they generally attend to the functions which contemporary structures and practices perform. Even when they are broadened to include an analysis of the conflict, tensions and struggles between different social groups, and incorporate the dynamics of class and gender, they still do not offer an adequate understanding of present-day structures and practices. For we also need to examine the historical origins of existing ideas and institutions. The current shape and character of psychiatry and of the mental health services which provide the context of psychiatry work, are as much a product of past needs, pressures and struggles as of present forces. It is for this reason that a full understanding of present-day psychiatry requires an analysis of its past development. It is to this task that I now turn.

Notes and references

1   See, for instance, Mills, 1959; Bottomore, 1966.
2   Miliband's work on power and the state (1966) illustrates this approach.
3   Illich, 1975 and 1977a.
4   Illich, 1977a, p. 11.
5   ibid., p. 11.
6   ibid., p. 271.
7   McKeown, 1976a; see also Dubos, 1959.
8   Cochrane, 1972, Chapters 5 and 6.
9   ibid., *passim*.
10   Illich, 1977a, p. 49.
11   ibid., p. 49.
12   Significantly the term medicalization is not explicitly defined or discussed by Illich; it merely appears in the chapter heading of the section of the book dealing with social iatrogenesis.
13   ibid., pp. 56–8.
14   Illich, 1975.
15   Illich, 1977a, p. 271.
16   ibid., p. 215.
17   ibid., p. 215.
18   ibid., p. 219.
19   ibid., pp. 254–5.
20   Illich, 1977b, p. 16.
21   See also Mills, 1959; Bottomore, 1966.
22   Illich, 1977a, pp. 172–3.
23   ibid., pp. 53–4.
24   ibid., pp. 255–6.
25   ibid., p. 56.
26   By the end of the 1970s about 90 per cent of all deliveries in Britain

took place in hospital (Brighton Women and Science Group, p. 167); see also Walsh, 1980; Strauss and Glaser, 1975.

27 Illich, 1977a, Part II, *passim*.

28 For twentieth century changes in British health services see Leichter, 1979; Walters, 1980, Chapter 2. The *Report as to the Practice of Medicine and Surgery by Unqualified Persons* of 1910 commented 'It is comparatively rarely that a general practitioner sees the child of working-class people until it has been purged and medicined for several days by the prescribing chemist.' Quoted in Carr-Saunders and Wilson, 1964, p. 89.

29 The class character of health care in the sixteenth and seventeenth century is discussed in Chapter 5.

30 The politics of its legalization are discussed by Greenwood and Young, 1976.

31 See Chapters 9 and 10.

32 For a useful analysis of the overall increase in public expenditure in the post-war period see Gough, 1979, Chapter 5.

33 Abel-Smith, 1976.

34 In 1974, for instance, labour costs constituted some 73 per cent of all National Health Service hospital expenditure (Levitt, 1976, Table 7, p. 181).

35 Some 40 per cent of all acute beds are occupied by persons over 65 (Ham, 1982, p. 45).

36 See Widgery, 1979, Chapter 8; Levitt, 1976, Chapter 8.

37 Navarro, 1976, Part II.

38 Navarro's ideas are discussed in more detail in the second section of this chapter.

39 Navarro, 1976, p. 112.

40 Freidson, 1970a and 1970b.

41 Freidson, 1970a, Chapter 4.

42 ibid.

43 ibid., pp. 23–4.

44 His account of the development of medicine as a profession is outlined in the first chapter of the book.

45 ibid., p. 21.

46 ibid., p. 72.

47 ibid., p. 83.

48 ibid., Chapter 4.

49 Parkin's discussion of social closure is of interest here (1979).

50 Freidson, 1970a, Chapter 14.

51 ibid., p. 346.

52 ibid., Chapter 13.

53 Gerth and Mills, 1948, p. 180.

54 Freidson, 1970b, Chapter 4.

55 ibid.
56 ibid., pp. 139–43.
57 ibid., Chapter 4.
58 ibid., p. 108 – the quotation is from Parsons' Introduction to Max Weber's *The Theory of Social and Economic Organisation*, (1964).
59 For instance, the National Health Service Act, 1946, provided that only registered practitioners could take up appointments within the National Health Service, and the Dangerous Drugs Act of 1920 provided that only registered doctors, dentists and veterinary surgeons could be in possession of dangerous drugs for the purpose of their practice. See Carr-Saunders and Wilson, 1964, pp. 88–9.
60 Freidson, 1970b, pp. 113–15.
61 This was part of their evidence to the Royal Commission on Doctors and Dentists Remuneration. Quoted in Robson, 1973, p. 415.
62 ibid., p. 414.
63 Freidson, 1970b, p. 84.
64 Johnson, 1972, p. 46, and pp. 77–86.
65 Although attempts to divert resources away from these areas of medicine generates considerable medical opposition, see Doyal, 1979, p. 213.
66 Direct financial controls, for instance, over the work of general practitioners, who have the status of independent contractors within the NHS, are limited.
67 Vaizey, 1962, p. 94.
68 Bodenheimer, Cummings and Harding, 1977.
69 ibid., p. 82.
70 Ehrenreich and Ehrenreich, 1971, p. 122.
71 Of course even if medical practitioners are salaried, economic and status considerations may 'distort' clinical judgements in this way.
72 Freud, 1935, p. 26.
73 Foucault's ideas are discussed by Sheridan, 1980, and Sedgwick, 1982, Chapter 5.
74 See, for instance, *The Order of Things*, 1970 and *The Archaeology of Knowledge*, 1972.
75 Kuhn, 1962.
76 Foucault asserts 'there is no power relation without the correlative constitution of a field of knowledge, nor any knowledge that does not presuppose and constitute at the same time power relations' (1977, p. 27).
77 See for instance Foucault, 1979, p. 67. He also uses the term psychiatrization (ibid., p. 105).
78 Foucault, 1967.
79 ibid., pp. 10–11.
80 Sheridan suggests his work contains both structuralist and anti-

structuralist features (1980, pp. 37–8, 89–91, 198–205).

81 For a recent discussion of Marxist conceptions of ideology see Larrain, 1983.

82 Sheridan discusses Marxists' reaction to Foucault's work, and their categorization of him as an idealist (1980, Conclusion).

83 Foucault, 1967; 1973; 1979.

84 Navarro's basic ideas about medicine are outlined in Part III of *Medicine Under Capitalism* (1976).

85 ibid., p. 136.

86 Miliband, 1969, Chapter 2.

87 Navarro, 1976, pp. 136–56.

88 He looks specifically, for instance, at the role of women in the health care labour force (ibid., pp. 170–9).

89 ibid., pp. 111–15.

90 Townsend and Davidson, 1982, Table 1, p. 57.

91 ibid., Chapter 5; Navarro, 1976, pp. 84–7.

92 Townsend and Davidson, 1982, pp. 61–3.

93 Parsons, 1951.

94 ibid., p. 285.

95 ibid., pp. 436–7.

96 ibid., p. 431.

97 ibid., p. 477.

98 Merton, 1968, Chapter III.

99 Navarro, p. 113.

100 ibid., p. 116.

101 ibid., Part IV.

102 ibid., p. 196.

103 ibid., p. 217.

104 Kovel, 1981.

105 ibid., p. 73.

106 ibid., p. 75.

107 ibid., p. 78.

108 Davis, 1938.

109 Scull, 1977 and 1979.

110 Scull, 1977, Chapter 8. The concept of the fiscal crisis of the state comes from O'Connor, 1973. Scull's argument in *Decarceration* is discussed more fully in Chapter 10.

111 Scull, 1977, p. 30.

112 Lockwood, 1981; Parkin, 1979; Giddens, 1981; Koch, 1980. See also Benton, 1984, pp. 220–5.

113 See Althusser's paper 'Contradiction and Overdetermination', (1969).

114 See, for instance, Dore, 1961.

115 Matthews, 1979.

116 Navarro, 1978.

117   ibid., p. 11.
118   Gough, 1979.
119   ibid., p. 64.
120   ibid., p. 57.
121   See, for instance, Young 1970 and 1977; Figlio, 1977 and 1978, and 1982; Cooter, 1981 and 1982.
122   Figlio, 1978, p. 592.
123   ibid., p. 589.
124   ibid., p. 592.
125   Figlio, 1982, pp. 176–7.
126   Berger and Luckman, 1966.
127   See, for instance, MacIntyre, 1962.
128   The problems of 'conventionalist' philosophy of social science are discussed by Keat and Urry, 1975, Chapter 3.
129   See Navarro, 1976, pp. 170–9.
130   ibid., see also Parry and Parry, 1976, Chapter 8.
131   Oakley, 1983, pp. 119–24.
132   ibid., pp. 103–9; Busfield, 1983.
133   Ehrenreich and English, 1974, 1976 and 1979.
134   A similar model is adopted by Oakley, 1976 and Versluysen, 1980. See also Donnison, 1977.
135   Ehrenreich and English, 1974, pp. 14–15.
136   ibid., p. 12.
137   ibid., p. 31.
138   Ehrenreich and English, 1979, p. 92.
139   Ehrenreich and English, 1976, p. 30.
140   Jordanova, 1982; Versluysen, 1980, pp. 190–7.
141   Jordanova, 1982, p. 125.
142   ibid., p. 125.
143   See Oakley, 1976; Versluysen, 1980; Donnison, 1977.
144   Gamanikow, 1978, pp. 100–1.
145   Seccombe, 1974; Gardiner, 1975; Molyneux, 1979.
146   Oakley, 1983; Busfield and Hart, 1978.
147   Busfield, 1983.
148   Goldberg and Huxley, 1980, p. 100.
149   Busfield, 1983; Cloward and Piven, 1979; Smith, 1975.
150   Busfield, 1983, pp. 127–31.
151   Phillips and Segal, 1969; Horwitz, 1977.
152   Busfield, 1983, pp. 127–31; see also Gove and Tudor, 1972.

part two
Historical Developments

5 The trade in healing and lunacy[1]

The emergence of psychiatry as a separate professional specialism within medicine can, with the benefit of hindsight, be identified as an event of the mid nineteenth century. It was then that the first official associations of doctors specializing in the care of mental diseases were set up, and the first journals devoted to insanity and psychological medicine were published. In England, for instance, the Association of Medical Officers of Asylums and Hospitals for the Insane was founded in 1841 and its journal – the *Asylum Journal* (which eventually became the *British Journal of Psychiatry*) was first published in 1854.[2] A few years earlier, in 1848, the rival *Journal of Psychological Medicine* had been founded by medical practitioners working outside the asylums.[3] In America, the Association of Medical Superintendents of American Institutions for the Insane was established in 1844, in Philadelphia, and its journal, the *American Journal of Insanity* (now the *American Journal of Psychiatry*) was founded the same year.[4] In Germany certain steps towards professionalization had occurred even earlier, although separate institutions for the insane were established relatively late.[5] A number of journals (albeit short-lived) devoted exclusively to the subject of mental disorders were published in Germany during the first two decades of the nineteenth century and the first Chair of Psychological Medicine was established at Leipzig in 1811.[6]

Psychiatry's emergence as a professional grouping within medicine was the result of a number of changes. Not least was the increasing professionalization of medicine as a whole, in which the rapidly expanding hospital sector played such an important role.[7] In England a major landmark of the increasing professionalization was provided by the Medical Act of 1858 which set up a single register of all legally qualified medical practitioners.[8] This followed important developments in medical training and scientific research in the previous two centuries, facilitated by the establishment of voluntary hospitals in the eighteenth century.[9] In the field of mental disorder it was, similarly, the development of the institutional care of the insane, first in voluntary and then, above all, in public asylums that provided the locus for the development of the new profession. Asylums offered new opportunities for the employment of medical practitioners as specialists in the care of the insane, consequently increasing the possibilities for the development of both expertise and claims to expertise, so crucial to successful professionalization. They provided a captive and clinically diverse clientele on which the skills of medical practitioners might be elaborated; they created opportunities for the development of training and research; and they offered employment for those with claims to specialist skills in the treatment and care of insanity. Hence they facilitated both the differentiation and amplification of knowledge, and the opportunities for employment so crucial to the profession's emergence. It was the asylum doctors who formed the core of the new profession.

However, while asylum doctors played a central role in the development of the new profession, the emergence of psychiatry as a professional specialism within medicine – the term psychiatry was first used in England in 1846 – did not occur without considerable negotiation and conflict.[10] There were a range of potential professional specialisms, each one differentiated from its parent medicine in a different and often far from clearcut way. The diversity of labels used to refer to the different practitioners working in areas that we would now embrace within the field of psychiatry reflects the range of conflicting groupings and the problems of boundary negotiation.[11] Comtemporary literature refers to alienists and neurologists, to mad-doctors and asylum doctors, to specialists in nervous diseases and specialists in medical psychology, as well as to psychiatrists. Many of these labels represented a different potential delineation of the emergent professional group, based variously on supposed differences in the type of illness, the causal aetiology, the physiological system involved, and the institutional location of the patients. As it is, what we now know as psychiatry represents something of an amalgam as well as a reconceptualization of these diverse groups, and the problems of boundary negotiation are far from settled.[12] Nevertheless, though the boundaries of specialisms are not exact, historically there can be no doubt that the development of separate asylums for the insane not only laid the foundations of psychiatry as a profession, but also exerted a profound influence on the structure of comtemporary mental health services.

The immediate antecedents of separate asylums for the insane are to be found, according to Foucault, in the ideas and practices of the Classical Age – the period from the middle of the seventeenth until the end of the eighteenth century – during which time a new critical consciousness committed to the values of reason, regarded madness as a form of unreason and sought to control it.[13]

A culture like that of the Classical Age, so many of whose values were invested in reason, had both the most and the least to lose in madness. The most because madness constituted the most immediate contradiction of all that justified it; the least, because it disarmed madness entirely, leaving it quite powerless. This maximum and minimum of risk accepted by Classical Culture in madness is perfectly expressed in the word 'unreason': the simple, immediate reverse side of reason; and this empty, purely negative form, possessing neither content nor value, which bears the imprint of a reason that has just fled, but which remains for unreason the raison d'être of what it is.[14]

The means of control was the 'great confinement' in which the insane were confined alngside the poor, sick, aged and dependent in new institutions. For Foucault it was the establishment of the Hôpital Général in Paris in 1656 that symbolized the new confinement. In England it was the workhouses, established in increasing numbers from the end of the seventeenth century, which confined the diverse group of indigent and dependent through the operation of the poor law.[15]

Yet while these developments in the public sphere were decisive, the emergence and growth of separate asylums for the insane in the nineteenth century can only be fully understood if they are also placed in the context of developments in the institutional provision for the insane in the private sector, and of developments within medicine more generally. It was the private madhouses in the seventeenth century that offered the first separate institutional provision for the insane – both rich and poor – and these private madhouses, and even more the charitable asylums that sprang up in the eighteenth century, not only offered the institutional base that contributed to the expansion of medical activity concerning the insane, but were also the locus for innovations in the conceptualization of insanity and its treatment. Some came to serve as the model for and the justification of the new public asylums.

In this chapter, therefore, I consider healing in the sixteenth and seventeenth centuries and the development of private madhouses. In the next I examine the development of the voluntary asylums in the eighteenth century, and the changes in ideas about insanity in the same period, in the context of changing medical ideas and practices. In the subsequent chapter I consider institutional provision in the public sector.

Healing and healers in the sixteenth and seventeenth centuries

Healing in sixteenth- and seventeenth-century Britain was characterized by its diversity: diversity in the social standing, background,
education, experience and official recognition of the healers, in their
ideas about the nature and causes of sickness, and in the treatments they
offered.[16] On the one hand there were the more organized and official
groups of healers, the hierarchically ranked physicians, surgeons and
apothecaries, vying with one another and with outsiders to strengthen
their monopoly position. All three were actively engaged in professiona-
lizing themselves through developing their respective occupational
organizations, which made more extensive training and qualifications
necessary for membership and also attempted to suppress unlicensed
practitioners. On the other hand there were the heterogeneous range of
'empirics' and unlicensed healers who catered for the sickness of the vast
bulk of the population who could not afford the services of the
licensed practitioners – the wise women, cunning men, herbalists,
magical healers, conjurers and sorcerers.[17] Together they constituted a
range of medical practioners striking in quantity as well as diversity. A
recent study estimated that at the end of the sixteenth century there was
one practitioner for every 400 persons in London (leaving aside
midwives, nurses and public health officials), and one for every 220 to
250 persons in Norwich.[18]

Throughout much of the period the ideas and practices of healers,
whether of high or low status, involved a mixture in which religion,
magic and science were inextricably interwoven, and illness was seen as
having both supernatural and natural causes.[19] The Church's involvement in healing was considerable, and the clerical and medical
professions were closely connected.[20] The Church was actively involved
in the licensing and regulation of healing and was especially concerned
about the use of magic in healing.[21] In addition many clergy were
themselves healers; on the one hand, seeing it as part of their charitable
duty to the poor, and on the other hand viewing the acquisition of
medical skills as a safeguard for their livelihood in a period of intense
religious conflict.[22] In this respect the clergy fitted into the general
pattern, for healing was to a large extent an entrepreneurial activity by
means of which individuals, often in combination with other activities,
hoped to make a living. Of course, the motives of the healers varied,
whether clergymen or not, as did their willingness to provide treatment
free for those who could not afford to pay for it; but the majority of
practitioners charged for their services, charges varying according to the

status of the practitioners and the pockets of those who sought their services and help. And the market for healing, despite the endeavours of the Church and the official medical organizations, was relatively free and unregulated, especially in the countryside.

London was the centre of organized medical practice and physicians led the field in the attempt to monopolize and professionalize medicine through restrictive licensing and efforts to control the activities of other licensed practitioners as well as unlicensed healers. The College of Physicians was established in London in 1518, with Thomas Linacre as its president, to supervise and license physicians in the City of London and within a seven mile radius.[23] Membership of the college was restricted to medical graduates of Oxford and Cambridge, thereby excluding women, and four years of practice were required before candidates were granted a fellowship. Members also had to pass an examination, but the content was more classical and academic than practical.[24] In the early years of the college there were only a dozen members; even by the middle of the seventeenth century the figure was only around forty. Meanwhile the population of London had increased sharply; it probably quadrupled during the sixteenth century, reaching some 200,000 persons by the end of the century.[25] By 1834 there were still only 113 fellows of the college and some 234 licentiates. The restrictive policy for membership ensured that there could be no real monopoly of medical practice, even in London, despite the acquisition of exclusive legal rights, and 'an inferior body, catering to the needs of the general public was bound by the mere logic of the situation to force its way sooner or later to a form of recognition'.[26] Nevertheless by the seventeenth century the members of the college 'constituted an extremely well-organized and vigilant medical elite'.[27] Outside London licensing was in the hands of the universities and the Church and the requirements for licensing were less restrictive. The numbers of licensed physicians was correspondingly greater, one list identifying 814 physicians licensed between 1603 and 1643.[28]

Medical training at Oxford and Cambridge, institutions which had strong links with the Anglican church, was lengthy, conservative and dominated by the classical humanistic traditions of Galenic medicine and humoral pathology, although during the seventeenth century there was an increasing emphasis on the study of anatomy and physiology, following the influence of William Harvey, a member of the College of Physicians.[29] Howver, other subjects such as astrology, which was part of natural philosophy, were included in the university curriculum and influenced the thought and practice of the physicians despite some hostility from the College of Physicians. Astrology was attractive not least for 'the ambitious scale of its intellectual pretensions':

It offered a systematic scheme of explanation for all the vagaries of human and natural behaviour, and there was in principle no question which it could not answer . . .. It was this comprehensiveness which made the art so compelling. In the absence of any rival system of scientific explanation, and in particular of the social sciences – sociology, social anthropology, social psychology – there was no other existing body of thought, religion apart, which even began to offer so all-embracing an explanation for the baffling variousness of human affairs. Nor had the sciences of medicine, biology and meteorology developed enough to offer a convincing and complete understanding of the world of nature. This was the intellectual vacuum which astrology moved in to fill, bringing with it the earliest attempts at a universal natural law. For a long time the alternative was stark; either one accepted astrological teachings or, as John Gadbury put it in 1674, one had to admit one's ignorance of the true causes of events, and 'be content to rank them among the occult qualities of nature of which no certain reason can be given'.[30]

Astrology reached the peak of its influence in the middle of the seventeenth century but after the Restoration in 1660 it began to decline and had all but disappeared from the circles of the intellectual elite by the end of the century. It had depended on a belief in the hierarchical subordination of earth to heavens and with the undermining of the distinction between terrestrial and celestial bodies such beliefs became untenable.[31]

Notwithstanding the importance of Galenic thought in the university medical curriculum, however, physicians were often relatively eclectic in their ideas about the causes of illness and its treatment, especially those practising outside London. Richard Napier, an Anglican clergyman and atrological physician practising in Buckinghamshire in the early decades of the seventeenth century, manifests this eclecticism. MacDonald, who has recently examined his case notes, argues:

The inadequacy of characterizing Napier, or any of his contemporaries, simply as a superstitious traditionalist or a progressive rationalist is nevertheless evident from his records. He accepted both traditional beliefs in witchcraft and magic and new arguments against their indiscriminate application. He regarded magic and science as alternative methods of evaluating individual cases, and did not view them as antagonistic belief systems. Depending upon the circumstances of a particular case, he emphasized either the natural or the supernatural causes of his client's main types of circumstances: troubled courtships, marital problems, bereavements and economic difficulties (a more important category for men than for women).[110] Some of these problems were attributed to the intervention of witches; a woman told Napier of a rejected lover 'One that haunteth her and sayeth that he will marry her, and she denieth him of a long time. She feareth that he hath bewitched her.'[111] Yet others had religious anxieties and spiritual problems.

The treatments Napier offered varied and often combined a number of different methods. There was little that was specific to mental disease in the general nature of the remedies, although there was perhaps a greater focus on 'psychological' healing and specific recipes were used for purges and vomits. The purges, vomits, and bleeding, adjusted according to age, sex and bodily condition, were supplemented by astrological and magical remedies, by exorcism and spiritual guidance.[112] His religious counselling seems to have consisted largely of 'comforting speeches', but he also urged regular church attendance and prayers.[113] He varied in his willingness to accept the validity of the witchcraft accusations of his patients, using 'every means available to him, angelic magic, witchcraft, and even folk rituals, to find out if his patients were bewitched'.[114] He then employed amulets, prayers and exorcism to deal with the malevolent spirits.

Napier, through his very eclecticism, illustrates the range of treatments which might be used to deal with the disturbances of mind that were brought to healers for cure. Some of the treatments, such as the use of purgatives and vomits, seem to have been relatively harsh, but they were not specific to complaints of mental disturbance. Napier did not use flogging as a means to control insanity and bring patients to their senses in the way that Willis was to recommend later in the century; however twenty of his patients had been chained or beaten at some time.[115] Village authorities could order the insane to be whipped, and those who flogged lunatics were exempted from legal punishment for assault.[116] However, it was not until the eighteenth century when the asylum system began to develop that the practice of beating the insane became more common. In order to analyse the development of that system we must turn to the private madhouses established in the context of the practices and ideas about healing which we have been examining.

Private madhouses

It is difficult to date the emergence of private residential care for the insane with any great precision. Houses catering for several insane persons seem to have been first established in the seventeenth century, although it had been the custom even earlier for those involved in healing, such as clergymen or other medical practitioners, to have an insane person lodging with them.[117] The real growth in the private madhouses seems to have followed the Restoration in 1660 and by the beginning of the eighteenth century the confinement of the insane in private madhouses was a well-established, albeit limited, practice.[118] In 1807 there were only some forty-five licensed private madhouses recorded. However, their numbers increased rapidly during the first half of the nineteenth century and there were 146 by 1849 when the number of houses reached its peak. From then on, as more public asylums were opened and existing asylums expanded in size, their numbers declined, so that in 1900 there were but seventy licensed houses.[119]

A large proportion of the private madhouses were located in the London area and during the second half of the nineteenth century when quantitative estimates for the whole country are available, they contained roughly half the total of all inmates of the private houses.[120] Outside London madhouses were more likely to be found in the more densely populated regions of the country.[121] The majority were small, although the metropolitan (i.e. London) houses were generally larger than the provincial ones.[122] In the nineteenth century, when the madhouse numbers were at their height, most provincial houses contained twenty-five inmates or fewer, and only a handful contained more than a hundred; hence the overall numbers they confined were small.[123] Even in the middle of the nineteenth century when the number of houses was at its peak, and the population some 18 million persons, the number confined was little more than 7000 as Table 14 shows.

The madhouses catered for two classes of inmate: on the one hand, for members of the affluent classes whose families could afford the relatively high cost of residential care – the private patients – and on the other hand, for those of low social standing forced into dependency on the poor law – the pauper patients – who were sent to the private madhouses under a system of contracting out developed by the poor law authorities.[124] Some of the private madhouses accepted only private inmates, others took both, providing different standards of accommodation and service for the two groups and charging a different weekly rate.[125] Pauper patients might be accommodated in the stables and outbuildings, while the private patients resided in the main house.[126] The proportion of private and pauper patients varied over time. Unfortunately the data on this matter even for the early decades of the nineteenth century is poor. Between 1844 and 1854 the returns show

Table 14   Number of patients in private licensed houses, 1819–70

Date	Provincial	Metropolitan	Total
1819	963	1,622	2,585
1825	11,321	1,761	3,082
1829	1,703	2,031	3,734
1831	1,742	2,345	4,087
1844	3,346	1,827	5,173
1848	3,949	3,081	7,030
1850	3,786	2,945	6,731
1860	2,356	1,944	4,300
1870	2,204	1,700	4,904

Note: The data for 1819–31 and for 1844–70 do not form a single time series since the original sources as well as the reliability of the data differ.
Source: Parry-Jones, 1972

more pauper than private inmates of the metropolitan and provincial licensed madhouses. From then on the number of pauper inmates declined quite sharply as more and more public asylums were opened, and the number of private inmates continued to increase slowly.[127]

Nineteenth-century data show that the largest percentage of inmates were said to be suffering from mania, perhaps some half to three-quarters of the total. Of the 250 cases admitted during the five years until the end of December 1843 to Duddeston Hall, a private madhouse near Birmingham, which admitted both private and pauper patients, some 190 (i.e. 76 per cent) were said to have mania, and only thirteen melancholia (5.2 per cent). The other cases were assigned to the categories of 'dementia consequent upon protacted mania' (eight persons), monomania (six), 'congenital idiocy' (one), general paralysis (sixteen) and epilepsy (sixteen).[128] For the same period the figures for Brislington House, near Bristol, which also admitted both private and pauper inmates, show mania accounting for 52 per cent of the 112 cases admitted and melancholia 21 per cent.[129] Private madhouses were, therefore, being largely used for the more severe forms of insanity as Willis, for one, had proposed – forms that, as we have seen, constituted only a relatively small proportion of Napier's mentally disturbed patients.

Throughout much of the nineteenth century men constituted a somewhat higher proportion of the inmates of the licensed madhouses than women, although returns from 1831 suggested that among the pauper patients there was a slight excess of females and this continued and increased as the century progressed.[130] Some madhouses were licensed for only one of the sexes; others admitted both, but kept men and women separate.[131] During the last two decades of the century the female excess was also found among the private patients.[132] The little material that has been analysed relating to gender and type of mental disorder for the private madhouses suggests no very marked gender differences for the different types of disorder, with the exception of melancholia where there was a clear female preponderance.[133]

The development of private madhouses can in many respects be seen as an extension of the entrepreneurial market in healing which characterized the sixteenth and seventeenth centuries. The madhouses were essentially commercial enterprises whose development and expansion were an aspect of the spread of commodity relations in an urbanizing and increasingly capitalist society, in which the market economy was advancing, and a growing number of goods and services could be bought in the market place. They were set up by private individuals who saw a potential market in the institutional care and treatment of the insane on a residential basis – a market that was initially free and unregulated. Charges varied considerably from institution to institution, but there is no doubt that the trade in lunacy was a reasonable and at times highly profitable business and that this was an important motive in setting up private residential madhouses.[134] Many of the houses, as with other business enterprises, were handed down within the family: they might pass from father to son, or they might be taken over by a wife on her husband's death.[135] Where purpose-built accommodation was provided, a practice more common in the nineteenth century than earlier but never the norm, considerable initial capital might be involved in the venture – Brislington House, opened in 1806, cost £35,000 to build.[136] More often the initial outlay might not be large and the return on the investment quite high.[137]

MacDonald suggests that the timing of the development of private madhouses can be related to the increasing secularization of ideas about sickness and healing among the intellectual elite.[138] It is no coincidence, he feels, that private madhouses began to be set up from the 1660s onwards, following the Restoration, when medical and religious ideas about sickness were declining and explanations of illness framed in entirely naturalistic terms were coming to replace them. However, the involvement of the medical elite in the establishment and running of madhouses was less important in the final decades of the seventeenth century, only really increasing from the middle of the eighteenth century as the professionalization of healing advanced. The early madhouses were set up and run by a more heterogeneous group of lay and medical practitioners, and the part played by the secularization of ideas about illness at the end of the seventeenth century is more debatable.[139]

In part the market for the private madhouses came from the poor law system whose general features are described in Chapter 7. With an increasing emphasis on the institutionalization of paupers as a condition of relief came the new problem of dealing with the sometimes disruptive and difficult insane paupers who had been institutionalized. Removing them to separate institutions away from the workhouse offered one solution to the problem, albeit entailing some additional expense, and the development of an institutional bias in the poor law system undoubtedly contributed to the development and growth of the private madhouses.[140]

But the establishment of private madhouses was not just a matter of making money out of catering for the pauper lunatics with which the poor law workhouses could not cope. Much of the attention of proprietors was directed towards attracting private inmates. It was common, as with other commercial ventures, for those who set up private madhouses to advertise their services. These advertisements, designed to attract private inmates, were published in various journals and as public circulars.[141] The following, circulated by one David Irish in 1700, provides an example:

This is to inform all Persons whom it may concern, That D. Irish doth and will (if God permit) instruct his Son in the best and speediest way of curing *Melancholy* and *Madness*. And likewise, those *Lunaticks* which are not curable, he will take them for term of Life, if paid Quarterly; such, and all others, he takes on Reasonable Terms, allowing them good Fires, Meat and Drink, with good attendance, and all necessaries far beyond what is allow'd at Bedlam, or any other place he has yet heard of and cheaper, for he allows the *Melancholly, Mad*, and such whose Consciences are Opprest with the sense of Sin, good Meat every day for Dinner, and also wholesome Diet for Breakfast and Supper, and good Table-Beer enough at any time: They have also good Beds and Decent Chambers, answerable to their Abilities: all which necessaries are daily allow'd and given them according to agreement during the time agreed for; they are all carefully look'd after by himself at his House in Stoke near Guildford in Surry, being a pleasant place and good Air; and such as please to be at Thorp, his son looks after them, and instruct his Son in the true Method of curing such distemper'd People.[142]

In marketing his services David Irish emphasizes three things: speedy cure (though he is willing to accept the incurable), good domestic standards (in keeping with the individual's status), and value for money. Value for money is the message of another advertisement issued the same year, where again the curative skills that the institution can provide are stressed.

> In Clerkenwell-Close, where the figure of Mad People are over the Gate; liveth one, who by the Blessing of God, Cures all Lunatick distracted or Mad People, he seldom exceeds 3 months in the Cure of the Maddest person that comes in his House, several have been Cur'd in a Fortnight, and some in less time; he has cur'd several from Bedlam and other Mad-Houses in and about this City, and his Conveniency for People of what Quality soever. No Cure no Money.[143]

An advertisement in 1779 of one William Finch asserts not so much speed as 100 per cent success: 'It is with the greatest satisfaction he can say, that every person he has had charge of, has, with the blessing of God, been cured and discharged from his house perfectly well.'[144]

   The claims about curability (for those considered curable), high domestic standards and competitive charges in these advertisements cannot be taken as an accurate description of what could be expected from private madhouse care. The quality of madhouses varied considerably as did the care meted out to different classes of patient, as subsequent investigations showed.[145] Rather the claims constitute the major selling points in the marketing of asylum care and as such they facilitated the acceptance and spread of the private madhouse system amongst the more affluent. Their importance must be understood in the context of the fact that the basic novelty of the product being marketed was the provision of care on a residential basis, and this service was being offered in a society where institutional care was viewed as a matter of last resort.[146]

   The selling of cures and treatments for insanity was, as we have seen, no novelty. But cures were either bought as goods in the market place in the form of herbal remedies, potions and so on, or might be provided as services at home or at the house of the healer.[147] The selling of care and treatment in institutions meant counteracting the general belief that institutions, whether workhouse or hospital, were places of last resort that confined only the poor, sick, aged and dependent without any proper alternative means of support.[148] This was not an issue with the pauper inmates who were driven by necessity and the dictates of the poor law system to accept institutional care; but the families of the private inmates had to be persuaded that to use private madhouses was acceptable – an acceptable necessity, if not intrinsically desirable. Hence there was a strong need to stress the positive features of the care offered for the insane in order to allay the anxieties and concerns of those who would have to pay for this care: to develop a more positive ideology of institutional care. The emphasis both on prospects of cure and high domestic standards served to do just this. For this characterization of private madhouses spoke both to the humane concerns of a family towards a prospective inmate, and to any fears of stigma and loss of status. Both genuine humanity – desires for cure and humane care – and anxieties about perceptions of inhumanity or familial inadequacy could be satisfied. In that respect the selling points were not only part of the competition between madhouses for clients, but also served to put an acceptable face on what might otherwise have been considered improper and inhumane. In so doing they contributed to new expectations about and perceptions of the institutional care of the insane.

This is not to say that the prospect of cure or good domestic standards account in themselves for the spread and use of the private madhouses, although they facilitated their acceptance. The early use of the private madhouses was undoubtedly prompted in large part by the custodial rather than the therapeutic service they provided. There is a range of evidence to support this view. First, custodial care was a paramount requirement in the case of the pauper patients sent to the private madhouses from the workhouses. It was the difficult and disruptive who were felt to be creating problems in the workhouses who were likely to be transferred; although the poor law authorities may have hoped that they might be cured there is no evidence that this was the dominant motivation or that they chose those whose chances of cure were greatest.[149] Second, the argument that residential care offered better prospects of cure, while it was common enough by the end of the eighteenth century, does not seem to feature in the early advertisement or discussions of the treatment of insanity. Cure was offered, but there were few specific claims that institutional care, though it was to be of high quality, significantly increased the chances of cure. Indeed residential care, the claims of the advertisements as to their curative powers notwithstanding, seems to have been viewed as particularly appropriate for long-standing cases of insanity where there was little prospect of cure. In his discussion of the treatment for madness Willis commented

In inveterate and habitual madness, the sick seldom submit to any medical Cure; but such being placed in Bedlam, or an Hospital for mad people, by the ordinary discipline of the place, either at length return to themselves, or else they are kept from doing hurt, either to themselves or to others . . . .[150]

There is here, however, a suggestion that the disciplined environment as well as time may slightly increase the low chances of cure.

Third, when criticisms of the private madhouses began to emerge in the eighteenth century they were presented largely as places where, because of the principle of profit, the unscrupulous could get rid of those they did not want, and not as institutions that failed to live up to claims about curative efficacy. Claims as to the accuracy of statements about cure were apparently a matter of little public concern.[151] Private madhouses were apparently serving their proper purpose if they provided care and custody of the insane, and them alone. In this period their curative efficacy was of much less public concern. Fourth, there is evidence that in the nineteenth century, when we can begin to quantify such matters, the private madhouses like the majority of other institutions, contained a high proportion of those considered incurable, both private and pauper. The 1844 Report of the Metropolitan Commissioners in Lunacy shows that in the provincial licensed houses only some 31 per cent were considered curable and that in the metropolitan houses the figures was roughly half that, with some 16 per cent considered curable.[152] Indeed, the metropolitan madhouses had the lowest proportion of cases considered curable of all institutions making separate provision for the insane, apart from the military and naval asylums. The data are presented in Table 15. For the incurable inmates the custodial function of the private madhouses was dominant.

We do not need to look far to locate the reasons for the demand for custodial care amongst the rich who could afford to pay for it. The notion

Table 15   Asylum superintendents' estimates of the number and percentage of curable patients in asylums in England and Wales in 1844

Type of Asylum	PRIVATE			PAUPER		
	Total patients	Number curable	Per cent curable	Total patients	Number curable	Per cent curable
Provincial licensed houses	1426	412	28.9	1920	637	33.2
Metropolitan licensed houses	973	153	15.7	854	111	13.0
County Asylums	245	61	24.9	4244	651	15.4
Charity Hospitals	536	127	23.7	343	59	17.2
Military/Naval	168	18	10.7	–	–	–
Bethlem	265	181	68.5	90	no estimate	
St Luke's	177	93	52.5	31	16	51.6

Source: Metropolitan Commissioners in Lunacy, 1844 Report, pp. 185, 187 (From Scull, 1979, p. 190)

of insanity was not created by the madhouse proprietors who sought to advertise their services, nor did they create a new sense that the insane constituted a problem, either for the immediate family or for society more generally. The symptoms of madness – wildness, rage, talkative babbling and violence – were enough in themselves to present problems for the families involved.[153] Hence the prospect of custody, let alone cure, for these awkward, difficult, sometimes violent, and certainly often burdensome people, in a place where their insanity would be less visible, was an attractive one, without any prospect of cure.

However, although private madhouses were attractive as much as places of custody as of prospective cure, the average length of stay of the inmates was not long when compared, for instance, with that of the stays of inmates of nineteenth-century public asylums.[154] There were two important reasons for this. Not least was the cost of private madhouse care, whether paid for by the private family or the public purse (at a lower rate). In the latter case, since private madhouse charges even for pauper patients were higher than the cost of workhouse care (the institutional alternative), there was pressure to send only the really difficult cases and to keep stays short.[155] Moreover, mortality rates in private madhouses were relatively high, even by the standards of the time, and a high proportion of 'discharges' were of inmates who had died.[156] Inmates were a selected group with higher chances of mortality than the population as a whole; moreover, at least in some private madhouses, as in the later voluntary hospitals, the institutional setting itself must have increased the chances of illness through infection.[157] Further, some of the treatments provided in the madhouses may have actually increased levels of mortality – the harsh effects of purgatives, for instance.[158]

The trade in lunacy attracted both lay and medical proprietors, some of them clergymen, some licensed practitioners, others not.[159] David Irish, whose advertisement was quoted above, described himself as a 'practitioner in physick and surgery' and for him, as for other medical practitioners of the time, the proprietorship of a madhouse was one way of securing an income from medical practice. When charitable and later public asylums were set up, the physicians who provided services in them also often had their own private madhouses to supplement their earnings.[160] With time, as official medicine's control over healing tightened, an increasing proportion of madhouse proprietors had some formal medical qualifications and were licensed medical practitioners. This can be seen rather clearly when madhouses passed from generation to generation within the same family, where early proprietors without formal medical qualifications were followed by descendants who obtained them.[161] By 1831 some forty-four out of the sixty-eight provincial madhouses had proprietors described as medically or surgically qualified.[162]

The advantage of formal qualifications and the acquisition of a medical licence in a world where the role and importance of official medicine was expanding was that these were official marks of recognition and legitimacy of the individual's therapeutic skills. Moreover, charges of profiteering and wrongful detention of inmates were more difficult to make against those persons with status and authority provided by these badges of official approval.[163] Medical practitioners were quick to emphasize their experience and knowledge and the lay proprietors' ignorance and profiteering in this competitive market. A physician writing in 1792 described lay madhouse proprietors, in contrast to medical men and the clergy, as:

men, who have just pecuniary powers sufficient to obtain a licence, and set themselves up keepers of private madhouses, alluring the public in an advertisement, that the patients will be treated with the best medical skill and attention . . . when at the same time, they are totally devoid of all physical knowledge and experience and in other respects extremely ignorant, and perhaps illiterate.[164]

Liable to such attacks it is not surprising that persons likely to inherit a madhouse obtained some medical qualifications, and that qualified persons were at an advantage in setting up a madhouse and attracting clients.

Proprietors with medical qualifications, especially if they involved a university medical degree, tended to rely on reference to their qualifications to lend status and authority to their advertisements for their madhouses, and made fewer specific claims about their curative skills or domestic standards: these could be taken for granted once their professional status was recognized. Nor did they stress value for money, and the commercial nature of the enterprise could pass unnoticed in the statement of professional skills and knowledge. The advertisement for Fishponds near Bristol issued in 1788, stated:

The public are respectfully informed, that the house at this place for the reception of the INSANE, which has been for many years conducted with the highest reputation and success, and which in point of situation, accommodations, and every possible advantage, yields to none of the kind in the kingdom: will henceforth be under the immediate care and direction of JOSEPH MASON COX, M.D. who proposes to confine his practice solely to cases of insanity, hypochondriasis, and other chronic nervous affections; these disorders having been the peculiar object of his studies and observations for several years past at the Universities of Edinburgh, Paris and Leyden.[165]

The tone and formality contrast markedly with that of David Irish and reflects the reliance on formal medical qualifications as a guarantee of skill and propriety.

The advantage of medical qualifications in claims about the standards of private madhouses was undoubtedly enhanced by increasing public anxiety during the eighteenth century about profiteering and exploitation.[166] The focus of concern was on wrongful detention arising out of the desire for financial gain, a concern that stemmed from eighteenth-century ideas and the value attached to the liberty of the individual.[167] In addition there was some concern about maltreatment and poor physical conditions.[168] Daniel Defoe, writing in 1728, was an early critic of the private madhouses. Here he describes how they could be abused in graphic terms:

This leads me to exclaim against the vile Practice now so much in vogue among the better Sort, as they are called, but the worst sort in fact, namely, the sending their Wives to Mad-Houses at every Whim or Dislike, that they may be more secure and undisturb'd in their Debaucheries: Which wicked custom is got to such a Head, that the number of private Mad-Houses in and about London, are considerably increased within these few years. This is the height of Barbarity and Injustice in a Christian Country, it is a clandestine Inquisition, nay worse. How many Ladies and Gentlewomen are hurried away to these Houses, which ought to be suppress'd, or at least subject to daily Examination, as hereafter shall be proposed? How many, I say, of Beauty, Vertue, and Fortune, are suddenly torn from their dear innocent Babes, from the Arms of an unworthy Man, who they love (perhaps too well) and who in Return for that Love, nay probably an ample Fortune, and a lovely Offspring besides; grows weary of the pure Streams of chaste Love, and thirsting after the Puddles of lawless Lust, buries his vertuous Wife alive, that he may have the greater Freedom with his Mistresses?[169]

The problem was that persons admitted to private madhouses could be detained there by the madhouse proprietors on the request of a family member, the only legal redress being a writ of habeas corpus. However, 'This procedure was seldom successful, since many devices – such as changing the patient's name, using secret cells which could not be detected by an investigator, or declaring that the patient had escaped

– could be used to defeat it'.[170] How common such cases were is difficult to assess, but they were sufficient to arouse the concern of a number of people, who felt that the fact that the proprietors could make money out of the situation was the underlying source of the problem.[171]

Defoe implies, too, that it was women who were more likely to be wrongfully detained than men, but again this is difficult to ascertain with any exactitude, although their relative lack of power and authority should make us suspect that this would be so. Certainly many of the cases of abuse that came to public attention were of women, though not all had been confined by their husbands.[172] It is true that overall there were more men than women in private madhouses, but such data do not help us quantify cases of wrongful detention.

The solution recommended by Defoe and others was the development of a system of licensed madhouses subject to regular inspection:

In my humble Opinion all private Mad-houses should be suppress'd at once, and it should be no less than Felony to confine any Person under pretence of Madness without due Authority. For the cure of those who are really Lunatick, licens'd Mad-Houses should be constituted in convenient Parts of the Town, which Houses should be subject to proper Visitation and Inspection, nor should any Person be sent to a Mad-House without due Reason, Inquiry and Authority.[173]

Any such system was likely to be opposed by the madhouse proprietors themselves, since it meant outside interference in the activities of the houses.[174] It also meant deciding who should be given the authority to license and inspect and to determine whether particular individuals were properly detained. Consequently, it raised issues about the freedom and autonomy of those who were pursuing their trade in lunacy.

During the eighteenth century there were various attempts to get legislation enacted regulating madhouses, but it was not until 1774 that the first act was passed.[175] It required the licensing of all private madhouses containing more than one lunatic, and set up a system of licensing and inspection for madhouses in London and the provinces. The system basically followed the model established for the licensing of medical practitioners.[176] For the London area five commissioners were to be appointed who were to be Fellows of the Royal College of Physicians. Outside London Justices of the Peace, accompanied by a medical practitioner, were to be responsible for licensing and inspection.

The act also introduced for the first time the necessity of certification on admission. It required that notice should be given of the admission of a lunatic within three days in the metropolitan area and fourteen days outside it, containing the name 'of the Person or Persons by whose Direction such Lunatick was sent . . . and . . . of the Physician, Surgeon, or Apothecary, by whose Advice such Direction was given.'[177] This certification procedure was, however, only required for private lunatics, not for paupers, wherever confined.

The act, therefore, assigned considerable responsibility to medical practitioners in the attempt to ensure that the private madhouse business be properly conducted. Medical practitioners (the act did not require that they should be licensed) were to be the judges of a patient's sanity: they were also to play an important part in the licensing and inspection of the madhouses. The restriction of the regional scope of the commissioners from the Royal College of Physicians was clearly a practical matter as it was with the medical licensing more generally: the number of members of the college was not large, travel was difficult, and the task would have been burdensome. As it was the Royal College approached some twenty years earlier about undertaking the licensing and inspection of private madhouses, had rejected the proposal, arguing that its implementation would be too difficult and inconvenient.[178] The requirement that the medical profession should be so heavily involved in the attempts at regulation of the trade in lunacy was more a mark of the success of some medical practitioners in building up a reputation as responsible experts in the field of insanity, and of the lack of any central state machinery for inspection and control, than of the active desire by the leaders of the medical profession as a whole to regulate the trade in insanity.

Overall, however, the act, because it ignored the pauper patients, because it exercised no more than 'a faint influence over provincial management', because it required little systematic inspection (it required houses to be inspected only once a year 'between the Hours of Eight and Five in the Day-time'), and because it gave only limited powers for the enforcement of better conditions and treatment, was not effective in regulating many of the abuses of the private madhouses.[179] The trade in lunacy continued to provide a focal point for reformers, and was an important argument in the campaign that developed in the nineteenth century for public asylums.

Notes and references

1 Sir George Clark in his *A History of the Royal College of Physicians of London*

suggests that the term 'trade' is appropriate for those whose service consists in buying and selling (Vol. I, 1964, p. 19). It therefore fits the activities of apothecaries (p. 6) but not that of surgeons or physicians. Echoing Parry-Jones (1972) I use the term to emphasize the commercial nature of much healing activity and thereby broaden it to include those who provide other services for a payment.

2   Walk, 1961.

3   See Hunter and MacAlpine, 1963, pp. 964–5.

4   Grob, 1973, p. 103, and pp. 137–40.

5   Doerner, 1981, Part III.

6   Hunter and MacAlpine, 1963, p. 1014.

7   Waddington, 1973; Jewson, 1976; Abel-Smith, 1964.

8   See Parry and Parry, 1976, p. 131; Berlant, 1975; Carr-Sanders and Wilson, 1964, p. 83.

9   The establishment of voluntary hospitals is discussed in the following chapter.

10   Oxford English Dictionary.

11   The conflicts between the asylum doctors and the neurologists in the United States are discussed by Rosenberg, 1968. See also Blustein, 1981.

12   As the two definitions of psychiatry given in the first chapter make clear.

13   Foucault, 1967.

14   Foucault, *Histoire de la Folie*, 1961 (the original longer version of *Madness and Civilization*), quoted in Sheridan, 1980. p. 31.

15   ibid., Chapter 2.

16   On healing and healers in this period see Thomas, 1973; Pelling and Webster, 1979; Webster, 1975; Clark, Vol. I, 1964.

17   The term empiric was often used as a derogatory epithet, like the term 'quack', to refer to unauthorized practitioners.

18   Pelling and Webster, 1979, p. 188 and p. 226.

19   Thomas, 1973, *passim*.

20   Pelling and Webster, 1979, p. 199.

21   Thomas, 1973, Chapter 9.

22   Pelling and Webster, 1979, p. 199.

23   Details of the foundation of the college are to be found in Clark, Vol. I, 1964, Chapter IV.

24   ibid., pp. 98–101.

25   Hill, 1969, p. 45.

26   Carr-Saunders and Wilson, 1964, p. 72.

27   Webster, 1975, p. 251.

28   Thomas, 1973, p. 12.

29   Webster, 1975, pp. 122–144.

30   Thomas, 1973, pp. 383–4.

31   Thomas, pp. 414–24.

32   MacDonald, 1981, p. 212.

33 Clark, Vol. I, 1964, p. 16.
34 See Cartwright, 1977, Chapter 1; Webster, 1975, p. 121.
35 MacDonald, 1981, p. 194.
36 ibid., p. 222.
37 Carr-Saunders and Wilson, 1964, pp. 68–9; Pelling and Webster, 1979, pp. 173–7.
38 Pelling and Webster, 1979, p. 188.
39 ibid., p. 175.
40 Thomas, 1973, p. 13.
41 Pelling and Webster, 1979, p. 177.
42 See Webster, 1975, pp. 252–4; Carr-Saunders and Wilson, 1964, pp. 72–83; Pelling and Webster, 1979, pp. 177–9.
43 However, Pelling and Webster comment, 'In the sixteenth century women could take out freedoms, run businesses and indenture apprentices, but it is not clear that they could do this in their own right, rather than in that of a deceased husband'. (1979, p. 222).
44 Hill, 1965, pp. 74–84.
45 ibid., p. 82.
46 Webster, 1975, p. 25².
47 ibid., p. 323.
48 This is Clark's estimate of the average charge in the later seventeenth and early eighteenth century (Vol. II, 1966, p. 436).
49 MacDonald, 1981, p. 51 and footnote 118, p. 261.
50 ibid., p. 53.
51 ibid., p. 20.
52 According to Clark 'the richest were very rich' (Vol. II, 1966, p. 436).
53 Abel-Smith, 1964, p. 3; Thomas, 1973, pp. 14–5.
54 ibid., Chapter 7.
55 ibid.
56 ibid., p. 211.
57 ibid., p. 218.
58 ibid., pp. 227–36.
59 ibid., Chapter 10.
60 ibid., Chapter 9. See also Clark, Vol. I, 1964, p. 24.
61 Thomas, 1973, p. 304.
62 Clark, Vol. I, 1964, p. 5.
63 ibid., pp. 54–7. The act remained on the statutes until 1948.
64 ibid., p. 60.
65 Pelling and Webster, 1979, pp. 191–5.
66 Thomas, 1973, p. 307.
67 ibid., pp. 678–80.
68 The College of Physicians alone took proceedings against 236 individuals for unauthorized healing activities between 1550 and 1600 (Pelling and Webster, 1979, pp. 182–3).

69   Thomas, 1973, pp. 533–4.
70   Clark, Vol. I, 1964, pp. 111–21; pp. 289–90, and *passim*.
71   Pelling and Webster, 1979, pp. 234–5.
72   Thomas, 1973, pp. 767–800.
73   ibid., p. 797.
74   ibid., p. 697.
75   MacDonald, 1981, p. 113.
76   ibid., p. 123.
77   ibid., pp. 121–32.
78   ibid., pp. 128–32.
79   ibid., Chapter 5.
80   ibid., pp. 173–8.
81   ibid., pp. 178–88; Jewson, 1974, p. 372.
82   MacDonald, 1981, Chapter 4.
83   ibid., p. 120.
84   ibid.
85   ibid., p. 148.
86   See for instance Foucault, 1967, Chapter V.
87   See the extracts from the writings of Bartholomaeus Anglicus and
     Philip Barrough in Hunter and MacAlpine, 1963, pp. 2–4, and 24–5.
     See also MacDonald, 1981, p. 185.
88   From Andrew Boarde's *The Breviary of Healthe*, 1552 (Hunter and
     MacAlpine, 1963, p. 14).
89   From Philip Barrough's *The Methode of Physicke, conteyning the causes,
     signes, and cures of inward diseases in mans body from the head to the foote*,
     1583 (ibid., p. 27).
90   ibid., pp. 27–8.
91   MacDonald, 1981, p. 10.
92   Foucault, 1967, Chapter 5.
93   See the extracts from Willis's writings in Hunter and MacAlpine, 1963,
     p. 191.
94   Foucault, 1967, pp. 125–6.
95   Hunter and MacAlpine, 1963, p. 191.
96   ibid., pp. 191–2.
97   ibid., p. 191.
98   MacDonald, 1981, pp. 150–60.
99   ibid., p. 151.
100 ibid., p. 152.
101 ibid., p. 161–2.
102 These percentages are derived from calculations on the data presented
     by MacDonald in Table 4:3 of *Mystical Bedlam* (ibid., p. 152).
103 On the difficulties of analysing present-day associations between
     class and mental illness see Hollingshead and Redlich, 1958, *passim*;
     Kohn 1968; Cochrane, 1983, Chapter 2.

104 MacDonald, 1981, p. 36.
105 ibid., p. 73.
106 For the present-day picture see Smith, 1975; Busfield, 1983.
107 See the classifications in Menninger, 1963, Appendix.
108 See Willis in Hunter and MacAlpine, 1963, p. 190.
109 MacDonald, 1981, p. 202.
110 ibid., p. 75. The classification is MacDonald's and the book docs not give us enough detailed data on individual cases to allow the reader to establish the appropriateness of the categorization or the concepts used to describe the men's and women's experiences.
111 ibid., p. 109.
112 ibid., Chapter 5.
113 ibid., p. 221.
114 ibid., p. 212.
115 ibid., p. 197.
116 ibid., p. 196.
117 Parry-Jones, 1972, pp. 7–8.
118 MacDonald, 1981, p. 11.
119 Parry-Jones, 1972, Tables 1 and 2, pp. 30–1.
120 ibid., Tables 11 and 12, pp. 54–5.
121 ibid., p. 33.
122 ibid., p. 43.
123 ibid., p. 40.
124 ibid., p. 7.
125 ibid., pp. 50–64, and Chapter 5.
126 ibid., p. 254.
127 ibid., Table 11, p. 55.
128 ibid., Table XVI, Appendix E, p. 330.
129 ibid., Table XII, Appendix E, p. 328.
130 ibid., pp. 48–50.
131 ibid., p. 49.
132 ibid., p. 50.
133 ibid., Tables III, XII and XVI, Appendix E, pp. 324, 328 and 330.
134 ibid., pp. 124–7, and pp. 84–90.
135 ibid., pp. 77–9.
136 ibid., pp. 85–6.
137 ibid., pp. 85–90.
138 MacDonald, 1981, pp. 9–12.
139 Parry-Jones, 1972, pp. 74–5.
140 The development of the Poor Law system is discussed in Chapter 7.
141 See Parry-Jones, 1972, pp. 102–12.
142 Hunter and MacAlpine, 1963, pp. 279–80.
143 ibid., p. 472.
144 ibid.

145   See, for example, the *Report of the Select Committee appointed to consider the Provision being made for the better regulation of madhouses in England*, 1815. See also Parry-Jones, 1972, *passim*.

146   Abel-Smith, 1964, pp. 3–4.

147   The home was the preferred locus of medical care (ibid., p. 2).

148   Cartwright, 1977, pp. 22–3.

149   Hodgkinson, 1967, Chapter 4; Parry-Jones, 1972, p. 217.

150   Hunter and MacAlpine, 1963, p. 192.

151   They do not feature in the public comment on the abuses and defects of private madhouses. See Parry-Jones, 1972, Chapter 8.

152   There are enormous difficulties in interpreting such comparative rates given the difference in the patient populations as well as variation in the criteria for assessing curability.

153   MacDonald, 1982, p. 123.

154   Parry-Jones, 1972, p. 207; See Chapter 8, pp. 264–5.

155   Though they were often longer than those of the private patients (Parry-Jones, 1972).

156   ibid., pp. 211–17.

157   Many of the inmates were in a poor state of physical health on admission (ibid., pp. 211–17). Parry-Jones also gives some data on the cases of cholera in the private madhouses (ibid., p. 153).

158   MacDonald (1982, pp. 190–3) discusses the hazards and inadequacies of the medical treatments of the time.

159   ibid., pp. 77–83.

160   ibid., pp. 77–9.

161   Hunter and MacAlpine, 1963, p. 472.

162   Parry-Jones, 1972, p. 78.

163   Scull, 1975.

164   Parry-Jones, pp. 81–2.

165   Hunter and MacAlpine, 1963, p. 595.

166   Parry-Jones, 1972, Chapter 8.

167   ibid.

168   ibid.

169   From his *Augusta triumphans; or, the way to make London the most flourishing city in the universe*, 1728 (Hunter and MacAlpine, 1963, pp. 266–7).

170   Jones, 1955, p. 31. See also Parry-Jones, 1972, p. 224.

171   ibid., pp. 241–2.

172   See the cases mentioned in Parry-Jones (ibid., Chapter 8) and Jones (1955, Chapter 3).

173   Defoe, *Augusta triumphans*, 1728 (Hunter and MacAlpine, 1963, p. 267).

174   Jones suggests that the Select Committee established in 1763 to inquire into the state of madhouses had to proceed discretely since 'a number of well-known members of the medical profession had financial interests in private madhouses' (1955, p. 34).

175 See Hunter and MacAlpine, 1963, pp. 451–6.
176 See Parry-Jones, 1972, pp. 9–10; Clark, Vol. II, 1966, pp. 584–7.
177 Hunter and MacAlpine, 1963, p. 456.
178 Parry-Jones, 1972, p. 9.
179 ibid., p. 10; Hunter and MacAlpine, 1963, p. 453.

6 Lunatic hospitals and moral treatment

Private madhouses were a product of an increasingly urbanized capitalist society, with the growing tendency for goods and services to be made available on a profit-making, commercial basis. They offered custodial care for the disturbed, difficult and unwanted from both the rich and the very poor. The voluntary hospitals for the insane, like other voluntary hospitals, were established in the eighteenth century and served socially intermediate groups, those in 'middling circumstances' and labouring classes. Both were funded on a charitable basis through public subscription, and both were the product of the social changes of the eighteenth century.[1] On the one hand, Enlightenment thought created a new sense of the human capacity to control nature and to deal with the problems of sickness and ill-health. It contributed new forms and patterns of philanthropy that directed money into institutions such as hospitals over which the donors had some control, and it encouraged a new more 'scientific' spirit among official healers, some of whom were in the vanguard of scientific advance. The new hospitals and asylums provided the collection of cases that could advance medical practitioners' opportunities for research and specialist training, as well as securing them status and prestige and access to a supply of private patients. On the other hand, increased urbanization and then the beginnings of industrialization provided both the concentrations of population necessary for hospital and asylum development, as well as increasing the need for financial and institutional support for those who could not earn a living because of sickness, handicap, old age or infirmity.

Voluntary hospitals designed to cater for the insane were one example of the specialist medical institutions, like the lying-in and fever hospitals which developed in the eighteenth century. The special hospitals shared many of the characteristics of the new voluntary general hospitals, and their existence was in part occasioned by the restrictive admission policies of the latter. To account for the development and character of the voluntary asylums we must, therefore, first consider the voluntary general hospitals.

Voluntary hospitals

The establishment of voluntary hospitals was not only the most visible but also the most important development within medicine in Britain during the eighteenth century. At the beginning of the century there were only a handful of hospitals in the country, and only two that were in any sense general hospitals – St Bartholomew's, founded in 1123, and St Thomas's founded in 1213, both in London.[2] Both were Royal or chartered hospitals, re-founded with charitable endowments in the sixteenth century. By the end of the eighteenth century in the region of forty new establishments had been added to this list, five in London, the rest in the provinces. The number of beds was still limited, some 4000 in all hospitals in England and Wales in 1800, at a time when the population has been estimated at some 9 million.[3] Numerically the expansion in hospital accommodation was far greater in the nineteenth century; in 1891, the number of beds for the sick in hospitals, infirmaries and workhouse institutions was over 100,000.[4] Nevertheless, the eighteenth-century voluntary hospitals had a profound impact on medical practice; their importance came less from any life-enhancing or life-saving powers than from their value as sites of medical learning and professionalization. There is plenty of evidence that their curative powers were limited and they may have contributed to rather than reduced mortality, particularly by facilitating the spread of infection by grouping together sick people in unhygienic conditions.[5]

The wave of eighteenth-century hospitals began in London with the opening of the Westminster Hospital in 1720.[6] This was the first voluntary hospital proper – that is, a hospital dependent for funds not on the income from the endowments of one or more wealthy benefactors often on their death, but on the subscriptions taken out by individual members of the community during their lives, or by organizations, which committed them to pay money to the institution over a period of time (something like a covenant).[7] The importance of this kind of financing lay not only in the need for ensuring the continuing support of benefactors if the institution were to remain financially viable (this could also be a problem for the endowed hospitals in the long term), but more importantly in the control subscribers had over the use of their benefactions. They were usually appointed governors of the hospital and could exercise patronage over admission of patients.[8] The old chartered hospitals and the new voluntary ones also differed in two other important respects. In the first place no fees were charged to those admitted to the voluntary hospitals, whereas it had been customary to charge some fee in the chartered hospitals. This made the hospitals more fully 'charitable': however, it also reduced the status and rights of the patients, who were no longer paying for a service, and the subscribers' power was complemented by the patients' powerlessness.[9] Second, apart from the resident apothecaries, the medical practitioners who worked in the hospital tended to have honorary appointments, whereas in the chartered hospitals they had been paid for their services (not necessarily especially highly).[10]

The opening of the Westminster Hospital in 1720 was followed by that of Guy's Hospital in 1725; this hospital was endowed by Thomas Guy in his will and was not dependent on voluntary subscriptions.[11] It was founded for incurables, but was allowed to accept other patients and they soon became predominant.[12] The next London hospital, St George's, a subscription hospital, was opened in 1733, and further voluntary hospitals were opened in London in the eighteenth century, the London Hospital in 1740 and the Middlesex in 1745. Outside London hospitals also began to be opened in the important centres of population, and the concentration of people in the expanding towns and cities was a precondition for the establishment of a new hospital. The first voluntary hospital to be opened outside London was the Edinburgh Royal Infirmary in 1729, and this was the first university town to have a hospital in Britain. The Winchester County Hospital was opened in 1736, to be followed in rapid succession by the Bristol Royal Infirmary (1737), the York County Hospital (1740), the Royal Devon and Exeter Hospital (1742), the Aberdeen Royal Infirmary (1742), the Bath General Hospital (1743) and many others. Despite generous benefactions from the physician John Radcliffe, who died in 1714, and another physician, John Addenbrooke, who died in 1719, the English university towns had to wait until the second half of the century before acquiring hospitals. Addenbrooke's Hospital opened in Cambridge in 1766, the Radcliffe Infirmary in Oxford in 1770.

The new voluntary hospitals were intended for those in middling circumstances and the labouring population; for those whose commitment to work, honesty and sobriety was held to make them justifiable objects of charity. Some might be considered poor, but they were deserving of support, since it was assumed that the rich could already afford to pay for the services of a physician or surgeon and would choose to receive medical attention at home, and that the destitute – the real poor – whose behaviour did not merit such charity – would fall within the provisions of the poor law system including the workhouses which were becoming more numerous as the eighteenth century progressed.[13]

The account of the establishment of the county hospital at Winchester, produced by the governors the year after its opening, sets out their assessment of the advantages of the new hospitals. It listed sixteen benefits, the eighth of which clearly circumscribes the limits of the governors' charitable intention:

It provides for the relief and comfort of Multitudes who are unable to be at the expense of Advice or Physick, but are not distinguished by the name of THE POOR, because They do not come under the care of a Parish or a Workhouse: and yet are the principal objects of this Charity, and most of all entitled to the regards of the Public; since They are in present want; and are of the diligent and industrious, that is, of the useful and valuable part of all Society.[14]

Such intentions to limit the object of the charity could be readily realized given the direct control that subscribers had over admission for 'The only method of a gaining entrance to an English voluntary hospital was by the recommendation of a subscriber unless the sick poor person had suffered an accident or was considered to be an urgent case for other medical reasons'.[15] In Scotland a group of managers could also recommend patients for admission.[16]

The subscribers' freedom to recommend for admission was itself precisely regulated so that departures from the basic policy in favour of the more disreputable poor would have been difficult. The regulations governing admission kept out the destitute quite effectively. In the first place there was a common ruling, like that at Winchester 'That No In-Patient be admitted without bringing a Security from some Substantial Person to defray the expenses of Burial or Removal', since 'the hospitals did not want the stigma that might arise if those who died were given pauper funerals nor were they willing to pay for the funerals themselves'.[17] And if that were not enough to deter the destitute, patients were supposed to arrive in a clean condition with a clean set of clothes. The Radcliffe Infirmary stated

It is particularly desired, that all subscribers recommending patients, do take care that they are sent clean, and free from vermin; and that they bring with them, at the time of admission, three shirts or shifts, and other necessaries for keeping them clean'.[18]

They might, too, have to pay for the laundering of bed-linen or be required to bring spare linen with them.[19] Paupers (that is, those in receipt of poor law relief) were, moreover, often specifically excluded from the hospitals; so too (usually) were apprentices and servants, the expectation being that their masters should pay for their medical treatment.[20]

While the procedures and regulations governing admission helped to determine the social standing of a patient admitted to the hospitals, a further set of regulations was intended to restrict the medical range of the cases admitted. The General Infirmary at Leeds, which opened in 1767, ruled:

That no Woman big with child, no Child under Six Years of Age, (except in extraordinary Cases, as Fractures or where Cutting for the Stone, or any other Operation is required) no Person disordered in their Senses, suspected to have the Small-Pox, Venereal Disease, Itch, or other Infectious Distemper; no Persons apprehended to be in a dying condition or incurable, be admitted as In-Patients, or if inadvertently admitted be suffered to continue.[21]

There was, however, variation in these rules especially concerning fever cases, with some hospitals admitting fever patients until later in the century and the Scottish hospitals having more liberal admission policies – both medically and socially.[22] Moreover, because of the limits of medical skills and knowledge cases that should technically have been excluded slipped through the net, sometimes to be tolerated, sometimes to be removed.[23] The underlying concern seems to have been to exclude two groups of patients: first, chronic cases (although there were occasionally specific wards for these) on the grounds of 'unnecessary expense' (they filled up beds and prevented the admission of persons for whom something could be done – albeit not necessarily to great effect); second, troublesome cases – troublesome because of infectious illness or its likelihood, for example, pregnancy where puerperal fever could develop, or because of behavioural problems and their management, as in the case of insanity.[24]

How do we explain the establishment of these voluntary general hospitals? Why were so many people willing to give money to help establish and run them? Why did hospitals rather than some other form of medical provision seem appropriate? A number of factors were involved. In the first place there was the identification of a group in need of medical services – those in middling circumstances and the 'deserving poor'. This apprehension depended on a complex set of ideas and judgements about official medicine and its potential value to the particular social groups. On the one hand it was felt that there were some people who could not afford much in the way of medical services, given their commercial nature, or rather that they could not afford the medical services provided by official medicine, especially the services of physicians and surgeons. We see here, therefore, an acceptance of the hierarchy of official medicine and an assumption of its superiority over the services of the empirics. The Winchester governors' list of the benefits of the hospital puts as the tenth,

It preserves Them from the ill usage of ignorant Quacks and Imposters Who too often take advantage of their Necessities; and not only insensibly drain them of the little Money Them have under the pretence of selling cheap Medicines; but frequently destroy their Health for want of Honesty or Skill.[25]

No doubt the decline of religious and magical beliefs about healing among the intellectual elite helped to discredit the activities of the unlicensed healers.

On the other hand it was believed that the health of this particular group of the population required attention. The motives of the philanthropists who subscribed to the hospitals manifest a definite instrumentalism about the value of a healthy population – more specifically a healthy workforce – which seems to derive from mercantilist ideas with their stress on economic interests and the wealth embodied in the natural resource of the people.[26] William Petty, for example, saw health as fundamental to prosperity, contending in 1676:

Now suppose that in the King's Dominions there be 9 millions of people, of which 360,000 dye every year, and from whom 440,000 are borne. And suppose that by the advancement of the art of Medicine, a quarter part fewer dye. Then the King will gain and save 200,000 subjects per annum, which valued at 20£ per head, the lowest price of slaves, will make 4 million per annum benefit to the Commonwealth.[27]

And he went on to propose that hospitals should be established to help improve the nation's health.[28] Such ideas were reflected in the arguments put forward by those involved in the establishment of the eighteenth-century voluntary hospitals. Urging the case for establishing a hospital in Edinburgh in 1721, Alexander Monro, a teacher of anatomy at the Surgeon's Hall, argued that not only did Christian duty require humanity and compassion to those who suffered, but 'That as the Relief of these is a Duty, so it is no less Advantage to a Nation, for as many as are recovered in an Infirmary are so many working Hands gained to the country.'[29] Similarly the Winchester governors' account of the establishment of their hospital adduces as the twelfth benefit of the hospital that 'It is a most certain means of increasing the number of the People; as well as of saving a multitude of Hands, who are often lost for want of timely assistance', adding that 'it deserves to be remembered, that a third part of what every labouring Man earns, is so much clear gains to the Public'.[30]

The case for hospital care rather than medical relief provided at home was based on a number of arguments. First, it seemed to offer a more economic and efficient use of resources – it seemed cheaper because of the accommodation of cases in one place, and because it provided a way of ensuring that resources were put to the use for which they were intended. This is what the Winchester governors had to say on the matter:

The expense of relieving a great number of Sick Persons in an Hospital, bears no proportion to that of assisting them at their separate Homes: And the Widow's Mite entrusted with Those who can dispose of it to the utmost advantage, will go farther toward answering the Ends of Charity, than a Sum of Money bestowed at random on such as are incompetent judges of the use of it, or of the proper manner of laying it out.[31]

Hospital care allowed a greater degree of paternalistic control to be exercised in the relief of the sick than did indiscriminate alms giving. This was not just a question of making certain that the money was spent on care for the sick person. It also meant looking after them in the right way – putting their care in the hands of licensed practitioners and controlling the physical and social environment in the desired way:

the care and neatness, as well as the simplicity and regularity of Diet, with which the Poor are kept in an Hospital, do all contribute much sooner to their Recovery, than their own way of living; and are often more effectual than Physic in the Cure of Several of the most inveterate Distempers.[32]

This claim is of especial importance since it stresses the positive merits of hospital based care and constitutes the beginnings of a pro-institutional ideology that would help to shift hospitals from their status as places of last to first resort, not only in the minds of charitable givers but also in the minds of the sick.

The other arguments for hospital care relate to the perceived advantages for the development of medical knowledge and skills which were held to be of potential benefit to patients. Part of William Petty's case for hospitals was in terms of the improvements in medical learning it would generate:

a man shall learn in a well regulated hospital where he may within halfe an hower's time observe his choice of 1000 patients, more in one yeare then in ten without it, even by reading the best Books that can be written.[33]

Petty stressed practical rather than academic learning, and pointed to the general gain from the enhancement of medical knowledge. The Winchester governors echo Petty very directly in the eleventh advantage they list: 'It is of infinite Use to All Other persons as well as the Poor, by furnishing the Physicians and Surgeons with more experience in one Year, than They could have in ten without it.'[34]

Both the argument for the medical and consequently general public advantage, and the argument that more direct control can be exercised over the use of resources and the care of the sick person in a hospital setting, strengthen the case for hospitals not only as a preferred alternative to relief at home, but also to the other alternative tried by the College of Physicians at the end of the seventeenth century, the dispensary. A dispensary for the sick poor of the City of London had been opened by the college in 1697, offering free advice and medicines at cost.[35] In part it was established by the college to try and deal with the threat of the growing power of the apothecaries, who during the seventeenth century had gained an increasing hold on the provision of medical care, both advice and medicines, for the poorer sections of the community.[36] This had occurred largely at the expense of the unlicensed healers, but still posed a threat to the physicians, since it broke the bounds of the tripartite division of labour the college sought to impose. The college's dispensary did not, however, survive for long, closing in 1725.[37] Perhaps this was because the advantages for the high status physicians who staffed it were few. Other dispensaries, opened under rather different auspices, were a significant feature of eighteenth-century medicine. John Wesley, for instance, opened a dispensary in the City of London in 1746, and one was opened in Westminster in 1715.[38]

The identification of a group in need, the sick among the middle ranks of society and the deserving poor, and the identification of the 'best' means of solving that need, the provision of hospitals, were not in themselves sufficient to ensure that new hospitals would be established. For the hospitals had to be funded. We need also, therefore, to consider the motives of those who were willing to provide the necessary money to

establish the hospitals, given a case could be made for their value. The
donors and public subscribers to the hospitals came largely from the
new, largely dissenting entrepreneurial class, people active in trade and
commerce.[39] They were a group who in the first half of the eighteenth
century did well financially and so had the necessary wealth to spend on
the new hospitals.[40] And the advantages of spending their money in this
charitable manner were numerous. Not only could they satisfy their
sense of religious duty and civic responsibility, but they could gain direct
benefits in status, power and prestige, and often some material benefits.
Social status, for instance, could be enhanced by becoming a subscriber,
since subscribers were often made governors, a position not only with
some esteem of its own, but also one offering opportunities for contact
with members of more aristocratic circles; it was common, for instance,
to secure one or two members of the nobility on the boards of
governors.[41] Then there was the power to elect hospital managers at the
annual meeting and to nominate beneficiaries to the institution, so
securing a form of patronage over workers and their families.[42] And
entrepreneurs, by their involvement with the hospital as subscribers,
might secure new business for themselves – either some contract to
build, maintain or supply the hospital in some way, or other work arising
from the social contacts they made.[43] It is not surprising, therefore, to
find that 'medicine was the most favoured object of the extraordinary
Protestant charitableness of the early British capitalists'.[44]

The initiative for the establishment of the voluntary hospitals often
came from lay rather than medical men, and the clergy with their long-
standing duty to help the sick constituted one important group of
advocates.[45] But the support of medical men was usually enlisted, and
sometimes medical men were actively involved from the start.[46] The
advantages to the medical men of the new hospitals were considerable.
Although their positions were normally honorary, the material advantages could be considerable and their duties were not normally
onerous.[47] The status and contacts gained from the honorary position
might provide a significant source of new private patients.[48] There were,
too, important new opportunities for teaching and research which
helped to enhance the individual status of the practitioner concerned
and brought direct financial returns in the form of fees for taking
students, as well as facilitating the overall professionalization of
medicine.[49] The numerous advantages of hospital work for medical
practitioners undoubtedly encouraged the establishment of the specialist
voluntary hospitals that began to be set up in the eighteenth century as well
as contributing to the growth and further expansion of the numbers of

general hospitals.[50] The medical exclusion policies of the general hospitals meant that there were important types of sickness not catered for by the general hospitals, and it was largely medical men seeking advancement in hospital work who took the initiative in founding specialist hospitals. Attracted by the glittering prizes the hospitals could offer, young practitioners often found the opportunities for advancement in general hospitals restricted (there were too many practitioners chasing too few senior posts), and the burden of work and their exploitation by their seniors considerable. Juniors were often expected to do most of the real work of the hospital; they were not usually allowed private patients in case they took them away from the senior practitioners, and they might not be allowed facilities for their own specialist work. Hence 'there accumulated in each hospital a group of exploited and frustrated young doctors' some of whom began to found specialist hospitals.[51] Apart from the voluntary hospitals for lunatics considered in the following section the most important group of specialist hospitals were the lying-in hospitals.[52] The first was opened in 1749, a second in 1750, the third in 1752 and the fourth and last of the eighteenth-century London lying-in hospitals in 1767.[53] Fever hospitals also began to be opened later in the century as more and more of the general hospitals excluded fever cases.[54]

The impact of the development of the voluntary hospitals on medical practice was enormous. First, they effected important changes in the nature of the relationship between medical practitioner and patient. Outside the hospital healing had been and still was an entrepreneurial activity involving a contract between individual healer and individual patient for which the patient was usually charged (the paradigmatic fee-for-service medicine). Hospital medicine in a voluntary hospital entailed a very different situation in which the practitioners' services were secured by the hospital (albeit without direct monetary reward) rather than by the individual patient, and no charge was made to the patient. Hence, on the one hand the immediate individual link between practitioner and patient was broken so that the practitioners' responsibilities and obligations to the patient were no longer direct but mediated through the institution of the hospital.[55] And on the other hand, the status and authority of the patient were reduced, since patients were the recipients of charity both from subscribers who exercised a clear element of patronage over them by nominating them for admission, and from practitioners who donated their services.[56]

The consequences of these changes in the nature of the practitioner–patient relationship were profound. Most obviously they increased the power of the practitioner and the passivity of the patient. A number of writers have argued that one of the key characteristics of medicine outside the hospitals in the eighteenth century and before was the power aristocratic clients had over their physicians. Despite the high standing of physicians within official medicine and their acceptance among the elite of society, their lack of landed property and their reliance on aristocratic clients for their living put them in a situation of some dependence.[57] This would have been true of all practitioners working for the aristocracy, and to a lesser extent for practitioners generally, where the competition for clients encouraged a tendency to please (though the degree of client power should not be over-emphasized). With the establishment of hospitals, however, medical power *vis à vis* this group of patients was increased, since the practitioners no longer owed their position directly to the individual patients but to the hospital (in the form of the governors responsible for making the honorary medical appointment).[58] Moreover the status differential between practitioner and patient came increasingly to favour the practitioner, as the honorary practitioners were of higher social status than the charitable recipients. Outside the hospitals the majority of sick persons would normally seek help from a healer whose status was not far from their own. In addition, medical practitioners had power and influence over decision making within the hospitals:

The governors had in theory complete authority over everything that happened in their hospitals. In practice, there were limits to the authority they could exercise over the senior professional men who were giving their services to the hospital. They were careful not to question the clinical judgement or examine the quality of the work of any of the doctors in the hospital unless they were forced to do so.

  Except where matters of finance were concerned, the doctors were left to run the medical side of the hospital. In teaching hospitals, the doctors selected their students, planned curricula and divided out the receipts from teaching. They also divided out the beds . . .. Each full staff member was responsible for the treatment of the patients in his beds. It was not the duty of the senior physician or the senior surgeon to exercise any supervision over the work of other full members of the staff.[59]

Placed in this situation of greater structural dependency, patients in voluntary hospitals had perforce to submit to the treatments and practices of the medical practitioners. Patients could, for instance, refuse a particular operation (operations were generally dangerous and painful), but if it was considered necessary they would either have to accept it or leave the hospital.[60] Nor were they in any position to object to being used as a case for teaching purposes; as Abel-Smith comments 'While the paying patient had a legitimate right to object to being observed and prodded by a group of students, a person in receipt of charity was hardly in a position to complain about such invasions of his privacy.'[61] And, as if to emphasize their powerlessness, patients' lives within the hospital were strictly regulated. At St Thomas's hospital they were not permitted 'to revile or miscall one another . . . nor abuse themselves by inordinate Drinking, nor incontinent living'.[62] Smoking and playing cards and games were not often permitted, though they were customary activities outside the hospitals, and ambulant patients were made to help with the work of the wards.

Second, the development of voluntary hospitals had a major impact on medical knowledge. Hospitals were the locus of major changes in medical thought and the shift to 'modern' medicine, that is, to the medicine whose characteristics I outlined in Chapter 1. The intellectual shift which has been summarily described as a shift from observation to examination or as the development of what Foucault calls 'the clinical gaze', is commonly said to have occurred in the state hospitals of Paris in the early decades of the nineteenth century following the French revolution.[63] It was there that the concept of localized pathology was introduced, and that 'hospital' as opposed to the preceding 'bedside' medicine was born.[64] The changes in the practitioner–patient relationship were, it has been suggested, crucial to these intellectual changes, since medical practitioners no longer had the same pressure to please the patient and to focus only on cure.[65] However, the complex interplay of forces that led to the development of the idea of localized pathology in Paris in the early nineteenth century cannot be examined here, nor can the details of intellectual developments in medicine in Britain during the second half of the eighteenth century when the voluntary hospitals were established.[66] What is clear, however, is that round the beginning of the nineteenth century major changes did occur in medical science which led to the gradual abandonment of the old Galenic medicine, and other monistic systems of medical thought fashionable in the eighteenth century, and that in this intellectual revolution the development of hospitals played a decisive part.

In turn, the establishment of hospitals was associated with marked changes in medical teaching. The advantages hospitals presented for medical training were asserted by those who advocated their establishment and were seen as prospective benefits not only to the medical profession itself but also to future patients. Initially teaching arrangements had generally followed the established pattern of apprenticeships and studentships, with honorary doctors taking 'house' pupils and charging them high fees for their attachment.[67] However, with the opening of the Edinburgh Royal Infirmary in 1729, encouraged by the College of Physicians in Scotland, Edinburgh became the first university medical school in Britain to include formal clinical training as part of medical education, and Edinburgh became the mecca of the aspiring medical student.[68] In England, despite the establishment of a number of private medical schools in the eighteenth century, the hospitals did not establish formal medical teaching schools until the nineteenth century when links between university medical teaching and clinical training were established.[69] Nevertheless, though slow to develop, formal clinical training was facilitated by the establishment of hospitals and the possibilities and requirements they generated for more systematic medical training. One consequence of the increasing formalization of medical training at the beginning of the nineteenth century was the exclusion of women from the ranks of official medicine, since women were not admitted to the new medical schools.[70] Hence in this period we can aptly talk not of medical practitioners but of medical men.

Finally, the establishment and then increasing importance of hospitals within official medicine transformed the hierarchical organization of the medical profession. The old hierarchy of official medicine had its three orders of physicians, surgeons and apothecaries. Within the new hospitals the hierarchy of physicians and surgeons and the conflict between them, though they did not disappear, began to be superseded by a new division between senior and junior hospital doctors.[71] But the major new division in the medical hierarchy was between the hospital doctors and those who worked outside them. With time, the former came to be viewed increasingly as specialists possessing superior knowledge who could be consulted in difficult cases, the latter as the general practitioners dealing with more routine medical matters.[72] This new hierarchy developed in part because of the changes occurring in the old tripartite division of labour outside the hospitals. In 1815 the apothecaries gained new licensing powers and introduced new educational requirements that both reflected and enhanced their increasing status within official medicine and signalled the failure of the physicians to enforce their own hierarchical model of the medical world.[73] The apothecaries' rights to advise and prescribe as well as to sell medicines were recognized, their range of activities broadened and they became 'general' practitioners, contributing to a situation where the salient distinction came to be that between the hospital doctor, a specialist consultant, and the general practitioner or family doctor. By 1858 when the Medical Act introduced a single register of all licensed medical practitioners (though no single licensing body) the new hierarchy was well established.[74]

Hospitals for lunatics

Unfortunately the establishment and activities of the charitable hospitals for the insane has, as yet, been subject to little systematic research. At this stage, therefore, any account of their development and operation is bound to be fragmentary and incomplete.

Prior to the eighteenth century, London, the only city with a population exceeding 50,000, was the one place with a separate institution for the insane. This was Bethlem Hospital – a chartered institution like St Bartholomew's and St Thomas's – more popularly known as Bedlam.[75] Originally a hospice or hospital in Bishopsgate run by the Order of St Mary of Bethlehem it was, like other medieval religious hospitals, a place of last resort for the sick and poor without means of support. Precisely when the hospital began to specialize in the care of mad people is not known, although the change seems to have taken place some time in the fourteenth century. Bethlem was not, however, used exclusively for the insane at this stage. In the fifteenth and sixteenth centuries there were struggles between the king and the City of London for control of the appointment of the Master, struggles that continued even after the granting of the custody of the hospital to the City by Royal Charter in 1546 following the Dissolution. Although funds for the hospital came from charitable endowments, fees were commonly charged for those who were admitted as they were in other chartered hospitals. In 1676 the hospital transferred to a new site in Moorfields that had been given to the hospital governors by the City of London, and remained there till 1815 when it moved once more, this time to St George's.

The establishment of further charitable foundations for the insane began in the eighteenth century. Norwich, the second most important city in England throughout the sixteenth and seventeenth centuries, with a reputation for schemes for dealing with poverty, had the first of these new hospitals – Bethel hospital, an endowed institution.[76] It was founded by one Mary Chapman in 1713, and on her death in 1724 it was placed under a governing body in accordance with the provisions of her will.[77] Further provision for lunatics occurred next in the form of special separate wards for lunatics within the new charitable general hospitals, for although these hospitals generally refused to admit lunatics, a few did make special provision for them, sometimes accommodating some lunatics in the basement. In London a ward was opened for twenty incurable lunatics at Guy's Hospital in 1728 under the provision of Thomas Guy's will.[78] The Edinburgh Royal Infirmary had twelve 'cells' for lunatics in its basement. The first proper voluntary hospital for the insane, and the second separate institution for lunatics in London, was St Luke's Hospital, opened in 1751 also at Moorfields.[79] During the second half of the eighteenth century other towns began to open special hospitals for lunatics, sometimes attached to existing general hospitals (sharing a physician, for instance) and sometimes completely separate.[80] Initially most were set up in the rapidly industrializing northern and midlands towns. Lunatic hospitals were opened in Manchester in 1766, in Newcastle-upon-Tyne in 1767, in York in 1777 – the first to be called a lunatic asylum, a term that soon came into common use for the charitable and later public institutions for lunatics.[81] Further asylums then opened in Liverpool in 1790 and in Leicester in 1794, and a second asylum at York, the Retreat, in 1796. Those in Manchester, Liverpool and Leicester were attached to the general hospitals opened in 1751, 1749 and 1771 respectively. In Scotland the first separate lunatic hospital, the Montrose Lunatic Hospital, was opened in 1781 (it was renamed the Royal Scottish Asylum in 1811). Other voluntary asylums opened in the first decades of the nineteenth century: at Exeter in 1801, at Lincoln in 1820 and at Oxford (the Warneford Hospital) in 1826.

Charitable hospitals for lunatics differed in character from private madhouses. In the first place they tended to be a little larger, increasing in size over time. The London asylums were the largest. Bethlem had 118 resident inmates in 1676, 130 in 1704, and by the beginning of the nineteenth century the figure had increased to an average of 250.[82] St Luke's, London, had 57 inmates in 1753 two years after its opening; it expanded rapidly and had 298 inmates by 1815.[83] Outside London the asylums started with smaller numbers, but again tended to expand. Manchester Lunatic Hospital had 22 places for lunatics in 1766 when it opened; Montrose Lunatic Hospital 37 in 1791, ten years after its opening.[84] In total the number of inmates was considerably lower than that in private madhouses since there were relatively few charitable asylums. The 1844 Report of the Metropolitan Commissioners in Lunacy gave a figure of 1442 lunatics in the category of registered hospitals.[85] The number continued to increase throughout the nineteenth century and there were some 4025 inmates in the registered hospitals by 1896.[86]

Second, the character of the inmate population differed in certain important respects from that of private madhouses. In particular the proportion of pauper patients was usually lower, although they were not excluded from all the lunatic hospitals (as was commonly the rule with the general hospitals). In 1844, for example, when the number of county asylums was still small, roughly one third of the inmates of the charitable asylums were paupers.[87] The presence or absence of paupers was usually a matter of specific policy, although the numbers were affected by the level of charges that might be made for their admission, for some of the subscription lunatic hospitals as well as the chartered institutions did require payments for certain categories of inmate.[88] St Luke's in London, for example, admitted lunatics without charge, but if after a year they were nor cured and wished to remain they could do so only for a weekly charge.[89] The social standing of those admitted as private patients was also somewhat lower than in the private madhouses, though it is difficult to be precise about this.[90] The 1844 Report shows slightly more women than men in the charitable asylums, a marginally larger difference than in the private madhouses.[91] By the end of the century, however, when women had come to predominate in the private madhouses, there were more men in the charitable asylums than women.[92]

Like the private madhouses the charitable lunatic hospitals mainly catered for cases of severe mental disorder and those diagnosed as having mania constituted the largest proportion of inmates (something in the order of 50 per cent of admissions).[93] Unlike the private madhouses, however, many of the charitable asylums were specifically intended for curable cases, though some had one or two wards, usually as a result of some special donation, for incurable cases. This was especially true of the chartered institutions since the subscribers' patronage over admissions in the voluntary lunatic hospitals made total exclusion of incurable cases more difficult.[94] During the eighteenth century, for instance, Bethlem only admitted curable cases, apart from two wings of the hospital that had been specially built for incurables as a result of the wishes of a benefactor.[95] Curability was measured in terms of recency and only cases where the onset had occurred within the previous year were considered curable.[96] Inmates not cured after twelve months would be discharged if no bed could be found for them on a ward for the incurables.[97]

The focus on curable cases paralleled that in the voluntary general hospitals, which Abel-Smith attributes to the wishes of medical men. Medical men, he contends, stood to gain from a focus on curable cases for a variety of reasons and managed by the beginning of the nineteenth century to impose their wishes over those who gave their money to provide care for the sick:

In the light of history, it may be said that the most significant change which occurred in the voluntary hospitals in the first half of the nineteenth century was the growing emphasis on the acute sick. To a considerable extent, the trend marked the triumph of the 'honorary doctors' over those of the charitable public. Many of the latter were content to have their money used to give relief and comfort to those in pain: help to a patient whose suffering was of long duration might even be preferred to constructive treatment for a patient whose stay was short. Pain was what mattered, not any 'economic' return for money spent. The doctors on the other hand and those lay governors who were influenced by them wanted to show results in terms of cure, and they were naturally reluctant to surround themselves with cases which showed the limitations of their professional skill. Doctors who taught particularly wanted to demonstrate success.[98]

However, the trend towards curable cases was apparent in many hospitals in the eighteenth century. It developed because of the coincidence of medical interests with arguments of economic efficiency. Incurable cases filled up hospital beds over long periods of time and prevented the admission of those for whom active medical intervention might have some benefit. Liverpool Infirmary, for instance, agreed in its early days to admit 'inveterate and desperate cases' but only 'while there was room', and without policies to exclude long-standing incurable cases there would have been little opportunity to admit cases that did afford a 'reasonable hope of cure'.[99]

Medical men were often involved in the initial establishment of voluntary asylums, as they were with other specialist hospitals, because of the possibilities these institutions offered for enhancing their position, (and so were in a better position to put admission policies that suited their interests into effect). William Battie, for example, the first physician at St Luke's in London, was an active participant in the establishment of the hospital.[100] The request for donations circulated in 1750 shows how the interests of medical men in gaining expertise and advancing research and training, and so securing a better basis for professional practice, could also be readily used as arguments to attract support for the asylums by pointing to the public gain from improvements in medical skills. The circular asserts

For more Gentleman of the Faculty, making this Branch of Physick, their particular Care & Study, it may from thence reasonably be expected that the Cure of this dreadful Disease will hereafter be rendered more certain and expeditious, as well as less expensive.[101]

And when St Luke's opened Battie used the hospital for teaching purposes although he did not introduce formal teaching there.[102]

Financial support was also encouraged, as with the general hospitals, by identifying groups in special need of charitable provision. The social groups were basically the same as for the voluntary hospitals, those in middling circumstances and the labouring classes who were neither very rich (they could afford the private madhouses) nor very poor (they were covered by poor law provisions); but there was an especial emphasis on the high financial costs of care for the insane, and the lack of existing support in other charitable institutions, that potentially broadened the range of those who would be helped by the establishment of charitable asylums. The St Luke's circular put the argument like this:

The Principal End . . . of establishing another Hospital for *Lunaticks* is evident, not only as they are incapable of providing for themselves and Families, are not admitted into other Hospitals or capable of being relieved (as in other Diseases) by private charity; but also as there must be Servants peculiarly qualified, and every patient must have a separate Room, and Diet, most of them, equal to Persons in Health. From hence it appears, that the Expences necessarily attending the Confinement and other means of Cure, are such as People even in middling Circumstances cannot bear, it generally requiring several Months, and often a whole Year before a Cure is compleated.[103]

There is the same stress on high domestic standards and curability as in the advertisements for the private madhouses, but with two important differences in what is said about cure. First the length and consequently expense of the time needed to secure a cure is stressed (in line with the objective of encouraging generous donations); second, confinement is explicitly viewed as a method of treatment in its own right. The argument, which is explicitly and fully formulated in the principles of moral treatment, is that care away from the home is likely to prove beneficial in itself. Again, therefore, attention is given to the problem of presenting institutions as places of first rather than last resort.

The importance of the new asylums stems, however, not only from their contribution to this ideological transformation, although during the eighteenth century asylums began to be seen by policy makers and medical men as the proper place for the treatment of lunacy. The charitable asylums (at least in England – in France the institutions were taken over by the state during the French Revolution) also provided the locus for the development and introduction of new ideas and practices of treatment. Private madhouses had emphasized the importance of cure, but the asylums by virtue of their stronger medical character (they were modelled on the general hospitals and often set up by medical men) were associated with a marked therapeutic interventionism, whose substance I will consider in the next section of this chapter. Not that all the innovation in treatment, if innovation it was, was distinctively medical in content, judged by the standards of modern medicine, or distinctively medical in origin; nevertheless, the therapeutic developments contributed to the abandonment of the old Galenic purges and vomits and helped to create a climate of therapeutic optimism concerning insanity that was of considerable significance in the reformers' case for the establishment of public asylums.[104] Nineteenth-century medical developments in the field of insanity that were in the mould of modern scientific medicine contributed, like those in medicine more generally, to an understanding of the organic aetiology of diseases, but initially had little direct therapeutic relevance.[105]

The new lunatic asylums also facilitated the specialization and professionalization of a group of medical practitioners – mad-doctors and alienists as they were commonly called – in the sphere of insanity, partly through the teaching, observation and treatment opportunities they provided. The honorary positions they offered, as in the general hospitals, were attractive to medical men and were filled by high status physicians, who continued with their private practice and might well have their own private madhouse as well, and often made an active contribution to official medicine. Battie, for instance, was one of the most eminent and successful in the eighteenth century.[106] A fellow of the Royal College of Physicians, he was elected its president in 1764, the year he retired as physician of St Luke's. As well as his *A Treatise on Madness*, he had written a book of physiology and a medical textbook. He was a governor of Bethlem Hospital and owned a madhouse in Islington Road. 'His success was such that although a self-made man his estate at his death was variously estimated at between £100,000 and £200,000.'[107] It was not, however, until the nineteenth century that such medical men began to set up the associations and journals that provide the mark of the emergence of new specialisms, and were the direct forerunners of the contemporary psychiatric profession, and by then they were joined by the physicians and medical superintendents associated with the new public asylums.[108]

Moral treatment

The treatment meted out to inmates of eighteenth-century charitable asylums and private madhouses has traditionally been described as harsh and brutal: its harshness and brutality was, it is usually suggested, transformed at the end of the eighteenth century by a new liberalism.[109] The supposed transformation in attitudes has been symbolized by Pinel's liberation of the lunatics at Bicêtre from their chains.[110] The argument is that during the eighteenth century the lunatic was perceived as a wild animal to be controlled by whipping, by instilling terror, and by chains; in the nineteenth century the lunatic, though disordered in mind, was, nevertheless, considered a person, amenable to the moderate methods of regulation and discipline epitomized by the new 'moral' treatment as well as what came to be called the system of non-restraint.[111] More recent historiography has questioned this transformation. On the one hand Foucault, while asserting that a real change in ideas did occur at the end of the eighteenth century, has pointed to the illusory nature of the new freedom:

The asylum of the age of positivism, which it is Pinel's glory to have founded, is not a free realm of observation, diagnosis, and therapeutics; it is a juridical space where one is accused, judged, and condemned, and from which one is never released except by the version of this trial in psychological depth – that is, by remorse. Madness will be punished in the asylum, even if it is innocent outside of it. For a long time to come, and until our own day at least, it is imprisoned in a moral world.[112]

On the other hand others have pointed to the continuity of the attitudes and methods of treatment of the 'new' liberalism with old ideas and practices.[113] Many of the details of the new moral treatment can be found in what was said and done in the seventeenth as well as the eighteenth century. Was there, therefore, any distinctive transformation at the end of the eighteenth century or even earlier? Did the principles of moral treatment constitute a decisive break with an old pattern of brutality and physical repression? What impact did the use of institutions as places for confining lunatics have on the way in which lunacy was perceived and treated?

The conception of insanity generally held to underly and occasion eighteenth-century brutality is the one that we have already encountered in the characterization of mania within the Galenic tradition – a characterization where medical and societal ideas about madness seemed to differ very little. Willis's description of madness emphasizes the wildness and animality of mania, and the treatments he recommends, with their emphasis on physical control and the inducement of fear, stem from this conceptualization.[114] Foucault, drawing on similar medical sources, describes the underlying perception of insanity like this:

Madness borrowed its face from the mask of the beast. Those chained to the cell walls were no longer men whose minds had wandered, but beasts preyed upon by a natural frenzy: as if madness, at its extreme point, freed from that moral unreason in which its most attenuated forms are enclosed, managed to rejoin, by a paroxysm of strength, the immediate violence of animality. This model of animality prevailed in the asylums and gave them their cagelike aspect, their look of the menagerie.[115]

The perception of animality occasioned both physical repression and apparent insensitivity to human sensibility. Since the insane were beasts they did not suffer from damp, cold or lack of food; indeed, lack of food might be positively beneficial since it was a way of controlling rage. Terror and mechanical constraint also tamed their animal passions. And like wild beasts, too, the ravings of lunatics constituted a public spectacle. A visit to see the lunatics at Bedlam was a popular Sunday pastime.[116]

The existence of this particular way of thinking about lunatics is not in doubt, not is the sense it makes of practices that by twentieth-century standards seem harsh and brutal. What is more controversial is the extent to which this conception of insanity was widely reflected in the behaviours and practices of those involved in dealing with insanity during the eighteenth century. The conceptualization did not arise in the eighteenth century: it appears in writings of the sixteenth and seventeenth centuries as well as the eighteenth century. However, there is evidence that the practices that it engendered were more common in the eighteenth-century lunatic hospitals and private madhouses than formerly.[117] Not that physical repression and harshness were specific to institutional contexts. We have already seen how some of Napier's patients had been flogged or chained and there is evidence, too, of the confinement and physical constraint of lunatics kept in individual houses (whipping, it should be remembered, was a standard punishment for many crimes).[118] But asylums and private madhouses provided a context in which the curative intentions of medical men were more likely to generate harshness and brutality, given their ideas about effective methods of treatment. Institutions for the insane justified their existence by claims about the therapeutic potential of the services they provided. Hence they were ideologically committed to try and take active steps to restore their inmates to sanity, and were therefore likely to follow the therapeutic prescriptions of authorities like Willis with some thoroughness and even ingenuity. Medical men, heavily involved as they were in the lunatic hospitals, often introduced treatments for insanity there that seem singularly unpleasant by our standards (though some were probably little worse than the purgatives and bloodlettings they routinely prescribed to all their patients, let alone the painful and dangerous surgical operations of the period). Believing that 'terror acts powerfully on the body through the medium of the mind, and should be employed in the cure of madness' or in Cullen's words that 'Fear, being a passion that diminishes excitement, may therefore be opposed to the excess of it; and particularly to the angry and irascible excitment of maniacs', they devised a range of treatments designed to shock and terrorize patients into sanity.[119] Lunatics were ducked into cold water baths, placed in machines that spun them through the air, and given electric shocks (a form of treatment revived in the eighteenth century).[120] The decline of magical and religious beliefs surrounding sickness among the medical elite undoubtedly contributed to this attempt to develop naturalistic forms of therapy for insanity which seem in many respects less humane than the therapeutic endeavours of the sixteenth and seventeenth centuries.[121]

A further factor contributing to the pervasiveness of apparently harsh and insensitive care in the asylums and madhouses of the eighteenth century was the sheer problem of management created by collecting together lunatics in special separate institutions, in particular lunatics whose behaviour had been considered violent, dangerous, difficult or uncontrolled. Order could have been achieved in a number of different ways, but economic and resource considerations as well as the framework of ideas within which those who managed asylums operated encouraged the imposition of social order by physically and mechanically coercive means, as well as contributing to some neglect of patients, especially those considered incurable.[122] Social order maintained along the principles of moral treatment, as we shall see, involved a much greater investment of resources.

The harshness and brutality that was common enough, though not all pervasive, in eighteenth-century asylums and private madhouses contrasts markedly with the form of treatment envisaged by those advocating moral treatment. The content and the principle of moral treatment have come to be associated with the work of the Tukes – a family of tea and coffee merchants – at the York Retreat, following an account of the Retreat published by Samuel Tuke, the grandson of the founder, William Tuke, in 1813.[123] Neither were medical practitioners. The Retreat had been opened in 1796 as a charitable asylum by a group of Quakers, including William Tuke, as a direct response to what they perceived as the harsh and brutal care in asylums following the death of a Quaker in York Asylum.[124] The new asylum, as its name was intended to indicate, was to be 'a place in which the unhappy might obtain a refuge – a quiet haven in which the shattered bark might find the means of reparation or of safety'.[125] The means of reparation was to be found in a 'mild system of treatment' that Tuke referred to under the heading 'moral treatment'. Intended as a general category, which included the use of fear, in opposition to medical treatment (i.e. the physical methods of treatment commonly used by doctors), the term came to serve as a label for a form of treatment designed to encourage self-restraint through what Tuke called 'the desire of esteem'.[126] The aim was to try and enhance individuals' own desires 'to struggle to conceal and overcome their morbid prepensities'.[127] Treatment consisted, therefore, in providing an environment that would facilitate this struggle for self-control, an environment that was itself well regulated and disciplined and governed by moral principles and moral authority. The power of physical coercion was to be replaced by the power of moral authority.

In order to achieve this ordered environment the conduct both of the superintendents and the attendants was considered crucial. Staff were to be carefully selected and all were to spend as much time as possible with the inmates, treating them humanely and offering them guidance. The superintendent was not, for instance, to converse with the patients as if they were children for

The natural tendency of such treatment is, to degrade the mind of the patient, and to make him indifferent to those moral feelings, which, under judicious direction and encouragement, are found capable, in no small degree, to strengthen the power of self-restraint; and which render the resort to coercion, in many cases, unnecessary.[128]

The extreme forms of repression were to be given up entirely 'Neither chains nor corporal punishments are tolerated, on any pretext, in this establishment'.[129] The use of fear was not, however, to be abandoned. Tuke considered it 'as of great importance in the management of the patients' but he argued that it was not 'to be excited, beyond that degree which naturally arises from the necessary regulations of the family'.[130]

The sort of moral order envisaged by Tuke and other writers required, therefore, a small asylum generously staffed with attendants who would treat the inmates with dignity and respect. The Retreat was initially designed for thirty patients. By the end of the first year there were fifteen and the staff consisted of a superintendent, a housekeeper, plus two men and three women servants. In addition a visiting physician came several times a week. By 1812, when an extension had been built, there were sixty-six residents and a staff consisting of one male and one female superintendent (his wife), her assistant, seven attendants and five domestic staff, as well as an occasional gardener.[131]

One component of this social order was the classification of patients according to their conduct

those who are violent, require to be separated from the more tranquil, and to be prevented, by some means, from offensive conduct, towards their fellow-sufferers. Hence, the patients are arranged into classes, as much as may be, according to the degree in which they approach to rational or orderly conduct.[132]

The inmates were also to be grouped according to sex, a common practice in madhouses and asylums as well as hospitals and workhouses.

As a moral order the properly run asylum had a positive value in its own right. It was no longer simply a place of physical and mechanical constraint or medical treatment and as such only of contingent value. It provided both a retreat from external pressures and an essentially therapeutic environment. Confinement had a double motive: it offered a movement away from an environment that had proved too difficult and troublesome for the individual and towards a moral order that would help heal and cure. Henry Maudsley, writing in 1868 on the subject of moral treatment in asylums, rehearses the former objective:

To remove the patient from the midst of those circumstances under which insanity has been produced must be the first aim of treatment. There is always extreme difficulty in treating satisfactorily an insane person in his own house amongst his own kindred, where he has been accustomed to exercise authority, or to exact attention, and where he continually finds new occasions for outbreaks of anger or fresh food for his delusions. An entire change in the surroundings will sometimes of itself lead to his recovery: if the patient is melancholic, he no longer receives the impressions of those whom having most loved when well he now mistrusts, or concerning whom he grieves that his affections are so much changed; if he is maniacal he is not specially irritated by the opposition of those to whose acquiescence he has been accustomed, nor encouraged by their submission to his whims and their indulgence of his follies.[133]

The belief that the environment was an important cause of insanity as well as a potential means of therapy was integral, therefore, to the conception of moral treatment. Tuke, for instance, catalogued a range of environmental factors – intemperance, disappointed affections, business losses and anxieties, family deaths, and so on – which could excite hereditary dispositions to insanity.[134] The list differs little from the pressures Napier's patients mentioned, though it excludes the magical and religious causes they cited. Tuke, indeed, like Napier and like many of his early nineteenth-century contemporaries, manifests a marked aetiological eclecticism at a time when hereditarian and environmental as well as physical and moral explanations of insanity were not regarded as incompatible. Indeed, an important feature of nineteenth-century hereditarian ideas was that acquired characteristics could be inherited.[135] Moreover, it was predispositions and potentials that were thought to be inherited and the heredity potential for a disease 'constituted the occasion for early and thoughtful prophylaxis'.[136] Hence an 'Absolute distinction between the innate and the acquired was a concept so novel, so contrary to traditional common sense, that it was not generally assimilated until the second decade of the twentieth century'.[137] In a similar fashion the increasing emphasis among medical men on the brain as the site of insanity during the first half of the nineteenth century did not exclude claims about an environmental or moral aetiology for the disorder.[138] According to one physician

Insanity arises from a disease of the brain, disturbing the healthy performance of its functions, and is exhibited in illusions, hallucinations, undue or morbid excitement of the feelings and propensities, perversions of the senses or estrangement of the moral feelings'.[139]

But he went on to add 'When the settled principles of religious faith and hope are discarded, when fanaticism predominates, and the established forms of religious worship are abandoned, then it is that the minds of the weak and excitable are distracted and made insane'.[140] Phrenological ideas, too, became increasingly fashionable among alienists in the first half of the nineteenth century and although they focused on brain functioning, were readily used to legitimate and support the principles of moral treatment.[141]

The attention to the social milieu of the patient for the purposes of therapy was seen by its proponents as largely replacing the physical methods of treatment usually recommended by medical men. Medical treatment was not considered undesirable in principle. It simply did not seem to work, at least the methods so far developed did not. The Retreat had, from its opening, employed a visiting physician to give medical treatment to the inmates but Tuke reported that they had been forced, none the less, 'to the painful conclusion, (painful alike to our pride and to our humanity,) that medicine, as yet, possesses very inadequate means to relieve the most grievous of human diseases'.[142] William Battie, writing more than half a century earlier, had made a similar point in recommending what he called the moral management of insanity, though he said less about the precise details of the regimen.

The Regimen in this is perhaps of more importance than in any distemper. It was the saying of a very eminent practitioner in such cases *that management did much more than medicine*; and repeated experience has convinced me that confinement alone is oftentimes sufficient, but always so necessary, that without it every method hitherto devised for the cure of madness would be ineffectual . . .. Nor does experience, which oftentimes supplies the defect of rational intention in many disorders that are hitherto inexplicable by general science and the common laws of Nature furnish us with any well attested remedy for Original Madness. For, altho' several specifick Medicines have by the merciful direction of Providence been of late successfully applied in some distempers otherwise incurable by art, such as Mercury in the venereal infection, Opium in pain and watchfulness . . . and altho' we may have reason to hope that the peculiar antidote of Madness is reserved in Nature's store, and will be brought to light in its appointed time; yet such is our present misfortune, that either that important secret hath been by its inventors withheld from the rest of mankind, or, which is more probable, hath never yet been discovered.[143]

There is here no principled objection to physical methods of treatment, nor indeed to medical men, but rather a concern to find an effective, humane method of treatment. Tuke, despite his scepticism about the value of existing medical treatment, thought that the physician still had an important role to play in the asylum:

It must not, however, be supposed, that the office of physician is considered at the Retreat of little importance. The physician from his office, sometimes possesses more influence over the patients' minds than the other attendants; and in all cases where the mental disease is attended by any bodily disorder; and more especially when it has supervened any obvious malady, however slight; judicious medical attention has been found of the greatest advantage.[144]

In their discussion of the ideas underlying moral treatment Bynum, and following him, Scull in his book *Museums of Madness*, have argued that moral treatment posed a threat to medical men's 'rather newly established place in the treatment of insanity', since it offered no clear role for the physician and did not call upon specifically medical skills.[145] However there are two problems with this argument. First, the extent to which it assumes medical men's interest and role in the treatment of insanity was relatively new. Bynum asserts that 'Despite the fact that physicians had frequently been concerned with what might be called the disease concept of insanity, the care, or custody at least of the insane was less frequently in their hands.[146] But this is surely because institutional solutions to insanity and illness were relatively new, not because medical men (whether licensed or not) did not have an established place in the treatment and care of insanity. Put another way I would suggest that medical men lacked an established place in the care of insanity only to the degree that they lacked an established place in healing more generally. Second, moral treatment can only be presented as a threat to the position of medical men in the newly developing institutional care of the insane by identifying medical practitioners of the day with a narrow set of physical procedures. Although in eighteenth-century official medicine the religious and magical therapies of the sixteenth and first half of the seventeenth centuries had disappeared, nevertheless the still influential Galenic tradition encompassed control of the patient's physical and social environment as well as direct therapies such as bloodletting, purgatives and vomits. Moral treatment did not, therefore, despite its criticism of existing physical therapies, pose such a clear departure in principles of treatment as some commentators have suggested.[147] It is true that during the nineteenth century the physical focus of medicine increased as 'modern' medicine developed and that this was advantageous in securing the professionalization of medicine. None the less during the first half of the nineteenth century when moral treatment was widely advocated it posed less of a threat to medical involvement in insanity than Bynum and Scull contend, simply because there was not the narrow identification of official medicine with physical methods of treatment.

The principles of moral treatment did not, therefore, involve a significant rupture in thought about the care and healing of sick persons in general; they were consistent with old traditions in medicine. The conceptual break was in ways of thinking about the insane in particular. The case for the use of moral treatment, as developed by writers like Tuke, involved a view of the insane as essentially human and amenable to more moderate and milder forms of control which emphasized the partial nature of insanity in many cases:

Insane persons generally possess a degree of control over their wayward propensities. Their intellectual, active, and moral powers, are usually rather perverted than obliterated; and it happens, not unfrequently, that one faculty only is affected. The disorder is sometimes more partial, and can only be detected by erroneous views, on one particular subject. On all others the mind appears to retain its wonted correctness.[148]

The insane still have 'a considerable degree of self command' and there is an advantage in 'treating the patient as much in the manner of a rational being as the state of his mind will allow'.[149]

But if the conceptual shift is clear enough we still have to consider whether there was a general transition in ideas concerning the insane around the turn of the eighteenth century, or perhaps half a century earlier. Doerner, for one, argues that Battie with his writing on moral management in his *A Treatise on Madness*, published in 1758, marks the turning point.[150] The argument for the continuity of conceptions of insanity embodied in the formulation of moral treatment with conceptions of the seventeenth and eighteenth centuries comes largely from two sources. First, it can be supported by the ideas about the care that was to be provided in some of the private madhouses. We have already seen how advertisements for the madhouses stressed that quality of attendance that would be provided, the high domestic standards, and a generally humane environment which do not suggest that the insane were regarded as little more than wild beasts (though there is equally, as we have seen, plenty of evidence of the use of harsh methods of treatment founded on a rather different conception of insanity in that period).[151] Second, medical and literary writings of the seventeenth and eighteenth centuries concerning melancholia show very clearly that melancholia far from being the sign of an animal nature was often considered a mark of civilization.[152] Can we reconcile these apparently contradictory observations?

First, it seems that the transition in conceptions of insanity concerned madness proper – that is mania, and perhaps other severe forms of insanity such as dementia. Melancholics and those troubled in mind had not been attributed a bestial nature during previous centuries. It is not, therefore, surprising that the locus of the transition should be asylums which largely confined lunatics rather than persons with milder forms of mental disturbance.

Second, and related to this, the transition largely concerns those of lower social standing, especially paupers. It was lower-class persons above all who had been considered animal in nature, lacking in sensibilities, and exposed to harsh and brutal treatment.[153] Thomas Monro, the physician of Bethlem Hospital, when giving evidence to a parliamentary committee in 1815 concerning the treatment of lunatics was asked about the use of chains and fetters as a mode of restraint and had this to say: 'They are fit only for pauper Lunatics; if a gentleman was put into irons, he would not like it . . .'[154] Asked to elaborate he continued:

In the first place, I am not at all accustomed to gentlemen in irons; I never saw any thing of the kind; it is a thing so totally abhorrent to my feelings, that I never considered to put a gentleman into irons.'[155]

The distinctions in the treatment of private and pauper patients, clearly evident in the private madhouses, even when both groups were confined in the same institutions, with pauper patients having less room, fewer attendants, a poorer diet and being more likely to be chained, were continued in the new asylums.[156] The harsher treatment of the pauper patients not only reflected the lack of respect accorded to their status but also the deterrent and almost punitive attitudes of the poor law system and the reluctance of poor law authorities to spend more than the minimum necessary on the care of any pauper. Lack of resources could also encourage physical restraint of poorer patients in charitable asylums even if they were not paupers. Thomas Arnold, the physician of Leicester Infirmary and Lunatic Asylum, commented 'Chains should never be used but in the case of poor patients, whose pecuniary circumstances will not admit of such attendance as is necessary to procure safety without them.'[157] In contrast the emphasis on humane care in private madhouses also had an economic motive in persuading families of the acceptability of using madhouses.

This is not to say that patients of higher social standing necessarily escaped harshness and brutality in the seventeenth and eighteenth centuries. The search for a cure could expose even those of highest social standing to the range of treatments, including physical restraint and intimidation, as well as the usual panoply of Galenic purges and bloodletting. George III, who was diagnosed as mad, did not escape the straitjacket when delirious, or the drugs, vomits, purges, cuppings and leeches recommended by medical men.[158] But the harshness was a matter of concern: 'Contemporaries hesitated at these therapies, not because they were harsh for a lunatic, but because they were harsh for a king.'[159] Being a gentleman or even a king was a status which could override that of being a lunatic and could moderate the harshness and brutality often meted out to such persons.

Nor is it the case that the conception of insanity propounded by the advocates of moral treatment had a sudden and all embracing impact on the way in which the insane of low as well as high status were treated. Although physical restraints such as chains and fetters did disappear from asylums by the end of the nineteenth century, and although moral treatment was quite widely introduced into asylums in the first half of the nineteenth century with considerable enthusiasm and interest, nevertheless, as we shall see in Chapter 8, by the second half of the nineteenth century asylums bore little resemblance to the places of refuge and moderate treatment its proponents envisaged.

Pinel's symbolic liberation of the insane from their chains at Bicêtre marks, therefore, not a radical transformation in ways of thinking about and treating insanity for people of all classes or for all types of mental disease. It represents more than anything else what its social context would suggest: an attempt to extend to mad people, including those of low status, ideas and practices that had already found their voice in other contexts. Likewise the principles of moral treatment developed at the York Retreat represent an attempt to theorize a form of mild care and therapy for lunatics that was supposed to be suitable for poor as well as rich and for maniacs as well as melancholics.[160] As with its predecessors, however, it did not succeed in eradicating differences in the way those of varied social standing were treated and cared for.[161]

Notes and references

1 On the eighteenth century and the Enlightenment see George, 1966; Porter 1982; Hill 1969, Part IV; Gay, 1973; Cassirer, 1955.
2 Abel-Smith, 1964, p. 4.
3 ibid., p. 1 gives this estimate of the number of beds. On the estimated population size see Cox, 1970, p. 322.
4 Abel-Smith, 1964, p. 200.
5 See Woodward, 1974, Chapters 8 and 9.
6 ibid., Appendix 1, p. 147. This Appendix lists the opening dates of all the eighteenth-century voluntary hospitals in England and Scotland.
7 ibid., p. 12.
8 ibid., p. 21.
9 Waddington, 1973.
10 Abel-Smith, 1964, p. 6.
11 Woodward, 1974, pp. 14–5.

12 ibid., p. 15.
13 ibid., Chapter 5.
14 ibid., p. 14.
15 ibid., p. 21.
16 ibid., p. 21.
17 ibid., p. 39; see also Abel-Smith, p. 12.
18 Woodward, 1974, p. 40.
19 ibid., p. 40.
20 ibid., p. 40.
21 ibid., p. 45.
22 ibid., Chapter 7.
23 ibid., pp. 61 and 63.
24 ibid., p. 45.
25 ibid., Appendix 2, p. 151.
26 Ogg, 1965, pp. 520–1.
27 Quoted in Woodward, 1974, p. 7.
28 ibid., p. 7.
29 ibid., p. 15.
30 ibid., Appendix 2, p. 151.
31 ibid., p. 150.
32 ibid., pp. 149–50.
33 ibid., p. 7.
34 ibid., Appendix 2, p. 151.
35 Clark, Vol. II, 1966, p. 446; see also Woodward, 1974, pp. 4–5.
36 Clark, Vol. II, 1966, Chapter XX.
37 ibid., p. 481.
38 ibid., p. 482. According to one estimate dispensaries in the London
    area were assisting 50,000 poor patients annually; see Woodward,
    1974, p. 145.
39 Cartwright, 1977, p. 36; Owen, 1965, Chapter 3.
40 Hill, 1969, Part 4, Chapter 2.
41 Abel-Smith, 1964, pp. 5–6; Woodward, 1974, pp. 20–1.
42 Abel-Smith, 1964, p. 6; Woodward, 1974, pp. 18 and 21.
43 Abel-Smith, 1964, pp. 5–6, 44.
44 Eckstein, 1959, p. 100.
45 Woodward, 1974, p. 17.
46 ibid., p. 18.
47 ibid., pp. 23–4; Abel-Smith, 1964, pp. 6–7.
48 Woodward, 1974, p. 23.
49 Abel-Smith, 1961, Chapter 2.
50 ibid.
51 ibid., p. 21.
52 ibid., pp. 22–3; see also Donnison, 1977, pp. 25–8.
53 Abel-Smith, 1964, p. 23.

54 ibid., pp. 23–4.
55 On mediation and the professions see Johnson, 1972, p. 46, and Chapter 6.
56 On doctor–patient relationships in eighteenth-century hospitals see Waddington, 1973.
57 Jewson describes this as a system of patronage (1974).
58 Waddington, 1973.
59 Abel-Smith, 1964, p. 33.
60 Waddington, 1973, p. 216.
61 Abel-Smith, 1964, p. 18, quoted in Waddington, 1973, p. 219.
62 Abel-Smith, 1964, p. 11.
63 Foucault, 1973; Waddington, 1973.
64 Jewson, 1976.
65 Waddington, 1973.
66 See Foucault, 1973; Waddington, 1973; Shryock, 1947, Chapter IX.
67 Abel-Smith, 1964, p. 18.
68 Clark, Vol. II. 1966, p. 543; Cartwright, 1977, pp. 47–8.
69 Holloway, 1964.
70 Parry and Parry, 1976, pp. 166–7.
71 Abel-Smith, 1964, pp. 20–1.
72 On the development of general practice see Brotherston, 1971; see also Abel-Smith (1964, Chapter 7) on the conflict between hospital and general practitioners.
73 See Carr-Saunders and Wilson, 1964, pp. 77–82; Holloway, 1966.
74 On the 1858 Act see ibid., pp. 83–9; Clark, Vol. II, 1966, Chapter XXXV; on the restructuring of the medical hierarchy, see Holloway, 1964, pp. 313–4.
75 The early history of Bedlam is described by Allderidge, 1979.
76 Hunter and MacAlpine, 1963, p. 462.
77 ibid., p. 462.
78 The relevant section of the bill is included in Hunter and MacAlpine's selection of materials (ibid., pp. 330–1.)
79 ibid., p. 402; an engraving of the austere fascade is also shown (p. 409).
80 ibid., pp. 405, 467, 512.
81 One of the first resolutions of the medical group that became the Association of Medical Officers of Asylums and Hospitals for the Insane in 1841 was 'That by the Members of this Association, the term *Lunatic*, and *Lunatic Asylum*, be abandoned, except for legal purposes, and the terms *Insane Person*, and *Hospital for the Insane* be substituted' (their own title notwithstanding) (ibid., p. 446).
82 ibid., pp. 302, 310, 645.
83 ibid., pp. 404, 632.
84 ibid., p. 512.

85   *Report of the Metropolitan Commissioners in Lunacy.* 1844 (ibid., Figure 176, p. 925).

86   *Special Report of the Commissioners in Lunacy on the Alleged Increase in Insanity*, 1897, Table 1, p. 6.

87   *Report of the Metropolitan Commissioners in Lunacy*, 1844 (see Hunter and MacAlpine, 1963, Figure 176, p. 925).

88   Charges were usually higher for private patients than for paupers, Donnelly, 1983, p. 38.

89   See Hunter and MacAlpine, 1963, p. 516.

90   Because of the charitable nature of the voluntary hospitals.

91   *Report of the Metropolitan Commissioners in Lunacy*, 1844 (see Hunter and MacAlpine, 1963, Figure 176, p. 925).

92   *Special Report of the Commissioners in Lunacy on the Alleged Increase in Insanity*, 1897, Table 1, p. 6.

93   Tuke, in his *Description of the Retreat* (1813, Chapter 6), states that 92 out of the 149 admissions in the years 1796 to 1811 had a diagnosis of mania.

94   According to the *Report of the Metropolitan Commissioners in Lunacy*, 1844, Bethlem had the highest proportion of curable cases of all types of institutions (see Table 15, Chapter 5 above).

95   Donnelly, 1983, p. 6.

96   Hunter and MacAlpine, 1974, p. 52.

97   Introduction of William Battie's *A Treatise on Madness* (Hunter and MacAlpine, 1962, p. 12).

98   Abel-Smith, 1964, pp. 44–5.

99   Woodward, 1974, p. 46.

100   See Hunter and MacAlpine, 1963, pp. 402–5, and their Introduction to Battie's *A Treatise on Madness* (1962, pp. 9–13); see also Doerner, 1981, pp. 39–48.

101   Hunter and MacAlpine, 1963, p. 404.

102   ibid., p. 404.

103   ibid., p. 404.

104   See Chapter 8.

105   ibid.

106   Hunter and MacAlpine, 1963, p. 402.

107   ibid.

108   The early history of the Association of Medical Officers of Asylums and Hospitals for the Insane is described by Walk, 1961.

109   See, for instance, Zilboorg, pp. 327–8; Scull, 1981, p. 110 talks of a rupture with the past.

110   The event is described in some detail by Zilboorg, pp. 321–3.

111   The term non-restraint is particularly associated with the ideas and work of John Connolly, physician at the Middlesex County Asylum at Hanwell from 1839 to 1852. His non-restraint system was elaborated

in a book *The Treatment of the Insane without Mechanical Restraints*, published in 1856.

112 Foucault, 1967, p. 269.
113 See, for instance, Porter, 1982.
114 See pp. 167–9 above.
115 Foucault, 1967, p. 72.
116 A charge of one penny or twopence was made. The practice was abolished in 1770 (see the Introduction to Battie's *A Treatise on Madness*, Hunter and MacAlpine, 1962, p. 10).
117 MacDonald, 1981, p. 11.
118 Ignatieff, 1978, pp. 20–1.
119 Benjamin Rush, *Medical Inquiries and Observations upon the Diseases of the Mind*, 1812 (see Hunter and MacAlpine, 1963, p. 669); William Cullen, *First Lines in the practice of physic*, fourth edition, 1784 (see Hunter and MacAlpine, 1963, p. 478).
120 ibid., pp. 534–7, pp. 600–1, and 650.
121 MacDonald, 1981, p. 11.
122 See Thomas Arnold's comment below (p. 218) on the cost of adequate attendance if chains were not to be used; see also Jones, 1955, p. 120.
123 Samuel Tuke, *Description of the Retreat*, 1813.
124 ibid., pp. 22–4.
125 See Hunter and MacAlpine, 1963, p. 685.
126 Tuke, *Description of the Retreat*, 1813.
127 ibid., p. 157.
128 ibid., pp. 159–60.
129 ibid., p. 141.
130 ibid., p. 141.
131 ibid., pp. 68–9 and p. 108.
132 ibid., p. 141.
133 Maudsley, 1867, p. 503–4. He is quoting from another unspecified author.
134 Tuke, *Description of the Retreat*, 1813, pp. 206–12.
135 Rosenberg, 1976, Chapter 1.
136 ibid., p. 29.
137 ibid., p. 47.
138 *Contra*, Scull, 1975 pp. 251–54. But see Rothman, 1971, pp. 110–19.
139 Hunter and MacAlpine, 1963, p. 703.
140 ibid.
141 See Cooter, 1981.
142 Tuke, *Description of the Retreat*, 1813, p. 111.
143 Battie, *A Treatise on Madness*, pp. 68, 71–2.
144 Tuke, *Description of the Retreat*, 1813, p. 115.
145 Bynum, 1981, p. 43; Scull, 1975.
146 Bynum, 1981, p. 40.

147   For example, Scull, 1975, pp. 228–9.

148   Tuke, *Description of the Retreat*, 1813, pp. 133–4. The notion of partial insanity is discussed more fully in Chapter 8.

149   Tuke, *Description of the Retreat*, 1813, pp. 139, 158.

150   Doerner, 1981, pp. 39–48.

151   See p. 171 above.

152   MacDonald, 1981, pp. 150–60.

153   Donnelly (1983, Chapter 6) attempts to begin to unravel the complex relationships between insanity and social class.

154   Hunter and MacAlpine, 1963, p. 703.

155   ibid., p. 703.

156   And also in the early public asylums where different categories of patient were clearly distinguished; see Walk, 1961.

157   Arnold, *Observations on the nature, kinds, causes, and prevention of insanity, lunacy, or madness*, 1782–6, (see Hunter and MacAlpine, 1963, p. 469).

158   Porter, 1981, p. 44; see also Hunter and MacAlpine, 1969.

159   Porter, 1981, p. 44.

160   The only exceptions mentioned by Tuke to the potential of moral treatment were 'cases in which disorder is chiefly marked by a mischievous malevolent disposition' but he does not associate such cases with persons of a particular social class (*Description of the Retreat*, 1813, p. 136).

7 The establishment of public asylums

The development of a system of public asylums throughout the country during the nineteenth century constituted a radical change in the institutional provisions for insanity. The Lunatic Asylums Act of 1845, which made provision of separate residential accommodation for the pauper insane mandatory for all local authorities, was the culmination of a series of acts specifically dealing with lunatics passed during the first half of the century. Together the acts gave local authorities powers to collect special rates for the purpose of providing separate accommodation for the pauper insane and set up a central inspectorate to regulate and control the public asylums as well as the private madhouses and voluntary asylums.

The insanity legislation of the first half of the nineteenth century was but one component of an increased state intervention in social problems manifest in a diverse range of legislation such as the Poor Law Act of 1834, the Factory Acts of 1833 and 1844, the Mines Act of 1842 and the Public Health Act of 1848.[1] All this legislation can be tied to the social changes associated with and summarily described by the term industrialization.[2] Rapid population growth, urbanization, a shift to factory work and higher levels of geographical mobility brought a range of social problems which demanded attention: inadequate housing, insanitary conditions, overcrowding, poverty, ill-health and exploitation. At the same time industrialization helped to transform the social and political orderings of society and people's consciousness of them. Not only did the new urban proletariat begin to develop a class consciousness and political organization, making them a greater political threat and a force that could not be entirely ignored, but the bourgeoisie acquired great political and economic power. Nineteenth-century industrialists and entrepreneurs often had different ideas about the efficient organization of society from the landed aristocracy to whose social position they tended to aspire; and although their individualist, *laissez-faire* ideology might seem antithetical to state intervention many were willing, nevertheless, to accept an increase in the intervention and power of central government, if it seemed necessary to sustain the social order considered essential to the maintenance of efficient and profitable business activity. They were willing to embrace new and what they considered highly rational solutions to the problems created by industrialization.

The impact of this reforming spirit on specific ideas about the treatment of insanity in the form of moral treatment have already been noted. Its impact on policies concerning the care of the pauper insane is the subject of this chapter. In order to understand and explain these policies, as well as the character of the public institutions that were established, it is necessary to examine the main features of the poor law system as a whole since it provided the context in which the new policies were formulated and the new institutions set up.

Tudor poor laws

Nineteenth century poor law had its origins in a series of poor laws enacted in the sixteenth century culminating in the famous Elizabethan Poor Laws of 1598 and 1601.[3] Above all these enactments were a response to the social disorder created by vagrancy which increased markedly during the period; they were an attempt to deal with the problem of those without adequate means of social support who became a social nuisance and a potential threat to the social order by virtue of begging, theft and violence, often carried out individually but, at times, on a more organized, collective basis.

Vagrancy itself was the result of the social upheaval and disruption of the sixteenth century – upheaval created in part by the decline of feudalism and the development of a new group of landless labourers dependent on wage labour for their means of survival. As Christopher Hill comments 'Wage labour and the Poor Law rise together and complement one another.'[4] The significance of the development of an economic system based on wage labour, the core of the new capitalist order, lay in the transformation it involved in the wage labourer's relation to the economic world. Wage labour created a dependence on the fluctuation and vagaries of the market economy. The landless labourer was at the mercy of unemployment, low wages and inflation. Families could usually only survive when wages were low and prices high by working long hours and by using the labour of all family members, men, women and children, and they were very vulnerable to economic disruption from the death, incapacity or disease of a family member (unless he or she could be rapidly replaced) or from unemployment or sudden price fluctuation.[5]

During the sixteenth century circumstances combined to prevent the market economy from operating in a smooth and stable manner. On the one hand there was relentless inflation. In England prices rose sixfold in the hundred years following 1520 – a level of inflation that was then historically unprecedented for European states.[6] On the other hand population growth was considerable, although the rate of growth was not as high as in the nineteenth century. It is difficult to measure the increase with any precision, but it has been estimated that the population of England grew from some 3 million in 1530 to some 4 million in 1600.[7] Population growth not only fuelled inflation, but also directly contributed to vagrancy by putting pressure on existing resources, land, jobs, houses, and so on and it may have encouraged enclosures of land. The result was greater dependence on wage labour, further increases in unemployment and an additional impetus to the growth of towns.[8] London, for instance, probably quadrupled in size during the sixteenth century.

Under these conditions poverty became increasingly pervasive: 'perhaps one third in the cities – one fifth in the rural districts' with women outnumbering men among the poor by some two to one.[9] Poverty was not, of course, a new phenomenon, but its extent and nature had changed.[10] Not only were there the increasing numbers of vagrants and beggars, people who had been dispossessed of their land, or had no land to take over, and were likely to steal or settle illegally on common land. But there was also the threat of riots and revolt – a threat that was not just a fear in the minds of the government and the aristocracy. The first local poor rate levied in Norwich – then the second largest town in England – in 1549 had been preceded by Ket's rebellion in which beggars had participated.[11] And the Poor Laws of 1598 and 1601 were preceded by food riots in 1596 following two years of wet summers and bad harvests.[12] Such rebellions clearly provided a spur for action. Christopher Hill describes the preconditions and the response:

Under all these circumstances – racking of rents, eviction and vagabondage, cutting down of great households, a wage freeze during a price rise, the poor flocking into towns, where the majority lived at or below subsistence level; a legally enforced retention of a pool of labour in the villages – poor relief was necessary to subsidise wages, if the lower orders were not to be forced into revolt by mass starvation.[13]

Undoubtedly, therefore, to quote one author 'the problem of poverty became an integral part of the problem of law and order, the maintenance of which was essential to the continuance of effective government'.[14] Poor law legislation was part of what can, in a broad sense be called the 'policing' of society.[15] It was also part of a range of interventionist measures in a period in which there was sufficient state power exercised through the monarchy for the state to intervene to control the economy in a number of ways – by attempts to control food supplies and prices, the mobility of labour and so on.[16]

Initial poor law legislation was directly repressive and punitive. An act of 1495 stipulated that 'beggars and other idle persons should be placed in the stocks for three days, fed on bread and water and subsequently whipped and returned to their places of origin'.[17] But the act was rarely put into force. The severe economic depression of the 1520s which increased unemployment and vagrancy led to further legislation. An act of 1531, recognizing some variation in the causes of poverty, introduced a distinction that was of particular importance in subsequent legislation, between the impotent and able-bodied poor.[18] The impotent poor – that is, those forced into dependency by virtue of sickness, old age and infirmity – were allowed to beg; vagrants and unruly persons were to be punished by the usual measures, harsh to modern eyes, that were meted out to deviants. The miscreant was to 'be tied to the end of a cart naked and be beaten with whips throughout the same market town or other place till his body be bloody by reason of such whipping'.[19] The law and its makers assumed that the able-bodied could find work if only they tried.

Within medieval society charity had been the traditional solution to the problem of poverty, and religious beliefs had sustained a pattern whereby the poor and the needy had been given gifts of food and alms to help them, and some had been placed in almshouses.[20] Early Tudor legislation tried to harness this traditional response. An act of 1536, for instance, attempted to ensure the local organization of charity for the impotent poor.[21] It also stated that children of the poor should be taught a trade and in due course set to work. Charity, however, was itself changing and becoming more secular; the poor law acts were designed to harness and direct it in more constructive, organized ways, as well as to supplement it.[22] Unorganized charity could not deal with the problems created by the poverty of a more mobile population in a society where the traditional ties between landowner and labourer were being disrupted.

Elizabethan legislation accepted, therefore, that the two basic solutions embodied in the earlier Tudor legislation of charity for the impotent poor and punishment for the able-bodied were inadequate in themselves.[23] Implicitly recognizing that poverty might not result from idleness but from some social upheaval, the loss of land and the difficulty of finding work, the Elizabethan acts introduced the principle that the able-bodied poor, including children, should be set to work by providing employment under supervision for adults and by arranging apprenticeships for children. The possibility of workhouses – places where the poor could be put to work was also envisaged. The wilfully idle were still to be punished either by whipping or by being put in a house of correction or common goal. Moreover, since charity did not always seem sufficient to provide for the impotent poor, arrangements were to be made by the parish for those who could not be supported by their families to receive poor law relief. This was to be financed by a compulsory rate. Abiding or poor houses for the impotent poor could also be provided following the precedent of almshouses that were a favoured object of charity in the Tudor and Stuart period.[24] The poor law system was to be administered by the parish under the organization of Justices of the Peace (who were usually members of the gentry) and the day to day management of overseers and magistrates. The precise levels of provision were to be set locally and the system was marked by extreme variability in the attitudes and practices of parish poor law authorities.[25]

Nevertheless, despite its apparently far-reaching implications, poor law relief was seen as essentially supplementary to private charity; throughout the period charity continued to make a far larger financial and material contribution to the relief of poverty than the poor law system.[26]

Early poor law institutions

During the early decades of the seventeenth century the poor law arrangements of the Elizabethan era continued to operate and they remained in force throughout the Civil War and Commonwealth, but there was something of a decline in private charity.[27] The Restoration brought a weaker monarchy and reduced the capacity of the state to intervene, increasing the liberty of men of property to act in their own interests subject to little governmental control.[28] The number of enclosures rose and many feudal tenures were abolished, changes that helped both to break down traditional agrarian relationships and substitute those of the market place and 'to harden the formation of England into two nations'.[29] New harsher attitudes to the poor developed which found expression in the legislation of the Restoration Parliament as a result of pressure from the parishes.[30] The legislation elaborated two features of Tudor poor law legislation that had previously been given little emphasis – a restriction of relief to those with rights of residence and an emphasis on the giving of relief on an indoor rather than an outdoor basis. In both cases the immediate goal was to keep the economic burden or poor law relief to a minimum.

A series of settlement acts, beginning with the Act of Settlement and Removal of 1662, made parishes responsible only for those with a right of settlement in the parish (a right that could be achieved in a number of ways which were themselves modified by different acts).[31] Those without the right of settlement could be removed from any parish where they lacked it, if they were likely to require poor law relief. The settlement acts were at times cruelly and harshly applied, but some parishes acted more humanely. The acts, like other poor law legislation, were also enforced unevenly. 'Single women, widows with children and deserted wives were most often removed. These were the most defenceless, and the most burdensome people.'[32] Single healthy men were the least likely to be removed since they might prove a useful addition to the labour force.

The establishment of a range of institutions within the poor law system had been envisaged by Elizabethan legislation: houses of correction for the wilfully idle, workhouses for the able-bodied, and abiding or poor houses for the impotent poor.[33] However, in view of the small size of parishes, there were economic obstacles to this policy. Although existing dwellings had sometimes been used, often for short periods of time, as poor law institutions, the institutional provision envisaged by the act required larger scale provision. A number of local acts were passed, therefore, creating poor law corporations with the necessary powers to provide institutions for groups of parishes.[34] Some purpose-built workhouses and poor houses began to be established at the end of the seventeenth century, although most used existing buildings, often rows of cottages.[35] The majority were small.[36] Houses were set up in Crediton, Tiverton, Exeter, Hereford, Colchester, Hull, Salisbury and London in 1698.[37] An act of 1722 which gave all parishes the necessary powers to join together to set up houses further facilitated their spread, and this and subsequent acts permitted the necessary aggregation of resources for the more permanent purpose-built workhouses.[38] The main stronghold of these eighteenth-century workhouses was the northern trade belt – Lancashire, Cheshire, Derbyshire, Nottinghamshire and the West Riding – many in textile areas where outwork could be readily provided.[39] In some cases manufacturers contracted with magistrates for the right to exploit the labour of the houses, introducing an element of private enterprise into the system, although 'The deal rarely proved profitable.'[40] Because of the concern to keep down the cost of the poor law system the institutions tended to combine the functions of workhouse, abiding house and house of correction, confining a diverse range of dependents so that the specialism of institutions envisaged in the Elizabethan legislation was rarely realized.

The new houses were intended, therefore, as much for the able-bodied as for the impotent poor, and many did initially admit the able-bodied and attempted to utilize their labour in activities like spinning and to instil discipline into supposed idlers. The houses were, consequently, run with some severity and the poor were reluctant to enter them, accepting lower allowances on outdoor relief and trying to manage on low wages in order to avoid the workhouse.[41] Viewed on a European scale Foucault calls this 'the Great Confinement' of the classical period, arguing that from the middle of the seventeenth century through to the end of the eighteenth the unemployed, the poor, the criminal and the sick were confined together in institutions designed to instil the virtues of labour and to punish idleness, as a way of policing them:

Confinement, that massive phenomenon, the signs of which are found all across eighteenth-century Europe, is a 'police matter'. Police, in the precise sense that the classical epoch gave to it – that is, the totality of measures which made work possible and necessary for all those who could not live without it . . ..[42]

It was not so much, he argues, that the institutions provided useful and profitable work for the poor, though some efforts were made to this end, but that they provided what Foucault describes as 'a certain ethical consciousness of labour, in which the difficulties of the economic mechanisms lost their urgency in favour of an affirmation of value'.[43] Their significance was moral and symbolic rather than practical. Their purpose was to proclaim the ethic of work. Children in particular were to be trained in the habits of work, it being assumed that habits impressed upon the child would continue throughout life. But direct training was less important in affirming the value of work than the symbolic presence of the institution as a place where those who failed to work might, of necessity, be forced to enter. Those who wished to avoid the routines, the harsh conditions and the degradation of the workhouse knew they must work. Moreover, though these institutions might confine the sick, they were not hospitals in the modern sense:

Before having the medical meaning we give it, or that at least we like to suppose it has, confinement was required by something quite different from any concern with curing the sick. What made it necessary was the imperative of labour. Our philanthropy prefers to recognize the signs of a benevolence toward sickness where there is only a condemnation of idleness.[44]

In England from the middle of the eighteenth century onwards, however, as prosperity increased and the economic advantages of putting people to work in institutions declined, fewer of the able-bodied were sent to the workhouses and their character tended to change. If work could be found relatively quickly there was little economic merit in sending the able-bodied to the workhouse, and those who did try to make a profit out of the workhouses found they could only do so by dishonest practices like pocketing part of the allowances for food.[45] Increasingly the impotent poor, especially the elderly, tended to be in the majority, and the able-bodied who were sent to the workhouse were those forced into dependency by the death of their spouses, or those considered wilfully idle or morally reprehensible in some other way:

The inmates lists show young deserted, unmarried and widowed mothers as the largest able-bodied group in most workhouses and there were very good reasons for bringing them in when they had small families. If they had no more than a couple of children, outdoor accommodation was likely to be costly and the woman's time used inefficiently because the need to care for the child would keep her from work. In a workhouse a few could look after the children while the remainder were set on useful tasks. In any case, nobody had any qualms about forcing unmarried mothers, whose plight aroused hostility rather than sympathy, into the workhouse.[46]

Moreover, since the labour of women could be readily exploited in the workhouse for the 'female' domestic tasks of cooking, cleaning, washing and nursing the sick, able-bodied women were more valuable in the workhouse than able-bodied men.[47] Indeed in the second half of the eighteenth century, as the proportions of able-bodied admitted to the houses declined, domestic work became almost the only work that was done in most houses, and their general strictness and severity were modified in line with the high proportion of impotent poor.[48] Research on Essex workhouses suggests that after the early decades of the century 'the spirit animating these and other early workhouses gave place to one of greater humanity within a short time'.[49]

The high proportion of women found in workhouses paralleled an overall excess of women in receipt of poor law relief.[50] This excess arose from the structural situation of women with their responsibility for children. Women with children were less free to work outside the home and to move to other areas to find work. Consequently they were more likely to be forced into dependency through the absence of an able-bodied male as a result of death, desertion, sickness or unemployment.

Although many workhouses and poor houses were set up during the eighteenth century, their usually small size and the short life of many of them meant that the overall numbers they contained were never very large.[51] Nevertheless, the early workhouses, intended as they were to discipline and provide work for the able-bodied, set a precedent for an institutional solution to the problem of the poverty not just of the elderly infirm – this had already been provided by the charitable almshouses – but also of the able-bodied who were capable of work. The disciplinary spirit of some of the early workhouses was reaffirmed and strengthened in the plans for reform of the poor law in the nineteenth century.

The New Poor Law

Nineteenth-century poor law reform, in the shape of the 1834 Poor Law Amendment Act, was prompted by two factors: on the one hand by the major social, economic and demographic changes associated with industrialization which transformed the problem of poverty during the second half of the eighteenth and the early decades of the nineteenth century; and on the other hand by the ideas and arguments of a number of different theorists and reformers whose ideas structured the way in which the problem of poverty was perceived during this period.[52] Especially influential were the writings of Thomas Malthus, whose argument in *An Essay on the Principle of Population*, first published in 1798, suggested the inevitability of poverty in any society; and of Jeremy Bentham, who contended that rationality and science should be applied to the social world with a view to obtaining a well-regulated and disciplined society.[53] Malthus' arguments offered a rationale for the abolition of the poor law system and this was the view put forward by many when the inadequacies of the poor law system in coping with the problems generated by industrialization became increasingly apparent.[54] It was, however, Edwin Chadwick, a Benthamite, who was the moving force behind the new legislation and was largely responsible for the 1834 Poor Law Report on which the 1834 act was based.[55]

Bentham advocated the development of new types of social institutions in which order would be maintained through discipline and surveillance. His design for an 'inspection house', the Panopticon, published in 1791, illustrated these principles.[56] The plan was for a circular construction of open 'cells' built around a central inspection tower from which both inmate and inspector alike would be placed under constant surveillance. Significantly he considered that this surveillance would make chains and other forms of physical restraint of difficult inmates unnecessary.[57] Inmates would, moreover, be expected to work and Bentham envisaged that they would work for a private contractor who would supervise the house and retain the profits of the enterprises, as had happened in some of the workhouses. Bentham considered his plan suitable for any institution, whether school, workhouse, prison, asylum or hospital and thought its value would be enormous:

Morals reformed – health preserved – industry invigorated – instruction diffused – public burthens lightened –economy seated as it were up on a rock – the gordian knot of the Poor Laws not cut but untied – all by a simple Idea in Architecture.[58]

The immediate problem with which the poor law reform was designed to deal was the increasing cost of making poor law provision. There were a number of reasons for this. The increased pace of urbanization meant that agriculture had to become more productive if the new towns were to be provided with adequate food, and so encouraged a further wave of enclosures, increasing both the proportion of landless labourers and rural unemployment.[59] And the move to the towns directly increased the proportions dependent on wage labour as well as breaking family and local ties which had provided a means of social support in times of unemployment, low wages or high prices. The situation was exacerbated not only by the rapid population growth associated with industrialization (between 1781 and 1851 the population more than doubled, from around 9 million to around 20 million), but also by wars, especially the French wars of 1793 to 1815, which made the impact of bad harvests greater because it was less easy to make up any deficiency with imports, and led to a sharp increase in prices.[60]

One response to the increase of poverty in rural areas, given the poor law authorities' reliance on outdoor relief for support of the able-bodied, was the development of a pattern, not unknown before, of subsidizing wages, the subsidy usually depending on the price of bread and sometimes on the size of family.[61] Schemes such as the famous Speenhamland system, named after the Berkshire village where it was introduced, were envisaged as temporary measures to tide the poor over a bad harvest or a sudden rise in prices. However, the conditions that created the increase in poverty did not prove temporary (the scheme itself probably fuelled poverty by keeping wages down), and the cost of poor relief to the parish became increasingly burdensome.[62] Indeed, it had been increasing from the 1770s, but it increased even more rapidly during the wars, rising according to one estimate from £2.6 million to £6.5 million between 1792 and 1812. By 1818 it had reached £8 million.[63]

The concern at these developments within the poor law system was a dual one. On the one hand there was the financial burden itself which was considered excessive. On the other hand the impact of the ideas of writers such as Malthus as to the inevitability of poverty made developments like the subsidizing of wages seem mistaken. They argued that such measures blurred the distinction between independence and pauperism by creating a category of workers whose wages were regularly subsidized.[64] Commentators contended that this provided an incentive to employers to pay low wages and permitted them to do so without conscience; and also, that it changed the labourers' expectations of poor law relief, making it seem more of a right, as well as giving them little incentive to work harder or find another job with higher pay (a familiar enough argument in our own time).[65] The force of these complaints about the poor law system was strengthened by the fact that expenditure on the subsidies was not proving at all successful in ensuring social order, the very thing the system had been designed to achieve. As one author comments:

What doomed the old Poor Law was that despite paying £7 million a year there still occurred the frightening Swing Riots of 1830. The burning of hay ricks and threats of spoliation of the South of England, coinciding apparently with the widespread use of the allowance system, convinced authority that reform must come. The Poor Law had not eradicted distress – indeed the rural populace had become disaffected and desperate.[66]

The anxieties about social order created by the Swing Riots were enhanced and heightened by the growing class consciousness of the period. On the one hand the perception of class was transformed and the very language of hierarchy changed from a language of orders and ranks to a language of classes.[67] On the other hand class consciousness and class conflict became more apparent, and new working-class organizations came into being.[68] This is how the historian E.P. Thompson describes the changes:

the outstanding fact of the period between 1790 and 1830 is the formation of the 'working class'. This is revealed, first, in the growth of class-consciousness: the consciousness of an identity of interests as between all these diverse groups of working people and as against the interests of other classes. And, second, in the growth of corresponding forms of political and industrial organisation. By 1832 there were strongly-based and self-conscious working-class institutions – trade unions, friendly societies, educational and religious movements, political organisations, periodicals – working-class intellectual traditions, working-class community-patterns, and a working-class structure of feeling.[69]

The increased working-class consciousness was particularly manifest in the early 1830s, which he describes as 'aflame with agitations'.[70] Such agitations contributed not only to the passage of the Reform Bill in 1832, which enfranchised a greater proportion of the bourgeoisie who were sympathetic to the case for poor law reform, but also to the setting up of a Royal Commission on the Poor Law in the same year. The commission was composed of nine members, including Edwin Chadwick and Nassau Senior, an economist of the classical school and also a protégé of Bentham who died the year the commission was established.[71]

The Poor Law Report, published in 1834, focused almost exclusively on the problem of the able-bodied poor.[72] It aimed to return the poor law to the Elizabethan principles from which it was held to have deviated.[73] Rather than advocating the total abolition of relief for the able-bodied, as some reformers had urged, it introduced the famous principle of less-eligibility which asserted that the situation of those relieved 'shall not be made really or apparently so eligible as the situation of the independent labourer of the lowest class'.[74] The means for enforcing this principle was the workhouse test, the report recommending that after a limited period no further relief should be given to the able-bodied 'otherwise than in well-regulated workhouses'.[75] Relief in aid of wages was to be abolished.[76] Parishes were to be incorporated into unions for the provision of workhouses and separate houses were to be built for *1* the aged and really impotent; *2* children; *3* able-bodied females; *4* able-bodied males.[77] There was also to be a central board of three commissioners to frame regulations for workhouses, to specify qualifications for officials and so on, but the parish was still to collect the poor law rates and the unions were to administer the relief.[78] The Poor Law Amendment Act itself, passed in the summer of 1834, laid down the administrative framework envisaged by the Poor Law Report but did not make specific reference to the workhouse test or the principle of less eligibility, and the commissioners were not assigned special powers to ensure that policies contained in the Poor Law Report were carried out.[79]

Nevertheless, the immediate consequences of the act were considerable: a large number of poor law unions were rapidly established (by the end of 1836 the commissioners had combined 7915 parishes into 365 unions covering about one tenth of the population, although after this the pace of unionization slowed down); the numbers in workhouses increased (incomplete returns showed an increase from 78,536 inmates in 1838 to 197,179 in 1843); and there was an immediate decline in the amount spent on poor law relief (between 1834 and 1839 some £11 million less was spent than in the previous five years, a reduction of over £2 million a year).[80] However, certain intentions of the Royal Commission were not realized. Only rarely were separate workhouses set up for different categories of inmate, and in most areas outdoor relief to the able-bodied continued.[81] There was, too, much opposition to the New Poor Law from labourers in the industrial areas of Northern England (riots occurring in 1837 and 1838), with the result that the Home Secretary urged the commission 'to exercise caution and delay in their extension of the New Poor Law to the area'.[82]

Although outdoor relief did not disappear, the 'ideological dogma' of the act had its impact; discipline and deterrence were, Thompson suggests, its guiding principles:

The doctrine of discipline and restraint was, from the start, more important than that of material 'less eligibility'; the most inventive State would have been hard put to it to create institutions which simulated conditions worse than those of garret-masters, Dorset labourers, framework-knitters and nailers. The impractical policy of systematic starvation was displaced by the policy of psychological deterrence: 'labour, discipline and restraint'. 'Our intention' said one Assistant Commissioner, 'is to make the workhouses as like prisons as possible'; and another, 'our object . . . is to establish therein a discipline so severe and repulsive as to make them a terror to the poor and prevent them from entering'. Dr. Kay recorded with satisfaction his successes in Norfolk; the reduction in diet proved less effective than 'minute and regular observance of routine', religious exercises, silence during meals, 'prompt obedience', total separation of the sexes, separation of families (even where of the same sex), labour and total confinement.[83]

Sickness was a matter of concern to the poor law system in so far as it created dependence. However, despite its recognized importance as a cause of poverty and the presence of Chadwick (he was to be one of the major proponents of public health reform on the grounds that 'sickness resulting from insanitary environments was a major charge on Poor Law expenditure'), it received little attention in the Poor Law Report, focusing as it did on the able-bodied.[84] None the less, the introduction of the New Poor Law had a significant effect on the provision of care for the sick. First, since it was the impotent poor who were most likely to end up in the workhouses, whatever the intention, the strengthening of the ideology of deterrence through discipline and restraint within the workhouses had most impact on the impotent poor including the sick and children.[85] Second, the importance attached to the classification of workhouse inmates and the provision of separate institutions for different groups of paupers provided an argument that could be used to legitimate the establishment of separate wards or infirmaries for the sick or separate asylums for lunatics. The fact that separate asylums began to be established before separate infirmaries is a matter of some interest. (The establishment of separate infirmaries largely followed the Metropolitan Poor Law Act of 1867.)[86]

Third, the report assumed that unions would appoint medical officers to provide medical services for the pauper sick (the practice had already developed in the midlands, the south and the east under the old poor law) and almost all the newly appointed Boards of Guardians did so.[87] (There were some 2800 by 1844.)[88] This occurred less because the report emphasized the necessity of so doing than because 'the new flexibility and enhanced financial strength of the unions compared with the feebleness of the old parish authorities' made it possible.[89] No doubt, as we shall see in the case of asylums, improvements in medical services came to seem an increasingly economic proposition for the poor law system at a time when advances in medical training and research were enhancing the status and position of medical practitioners.[90]

Separate public asylums were established within the context of the poor law system, and were as much affected by the ideology and practices of the New Poor Law as by those of the developing medical profession: it is to the development of these institutions that we must now turn.

The campaign for public asylums

Before the nineteenth century the poor law did not itself make any separate institutional provision for pauper lunatics. Some were given outdoor relief, others were grouped together with vagrants, the wilfully idle, the elderly and the infirm in the workhouses, although their insanity might mean certain differences in their treatment. Those considered dangerous were subject to greater curtailment of their liberties and greater restraint, some were chained and confined in the worst of circumstances. Others, if they were confined in an institution and considered harmless, would be set to work along with other inmates. The few pauper insane sent to private madhouses or voluntary asylums that accepted paupers were usually those considered troublesome or dangerous, and if they became less difficult they might well be returned to the less costly workhouse.[91]

In England the earliest legislative attention to the special problems created by lunatics within the poor law system was an Act of 1714 which referred to 'Persons of little or no Estates, who, by lunacy, or otherwise, are furiously Mad, and dangerous to be permitted to go Abroad', and directed that they 'be Apprehended, and kept safely Locked up, in such secure place within the County where such Parish or Town shall lie . . . and (if such Justices find it necessary) to be there Chained. . . .'[92] The cost of confining pauper lunatics was to be paid for by the parish of settlement. A further act in 1744 made the parishes liable for the cost of 'curing such Person during such Restraint', the first legislative reference to cure.[93] Any lunatics who were confined under these provisions would be confined within existing institutions, and these provisions were invoked when paupers were sent to private madhouses or voluntary asylums.

At the end of the eighteenth century, however, a campaign began to develop to reform the arrangements for lunatics within the poor law system and outside it. The reformers were mostly successful entrepreneurs and merchants, and mostly religious dissenters – Quakers and Evangelicals. They advocated two major reforms: the further regulation and control of existing asylums and madhouses; and the provision of public asylums for the pauper insane.[94] Both objectives sprang from a common source: the belief that much of the existing provision for the insane, whether they were confined alone or along with other groups, was inadequate, not only in quantity, but also, equally importantly, in quality. There were too few asylums (it was difficult to secure the necessary charitable support for them); inmates were too often harshly treated; the madhouse proprietors were more concerned about making a profit than about the care of their inmates; many pauper lunatics were kept in mixed work and poorhouses, and so on. What was needed was a system of public asylums to ensure that the necessary public funds would be allocated to the care of lunatics, and those and all other institutions housing lunatics must be subject to public inspection.

The type of deficiencies worrying the reformers were documented by a Parliamentary Select Committee in 1815–16, which produced four reports over two years. It provided ample evidence of a catalogue of defects in existing provision: overcrowding, too few attendants, mixing of 'outrageous' patients with the 'quiet and inoffensive', a lack of medical assistance, excessive use of mechanical restraint, poor conditions of pauper patients, wrongful detention, inadequate certification procedures, and defective visitation of private madhouses.[95] The committee concluded that:

inquiries . . . have convinced them that there are not in the Country a set of Beings more immediately requiring the protection of the Legislature than the Persons in this state . . . .. If the treatment of those in the middling or in the lower classes of life, shut up in hospitals, private madhouses, or parish workhouses, is looked at, Your Committee are persuaded that a case cannot be found where the necessity for a remedy is more urgent.[96]

Underlying these comments and the reformers' campaign was the ideological change I considered in the previous chapter: the belief that all types of lunatics, maniacs as well as melancholics, paupers as well as gentlemen, were people with human feelings and should be treated humanely.

A change in consciousness that led to the view that many of the insane were harshly and cruelly treated was not, however, sufficient in itself to ensure the success of the reformers' campaign, although it was an essential pre-condition. There was opposition from a number of quarters: from madhouse proprietors who did not want any interference in the running of their business; from medical practitioners who saw the reformers' proposals as 'an assault on medicine's professional preroga- tives'; from a rural aristocracy averse to any increased involvement of central government in local affairs; and from local authorities themselves anxious about demands for them to spend more money.[97] The setting up of new public asylums meant extra expenditure on a group of low status dependents. Not only was there the capital cost of the new public asylum to be found, but the weekly cost of maintaining a lunatic was likely to be greater there than in a workhouse. In 1837, for instance, the cost per week of maintaining a pauper lunatic in a county asylum was 6s.6d., in a private madhouse 9s.3d., and in a workhouse or on outdoor relief 3s.6d.[98] If local authorities were reluctant enough to send pauper lunatics to the private madhouses on grounds of cost, they were likely to be even more reluctant to set aside the necessary sums of money for the capital and recurrent expenditure needed to set up a public asylum.[99]

The initial steps towards reform were limited. A Select Committee of

Parliament was set up in 1807 to investigate 'the State of Criminal and Pauper Lunatics in England and Wales' and produced a rather brief report the same year.[100] It requested some information from madhouse proprietors and asylum doctors but did not itself collect any direct evidence by visiting asylums.[101] The committee, under the chairmanship of Charles Williams Wynn, included several active reformers such as William Wilberforce and Samuel Romilly and had been set up as a result of the efforts of a Gloucestershire magistrate, Sir George Onesiphorus Paul, whose family had made their fortune in the woollen trade.[102] Paul, who had been involved in the establishment of a penitentiary in Gloucestershire, was a prison reformer and disciple of John Howard and Bentham, although he did not agree with all Bentham's ideas (he did not think, for instance, that penitentiary work should be run on a commercial basis). He was particularly concerned about the treatment of criminal lunatics and had also been involved in the plans to try and establish a subscription asylum for private and pauper lunatics in Gloucester during the previous decade; however, no asylum had been built owing to the lack of public support, although funds were still being collected for that purpose, and he wanted to secure government backing for the establishment of this institution and others like it.[104]

The Select Committee viewed the new voluntary asylums at York, Liverpool and elsewhere as the model for further provision for pauper and criminal lunatics, and recommended the establishment of public asylums similar to them:

the Measure which appears to Your Committee most adequate to ensure the proper care and management of these unfortunate persons and the most likely conducive to their perfect cure, is the erection of Asylums for their reception in the different parts of the kingdom, a measure which has already been adopted with great success at York, Liverpool, Manchester, Exeter, Hereford, Norwich and Leicester.[105]

These asylums would be funded from the county rates in conjunction, perhaps, with public subscription, and could be considered an economic investment, the report contended, because of the improved chances of cure they would offer.

Even if the condition of the persons so confined in Poor Houses were not so revolting to humanity, as from the evidence of Sir George Paul, and from the observation of different Members of your Committee, it appears frequently to be; Your Committee are of opinion, that there are other sufficient inducements to provide proper places expressly for the reception of Lunatic Paupers. In their present situation there is no probability of their cure, and they remain a burden upon the public as long as they live. In the Asylum which has for twenty years been established at York, nearly one half of the patients admitted have been discharged cured, and at St Luke's a still larger proportion.[106]

The committee considered the case for public asylums sufficiently powerful that in the first instance it was necessary only to commend and assist their establishment.[107] It recognized, however, that the cost of an asylum was not inconsiderable and pointed out that a relatively large asylum might be more economic: 'it would be highly desirable for the purpose of preventing unnecessary expense, that each building should be calculated to contain as large a number as possible, not exceeding three hundred'.[108] It also recommended siting any asylum where it would have ready access to medical assistance.[109]

The Lunatics Act, passed the following year, and commonly referred to as Wynn's Act, authorized but did not compel counties or groups to erect asylums for pauper and criminal lunatics and empowered them to collect a county rate for this purpose.[110] The first of the new county asylums was opened in Nottingham in February 1812, the second in August of the same year in Bedford, the third in Norfolk in May 1814 and the fourth in Lancaster in July 1816.[111] By 1824 eight counties had established new asylums and an institution in Bristol had been incorporated under the act – a number that is small in absolute terms but not insignificant in relation to the existing number of charitable asylums, by then eleven.[112] The new county asylums were, moreover, relatively similar in character to the voluntary asylums as the 1807 Committee had intended. Several of the new institutions were partly funded by subscription and admitted private as well as pauper patients; most of them at this stage were much smaller than the committee's suggested limit of 300 patients (close to 100 was the average size) and some tried to institute the principles of moral treatment.[113] Indeed, to a large extent they were an extension of the voluntary asylum movement (despite the significance of the involvement of local authorities and the commitment of public funds) and the pattern of their growth was complementary to that of the voluntary asylums. Public asylums tended to be set up by towns that had not managed to secure a voluntary asylum. The Nottingham asylum, for instance, had already been planned prior to Wynn's Act and with the passing of the act the existing voluntary committee joined with the town and the county to establish the new asylum, which had three classes of patient as originally envisaged, ninety in all: paupers; patients who paid a fee sufficient to subsidize a third group of charity patients who were charged a relatively low fee.[114] Similarly, in Gloucester the voluntary committee joined with town and county following the passage of the act and after some delay an asylum was opened in 1823 for 110 patients, again for three classes.[115] As a result the new act extended the pattern followed by the voluntary asylums, and asylums were built to serve places with the large concentrations of population that urbanization was producing.[116]

The 1815–16 Parliamentary Select Committee included several members of the 1807 Committee and was set up following scandals concerning treatment at York Asylum (partly activated by the publication of Tuke's *Description of the Retreat* in 1813) and at Bethlem.[117] It attempted the first detailed investigation of lunatics of all types (not just pauper and criminal lunatics) and pointed to many defects and deficiencies in existing provision. However, although the committee's four reports led to further pressure for action to control abuses and resulted in a number of parliamentary bills between 1816 and 1819 which sought in particular to establish a central inspectorate, all were successfully opposed by an alliance of forces hostile to reform.[118] It was not until 1828, following a further Select Committee set up to inquire into the conditions of Metropolitan madhouses, that further legislation was passed, this time largely because it modified and weakened the earlier bills' proposals on central inspection. The 1827 Select Committee was established on the initiative of a member of the 1815–16 Committee, Lord Robert Seymour, a Middlesex magistrate anxious to secure a public asylum for the county.[119] The Committee focused its attention on a large private madhouse at Bethnal Green, Warburton's White House, revealing neglect, ill-treatment and abuse. Lord Ashley, later the 7th Earl of Shaftesbury was a member of the committee.[120] He was a Tory landowner and Evangelical who was also actively involved in securing the passage of factory legislation through Parliament in the 1830s. Under the provisions of the 1828 legislation he was made one of the new Metropolitan Commissioners in Lunacy, remaining a commissioner until his death in 1885.

The 1828 Madhouse Act repealed the 1774 Act, and set up an improved system of licensing and inspection, though only of private madhouses in the metropolitan area.[121] Fifteen part-time Metropolitan Commissioners, including five physicians, were to replace inspection by five members of the College of Physicians. They were given powers to license and inspect madhouses, but as before, outside London magistrates were to license and inspect, though the inspectors now had to include one medical man. The new Metropolitan Commissioners were, however, in a position to campaign for further reform including a permanent central inspectorate.[122] The County Asylum Act passed the same year, required the asylums to send returns of admissions, discharges and deaths to the Home Office, and gave powers of visitation to the Secretary of State.[123] It further, and more importantly, required any county asylum with one hundred patients or more (by then the majority of them) to have a resident medical officer. The smaller institutions were to be visited by a medical practitioner not less than twice a week. Restraint was only to be imposed by the order of a medical attendant, who might be a physician, surgeon or apothecary. The act also extended the procedure for certification. The admission of private patients now required two medical certificates, the admission of pauper patients an order signed by two magistrates or by an overseer and a clergyman of the parish together with a medical certificate.

It was, however, legislation in the 1840s that finally made the provision of public asylums mandatory and set up a central inspectorate for the whole country. An act in 1842, the Lunatic Asylums Act, for the first time extended the range of the powers of the Metropolitan Commissioners to the provinces, requiring them to visit and inspect all public and private asylums in England and Wales for the purpose of preparing a report to Parliament.[124] The important 1844 Report of the Metropolitan Commissioners in Lunacy which followed was written by Lord Ashley.[125] It provided the first national, relatively systematic quantitative data on lunatics in all types of institutions. At this stage there were seventeen public asylums, eleven charitable asylums, two military and naval hospitals for lunatics, ninety-nine provincial licensed madhouses and thirty-nine metropolitan licensed houses. The report argued both for a national inspectorate and for the advantages of county asylums. It provided data showing that of the close on 21,000 lunatics in existing establishments (including nearly 300 'single' patients under the commission's purview) nearly half were confined in 'workhouses and elsewhere', and argued that:

We think, however, that the detention in Workhouses not only of dangerous lunatics, but of all lunatics and idiots whatsoever, is highly objectionable . . . . Although a patient may not be violent or raving, he may require medical treatment, and it is at the beginning of attacks of insanity, when the causes of the disease are in most powerful operation, and the symptoms are developing themselves, that the skill of a medical officer experienced in this disease is most required. Our objection to the clause of the Act to which we have referred is, that it has a tendency to impress upon those who have the care of the poor, the belief that there is no harm in keeping lunatics away from Asylums so long as they are not dangerous, and thus to combine with the other causes which we have pointed out in producing that incurable condition in which pauper lunatics are so often sent to Asylums.[126]

Although the commissioners were keen for lunatics to be sent to asylums early in their illness, before the condition became incurable, they argued that licensed houses should receive only insane persons 'and the reception of nervous, imbecile, and dejected persons, amongst those who are Insane, and often dangerous, is for obvious reasons open to serious objection'.[127]

The recommendations of the 1844 Report were incorporated into two acts passed in 1845. The Lunatics Act established a permanent central regulatory body, the Lunacy Commission, to visit and inspect all types of asylums in the whole country.[128] There were to be eleven commissioners, five lay, including a full-time, unpaid chairman (Lord Ashley was the first), three salaried medical practitioners and three legal men. Licensing in the provinces was to continue in the hands of magistrates, but subject to the overall supervision of the commission. The powers of the commission were not, however, extensive: in particular they could not compel compliance to directives concerning the running of asylums. A further act in 1845, the Lunatic Asylums Act, made the erection of county and borough asylums mandatory.[129] It also authorized counties and boroughs, following a recommendation of the 1844 Report, to build separate, less costly asylums for chronic lunatics, but none did so under the provisions of this act.[130] Following the new legislation the number of county and borough asylums increased more rapidly. There were twenty-four in 1850, forty-one in 1860, fifty in 1870 and seventy-seven by 1900.[131] And their character began to change; the asylums expanded in size, private patients were moved out to the charitable asylums, and there was little active attempt to put the principles of moral treatment into effect.[132] The nature and cause of such changes will be considered in the next chapter.

Explaining the legislative success

The success of the lunacy reformers' campaign in securing mandatory legislation requiring all counties to make provision for pauper lunatics is in many respects surprising, given the financial outlay and central intervention it required. It can be attributed to a number of factors. First, and perhaps most important of all was the argument that the development of separate asylums could provide an efficient and effective long-term solution to the problem of insanity. Of greater salience here than any widespread acceptance of the argument that the insane, even the pauper insane, should be treated less harshly and repressively, was the rhetoric of curability with which lunacy reform was associated.[133] What has been called the 'cult of curability' was based more on the optimism of reformers, and the inexpert and often confusing presentation of statistics by asylum superintendents anxious to demonstrate their success, than on any firm basis in objective fact.[134] Yet the belief that asylums could achieve high rates of cure was little questioned until the middle of the nineteenth century.[135] The belief was first evidenced in the claims made in the private madhouse proprietors' advertisements designed to attract inmates to their houses. It was then given further sustenance not only by medical men in voluntary asylums anxious to demonstrate their success, but also by the climate of therapeutic optimism created by moral treatment. The statistics and claims presented in the reports of these asylums became, in turn, the authorities on which reformers could rely for their assertions about the curability of insanity.

The type of therapeutic optimism widespread in the first half of the nineteenth century is illustrated in the comments on cure made by William Browne, medical superintendent of Montrose Asylum in a pamphlet *What Asylums Were, Are and Ought to Be*, published in 1837:

Drs. Monro, Burrow, and Ellis, declare, however, that they cure ninety out of every hundred cases. Such a result proves . . . that instead of being the most intractable it is the most curable of all diseases. The declaration, however, applied only to recent cases, which have not existed for more than three months, and which have been treated under the most favourable circumstances . . . . But even where poverty, popular prejudice, indifference or other obstacles, have deprived the insane of many of those means which it is in the power of benevolence and art to bestow, the proportion of cures is such as to dispel the disheartening and unworthy conviction that this affliction must continue to baffle human skill . . . . That proportion . . . does not depend upon, or vary with, local circumstances; it is the same in Italy as in England; it bears little relation to the occupation, sex, or age of the patient, and less to the cause of the malady unless that be organic . . . . If all asylums have advanced to that stage of improvement to which they will ultimately be forced by the irresistible impetus of public opinion; and were patients placed under treatment on the very first and slightest indication . . . the proportion given by Ellis would become universal. Even now, contending, as physicians to the insane have almost everywhere to do, with errors and difficulties which none can appreciate save those who have tried to put the moral machinery of an asylum into operation; and taking all cases as they are presented of long or short duration, simple or complicated with malformation of the head or organic disease, the average number is about one-half.[136]

This passage brings out two components of the argument about curability that are of especial interest. First, Browne suggests that people of any rank of life, age, or sex can be cured. Hence the pauper insane, no less than the rich, can benefit from asylum care. This is the corollary of the changing perception of the need for humanity in the care of people of all social positions. Second, it manifests the belief, continually affirmed by medical men and those involved in lunacy reform, that early treatment enhanced the chance of cure.[137] The implication of this (given the assumption that cure required institutional care) was to define institutions as places of first rather than last resort, first in time as well as the first and preferred location for cure.

The belief in the curability of insanity was essential to the reformers' success because it made the social problems created by insanity seem soluble. From the point of view of the poor law authorities the problem created by the pauper insane was two-fold: their social disruptiveness and their long-term dependency. The workhouse was a poor solution, not only because the insane could be difficult and even dangerous and disturbed the smooth running of the institution, but also because they were often a long-term burden on the institution. The appeal of the claims about curability was the possibility that insanity could be transformed into short-term dependency and the long-term build up of cases in the workhouses could be avoided. The immediate cost might be more, which was an obvious disadvantage, but it seemed that in the long-term the overall cost would be less. The establishment of public asylums looked, therefore, like a cost-effective solution to the problem of insanity as the 1807 Committee suggested. The case is similar to that made for charitable hospitals and asylums in the attempt to gain subscriptions, and it was also used in the debates about infirmary provision for the pauper sick in the workhouse: 'the time saved in illness was beneficial to the parish'.[138] And in this case, too, early institutional treatment was presented as an economic proposition since it was held to increase the chances of cure by providing treatment at the right time (early enough), in the right place (away from the disease producing environment), and of the right type (under proper medical supervision). It was considered a mistake to leave the insane or the sick at home or without proper care in the workhouse 'until the disease has become inveterate and recovery hopeless'.[139] The argument had more immediate effect in the context of the poor law when applied to asylums than to infirmaries, not only because the long-term burden of insanity was more obvious (the sick often either returned to health or died) but also because the therapeutic optimism associated with moral treatment gave the argument added conviction. In addition the difficulties and problems created by 'refractory' lunatics in the workhouses made some separate provision for lunatics seem more necessary.

One consequence of the widespread optimism about the curability of insanity was that although some qualifications were made about the conditions under which greater chances of cure could be achieved, the general optimism made compromise on the precise characteristics of asylums easier to achieve – compromise as to size, levels of staffing, quality of care and so on. Some compromise on these characteristics was important in gaining acceptance for the policy of setting up asylums in the face of the financial concerns of local authorities, for it helped to legitimize departures from the ideals of the model asylum and so to reduce their costs.[140] Any asylum it seemed, even one that was larger, less well staffed and more bureaucratically regulated than the ideal, could offer better prospects of cure than leaving the insane without asylum care. The provision of an asylum could become an end in itself and little attention need be paid to its precise characteristics.

The second factor contributing to the eventual success of the lunacy reformers' campaign was the reform of the poor law system in the 1830s. At first sight the changes in poor law policy would seem to have militated against the introduction of separate asylums for the insane, since a major pressure for the reform of the poor law was anxiety about the increasing cost of the poor law provisions. However, the workhouse test, by affirming the belief in institutional solutions to social problems, contributed to a climate of opinion that accepted the costs of institutional care as essential to the overall operation of the system. Of course within poor law ideology, as we have seen, institutions were places of last resort with explicit deterrent value, whereas lunacy reformers affirmed their positive advantages for the insane; nevertheless, both sides could concur in their value as a means for dealing with social problems. Consequently lunacy reformers found a strong pro-institutional ideology within the poor law system on which to base their case for separate public asylums.

The Poor Law Report itself paid no specific attention to the problems of the lunatic insane. However, the Poor Law Amendment Act affirmed that any dangerous lunatic, insane person or idiot should not be detained in a workhouse for longer than fourteen days.[141] The Poor Law Commissioners argued that asylums for pauper lunatics attached to a large workhouse should be established. In this proposal economy and the interests of the insane persons were seen to be happily combined; it would be preferable to

sending these unfortunate persons to private institutions, in which it is in the interests of proprietors that they remain . . .. It would also be better as point of their economy, the price paid to asylums being 10s. to 12s. weekly, whilst in the poor house they could be kept to less than half that amount.[142]

Separate provision was acceptable, but not any increase in cost.

A third factor that contributed to the success of the campaign for lunacy reform was the deficiency of existing provision for the insane, rich as well as poor. In the first place, although it might be widely accepted that sensibility was associated with social rank and that those of higher status merited a degree of respect and standards of care that the pauper did not, nevertheless, as we have seen, influence and high status were no guarantee of freedom from cruelty and exploitation in a private madhouse or charitable asylum. This was one reason for the calls for the better regulation and inspection of those institutions and asylums. Combined, however, with a further belief that the quality of care was often adversely affected by the desire for profit, it became a significant argument in the campaign for public asylums. Charitable asylums financed by private subscriptions did offer an alternative to the private madhouses, but they were relatively few in number and there seemed little hope of much expansion because of the difficulty of obtaining the necessary finance from public donations. Consequently public asylums were also supported by those who believed that 'the judgement and conduct of those running them could not be perverted by considerations of personal profit', as well as by those who could not afford the charges of either private madhouses or charitable asylums, but wanted to avoid the stigma of the workhouse.[143] Of course, all patients admitted to public asylums without charge were categorized as pauper patients, but those who advocated the development of public asylums often planned for asylums that would provide for different classes of patients, rich, charitable and pauper with different standards of accommodation, and, as we have seen, early public asylums were designed on these lines.[144]

The final set of factors contributing to the success of the lunacy reformers' campaign relates to the political changes that were a part of the social transformations associated with industrialization and the development of industrial capitalism. A 'triumphant' bourgeoisie of merchants and traders, now swelled by the addition of industrial capitalists, was gaining greater political power alongside the aristocracy, a change symbolized by the passing of the Reform Bill in 1832.[145] This enhanced political power was important for the cause of lunacy reform since the reformers, as we have seen, tended to be drawn from the bourgeois class. Three groups of reformers were of particular importance: the Quakers, such as the Tukes; the Evangelicals, such as Lord Ashley; and the Benthamites such as Sir George Onesiphorus Paul.[146] All drew much of their support from the bourgeoisie, and with the increased political power of that group the policy reforms they proposed had a greater chance of success. The Evangelicals were of particular significance as they remained within the Church of England and so 'constituted a link, effected a transition between Anglicanism and Dissent, between the governing classes and the general public, as represented by the great middle class'.[147] What these reforming groups represented was an alliance of two opposing tendencies, capitalism and philanthropy: 'There came into existence a class of austere men, hard workers and greedy of gain, who considered it their two-fold duty to make a fortune in business and to preach Christ crucified'.[148] By the middle of the nineteenth century the government was no longer merely in the control of the aristocrats, rather it was one in which the aristocracy had been forced to share some of their power with the bourgeoisie and in which, therefore, bourgeois interests were well represented.

Lunacy reform, moreover, required a greater degree of central control, and here too the increased power of the bourgeoisie was important, since they did not have the same degree of opposition to greater centralization as the aristocracy. Part of the power of the aristocracy stemmed from the control they could exercise locally; they therefore tended to be opposed to policies that took decision making away from the local areas.[149] The bourgeoisie, on the contrary, despite their commitment to the ideology of *laissez-faire*, and some acquisition of power at a local level, accepted that some government intervention was necessary 'to create and maintain the best conditions for capitalism, which is regarded as an essentially self-regulating and self-expanding system which tends to maximise the "wealth of the nation"'.[150] Industrialization in the first half of the nineteenth century brought a new range of social problems and led to greater, though relatively circumscribed, state intervention to remove certain obstacles to the operation of the free market economy: to cut down, for instance, the power of the vested interests of the landed classes and to cut down the social obligations to the poor. With the growing importance of the bourgeoisie came a new willingness to intervene to create a social order suitable for capitalism and this included a new moral order among the working classes. In terms of the poor law ideology it meant not only keeping the cost of poor law relief down to a minimum but also driving unemployed labour resources onto the free market to keep wages low. Lunacy reform was one component of this new order, backed by central government against the local landed gentry and aristocracy. Its institutional form in the public sphere reflected a coincidence of medical and poor law ideology.

Notes and references

1 For more detailed discussions of these acts see Finlayson, 1969; Fraser, 1984.
2 On industrialization see Hobsbawm, 1969; Landes, 1969.
3 Tudor poor laws and the factors that gave rise to them are discussed by Pound, 1971; see also Beier, 1983.
4 Hill, 1969, p. 45.
5 Pound, 1971, p. 15; on the development of family wage labour see Tilly and Scott, 1978.
6 Mann, 1980, p. 186.
7 Hill, 1969, p. 44.
8 ibid., pp. 45–6.
9 Pound, 1971, p. 15; Beier, 1983, p. 5.
10 ibid., pp. 25–30.
11 Pound, 1971, p. 60.
12 ibid., pp. 48–53.
13 Hill, 1969, p. 58.
14 Oxley, 1974, p. 15.
15 In the sense that Foucault uses it of 'the totality of measures which make work possible and necessary for those who cannot live without it' (1967, p. 46).
16 Mann, 1980.
17 Pound, 1971, p. 39.
18 ibid., p. 39.
19 ibid., document 14, p. 103.
20 ibid., Chapter 6; see also Jordan, 1959.
21 Pound, 1971, p. 40.
22 Jordan, 1959, *passim*.
23 Pound, 1971, Chapter 4.
24 Jordan, 1959.

25 Fraser, 1984, pp. 33–4.
26 Pound, 1971, pp. 75–6.
27 Beier, p. 29; Jordan, 1959.
28 Hill, 1969, pp. 142–5.
29 ibid., pp. 149 and 144.
30 Oxley, 1974, p. 19.
31 ibid., pp. 19–21; Fraser, 1984, p. 34.
32 Henriques, 1979, p. 14.
33 Fraser, 1984, p. 35.
34 ibid., Oxley, 1974, p. 22.
35 Oxley (ibid., p. 84) suggests that the construction of purpose-built houses became more common from 1760 onwards.
36 ibid., p. 85.
37 ibid., p. 81.
38 Fraser, 1984, p. 35.
39 Oxley, 1974, p. 88.
40 Ignatieff, 1979, p. 111.
41 Brown, 1969, p. 148.
42 Foucault, 1967, p. 46.
43 ibid., p. 55.
44 ibid., p. 46.
45 Ignatieff, 1979, p. 111.
46 Oxley, 1974, pp. 90–1.
47 ibid., pp. 89–92, and p. 94.
48 ibid., Chapter 6.
49 Brown, 1969, p. 148.
50 Women were predominant until the last years of the old poor law system when schemes such as the Speenhamland system brought in a higher proportion of men; see Oxley, 1974, pp. 59–60; See also Beier 1983, p. 5. Women also predominated among those receiving relief under the New Poor Law: see Thane, 1978.
51 Oxley, 1974, p. 36. The Poor Law Commissioners estimated that there were 3765 workhouses in 1803 (Crowther, 1981).
52 For the social and ideological context of poor law reform see Checkland and Checkland, 1974, Introduction; Fraser, 1984, pp. 37–48; Brundage, 1978.
53 See Checkland and Checkland, 1974, Introduction, pp. 20–3; Henriques, 1979, pp. 22–4.
54 Fraser, 1984, pp. 38–9.
55 Henriques, 1977, p. 26.
56 See Ignatieff, 1979, pp. 109–13; Donnelly, 1983, pp. 57–65.
57 Clearly there is a parallel here with the belief amongst proponents of moral treatment that such a system of treatment of lunatics would make mechanical restraints largely unnecessary.

58 Quoted in Ignatieff, 1979, p. 112.
59 Henriques, 1979, pp. 18–9.
60 ibid.
61 ibid., p. 18; Checkland and Checkland, 1974, pp. 90–102.
62 Fraser, 1984, p. 36; Checkland and Checkland, 1974, Introduction, p. 19.
63 Henriques, 1977, p. 19.
64 Checkland and Checkland, 1974, Introduction, p. 19.
65 Fraser, 1984, p. 44.
66 ibid., p. 41.
67 Morris, 1979, p. 19.
68 Thompson, 1963, *passim*; Morris, 1979, Chapter 6.
69 Thompson, 1963, p. 194.
70 ibid., p. 203.
71 Checkland and Checkland, 1974, Introduction, p. 29.
72 On the grounds that 'The great source of abuse is the out-door relief afforded to the able-bodied on their own account' (ibid., p. 82).
73 Henriques, 1979, p. 27.
74 Checkland and Checkland, 1974, *The Poor Law Report of 1834*, p. 335.
75 ibid., p. 375.
76 ibid., p. 376.
77 ibid., p. 429. This was preferable, the commissioners claimed, to classification within a single large workhouse and necessary for proper discipline. However, whether within or between institutions, such classification would result in the separation of family members (see Crowther, 1981, pp. 37–43).
78 Checkland and Checkland, 1974, pp. 398–471.
79 ibid., Introduction, pp. 42–3; Fraser, 1984, pp. 48–9.
80 Henriques, 1979, p. 42; Thompson, 1963, p. 268.
81 Crowther, 1981, p. 37; Fraser (1976, Table II, p. 18) provides data showing that in 1859 only some 14.5 per cent of all paupers were in receipt of indoor relief.
82 Rose, 1972, p. 10.
83 Thompson, 1963, p. 267.
84 Flinn, 1976, p. 48.
85 In 1859 only some 16 per cent of those in receipt of indoor relief were able-bodied adults. Some 38 per cent were children (Fraser, 1976, Table I, p. 5).
86 See Abel-Smith, 1964, Chapter 6; Flinn, 1976.
87 ibid., p. 47.
88 ibid., p. 49.
89 ibid., p. 49.
90 Holloway, 1964.
91 Hodgkinson, 1967, Chapter 4.

92 Its full title was *An Act for Reducing the Laws relating to Rogues, Vagabonds, Sturdy Beggars, and Vagrants, into One Act of Parliament; and for the more effectual Punishing such Rogues, Vagabonds, Sturdy Beggars, and Vagrants, and sending them whither they ought to be sent* (see Hunter and MacAlpine, 1963, pp. 299–301).
93 ibid., p. 300.
94 See Scull, 1979, pp. 54–9.
95 *Parliamentary Inquiry into Madhouses 1815/16* (see Hunter and MacAlpine, 1963, pp. 696–703).
96 ibid., p. 697.
97 Scull, 1979, p. 83.
98 Hodgkinson, 1967, p. 181.
99 Hence the need for mandatory legislation.
100 See Scull, 1979, pp. 59–60; Donnelly, 1983, pp. 21–2; Hunter and MacAlpine, 1963, pp. 621–6.
101 It heard evidence from some of those in charge of madhouses and asylums or associated with them including Sir George Onesiphorus Paul, Thomas Dunston, Master of St Luke's Hospital, R.D. Willis one of the Royal College of Physicians' Commissioners in Lunacy, and John Nash an architect who gave information on the building of asylums (ibid., p. 622).
102 Scull, 1979, p. 59.
103 On Paul, see Walk, 1961, pp. 604–6, and Ignatieff, 1978, pp. 98–109.
104 Walk, 1961, p. 605.
105 *Report of the Select Committee appointed to enquire into the State of Criminal and Pauper Lunatics in England and Wales, and of the Laws relating thereto*, 1807, p. 6
106 ibid., p. 6.
107 ibid., p. 6.
108 ibid., pp. 6–7.
109 ibid., p. 7.
110 *An Act for the better care and maintenance of lunatics, being paupers or criminals in England*, 1808.
111 *Report of the Metropolitan Commissioners in Lunacy*, 1844 (see Hunter and MacAlpine, 1963, Figure 175, p. 924).
112 ibid.
113 Jones, 1955, p. 116.
114 Walk, 1961, p. 606.
115 ibid., p. 606–7.
116 While Scull (1979, pp. 14–5) is right to reject 'simplistic' explanations linking lunacy reform to urbanization (or industrialization), his argument that the institutional response to insanity 'bore little or no relationship to the degree of urbanization of its population' (p. 29) cannot be accepted, since he looks only at the location of county asylums and ignores the geographical distribution of the already

established voluntary asylums or indeed the private madhouses.

117 See Scull, 1979, pp. 73–82; Donnelly, 1983, pp. 24–6; Jones, 1955, Chapter 6.
118 Scull, 1979, pp. 82–6; Jones, 1955, pp. 108–11.
119 ibid., pp. 133–41; Donnelly, 1983, p. 26; Scull, 1979, pp. 86–8.
120 Jones, 1955, pp. 133–4.
121 ibid., pp. 141–3; Scull, 1979, pp. 88–9.
122 See Hunter and MacAlpine, 1963, p. 923.
123 Jones, 1955, p. 143; Parry-Jones, 1972, p. 17.
124 Jones, 1955, pp. 171–4.
125 ibid., pp. 175–84; see also Scull, 1979, pp. 108–12.
126 *Report of the Metropolitan Commissioners in Lunacy*, 1844 (see Hunter and MacAlpine, 1963, p. 929).
127 ibid.
128 *An Act for the Regulation and Treatment of Lunatics*, 1845; see Scull, 1979, pp. 112–13.
129 Jones, 1955, pp. 191–5.
130 *An Act to amend the Laws for the Provision and Regulation of Lunatic Asylums for Counties and Boroughs, and for the Maintenance and Care of Pauper Lunatics*, 1845; see Scull, 1979, p. 113.
131 Jones, 1960, Appendix Two, p. 210.
132 The character of the asylums is discussed in the following chapter.
133 See Scull, 1982, p. 12; Donnelly, 1983, pp. 83–4.
134 ibid.
135 Isaac Ray, an American physician and medical superintendent, in an article 'Statistics on Insanity' published in the *American Journal of Insanity* in 1849, was one of the first to point to some of the problems with statistics on cure (see Hunter and MacAlpine, 1963, pp. 974–8).
136 See ibid., p. 867.
137 Scull, 1979, p. 111.
138 A claim made by the chairman of West Ham Poor Law Union in 1844 quoted in Hodgkinson, 1967, p. 154.
139 This was the assertion of W.J. Gilbert, an Assistant Poor Law Commissioner in a report on Devon (ibid., p. 178).
140 Scull, 1979, pp. 113–14.
141 Jones, 1958, pp. 161–2.
142 Quoted in Hodgkinson, 1967, p. 179.
143 Scull, 1979, p. 111.
144 Walk, 1961, p. 606; Donnelly, pp. 38–9.
145 Hobsbawm, 1969, pp. 82–3; Thompson, 1963, pp. 807–27.
146 Scull, 1979, pp. 54–9.
147 Halevy, Vol. I, 1960, p. 458.
148 ibid., p. 284.
149 Scull, 1979, pp. 84–6.
150 Hobsbawm, 1969, pp. 226–7.

8 Custodial institutions

The public asylums established under the legislation of the first half of the nineteenth century bore little relation to the vision of the lunacy reformers. They had argued for asylums that would restore the inmates to health and to work and make them no longer dependent on the financial resources of the community. Many envisaged asylums run in accordance with the principles of moral treatment where the skills, understanding and expertise of the staff would create an ordered and humane environment. Such asylums would be the desirable and chosen locus of care for the insane and would normally receive people for treatment in the early stages of their disorder. In the event, although some asylums did, in the earlier years of their existence, actively attempt to promote the principles of moral treatment, the public asylums increasingly became large-scale, regimented institutions, places of last resort for the unwanted and chronically dependent.[1] Few attempted much either in the way of moral treatment or of any more specific medical therapy. Typically, the inmates' chances of cure were low and their chances of a lengthy stay, often until death, were high. The asylums were essentially custodial institutions, sometimes little better than the workhouse in the standards of care they offered, and equally, if not more, stigmatizing.

How do we account for this departure from the reformers ideals? Why did the asylums seem to promise so much and yet offer so little? Why did the presence and superintendence of medical men not make them more therapeutic institutions? Before considering these questions further the custodial character of the public asylums needs to be described more fully.

Custodial features

The first and most obvious respect in which public asylums took on a custodial character was that they had, from their inception, legal powers of custody over all inmates. These legal powers of custody had their origins in the earliest legislation specifically concerned with the pauper insane. The act of 1744 had given local Justices of the Peace powers to detain both criminal and dangerous lunatics, and the 1808 Act, authorizing local authorities to provide public asylums, applied the legal powers of detention to all those admitted to asylums. The act stated that:

All lunatics, insane persons or dangerous idiots so committed to such asylums shall be safely kept . . . no such person shall be suffered to quit the asylum or be kept at large until the visiting justices, or the greater part of them shall order the discharge of such person . . ..[2]

Asylum attendants could be fined for permitting inmates to escape.[3] At this stage admission and discharge of pauper lunatics to county and borough asylums were in the hands of Justices of the Peace, admission initially requiring a warrant from two justices, while discharge had to be agreed upon by the committee of visiting justices on recovery. Subsequent legislation required a medical certificate for the admission of pauper lunatics (a procedure made compulsory by the 1774 Act for private lunatics) and enabled discharge to be made by two visiting justices. The only means of redressing any abuse of these powers was, as with the inmates of private madhouses, by way of a writ of habeas corpus.

Throughout the nineteenth century the complex procedures of certification which developed to regulate the powers of compulsory detention were continually modified. However, certification continued to be a legal requirement for all inmates of public asylums throughout the century and it contributed, as we shall see, to the custodial character of the public asylums, since the requirements for clear evidence of insanity for admission, and of recovery for discharge, served as a deterrent both to the early admission of cases and to their early discharge. Consequently they affected the type of cases admitted and the possibilities of cure.

The asylums' legal powers of custody were reflected in the physical design of the buildings which embodied a concern for security and added a second custodial dimension to the institutions. An effort was usually made to make asylums appear outwardly attractive, even stylish, and to avoid the appearance of a prison. But the sometimes ornate and often impressive facades – impressive in part because of the size of the institutions – could not entirely disguise the attention to security. Colney Hatch, opened in 1851, was surrounded by a boundary wall 10 foot high constructed of brick, except for one section near the railway 'where 6 foot iron railings were mounted in a 4 foot stone curb to allow travellers a sight of the asylum'.[4] Access to the asylum was also strictly controlled:

There was only one entrance other than the railway siding 'so that every body and every thing entering or leaving the Asylum must come under observation of the Porter at the Entrance Lodge . . . situated to the left within the Entrance Gates'. The lodge also housed 'a Waiting-room where Visitors produce their orders for admission; Tradesmen and all other persons explain their business and are instructed by a Porter how and where to proceed'.[5]

Even if these external custodial features in the design of asylums escaped the observer's eye, the contrast between the elaborate facade and the drabness within was clear enough. Colney Hatch provided just such a contrast, as one contemporary writing in 1857 noted:

The enormous sum of money expended upon Colney Hatch . . . prepares us for the almost palatial character of its elevation . . . the whole aspect of the exterior leads the visitor to expect an interior of commensurate pretensions. He no sooner crosses the threshold, however, than the scene changes. As he passes along the corridor, which runs from end to end of the building, he is oppressed with the gloom; the little light admitted by the loopholed windows is absorbed by the inky asphalt paving, and, coupled with the low vaulting of the ceiling, gives a stifling feeling, and a sense of detention as in a prison.[6]

Little was done, especially in the early years, to relieve the gloom of the buildings, as the same observer went on to complain: 'Upwards of a quarter of a million has been squandered principally upon the exterior of this building; but not a sixpence can be spared to adorn the walls within with picture, bust, or even the commonest cottage decoration'.[7] The Commissioners in Lunacy almost a decade later (1865) echoed his complaints in their description of the so-called 'refractory wards'.

The gloom is unrelieved by comforts of furniture of the commonest description; the seats, notwithstanding the many paralysed and feeble persons, are fixed wooden settees in the windows, or long unbacked benches on either side of the dining-tables. A chair and a small table is hardly anywhere to be seen, and there are only a very few scanty prints on the walls.[8]

The lack of furniture and of knives and forks in the male refractory wards was explained by attendants on the grounds that 'the men were all

Table 16   The size of mental hospitals (county asylums)

Jan 1	No. of county, county borough and city asylums	Total patients in public asylums	Average no. of patients per asylum
1827	9	1,046	166
1850	24	7,140	297
1860	41	15,845	386
1870	50	27,109	542
1880	61	40,088	657
1890	66	52,937	802
1900	77	74,004	961
1910	91	97,580	1,072
1920	94	93,648 (104,298)	996 (1,109)
1930	98	119,659	1,221

Note: Figures in parentheses for 1920 are for total numbers of beds available, as distinct from the total number of beds occupied. Many beds had then recently been freed from use as emergency beds for war cases, and the normal flow of civilian cases had not yet been resumed. *Source*: Jones, (1960) p. 210

of them too dangerous to be trusted' –a justification the commissioners called into question.[9] Other features, justified either on the grounds of security or from the need to stop inmates hurting themselves, contributed to the prison-like nature of the institution:

Thoughtfully 'the whole of the Angles throughout the Building have circular bricks, to prevent Patients injuring themselves'; the open fire places (three in each ward) had locked fire guards; and windows were so constructed that they could only 'be opened or closed, and locked in either position, by the Attendants'.[10]

Part of the problem was the sheer scale of the institutions. Some of the first public asylums had been built to house around 100 inmates, but by the middle of the century some were being built for as many as 1000. Colney Hatch, for instance, was designed for 1000 and was enlarged to cater for 1250 while still under construction. By the end of the century the average size of the public asylums was 1000 inmates as Table 16 shows; some contained 2000.

The 1808 act had recommended an asylum size of not more than 300 inmates, a figure that was a compromise in relation to the ideal, justified on grounds of economy.[11] But whatever the number of beds available demand never seemed to match supply and the size needed perpetually outstripped expectations and plans, as many contemporaries noted:

notwithstanding very considerable pains have been taken, on the proposition to build a new asylum, to ascertain the probable number of claimants, and a wide margin over and above that estimate has been allowed in fixing on the extent of accommodation provided, yet no sooner has the institution got into operation, than its doors have been besieged by unheard of applicants for admission, and within one third or one half of the estimated time, its wards have been filled and an extension rendered imperative.[12]

Asylums that had begun relatively small rapidly expanded to cope with the ever increasing numbers. Inevitably, the sheer size of the institutions contributed not only to the scale and impressiveness of their exteriors but to the prison-like nature of their interiors, since they were designed as one large, single building. Colney Hatch, for instance, had some 6 miles of corridors.

But it was the management of these large-scale institutions as much as their physical design that contributed to their custodial character. Instead of a system designed to achieve controlled and ordered conduct through individual self-control in the way that moral treatment had envisaged, a system emerged that achieved control by regimentation and routine and the creation of passivity and dependence. J.T. Arlidge, writing in 1859 of the evils of gigantic asylums, conveys vividly the way in which social order was attained in such institutions without mechanical restraint:

In a colossal refuge for the insane, a patient may be said to lose his individuality, and to become a member of a machine so put together as to move with precise regularity and invariable routine; – a triumph of skill adapted to show how such unpromising materials as crazy men and women may be drilled into order and guided by rule, but not an apparatus calculated to restore their pristine condition and their independent self-governing existence.[13]

The precise routines used to order the lives of the patients depended on assessments of their physical and mental condition. Inmates were classified – a matter not so much of medical diagnosis as of grouping into categories relevant for management along the lines envisaged by the poor law – by age, sex, social class, curability, quietness and amenability.[14] As in the workhouses themselves, those considered suitable by virtue of their age, sex, physical health, mental condition and previous occupation would usually be given work that contributed to the running of the institution and helped to keep costs down, as well as maintaining an orderly, routine organization of the inmates' lives. The second Annual

Report of the Colney Hatch Asylum detailed the occupation of patients in 1853:

75 Males are weekly employed on the Farm and Garden, and 144 more in other ways; while of the Females 62 are engaged in the Laundry, 6 in the Kitchen, 96 are Helpers in cleaning the Wards and Corridors, 2 at the Officers' Residence, 151 in Needlework, and 11 in Fancy work . . . . The whole of the Brewing and Baking for the Establishment have been done by the Patients, with the assistance of only two paid servants.[15]

At this point some 43 per cent of male inmates and some 45 per cent of female inmates were in employment. In 1881 38 per cent of the men and 54 per cent of the women were 'usefully employed'.[16]

Inmates who could be put to work were those considered more amenable and trustworthy and they might also be offered occasional entertainments and given some liberty – visits to shops in the local town might even be permitted. For inmates of this 'more favourable class' the physical comforts would generally be somewhat greater. For others the routines, as well as the physical comforts, were more restricted. The more difficult and awkward were confined to their wards, and although many of the public asylums abandoned the use of mechanical restraints such as chains, they were still liable to restraint in padded rooms. Some were given sedatives at night. Moreover, some medical officers continued to use certain physical forms of constraint such as confining patients with belts, wrist straps and locked gloves. Later in the century some returned to the old mechanical devices.[17] The elderly and infirm would lie in bed, or remain in the wards; little was done to enliven the daily routine.

Work, exercise and amusement for the more amenable inmates and the absence of mechanical restraints did not mean, however, that the principles of moral treatment had been put into effect. These demanded much more in the way of individual attention from staff and a much less routinized and regimented organization of the inmates' daily lives. But staffing levels were grossly inadequate and although inmates took over much of the domestic labour of the institution, the number of medical men and attendants was not enough to give the inmates anything like the individual care and attention that the principles of moral treatment demanded.

The medical superintendent of a public asylum, although the key figure in the day-to-day running of the institution, played a largely administrative role: he might have the help of one or two medical assistants but none of them would have much time for strictly clinical work. Colney Hatch, with its initial 1250 beds, had two resident medical officers, one for the male and one for the female side. By 1859 four assistant medical officers had been appointed to help them and these six had to cover what by then had become 2000 beds. As one contemporary noted in a letter written in 1850, the time of the two chief officers was, perforce, largely taken up by bureaucratic tasks:

If the medical superintendent be required simply to walk through the wards mechanically every day, to enter the names of the patients as they presented themselves at the establishment, then it is possible all may go on smoothly. . . . If the patients are to be treated according to the most improved method, it will be impossible for the medical officer to examine with that degree of minuteness each individual case. . . . Independently of his purely professional, let us look at his collateral duties. . . . He will be required, by the provisions of the Act of Parliament, to attend all certificates of admissions and discharges, sending in copies of each to the Commissioners in Lunacy: he will be required to enter these in the registers prescribed, and also keep up his weekly reports; he will, furthermore, be required to enter into a case-book a minute history of each case, detailing its origin, early symptoms, progress, treatment, etc.; and if the medical officers are to discharge their duties efficiently, it will be imperative upon them to institute, with care, a post-mortem examination of all who die in the Asylum. . . . In addition . . . [he] will be required to attend the meetings of Magistrates on Board days; and furthermore, if the establishment is to be rendered useful in a scientific and education point of view, he will be called upon to preside over a school of Mental Pathology, and communicate to his class the results of his observations. How, in common sense, can the two medical men, having, day and night charge of a thousand patients, accomplish such multifarious duties . . ..?[18]

The same applied to the medical assistants, who were not given clinical responsibility for inmates and largely assisted with statutory duties like keeping casebooks, journals and registers.[19] Nor was the number and quality of attendants employed on the wards sufficient to make good this deficiency. They were few in number and faced harsh conditions and low wages, lower in some areas than 'that which is required by ordinary servants in gentleman's families'.[20] Even where wages were higher, as they were in some asylums, staffing levels were still poor.[21] In this situation the scope for developing the self-control of inmates through working on their self-esteem was limited, even if the asylum had been committed to putting the principles of moral treatment into force. As it was, by the second half of the nineteenth century the commitment to moral treatment and to 'non-restraint' had waned.[22]

If the management of inmates did not conform to the dictates of moral treatment in many of the ways envisaged by its original proponents, neither was there much in the way of distinctively medical treatment. Some inmates, it is true, because of their physical infirmities would be bedridden and require nursing care, which the poor staffing levels made difficult; but there was generally little in the way of medical treatment for insanity itself. Some, as we have seen, were given sedatives or purgatives, but the majority were not.[23] Hydrotherapy was popular in some institutions, and attention was often paid to diet, though the concern was more for its general adequacy than its appropriateness for the management of individual patients. Of the other medical activities of the institution, the initial assessment and case history, together with autopsies, were considered especially important. The initial assessment provided the basis for classification for management purposes and for medical diagnoses. These were used as the basis for figures on admissions and discharges given in annual reports and for returns to the Commissioners in Lunacy. The commissioners were themselves anxious to encourage the practice of performing post-mortems on all patients who died in asylums and 'Anything less than an 80 per cent autopsy rate came in for comment.'[24] The rationale was the potential contribution to medical knowledge: autopsies, the Commissioners in Lunacy in their report of 1870 argued, should be performed:

With the all-important view of advancing the knowledge of the pathology and treatment of the various forms of insanity . . . and also in showing that insanity is not solely a disease of the mind, but is frequently associated with bodily lesions, and within the reach of medical treatment. . . .[25]

Such activities did not, however, transform asylums into active therapeutic environments – hospitals in the contemporary sense. Nor was this the intention of many directly associated with them: 'It must be remembered that we are an asylum rather than a hospital' asserted the chairman of the Committee of Visitors of Colney Hatch in 1859.[26]

The custodial character of nineteenth-century public asylums is evidenced both by the low rates of cure and the lengthy stays of many of the patients. Data on rates of cure must be treated with extreme caution, especially if comparisons are made over time or between different institutions. Not only did the criteria used by medical men differ over time and place, but even had similar criteria been applied, rates of cure obviously depend on the composition of the inmate population. Where

Table 17   Percentage of stated recoveries of all certified lunatics to the total
number under treatment, 1869–1908

Year	Males	Females	Total
Averages 1869–78	8.17	9.13	8.67
Averages 1879–88	7.63	8.57	8.14
Averages 1889–98	7.47	8.12	7.82
Averages 1899–1908	6.67	7.14	6.92

Source: 64th Annual Report of the Commissioners in Lunacy, 1910, Table V, Appendix A.

the population consisted largely of those with chronic complaints of long standing, far less could be hoped in the way of cure than with an inmate population restricted to acute cases. Comparisons of rates of cure or the percentage of inmates considered curable, often tell us, therefore, more about the type of inmates admitted and the judgements made of them than about the actual efficiency of the institution. Low cure rates and low proportions of curable inmates indicate an assessment that little could be achieved therapeutically, whether because the cases admitted were especially difficult and intractable or because the therapeutic potential of the institution was limited.

The 1844 Report of the Metropolitan Commissioners in Lunacy indicated that the percentage of paupers in public asylums considered curable was only some 15.4 per cent of the current inmates. Moreover, the proportions of those lunatics stated to have recovered as a percentage of inmates was low, and declined throughout the century. The figures are given in Table 17.

That stays were long in public asylums was apparent from early in their history. Hanwell, the first Middlesex asylum, was opened in 1831. The 1844 Report gives data on the length of stay of its 918 inmates in 1841. By then some 42 per cent of inmates had been there more than five years, as Table 18 shows. Unfortunately the Commissioners in Lunacy did not present data on the length of stay of inmates in public asylums as a whole, so the general pattern can only be inferred from fragmentary data such as this.

The overall picture that emerges of nineteenth-century public asylums is of institutions which, despite some variation over time and place, largely performed a custodial role in relation to their inmates. Those who resided there would probably be reasonably fed: they would, especially if they were not difficult or violent, be given work

Table 18   Length of stay of patients at Hanwell Asylum 1841

	NUMBERS			PER CENT OF INMATES		
Length of stay	*Male*	*Female*	*Total*	*Male*	*Female*	*Total*
Not more than 6 months	37	57	94	9.6	10.7	10.2
Not more than 1 year	29	38	67	7.5	7.2	7.3
Not more than 2 years	61	57	118	15.7	10.7	12.9
Not more than 5 years	99	157	256	25.6	29.6	27.9
More than 5 years	161	222	383	41.6	41.8	41.7
Total	387	531	918	100.0	100.0	100.0

Note: these categories are exclusive
Source: *Report of the Metropolitan Comissioners in Lunacy, 1844.*

and perhaps some entertainment and visits outside the asylum; but active therapy either along moral or medical lines would probably be minimal. Some would be discharged, as often as not without having been cured; many, however, could expect to spend long periods of time in an environment that ordered and organized their lives in a routinized way – a life not so much actively harsh or cruel as dull, monotonous and sapping of independence. This was recognized by contemporary critics – and there were many – who attacked public asylums not for their harshness and brutality but for their custodial character; as Henry Maudsley put it, instead of being 'hospitals for the insane' they had become 'vast receptacles for the concealment and safe keeping of lunacy'.[27]

Why custodialism?

How do we explain this departure of nineteenth-century asylums from the ideals of the lunacy reformers? Why was so little attempted or achieved in the way of therapy? The custodial character of nineteenth-century public asylums is to be explained above all by their location within the poor law system. Public asylums were first and foremost poor law institutions and it was the character of the poor law that largely determined their nature. It affected the numbers, flow and characteristics of the inmates to be found within them; it affected the size and scale of the institutions; it affected the resources available to them including the numbers, qualifications and attitudes of the medical men and the attendants who worked within them; and it affected the responses to policy initiatives to improve and reform them. This is not to say that the private madhouses and voluntary asylums outside the poor law system were entirely devoid of the custodial features of the public asylums; indeed they shared many of them. But private madhouses differed in many important respects; in their size, staffing, and care of inmates, and in their procedures and policies of admission and discharge. Though rates of cure were not high, in the better ones many of the worst custodial features of the public asylums were absent: the physical environment was far more pleasant, life was less routinized and there were more active attempts at therapy.[28]

The all-pervasive impact of the poor law system on public asylums is apparent if we look at some of the specific factors contributing to the custodial character of the asylums. Two key factors affecting the nature of the public asylums were the number and the type of inmates with which they had to deal. The two were closely related; the huge increase in numbers confined within public asylums being in part the result of the type of patients admitted. The rapid expansion in the numbers of inmates of the public asylums in the nineteenth century emerges clearly from Table 19 which shows the distribution of all known lunatics in various locations up until the Second World War.

Data for the number of lunatics before 1844 is inexact. The 1807 Select Committee on pauper and criminal lunatics identified, on the basis of local returns from poor law guardians, some 2248 pauper lunatics in poor-houses, houses of industry or in private custody, but commented that the returns were 'so evidently deficient in several instances, that a very large addition must be made in the computation of the whole number'.[29] Moreover, there was no attempt to estimate the number of non-pauper lunatics or to provide a comparable figure for criminal lunatics. What is clear from Table 19, however, is that the rapid expansion in the numbers in public asylums did not simply result from an expansion of public asylums at the expense of alternative places of residence for the insane. The number of known lunatics located in workhouses, for instance, continued to increase, although they constituted a declining proportion of all lunatics. By 1889 there were more than 17,000 pauper lunatics and persons of unsound mind to be found in the workhouses, a figure that easily exceeds the total number of publicly known cases of insanity in 1807, even allowing for the major deficiencies of the 1807 estimate. By 1848, it is true, the numbers of lunatics in private madhouses had reached its peak, both absolutely and relatively, but their subsequent decline can

Table 19   Number and distribution of all reported lunatics, idiots and persons of unsound mind in England and Wales on 1 January of selected years from 1844 to 1896 and 1939

	1844	1859	1869	1879	1889	1896	1939
County and borough asylums	4,489 (21.5%)	15,844 (43.1%)	26,867 (50.5%)	38,871 (55.6%)	51,694 (61.3%)	63,957 (66.3%)	133,827 (84.3%)
Registered hospitals	1,422 (6.9%)	1,855 (5.0%)	2,352 (4.4%)	2,837 (4.1%)	3,511 (4.2%)	4,025 (4.2%)	2,507 (1.6%)
Metropolitan and provincial licensed houses	5,173 (24.8%)	5,016 (13.6%)	4,796 (9.0%)	4,635 (6.6%)	4,347 (5.2%)	4,336 (4.5%)	2,859 (1.8%)
Naval and military hospitals and Royal India asylums	168 (0.8%)	164 (0.4%)	209 (0.4%)	342 (0.5%)	289 (0.3%)	208 (0.2%)	282 (0.2%)
Broadmoor Asylum (opened 1861)	–	–	461 (0.9%)	483 (0.7%)	618 (0.7%)	641 (0.7%)	779 (0.5%)
Workhouses including metropolitan district asylums/public assistance hospitals	9,621 (46.0%)	7,963 (21.7%)	11,181 (21.0%)	15,005 (21.5%)	17,509 (20.8%)	16,945 (17.6%)	14,634 (9.2%)
Residing with relations or others		5,920 (16.1%)	7,311 (13.7%)	6,702 (9.6%)	6,372 (7.6%)	6,334 (6.6%)	3,835 (2.4%)
Total	20,893 (100%)	36,762 (100%)	53,177 (100%)	69,885 (100%)	34,340 (100%)	96,446 (100%)	158,723 (100%)

Source: Report of the Metropolitan Commissioners in Lunacy, 1844; Special Report of the Commissioners in Lunacy on the Alleged Increase of Insanity, 1897, Report of the Board of Control, 1939.

in no way account for the enormous expansion in numbers confined in public asylums in the second half of the nineteenth century.

Nor can the rapid increase in the numbers of persons in public asylums be accounted for by the population growth of the nineteenth century. Population growth was considerable, but the ratio of lunatics and idiots to the total population continued to rise, as Table 20 indicates. Aggregate figures of population growth can hide important changes in the age structure of the population which could also have affected levels of insanity, since these vary with age. Of particular interest are changes in the proportion of children and elderly people in the population since

Table 20   Total population, total number officially identified as insane, and
rate of insanity per 10,000 people in England and Wales

1 Jan.	Population	Number officially identified as insane*	Rate per 10,000	Source of data on number insane
1807	9,960,000	2,248	2.26	House of Commons 1807
1819	11,106,000	6,000	5.40	Burrows 1820
1828	13,106,000	8,000	6.10	Halliday 1828
1829	13,370,000	16,500	12.34	Halliday 1829
1836	14,900,000	13,667	9.18	Parliamentary Return 1836
1844	16,480,000	20,893	12.66	Metropolitan Commissioners in Lunacy
1850	NOT AVAILABLE			
1855	18,786,914	30,993†	16.49	Commissioners in Lunacy
1860	19,902,713	38,058	19.12	Annual Reports
1865	21,145,151	45,950	21.73	
1870	22,501,316	54,713	24.31	
1875	23,944,459	63,793	26.64	
1880	25,480,161	71,191	27.94	
1885	27,499,041	79,704	28.98	
1890	29,407,649	86,067	29.26	

Notes:
* Includes lunatics confined in asylums, but also those in workhouses, at large in the community, etc.
† The Commissioners found 20,493 lunatics in asylums of all types in 1855; lacking a complete enumeration of all lunatics not so confined, they estimated that these amounted to some 10,500 persons. (Commissioners in Lunacy Annual Report 1855, Vol. 9, p. 39.)
Source: Scull, 1979, p. 224.

admission rates were almost negligible among the former, and quite high among the latter. However, although over that part of the nineteenth century for which there are adequate data the proportion of those under 15 declined (from 36.2 per cent of the population in 1841 to 32.5 per cent in 1901) and there was a very small rise in the proportion of those over 60 (from 7.2 per cent in 1841 to 7.4 per cent in 1901), these changes were not in any way sufficient to account in themselves for the increased numbers or rates of asylum inmates.[30]

Indeed the expansion of the numbers confined within asylums was only partly due to increasing rates of admission. A further important factor in the long term was the build-up of cases in the asylums, that is, the tendency for those admitted to stay for long periods of time and fill up the institutions. It was this trend, as well as increasing admission rates, which increased the numbers of inmates so sharply. The rise in admission rates is shown in Table 21 and the increase in rates is proportionately smaller than that in the total number of lunatics. The increase in the latter was some 77 per cent; in the former some 56 per cent.

Table 21   Total population, total admissions into all asylums in the year, and admissions expressed as a rate per 10,000 of the total population of England and Wales, 1855–90

	Population estimated for middle of year	Total admissions excluding transfers	Rate of admissions per 10,000
1855	18,786,914	7,366	3.92
1860	19,902,713	9,512	4.77
1865	20,990,946	10,424	4.96
1870	22,501,316	10,219	4.54
1875	23,944,459	12,442	5.19
1880	25,480,161	13,240	5.19
1885	27,499,041	13,354	4.85
1890	29,407,649	16,197	5.51

Source: Scull, 1979 p. 232

The rapid expansion in public asylum inmates was due in part, therefore, to the fact that many of those admitted stayed, as we have seen, relatively long periods of time. These long-term inmates filled up the available beds and created a pressure for further expansion if any more admissions were to be possible. The problem is familiar enough; it needs only a relatively small proportion of those admitted to an institution to stay for a long period of time, for whatever reason, and the available accommodation is soon filled by the long stay cases, leaving little room for further admissions without over-crowding or further expansion.[31] And with a high proportion of long-stay inmates custody rather than cure is likely to become the predominant activity of the institution, since it will be largely filled with precisely those persons whose illness seems difficult, if not impossible, to cure.

Why did many inmates stay so long in the asylums? It would be easy to place all the blame on the therapeutic deficiencies of the institution for the often lengthy stays of patients, and it is of course true that the institutions failed to cure many of those admitted. However, low rates of cure were not simply due to the obvious limitations of the public asylums and their departure from the ideals of moral treatment in terms of size, staffing levels and individual attention. There is evidence that even in those private madhouses which corresponded most closely to the ideals of moral treatment many inmates were not cured.[32] The low rates of cure in the public asylums as in the private madhouses were also due to the fact that the problems of those admitted often only received medical attention when they were either especially severe or already 'long-standing'. And this was particularly true of those admitted to public asylums. It was a widely held belief that early, acute cases were more amenable to treatment, and that some cases were easier to cure than others.[33] Yet the problems of those admitted to public asylums were very likely to be of an already chronic nature, making therapy more difficult, if not impossible (given existing therapeutic techniques), and further contributing to the custodial character of the public asylums.

Public asylums departed very quickly from the reformers' intention that they should restrict themselves to acute, potentially curable cases in the early stages of illness. The reasons for this are not hard to seek. In the first place, the principles of the poor law system militated against the admission of early, acute cases. The underlying philosophy of the Poor Law Act of 1834, was as we saw in the previous chapter, one of deterrence; relief was a matter of last resort.[34] Only the destitute, whether sick and infirm, or without any hope of work, were permitted to turn to the public authorities for support and there was to be no incentive to rely on public relief. The 1834 Poor Law Report embodied these attitudes to the poor in the principle of less eligibility and the workhouse test: only those willing to enter the workhouse were to be given any relief. In practice the harsh principles of the 1834 Poor Law were sometimes mitigated by the humanity of certain poor law officials, and in many areas outdoor relief, which the 1834 Report had intended to abolish, did not disappear completely.[35] Nevertheless, the philosophy embodied in the legislation ensured that pauper institutions, whether workhouses or public asylums, were places of last resort. Moreover, since public asylums were actually more expensive than workhouses, the motive for economy was two-fold: first, to keep a person from receiving any form of relief, and then, if that could not be avoided, to keep him or her in the workhouse rather than the public asylum.[36] The result was that by the time the individual was sent to the asylum his or her problems were chronic and long-standing. A number of commentators noted these tendencies; an assistant Poor Law Commissioner commented:

At the moment we do not know what to do with the pauper lunatic . . . the expense of sending them to the asylum is so great that they have been kept in the workhouse until they become troublesome and . . . until the disease has become inveterate and recovery hopeless.[37]

The Report of the Metropolitan Commissioners in Lunacy in 1844 also drew attention to the same problem:

The Asylums in which the lunatic poor are received . . . are, we regret to say, filled with incurable patients, and are thus rendered incapable of receiving those whose malady might still admit of cure. It has been the practice in numerous instances to detain the insane pauper at the workhouse or elsewhere, until he becomes dangerous or unmanageable; and then, when his disease is beyond all medical relief, to send him to a Lunatic Asylum where he may remain during the rest of his life, a pensioner on the public. This practice, which has been carried on for the sake of saving, in the first instance, to each parish some small expense, has confirmed the malady of many poor persons, has destroyed the comfort of families, has ultimately imposed a heavy burthen upon parishes and counties and has, in a great measure nullified the utility of public Asylums, by converting them into a permanent refuge for the insane, instead of hospitals for their relief or cure.[38]

In their Annual Report published the same year the Poor Law Commissioners expressed the same concern. 'We are deeply convinced', they asserted, 'that the paupers of unsound mind should, where there is a chance of cure, be sent to an asylum as soon as possible after the commencement of the malady.'[39] To this end they circularized clerks of all Boards of Guardians calling their attention 'to the extreme importance of suffering no motive of economy to deter the Guardians from sending pauper patients to an asylum where they might receive proper treatment as early as possible'.[40] The Local Boards of Guardians, however, whilst they might recognize the argument for sending cases as early as possible, operated a system whose general philosophy and financial interest militated against such action.

It was the moral and economic parameters of the poor law system, rather than procedures designed to select curable cases, which determined the type of people admitted to the public asylums. This is apparent in the following negative evaluation of inmates of the asylums given by Granville, a medical man commissioned by *The Lancet* to prepare a report on lunatic asylums, published in 1877:

No one carefully examining the inmates of asylums, generally, can fail to notice that a large part of the multitude is made up of individuals of all ages, who are either physically disabled or disinclined for work. Vicious young persons of both sexes, sullen middle-aged people with grievances and a grievous intolerance of laborious or sustained exertion of any kind, with poor old folk in whom the light or reason has begun to wane; a few idiots, more cheaply maintained in an asylum than at a suitable training institution, as the law directs; and a crowd of confirmed epileptics, for whom little good can be effected, make up the population of most county and borough asylums.[41]

As far as the poor law system was concerned the criterion for admission was chronic economic dependence arising from diverse sources, not the possibility of cure.

The certification procedures surrounding admission and discharge further compounded the tendency for asylums to become places for chronic and incurable cases and affected the private madhouses as well as the public asylums. Complex certification procedures designed to protect the rights of the individual citizen militated against any attempt to secure the admission of early, acute and curable cases or to discharge them relatively quickly. Certification required clear evidence of insanity for admission and clear evidence of a return to sanity before discharge. Consequently there was, on this ground alone, a tendency to wait till cases were as clearly established as possible before admission and to delay discharge – a tendency that the inevitable stigma associated with certification encouraged. Medical men, of course, played an important role in certification, and at least in theory it might have provided them with the opportunity to control admissions in favour of acute, potentially curable cases. However, the legal procedures of certification only required medical men to agree that there was clear evidence of insanity, not to assess the possibilities of cure, and there was little scope to restrict admission to acute, curable cases through the procedures of certification. Chronic mental infirmity no less than acute mania was insanity in medical as well as public eyes and the certification procedures controlling admission and discharge did not provide a mechanism for restricting admission to acute early cases or for discharging those who could not be cured.

But if the public asylums even more than the workhouses were places of last resort, why did the numbers admitted to the asylums actually expand quite rapidly over the nineteenth century? The philosophy and practice of the poor law system can account for the chronic state of those admitted and the departure from the original intention that asylums should be places for acute sickness. But one might argue that these very same features would entail a low level of admission. In fact, however, the poor law system, for all its stress on deterrence, itself contributed to the expansion in numbers admitted. The reluctance of the poor law officers to spend money on asylums was undoubtedly matched by a common reluctance of the poor to have a member of the family admitted to either the workhouse or the asylum, so that a person would be admitted only after 'the remedial resources at the command of their friends, or the parishes, have been previously exhausted' and 'the severity and chronic nature of the symptoms at length rendered their removal compulsory'.[42]

Nevertheless, the unwillingness of the poor law officials to provide an alternative form of support on a non-institutional basis, especially for those needing it over the long term, helped to ensure that acceptance of institutional support became a matter of necessity. It was not so much, as Scull suggests, when he talks of asylums as a dumping ground for the awkward, difficult and unwanted, that the development of the asylums decreased the community's tolerance for the troublesome and dependent and provided a way of getting rid of such people, but that the institution was often the only form of support available within the poor law system.[43] It was not lowered familial tolerance but economic and practical necessity that led to the expansion in admissions. And since the economically dependent included the awkward, difficult and mentally infirm, asylums no less than workhouses increased their numbers.

The poor law system, consequently, through its reluctance to provide outdoor relief and the inadequacy of its outdoor provisions, structured the response to the economic dependence of those with chronic infirmities. And the need for some form of public support for lunatics was itself undoubtedly increased by the enormous social and economic changes of the nineteenth century. On the one hand the continuing growth of wage labour, the still low level of wages for many, and the increasing reliance of families on the wages of both husband and wife and often children, increased the vulnerability of families to economic adversity and the loss of the wages of an individual through sickness or unemployment.[44] On the other hand the capacity of the family to provide the practical and personal care for an infirm or difficult family member also declined with the shift of productive activity away from the home, the geographical mobility separating kin one from another, and the pervasiveness of poverty.[45]

Scull contends that by serving as a dumping ground for people whose problems were essentially those of dependency, the public asylums broadened the notion of insanity.[46] No longer was the insane person only the raving lunatic or madman: the term now embraced the mental infirmities of age, the social problems of the epileptic and the imbecile and all other types of chronic incapacity and infirmity, both mental and physical. He argues, too, that it was the very vagueness of medical definitions of insanity that contributed to this situation. Indeed, he suggests, it was the medical tendency to solve boundary problems of insanity by incorporation rather than exclusion that was a major factor in the nineteenth-century rise in the number of people identified as insane. His argument raises a number of issues. In as far as he suggests that the asylum doctors played a largely passive role in directly determining the boundaries of their asylum populations I would agree with him. Formal certification procedures controlling admission gave, as we have seen, little scope for medical control of the flow of inmates through the asylums, though medical work on the labelling and categorization of specific types of mental illness played a part in the way in which particular types of problems might be viewed as evidence of insanity and suitable for asylum care. However, in as far as his argument suggests that the types of dependency leading a person to eventual asylum care had formerly been outside the boundaries of what might be regarded as insanity or mental disease it is not, I believe, correct. Epilepsy, dementia and imbecility were old categories, by no means new to the list of types of lunacy: what was new was that they should be both matters for official identification and the grounds for asylum care.[47]

Specialists in insanity did introduce some new concepts in the nineteenth century that affected societal perceptions of conditions and problems suitable for asylum care. One given some importance by medical men was 'partial insanity' or 'monomania'.[48] The idea that insanity might be limited or partial in nature was an old one, and had been particularly mentioned in connection with melancholia, a condition that did not itself clearly fall within the bounds of insanity proper. Casaubon, a seventeenth-century divine, developed the idea of a form of insanity restricted in its object:

There is a sober kind of distraction or melancholy: not such only wherein the brain is generally affected to all objects equally; never outrageous, nor out of reason, as it were, to outward appearance; but also where the distemper is confined to some one object or other, the brain being otherwise very sound and sober upon all other objects and occasions . . . there is not any Physician, either ancient or late, that treateth of Melancholy, but doth acknowledge it, and hath several examples . . . I my self in my life time, have known one, (yet alive for ought I know,) who upon apprehension of great wrong done unto him by some in Authority, fell into some hypochondriacal conceits much of that nature, sober and discreet otherwise, in all his conversation: only upon that subject he would be very earnest; and if opposed, grow fierce.[49]

He goes on to consider whether it is reasonable to call this a distemper of the imagination alone, or whether it is 'a depravation of the Understanding, as well as of the Imagination?'[50] It was Esquirol, however, who drew the attention of nineteenth-century medical men to the idea of partial insanity or monomania in his effort to develop a more precise terminology of mental diseases. In a paper published in France in 1820, he argued that there had been a tendency to broaden the notion of melancholy from its old Galenic bounds of a form of delirium characterized by 'moroseness, fear, and prolonged sadness' arising from a 'depraved condition of the bile' to cover 'every form of *partial* delirium, when chronic, and unattended by fever'.[51] He proposed a division between lypemania or melancholia – 'a cerebral malady, characterized by partial, chronic delirium, with fever, and sustained by a passion of a sad, debilitating or oppressive character' – and monomania or partial insanity proper which 'corresponds with maniacal melancholy, maniacal fury, or with melancholy complicated with mania'.[52] The potential breadth of these two forms of insanity is apparent in Esquirol's comment on the general category of partial insanity or monomania:

Monomania is of all maladies, that which presents to the observer, phenomena the most strange and varied, and which offers, for our consideration, subjects the most numerous and profound. It embraces all the mysterious anomalies of sensibility, all the phenomena of the human understanding, all the consequences of the perversion of our natural inclinations, and all the errors of our passions. . . .[53]

The concept of moral insanity was introduced by the English physician Prichard in his *Treatise on Insanity and other Disorders Affecting the Mind*, published in 1835.[54] He distinguished three basic types of mental disease according to the mental faculty that was disordered: 'those of feeling or sentiment, the understanding, and the will'.[55] The concept of moral insanity referred to disorders that combined 'disorders of affection or feeling' with 'those of the active powers or propensities' and was outlined by him in the following terms:

This form of mental derangement has been described as consisting in morbid perversion of the feelings, affections, and active powers, without any illusion or erroneous conviction impressed upon the understanding: it sometimes co-exists with an apparently unimpaired state of the intellectual faculties. . . .

The term which I have adopted as designating this disease, must not be limited in its use to cases which are characterized merely by preternatural excitement of the temper and spirits. There are many other disordered states of mind which come under the same general division. In fact, the varieties of moral insanity are perhaps as numerous as the modifications of feeling or passion in the human mind. . . .[56]

The concept was much attacked for its imprecision, but was accepted and used by many medical men and, like the notion of partial insanity, helped to support a broader interpretation of the cases suitable for asylum care (though not of the range of mental troubles considered suitable for medical intervention). In both caes, however, we should see the new conceptualizations as a product of medical efforts to make sense of and structure their interactions with the increasing numbers of patients to be found in asylums. It was not that medical men broadened their notions of insanity and as a result were willing to admit more individuals to asylums. Rather, as a more diverse range of people were admitted to asylums, medical concepts of insanity themselves diversified and expanded, and this in turn was one factor affecting the subsequent flow of inmates to the institutions.

The accumulation of long-stay, incurable cases in the asylums was also affected by declines in the death rate during the nineteenth century, though their precise impact is difficult to assess. Overall the decline in mortality is clear enough (from a crude death rate of about twenty-seven per thousand in England in 1801 to about twenty-two per thousand in 1871).[57] The effect of this on the age structure of the population was not, as we have seen, very large; nevertheless there were significant declines in the mortality of the adult population which must have increased the chances of survival of those with chronic mental infirmities. It is possible that there was a differential improvement in the mortality of the latter, so increasing the potential asylum population and the tendency for those admitted to stay for long periods of time.

Asylum inmates, it is true, tended to have generally higher death rates than the general population; an analysis in 1895 by the Commissioners in Lunacy comparing the mortality by age of lunatics and idiots with those of the total population of England and Wales showed 'the vastly higher mortality among lunatics as compared with that of the entire population of the country'[58] But the death rates of asylum inmates did decline and this contributed to the build-up of cases. The 49th Report of the Commissioners in Lunacy attempted to assess the effect of the declines in mortality over the period 1859 to 1894, calculating that 6800 persons would have been removed by death if the death rate had remained at the earlier level.[59]

Given the way in which the poor law system, as well as the procedures of certification, operated to assign many with chronic and incurable problems to the public asylums, the only alternative to the relentless accumulation of cases would have been the introduction of specific policies to exclude the incurable, either by preventing their admission or by the active discharge of such persons after a certain period of time.

This is what happened in some of the voluntary asylums, where stricter criteria were applied on admission and cases not cured by the end of one year would be discharged. But the voluntary asylums could operate such a policy without having any responsibility for those they did not admit or for those discharged uncured. This did not apply to the public asylums which, as a component of the poor law system, were part of a system that had to offer some alternative provision if the chronic cases were not admitted to the asylums. The workhouses themselves did not offer much of a solution, since their reluctance to deal with disturbed and difficult people had been one factor leading to the initial development of the asylums.

Commentators in the second half of the nineteenth century put forward a number of proposals for dealing with chronic cases. Henry Maudsley, a well-known private physician with an interest in asylums, advocated a system of boarding out harmless lunatics in private families:

Many chronic insane, incurable and harmless will be allowed to spend the remaining days of their sorrowful pilgrimage in private families, having the comforts of family life, and the priceless blessing of the utmost freedom that is compatible with their proper care.[60]

But this solution ran counter to the institutional bias of the nineteenth-century poor law and so had little chance of adoption.

Granville, in his *Lancet Report*, recommended a tri-partite institutional structure. His plan was:

To provide in every district an hospital, properly so called and thoroughly furnished with all necessary appliances for the physical and moral treatment of insanity. Attached to this hospital, so far as the control of its general arrangements is concerned, construct an institution – or, if necessary, more than one – to which patients not either requiring, or likely to be benefited by, active personal treatment, but still needing medical care, may be removed, when in the course of each individual case, it becomes apparent, that this transfer will not prejudice the final chances of recovery. In connection with the workhouse, or in some appropriate institution – for example, a 'workhouse asylum' – provide suitable wards for the senile and infirm, whose recovery is impossible, and who tarry only for death.
This threefold system being efficiently organized, the necessary circulation of cases may be readily maintained, without either indefinitely multiplying costly buildings, or allowing the curative establishment to become blocked against recent and curable, by the stagnation of chronic, cases.[61]

He too thought that some chronic, harmless cases could be boarded out with the relatives 'under proper supervision'.[62]

The solution proposed by the Metropolitan Commissioners in Lunacy in the 1844 Report was not dissimilar, recommending, as it did, the establishment of separate asylums for incurable cases:

The disease of Lunacy, it should be observed, is essentially different in its character from other maladies. In a certain proportion of cases, the Patient neither recovers nor dies, but remains an incurable lunatic, requiring little medical skill in respect to his mental disease, and frequently living many years. A Patient in this state requires a place of refuge; but his disease being beyond the reach of medical skill, it is quite evident that he should be removed from Asylums instituted for the cure of insanity, in order to make room for others whose cases have not yet become hopeless. If some plan of this sort be not adopted, the Asylums admitting Paupers will continue full of Incurable Patients; and those whose cases admit of cure, will be unable to obtain admission, until they themselves become incurable; and the skill and labour of the physician will thus be wasted upon improper objects.[63]

This recommendation was incorporated into the Lunatics Asylums Act of 1845, which gave local authorities power to erect separate asylums for chronic cases. However, none used their powers under the act to do so. Scull has drawn attention to the opposition to this proposal from the asylum doctors themselves.[64] They claimed it would create avowedly custodial institutions with all the deficiencies and abuses the new public asylum had been designed to avoid. Scull contends, however, that their opposition was also self-interested. The development of special asylums for chronic lunatics would, he suggests, have constituted direct competition for funds, would have dispensed with medical staff, and stopped the asylum doctors using the excuse of the presence of so many chronic patients to account for their low rates of cure. However, medical opinion was divided on the matter. While the public asylum doctors tended to be hostile to such schemes, medical men working in the private sector, such as Maudsley and Granville, tended, as we have seen, to be their strong advocates. And the decisive factor was not so much the asylum doctors' hostility to the proposal, for their low status reduced the force of their opposition, but the reluctance of the local authorities to incur the additional capital expense of a separate institution. It was cheaper to extend and crowd an existing institution than to build a new one.

Three Metropolitan District Asylums were, in fact, established near London in 1870 under the powers of the Metropolitan Asylums Board set up in 1867.[65] The board aimed to provide services for 'harmless persons of the chronic or imbecile class as could be lawfully detained in a workhouse', not for the dangerous or curable who 'under the statutes . . . require to be sent to a lunatic asylum'.[66] These asylums were much criticized by Granville in his report and did not correspond to his plan for workhouse asylums for chronic patients since they received patients directly, without prior admission to the public asylums, and without the normal procedures of certification. Although they housed some chronic inmates, they did not provide sufficient accommodation to prevent the further expansion of the public asylums and had no real impact on the problem of chronic cases outside the metropolitan area.

The long-term increase in inmates within the public asylums was, therefore, largely a result of the fact that public asylums were part of a poor law system designed to provide institutions of last rather than first resort. They were, none the less, the only alternative for those whose poverty and familial circumstances meant that care within the family was impossible. As a result they were filled with long-stay, chronic cases for whom little could be hoped in terms of cure. The chances of providing therapeutic help for such people were further reduced by the fact that it was almost impossible to create much in the way of a therapeutic environment and therapeutic facilities within institutions operating within the framework of the poor law system. Both the philosophy of the system and its economic concerns contributed to the custodial character of the public asylums. That inmates should be fed and clothed was all that was considered necessary and desirable to poor law guardians anxious to keep the cost of the asylum to a minimum, and the bleakness and lack of comforts of the asylum reflected the principle of deterrence. The weekly cost of maintaining inmates was a matter of great concern and any reduction 'however small was a matter of pride'.[67] The Committee of Visitors in the year when the Middlesex magistrates handed over Colney Hatch Asylum to the London County Council reported that 'The excellence of the financial arrangements . . . is sufficiently shown by the fact that the weekly rate has diminished from 10s 2½d. in the year 1862 to 8s 9d. at the present date.'[68] While employment was considered an important form of therapy for inmates, it was also important to the economy of the institution, and was consistent with the poor law philosophy 'that all who receive relief from the parish should work for the parish exclusively, as hard and for less wages than independent labourers work for individual employers'.[69] The size and scale of institutions, too, resulted from motives of economy.

Levels of pay for staff were also kept as low as possible and this, together with the low status of the institutions and the patients, affected the quality of staff, as well as directly contributing to the routinization and regimentation and the lack of individual attention from attendants and medical staff.[70] Work in the public asylums was not especially attractive and although in some areas the nature of the local labour market might be such that asylums had no difficulty finding attendants, nevertheless the attendants' character, behaviour and lack of education were often matters for concern. They were, according to one contemporary, 'the unemployed of other professions . . . if they possess physical strength and a tolerable reputation for sobriety, it is enough; and the latter quality is frequently dispensed with. They enter upon their duties completely ignorant of what insanity is.'[71]

But it was not only the quality of attendants that was at issue. The conditions of public asylum work meant it tended to be a relatively unattractive proposition within the medical profession. Consequently it attracted relatively low status and less dynamic doctors. The position of medical superintendent did offer powers and status within the asylum as well as job security, but there were important disadvantages: the necessity of residing at the asylum; the diminution in status entailed by work with low status patients; the high proportion of administrative rather than strictly medical tasks, and a heavy work load.[72] The post was salaried and this together with job security was an advantage, but the constraints on the work were considerable, not least the constraints imposed by the exigencies of the poor law system. Consequently, after the initial reforming enthusiasm of the early part of the century (when non-resident physicians were often employed), the medical men who came to work in asylums tended to be those of lower status in terms of training and background (surgeons rather than physicians) and to secure lower status by virtue of their work. All this further reduced their power in any conflicts with the local authorities and Boards of Guardians and their chances of attempting to make public asylums therapeutic rather than custodial institutions. The doctors had the power to run and organize their institutions on a day-to-day basis and had considerable power within them, but they did so within the limits set by the local magistrates, and these limits were in practice highly restrictive. Their reluctance to rid themselves of their chronic patients and to campaign actively, unlike the specialists outside the public asylum system, for reforms that would have given asylums a less custodial character, has more to do with the selection processes which operated to determine the type of men who worked in the public asylums and the constraints within which they worked than with any need to blame their therapeutic ineffectiveness on the presence of so many incurable cases. The need for medical men in the running of any asylum was already established and did not depend on their therapeutic abilities as Scull describes:

Fortunately for the psychiatric profession, their inability to produce significant numbers of cures was of only slight concern to their sponsors. For there had emerged a widespread consensus among local and national élites on the value of a custodial operation, so that the impact of the occasional grumbling about the asylum doctors' performance was muted, and the sort of sustained criticism which might have undermined their position simply failed to materialize. Moreover, their ability (or lack of ability) to produce cures by no means exhausted the asylum doctors' usefulness. They were, after all, no worse than anyone else as administrators, and their medical skills were useful in ministering to the numerous physical ailments of the decrepit specimens the asylums were continuously receiving. And by sustaining the illusion that asylums were medical institutions, they placed a humanitarian and scientific gloss on the community's behaviour, legitimizing the removal of difficult and troublesome people whose confinement would have been awkward to justify on other grounds.[73]

To an extent the imprecision of the principles of moral treatment facilitated this focus on management by routinization and regimentation:

the bourgeois emphasis on the virtues of self-discipline and regularity which was so prominent a feature of the ideology of moral treatment was not always carefully distinguished, even in the minds of its principal advocates, from a celebration of order and obedience for their own sakes – and such a perversion of the original intent was particularly likely to occur and to be overlooked once asylums began to deal with an essentially lower-class population. In a sense, the potential for its transformation into an instrument of repression was always latent in moral treatment.[74]

Nevertheless, by the second half of the nineteenth century many asylum superintendents were not even paying lip-service to the principles of moral treatment and any inherent weakness of its principles due to imprecision in their formulation was of little importance in comparison with its incompatibility with the principles of the poor law system, which structured and organized the asylum doctors' thought and practice as well as the lives of the inmates.

Moreover, the changes in medical thinking about illness during the nineteenth century meant that the intellectual foundations on which medical support for moral treatment had been built were crumbling.

Medical support had rested on a foundation combining Galenic concern for managing the patient's physical and social environment with the Protestant, bourgeois concern for discipline and regularity.[75] The intellectual revolution in clinical medicine associated with the Paris school at the beginning of the nineteenth century and the concept of localized pathology began to shift medical attention away from the creation of a therapeutic environment towards identifying the pathological lesions assumed to be the cause of mental diseases. The success of Bayle and others in Paris in the 1820s in showing that the psychological symptoms of a progressive dementia and the neurological symptoms of paralysis were symptoms of a single distinct disease, termed general paralysis or paresis of the insane (GPI) and the result of the chronic inflammation of the meninges covering the brain, sustained and supported this type of approach.[76] Further research later in the century indicated an association between syphilitic infection and GPI, but the aetiology was only finally demonstrated in the early years of the twentieth century when syphilitic micro-organisms were detected in the brain.[77]

GPI was the most notable success in the search for pathological lesions of the brain but other work helped to identify specific forms of dementia associated with specific types of brain pathology.[78] Such work contributed to the acceptance of autopsy as a standard procedure for those dying in asylums, but it was not of much immediate therapeutic value to the patients, for the research focused almost entirely on brain pathology and little attention was paid to therapeutics.[79] The same had been true of medicine in France at the beginning of the nineteenth century when the important advances in the localization of diseases had been associated with a marked therapeutic nihilism.[80] Shryock, in his standard history of medicine, asserts that medicine around the middle of the nineteenth century 'seemed to have come to a dead end on the high road to human betterment'.[81]

Medical practitioners working in public asylums, in as far as they oriented themselves to the medical world outside the asylums and to the world of medical research, consequently had their attention directed away from therapy; and this, too, reinforced their custodialism and their lack of concern for the principles of moral therapy.

The 1890 Lunacy Act

Nineteenth century custodialism found legislative expression in the Lunacy Act passed in 1890.[82] The critics of the asylums in the second half of the nineteenth century argued for a variety of reforms aiming to make the asylums more therapeutic and less custodial. They argued in particular for the introduction of treatment in asylums without certification, and for the dvelopment of special facilities for the early treatment of cases, as well as for the boarding out of chronic cases. But their arguments were ignored, and the 1890 Act did not concern itself with trying to improve the treatment and care of lunatics in asylums: rather it focused on the long-standing concern about wrongful detention, seeking to protect the interests of those outside the asylums – to protect their right to liberty. The act paid particular attention to the procedures governing detention, systematizing them and tightening the safeguards against wrongful detention. (It was a composite of two earlier bills, one of which was designed to consolidate previous legislation, the other to introduce certain amendments.) It introduced the necessity for a magistrate's order as well as medical certificates in every certified case, other than on an 'urgency order' for not more than seven days – a proposal that Lord Shaftesbury, who had died in 1884, had particularly opposed.[83] All orders for detention were, however, to cease to have effect at a specified time, unless renewed. 'This placed the onus of continued detention on the shoulders of the medical profession, rather than leaving the question of discharge to their initiative'.[84] Reception orders, the main category of orders for detention, were to last for one year, renewable for periods of first two years, then three years, then successive periods of five years. The act also strengthened the Commissioners in Lunacy's powers of visitation, and it gave legal protection to medical practitioners and others 'against vexatious actions where they have acted in good faith'.[85] This clause was a gesture to medical practitioners who were concerned about their situation following the case of *Weldon v. Winslow*. One Mrs Weldon had in 1877 sued Forbes Winslow, an eminent specialist in mental disorders, for libel, assault, wrongful arrest, false imprisonment and trespass, after she had been forcibly detained in his private asylum in Hammersmith, and she had managed to win some of these legal battles.[86]

Kathleen Jones, in her history of mental health services, sees the 1890 Act as a triumph of legalism, an act that 'bears the heavy impress of the legal mind' in which 'Nothing was left to chance, and very little to future development.'[87] She explains this triumph in terms of the power and status of the legal profession and identifies three possible channels for further reform in the period after the 1845 Act: social and humanitarian, following the model of the Retreat; medical, in which the distinction between mental and physical disorders would be blurred and 'the great developments which characterized general medicine in the second half of the nineteenth century' would be shared; and legal, with legislation 'piling safeguard on safeguard to protect the sane against illegal detention, delaying certification and treatment until the person genuinely in need of care was obviously (and probably incurably) insane'.[88] The actual outcome was, she contends, a matter of the relative power of the groups that could pressure for these reforms:

The movement for further reform of the law became an affair of pressure groups – and the pressure groups were unequal. The legal profession had been fully established for centuries. Medicine was engaged in throwing off the shackles of a long association with barbering and charlatanism, and did not achieve full status until the passing of the Medical Registration Act of 1858, which set up a register of doctors who had passed prescribed examinations. Social work and social therapy were to remain occupations for the compassionate amateur until well into the twentieth century. It is therefore not surprising that the legal approach took precedence, to be followed after 1890 by the medical approach. It is only now, when the social sciences have developed a comparable professional status, that the social approach is coming into its own again.[89]

This liberal–scientific interpretation of the history of mental health legislation and services, with its model of competing pressure groups, fails to locate the activities of medical and legal men in relation to the broader social, economic and political features of society.[90] The direction of reform and change is not a matter of the relative professional advance of competing groups, although the professional advance of one group may be an important factor shaping the development of a particular policy. Medical men had been given important powers in relation to lunacy, not only of certification but also of inspection, at the end of the eighteenth century when, according to Jones, they had not achieved full status as a profession. The passing of the 1890 Lunacy Act did not result from the power of the legal profession, but rather on the one hand from a desire to strengthen legal safeguards (which necessarily involved the legal profession), and on the other hand because of major obstacles to reform in the direction advocated by men like Maudsley. The desire to strengthen legal safeguards was enhanced and reinforced by the custodial character of the asylum system which had developed in the second half of the nineteenth century. The very powers of detention, the separation from the community, and the lack of prospects of cure, all created a concern for the protection of the individual in a society where the bourgeois ideology of individualism, with its concern for freedom and liberty, was still at a premium.[91] The obstacles to reform came from the philosophy and practices of the poor law system which helped to create and sustain the custodial character of the public asylums, and to ensure that there was little scope for reforms which would transform them into more therapeutic institutions. Not until the poor law philosophy began to be undermined and the system itself broken down would the reforms be accepted. It is to these developments that I now turn.

Notes and references

1 See for instance the account of Lancaster Asylum in the years 1816 to 1870 (Walton, 1981, pp. 166–97).

2 *An Act for the better care and maintenance of lunatics, being paupers or criminals in England*, 1808.

3 Jones, 1955, p. 76; Hunter and MacAlpine, 1974, p. 97.

4 ibid., 1974, p. 27. This study provides a detailed history of Colney Hatch Asylum (now Friern Hospital and due to be closed).

5 ibid., pp. 26–7

6 ibid., p. 136.

7 ibid.

8 ibid., p. 137.

9 ibid.

10 ibid., p. 28.

11 The Report argued that 'it would be highly desirable, for the purpose of preventing unnecessary expense, that each building should be calculated to contain as large a number as possible, not exceeding three hundred'. (*Report of the selected Committee appointed to enquire into the state of Criminal and Pauper Lunatics in England and Wales, and of the Laws relating thereto*, 1807).

12 Quoted in Scull, 1979, p. 248.

13 From *On the state of lunacy and the legal provision for the insane, with observations on the construction and organization of asylums*, 1859 (see Hunter and MacAlpine, 1963, p. 1029).

14 Hunter and MacAlpine, 1974, p. 17, and pp. 77–8.

15 Hunter and MacAlpine, 1974, p. 37.

16 ibid., p. 130.

17 ibid., p. 86. See also Walton, 1981, pp. 186–7.

18 ibid., p. 72.

19 ibid., p. 77.

20 ibid., p. 88. The second comment was made by the Commissioners in Lunacy in their Report for 1859.

21 Walton, 1981, pp. 180–1.

22 ibid., pp. 183–91; Scull, 1979, p. 194.

23 Hunter and MacAlpine, 1974, pp. 91–2; Walton, 1981, pp. 185–6.

24 Hunter and MacAlpine, 1974, p. 245.

25 ibid., p. 244. Underlying this stress on the importance of autopsies were

developments in medicine during the first half of the nineteenth
century. These are discussed briefly in the final section of this chapter.

26 ibid., p. 18.

27 Maudsley, *The Physiology and Pathology of Mind*, 1867, p. 501.

28 Scull, 1979, pp. 204–8.

29 *Report of the Select Committee*, 1807, p. 5.

30 Cox, 1970, p. 324.

31 For instance, according to one calculation made in 1972, half of all
district general hospital beds would be filled up after only seven years
if chronic patients represented only 1 per cent of all acute admissions
(MIND, 1974, p. 7).

32 Scull, 1979, p. 208.

33 The belief in the importance of early treatment is discussed more fully
in the following chapter.

34 See pp. 233–8 above.

35 Rose, 1972, p. 11.

36 Hodgkinson, 1967, Chapter 4.

37 ibid., p. 178.

38 *Report of the Metropolitan Commissioners in Lunacy*, 1844, p. 6.

39 Quoted in Hodgkinson, 1967, p. 180.

40 ibid., p. 180.

41 Granville, *The Care and Cure of the Insane*, 1877, Vol. I, p. 173.

42 Quoted in Hunter and MacAlpine, 1974, p. 173.

43 Scull, 1979, pp. 239–45.

44 On family wage labour see Tilly and Scott, 1978.
Geoffrey Best estimates some 30 per cent of the population were in
'painful poverty' in the 1850s and 1860s (1979, p. 144.)

45 Michael Anderson, in his *Family Structure in Nineteenth Century Lancashire*
provides local data on patterns of migration in the middle of the
century (1971, pp. 34–42). The book also offers an illuminating
analysis of the factors that undermined kinship support.

46 Scull, 1979, pp. 233–9.

47 See the classifications collected together by Menninger (1963,
Appendix).

48 On nineteenth century concepts of insanity, see Donnelly, 1983, pp.
68–77; Skultans, 1979; Dain, 1964.

49 From *A treatise concerning enthusiasme, as it is an effect of nature: but is
mistaken by many for either divine inspiration or diabolical possession*, 1655
(see Hunter and MacAlpine, 1963, p. 146).

50 ibid., p. 147.

51 *Lypemania or Melancholy*, 1820 (see Hunter and MacAlpine, 1963, p.
735). Tuke in his *Description of the Retreat* also asserted that insanity was
often partial. See the quotation on p. 217 above.

52 Hunter and MacAlpine, 1963, p. 735.

53 ibid.,
54 See Hunter and MacAlpine, 1963, pp. 836–42.
55 ibid., p. 837.
56 ibid., p. 839–40.
57 Wrigley and Schofield, 1981, Table A 3.1.
58 *49th Report of the Commissioners in Lunacy*, 1895, p. 6.
59 *Special Report of the Commissioners in Lunacy to the Lord Chancellor on the Alleged Increase in Lunacy*, 1897, p. 26.
60 Maudsley, 1867, p. 501.
61 Granville, 1877, Voll. II, p. 134–5.
62 ibid., Vol. I, p. 338.
63 *Report of the Metropolitan Commissioners in Lunacy*, 1844, p. 92.
64 Scull, 1979, pp. 188–94.
65 The work of the Board is described by Powell, 1930.
66 Hunter and MacAlpine, 1974, p. 56.
67 ibid., p. 57.
68 ibid., p. 68.
69 *The Poor Law Report of 1834* (Checkland & Checkland, 1974, pp. 375–6).
70 On asylum nursing in the nineteenth century see Carpenter, 1980.
71 Quoted in Scull, 1979, p. 122.
72 ibid., pp. 171–80.
73 ibid., p. 173.
74 ibid., p. 209.
75 See Foucault, 1973; Waddington, 1973; Shryock, 1947, Chapter IX.
76 See Hunter and MacAlpine, 1963, pp. 779–83.
77 ibid.
78 Shryock, 1947, pp. 293–5.
79 ibid., p. 294.
80 Waddington, 1973, pp. 217–8.
81 Quoted by Waddington (ibid., p. 217).
82 See Jones, 1960, Chapter 2.
83 ibid., p. 31.
84 ibid., p. 32.
85 ibid.
86 ibid., pp. 25–8.
87 ibid., p. 40, and p. 35.
88 ibid., p. 10.
89 ibid.
90 See the comments in Bean, 1980, pp. 32-8.
91 Taylor, 1972, *passim*. Taylor notes that most historians have seen a growth of collectivist ideas in the final quarter of the nineteenth century, but such ideas were not pre-eminent and Government intervention was still relatively limited.

9 Inside and outside the asylum

The twentieth century has witnessed marked changes in the character of mental health services. Four have been of especial importance. In the first place the underlying structure of the mental health services has been transformed. In the nineteenth century the pattern of care for the insane was of single specialist institutions, whether public or private, set apart from the community and designed to provide both a refuge from the pressures and stresses of the everyday world and an ordered therapeutic environment that would restore the insane person to health. Asylums and madhouses provided the main locus for specialist care, and the only alternative form of treatment would be that offered in the market by a private practitioner, whether of a more specialist or more general nature. The twentieth-century pattern of care is of a diverse range of services, both residential and non-residential, modelled on the general health services and designed to cover the different stages of the patient career – all of them integrated as far as possible both into the community and into the rest of the health services.[1] Specialist services are available not only for residents in asylums but also in psychiatric units in general hospitals, psychiatric outpatient clinics, and in child guidance clinics, and there is a broad base of non-specialist primary care as well as some after care facilities. The asylum, though it continues to exist, is but one component of a range of services, many of them provided by the state. This general pattern of services can be described as one of community care, a loose term, often largely defined negatively to mean all forms of care other than residential care in an asylum, but one that can embrace the diversity of services now available for the mentally ill.[2]

The shift from asylum care to a more diverse pattern of community care has been associated with a second important change: a marked expansion in the numbers receiving some form of professional medical treatment, specialist or otherwise, for problems considered psychiatric. From the beginning of the nineteenth century until the mid 1950s the expansion took the form of large increases in the numbers of residents of psychiatric beds. During the post-war period, despite a decline in the

Table 22 Resident population of mental hospitals in England and Wales, 1951–70

Year	Thousands	Year	Thousands
1951	143	1961	135
1952	145	1962	134
1953	147	1963	128
1954	148	1964	127
1955	147	1965	123
1956	146	1966	122
1957	143	1967	119
1958	143	1968	116
1959	139	1969	106
1960	136	1970	103

Source: Scull (1975) *Decarceration*, Table 4.3

total number of residents, admissions rates have continued to increase. However the major expansion has been in the numbers attending day hospitals, psychiatric clinics or visiting general practitioners for some medically identified psychiatric problem.[3] Tables 22 and 23 give some data on the post-war pattern of the resident population of psychiatric beds and of admissions. It is sometimes suggested that the increase in admissions since the 1950s can simply be accounted for by the development of a 'revolving door' phenomenon – a shift from a pattern of long, continuous stays to one of admission, discharge and then readmission. Data distinguishing first from subsequent admissions is only available from 1964 (see Table 23), but it is clear that until the end of the 1960s first admissions were continuing to grow quite rapidly and were contributing more to the overall increase in admissions than readmissions. Not until 1970 did the number of first admissions start to decline. The most recent figures for England show that first admissions have dropped to some 28 per cent of all admissions.[4] The figures in Table 24 give the growth in day-patients and out-patients. The expansion in

Table 23 Admissions to mental illness hospitals (England and Wales) 1964–72

Year	Total admissions	First admissions	Non-first admissions
1964	158,861	76,194	82,667
1965	159,452	80,566	78,986
1966	163,980	82,305	81,675
1967	168,438	85,780	82,658
1968	172,485	89,021	83,464
1969	174,709	89,931	84,778
1970	176,163	65,552	110,611
1971	176,028	65,563	110,465
1972	185,131	63,838	121,293

Source: Clare (1976), p. 375.

Table 24   Day-patients and out-patients, Great Britain, 1961–76

	DAY-PATIENTS MENTAL ILLNESS AND HANDICAP		OUT-PATIENTS MENTAL ILLNESS	
	New	Attendances (thousands)	New	Attendances (thousands)
1961			187.7	1368.5
1962			198.9	1479.0
1963	11.7	708.8	209.3	1517.6
1964	12.6	863.1	213.3	1536.6
1965	14.7	1010.3	222.9	1555.2
1966	16.9	1216.8	230.5	1580.9
1967	18.2	1320.9	244.2	1641.0
1968	19.7	1486.1	247.1	1667.5
1969	21.5	1652.7	254.0	1698.5
1970	24.1	1813.5	250.2	1748.0
1971	27.9	2177.7	248.9	1802.4
1972	30.9	2512.2	248.5	1834.4
1973	34.6	2707.1	245.6	1853.6
1974	36.3	2737.5	237.2	1835.3
1975	37.5	2852.1	225.7	1802.7
1976	44.3	1383.4	234.4	1859.6

Source: Digest of Health Statistics, 1971; Health and Personal Social Statistics, 1977.

contacts with general practitioners for conditions diagnosed as mental disorders, though more difficult to document, has been especially rapid. The general practice morbidity survey of 1956–7 produced an incidence figure of some fifty cases per 1000 persons at risk. A similar study carried out in 1970–1 yielded an incidence rate of almost 300 cases per 1000 persons.[5]

Both the shift in the pattern of mental health services and the expansion in the numbers receiving treatment have been associated with a third major area of change, a shift in the balance of psychiatric activity in terms of the type of problems that receive attention. The development of non-residential forms of care has generally been associated with a shift away from what are now categorized as psychotic and organic conditions (schizophrenia, senile dementia, manic-depressive psychoses), that is, the more severe and potentially chronic forms of mental disorder, towards neurotic conditions and personality disorders (anxiety neuroses, neurotic depression, phobias, drug addiction, alcoholism), which are considered less severe, and in the case of the neuroses, less liable to lead to chronic disability.[6] (The obvious exception in this respect is the day hospitals which deal with a high proportion of psychotic and organic conditions.)[7] Although this shift of attention has been associated with the development of new conceptualizations of the less severe mental disorders it does not represent any marked broadening of the boundaries of medical interest. It is the distribution of the type of complaints that has changed. Medical professionals have long dealt with the type of complaints that are now assigned to the neurotic category, but they have done so in the context of private practice, particularly for the restricted group who could afford the services of a physician.[8] With the establishment of non-residential services in the public sector the balance of medical activity in relation to mental health problems has changed. In the nineteenth century the public asylums and the organic and psychotic cases were dominant; now the neuroses and personality disorders play a far larger role throughout the mental health services, not just in the private, non-residential sphere.

Fourth, the changing structure of services has also meant a change in the social character of patients. Public asylums that held the majority of psychiatric inmates dealt primarily with pauper patients. They confined the poor who could neither afford the cost of a private madhouse nor had the patronage and respectability to secure admission to one of the few charitable hospitals. Middle-aged men and women were the typical inmates. During the present century the proportion of elderly inmates in psychiatric beds has increased dramatically (from 10.5 per cent in 1895 to some 54 per cent in 1981). The evidence suggests, however (although we do not have precise information), that, with the exception of the day hospitals, non-residential services deal with a higher proportion of younger, more middle-class people, and with a higher proportion of women.[9]

These structural changes in the character of mental health services are the outcome of the development, acceptance and implementation of specific policy objectives for the mental health services. Two basic, interrelated policy objectives can be distinguished, that to a large extent followed one another chronologically. The first, which dominated policy making up to the 1930 Mental Treatment Act, was to transform the custodial asylums into proper hospitals. The second, which emerged in the period after 1930 and became widely accepted after the war, was to develop a broader system of community care – a policy of moving away from the asylums as the major locus of treatment. In order to understand the changes in the pattern of care between the nineteenth and twentieth centuries, therefore, it is convenient to consider these two policy objectives in turn. In this chapter I examine the moves to transform asylums and in the next I consider the policy of community care.

Transforming the asylum

Medical critics of the custodial asylums and lunacy reformers of the second half of the nineteenth century had one clear objective: to transform asylums into hospitals. In Maudsley's words 'the vast receptacles for the concealment and safe keeping of lunacy' should become 'hospitals for the insane'.[10] The problem was how to achieve this objective. One necessary condition was to find some alternative form of care for chronic and incurable cases and, as we have seen, a number of proposals were put forward to deal with the problem of long-term patients. But getting rid of chronic cases was not enough.[11] It might be possible to get rid of long-stay patients, but a way had also to be found to ensure that the acute cases, regarded as the proper population of a hospital for the insane, would come forward to receive treatment in the new therapeutic environment. And this meant getting patients into treatment early, at the point when the disease was in its acute stages, before it had become chronic. Early treatment was considered the key, since it would not only ensure that asylums engaged in their proper work of restoring the insane to health, but it would also help to prevent the long-term build-up of cases that deflected asylums from their proper task.

The belief that early treatment improved the chances of cure and was indeed the *sine qua non* of successful therapy was both long standing and widely accepted by medical practitioners. Maudsley commented:

No point is more clearly established in the history of insanity than this, that the facility of cure and the proportion of recoveries bear a distinct ratio to the shortness of time that has elapsed from the origin of the complaint to the commencement of treatment. If the interval be brief, the probability of cure is great.[12]

The belief was not specific to medical men. It was being urged in the early reports of the Retreat at York, and in those of the Poor Law and Lunacy Commissioners when they began to be published.[13] Recent onset had become the main criterion of curability and curable cases were judged to be those within a year of onset; cases of longer duration were generally considered incurable.[14]

The proposals put forward by the asylum critics of the second half of the nineteenth century, designed to facilitate early treatment, focused on two points: certification and the establishment of special services for acute, early cases. Certification, as I have already indicated, was considered a definite obstacle to early treatment and critics suggested a number of ways in which the barrier might be reduced. Granville, in his Lancet Report, put forward one relatively modest proposal for change in certification procedures. He argued that certification should take place after rather than before admission, and that lunatics should be admitted for treatment into special admission rooms of public asylums without certification, where they could be held for three days and certification could take place.[15] This would not only mean that the medical superintendent of a public institution would be involved in certification (with advantages, Granville contended, in expertise and the lack of financial interest in the case), but also that treatment could begin without the usual delays that were considered so disadvantageous:

The early hours, almost minutes, of an attack of mental disease are often of the highest moment to the issue. While friends are faltering in their resolution to take so grave a step as placing a man or woman under certificate, the chances of cure are slipping away. The first effort should be to treat the case, not to talk and write about it. Imagine the consequences of waiting to obtain a parcel of legal documents before you began to treat a man for apoplexy. At such a moment it is impossible to introduce practitioners even singly, into the presence of a patient and expose him to their interrogatories without the danger of irritation, and perhaps permanent injury.[16]

The comparison in the passage with what happened in cases of physical illness is typical of the literature of the period.

Granville's proposal in this instance only involved the timing of the certification procedures. However, he also argued that some cases should be admitted without certification and this was a major objective of many lunacy reformers: 'patients labouring under mental derangement should be removable to a public or private asylum, as to an hospital for ordinary disease, *without certificate*'.[17] He further argued that 'the power of signing certificates of lunacy should be withdrawn from ordinary medical practitioners, magistrates and clergymen'.[18] In this latter suggestion Granville nicely combined professional interest with public concern about wrongful detention, contending that only medical men with special knowledge of mental disease should determine matters of certification. Lord Shaftesbury, however, was against any further restriction in certification procedures, considering it a hindrance to early treatment. 'It sounds very well to say that persons acquainted with lunacy should be the only ones to sign certificates' but 'What follows from this course? Why, that the cases are very far advanced, and have got pretty nearly into the category of the incurable.'[19]

Maudsley used the public concern for the liberty of the individual to argue that certification and sequestration in an asylum (he assumed the two went hand in hand) should be more limited and in so doing he tried to specify the principles of confinement.

The true principle to guide our practice should be this – that no one, sane or insane, should ever be entirely deprived of his liberty, unless for his own protection or for the protection of society . . . in dealing with the insane, who are suffering from disease, there can be no question of punishment, but we confine them in order to apply proper means of treatment, and to cure them, if possible; and, secondly, to protect themselves and society from their violence.[20]

Asylums should be kept for cases that could be cured and many chronic and incurable cases should be boarded out. But he, too, was soon putting the case for admission without certification not into existing asylums but into special institutions for the treatment of early cases.[21] Samuel Gaskell, Commissioner in Lunacy and a medical man, had made a similar proposal in an article in the *Journal of Mental Science* in 1860. It was, he argued,

desirable to extend legal sanction to a class of houses into which patients should be allowed to place themselves voluntarily, or be admitted on less complicated and stringent documents . . . Such places offering an agreeable change of scene, quiet and retirement, as well as the benefit of good advice, would afford a means of treatment much to be desired for incipient and transient cases. For those also convalescent from the more severe forms of the malady they would prove of great benefit as probationary houses, intermediate between the asylum and home . . . Abodes such as are here contemplated, marked by an entire absence of offensive objects, sounds, or restrictive contrivances would invite early treatment, and prevent the malady running on to an incurable extent.[22]

The echoes of the model asylum advocated by the reformers earlier in the century are very clear. Now, however, the previously taken for granted legal compulsion is explicitly and consciously abandoned.

Precedents for treatment of incipient cases without certification came first in the private sector. On the one hand, a few private unlicensed establishments, technically illegal, provided care for less serious nervous maladies without the formal procedures of certification. On the other hand some legal changes were introduced in the second half of the nineteenth century to permit admission without certification under certain restricted circumstances or with a modified form of temporary certification. In England an Amending Act of 1853 permitted inmates of private licensed houses to remain as voluntary boarders if they had earlier been certified, had recovered sufficiently to no longer require or justify certification, but wished to remain for further treatment.[23] Soon this was extended to those seeking re-admission who had been certified within the previous five years, and in 1890 the Lunacy Act allowed voluntary boarders to be admitted to licensed houses without previous certificate.[24] The act required that they be discharged within twenty-four hours of their indicating their intention to leave. In Scotland voluntary boarders could be admitted to public institutions 'though financial considerations appear to have deterred the local authorities from fully utilising this provision', and from 1857 private madhouses in Scotland could admit patients for a period of up to six months with one medical certificate to the effect that 'the patient is afflicted, but that the malady is not confirmed'.[25]

Maudsley himself endeavoured to put his own ideas about the treatment of early cases without certification into practice when, in 1907, he gave the London County Council £30,000 towards the establishment of a new mental hospital specifically for early cases on both an in- and out-patient basis without certificate.[26] Special legislative permission to admit patients without certification was secured in 1915, the year the hospital opened. However, by then the war had begun and it served as a war hospital under the Ministry of Pensions during its first years, dealing largely with cases of the newly identified shell-shock.[27] It continued to take shell-shock cases for the Ministry of Pensions until 1923. The need to deal with shell-shock cases and other cases of 'war neuroses' was also an important factor in the establishment of psychiatric clinics for early, acute cases, at some of the voluntary general hospitals:

Notice had been taken both by the medical world and the lay public of the striking reports of how victims of war neuroses had been cured by suggestion, hypnosis, catharsis and so-called analysis. Cases of neurosis were usually referred to the neurological departments of hospitals, often by other hospital departments, but also by practitioners outside the hospital. Such patients sometimes caused embarrassment; there were few satisfactory facilities for treatment; adequate disposal was difficult and these cases were apt to become chronic hangers-on, returning again and again for their bottle of medicine, varying little their recital of symptoms and complaints, yet somehow sustained by a faith in the hospital.[28]

Clinics, some taking in- and out-patients, some only the latter, were set up at a number of voluntary hospitals. Although one or two hospitals had taken psychiatric out-patients since the 1880s, during the First

World War and immediately after a number of psychiatric clinics were established, usually in connection with teaching hospitals: there were clinics in Manchester, Birmingham, Sheffield, London, Cardiff and Oxford.[29] Although located in general hospitals the work was often carried out under the supervision of the medical superintendent of the local asylum.[30]

In general, however, even after the war, the possibilities for admission without certification were limited, especially in the public sector. Some public asylums apparently manipulated the certification procedures to allow for the admission of patients for short periods without certification, delaying the completion of certification so that the patient could be discharged before full certification had occurred, but this could only be done in the minority of cases.[31] And despite the backing of some eminent medical men the reformers' early attempts at securing legislative change were unsuccessful. A bill was introduced into Parliament in 1915 concerning early treatment referring to the treatment of cases of shell-shock, but it was withdrawn before its second reading owing to lack of support, and a further bill introduced in 1922–3 also failed to pass through Parliament.[32] In 1924, however, a Royal Commission on Lunacy and Mental Disorder was established under the Chairmanship of H. P. Macmillan (later Lord Macmillan), the Lord Advocate for Scotland.[33] The establishment of the commission was occasioned less by a recognition of the need for reform in the direction of voluntary admission and early treatment than by a new wave of public concern about wrongful detention, provoked in the first instance by the publication in 1921 of a book by Dr Montague Lomax, *The Experiences of an Asylum Doctor*, about a public mental hospital at Prestwich.[34] The public reaction led the Minister of Health to set up a committee 'to enquire into the administration of Public Mental Hospitals'.[35] However, the powers of the committee were restricted and its conclusions limited. The work of the committee does not seem to have been successful in quelling public concern about either the administration of public mental hospitals, or the issue of wrongful detention or the problem of harsh and cruel treatment. The Royal Commission was prompted by these continuing worries.

The Macmillan Commission, whose terms of reference were broad, 'was certainly aware of the circumstances surrounding its appointment, but it chose to ignore them. It interpreted the criticisms of existing legislation as demands for some measure of change, not as demands for additional legal safeguards'.[36] Most of the initial twelve members of the commission, including the chairman, had legal qualifications and only two were medically qualified (one of these was Sir Humphrey Rolleston, the then President of the Royal College of Physicians). None the less the commission's report, published in 1926, advocated a largely medical approach to the problems of lunacy and insanity. Its central message was 'The keynote of the past has been detention; the keynote of the future should be prevention and treatment.'[37] This it viewed as the 'enlightened approach' to lunacy and mental disorder.[38]

The commission took as a basic assumption the point, constantly reiterated by twentieth-century policy makers in the field, that there is a close interrelationship between mental and physical illness. In an oft-quoted passage the report contended:

It has become increasingly evident to us that there is no clear line of demarcation between mental illness and physical illness. The distinction as commonly drawn is based on a difference in symptoms. In ordinary parlance a disease is described as mental if its symptoms manifest themselves predominantly in derangement of conduct, and as physical if its symptoms manifest themselves predominantly in derangement of bodily function. This classification is manifestly imperfect. A mental illness may have physical concomitants; probably it always has, though they may be difficult of detection. A physical illness on the other hand may have, and probably always has, mental concomitants. And there are many cases in which it is a question whether the physical or mental symptoms predominate.[39]

The report went on to argue that the 'rough and ready distinction drawn by the public between mental and physical ailments' had had 'an undue influence in the development of our lunacy system'.[40] Rather than emphasizing the differences and keeping the two apart they should be treated as far as possible in a similar fashion. And this would inevitably mean a greater role for the medical profession: 'The more mental illness is assimilated to physical illness the more the public must rely on the medical profession.'[41]

The case for voluntary treatment was a further important corollary:

an anomaly which has much struck us is that except in the case of registered hospitals and licensed houses the doors of our institutions for the treatment of the mentally afflicted are closed to all but certified cases. In order that a patient may qualify for the benefit of treatment in any of the mental hospitals maintained with public money . . . he must first be certified. But pre-requisite of certification is that the patient's disease shall be so definite and well-established that he can be declared by a medical practitioner to be actually of unsound mind and in a condition justifying compulsory detention. In the case of every other type of institution for the treatment of disease the aim is to get in touch with the patient at the earliest possible stage of his attack and by care and treatment to ward it off or at least mitigate its effects. Not so in the case of insanity. Contrary to the accepted canons of preventive medicine, the mental patient is not admissible to most of the institutions provided for his treatment until his disease has progressed so far that he is become a certifiable lunatic. Then and only then is he eligible for treatment. It is not perhaps remarkable in these circumstances that the percentage of recoveries in public mental hospitals is low.[42]

Voluntary admission, the commission believed, should be encouraged wherever possible, but was not feasible in all cases. It required volition and should not be extended to a person 'who does not clearly comprehend the nature of the act'.[43] Compulsory detention was necessary in cases where individuals 'who may do injury to themselves or to others' were unable to co-operate intelligently in their own treatment and cure.[44] But the compulsory detention should not be a 'deterrent punishment', it 'ought to have one object and one object only, the protection, treatment, and, if possible, cure of the patient'.[45] Hence the commission's explicit rationale for the existence of compulsory detention (the acceptance of the principle of voluntary admission necessitated attention to this matter), although referring to the public interest focused on the potential benefits to the individual of in-patient admission. Assimilation of the care of the lunatic to that of the physically ill was the goal.

The association of the lunacy system with the poor law was similarly condemned with the argument that it differentiated the mentally ill from those with other forms of sickness:

Without in any way disparaging the great services rendered by boards of guardians and poor law officials in the administration of the lunacy laws we cannot but feel that this association is unfortunate. It is another of the causes which have tended to accentuate the differentiation of the mentally afflicted from other sufferers. Many households make their first acquaintance with the relieving officer in connection with the occurrence in the family of a mental case. It is not a concomitant of other illnesses that the patient in order to obtain treatment must necessarily become in law a pauper. . . . There runs, moreover, through the whole lunacy code a distinction in procedure between the pauper case and the private case, the justification for which has largely disappeared under modern social conditions.[46]

The report also argued for proper separation of new cases from old, for better after-care facilities, and for the development of clinics for both in- and out-patients attached to general hospitals.[47]

The Mental Treatment Act, introduced into the House of Lords in November 1928 and eventually passed in 1930, gave legislative form to some, though not all of the 1926 Report.[48] It introduced the principle of voluntary admission, but instead of restricting admission to two categories, voluntary and involuntary, as the commission had suggested, introduced three: voluntary, temporary and certified. The procedures for admission of certified patients followed those of the 1890 Lunacy Act. Voluntary patients could be admitted under the following procedures: 'Any person who is desirous of voluntarily submitting himself to treatment for mental illness and who makes a written application for the purpose to the person in charge, may without a reception order, be received as a voluntary patient. . . .'[49] Such patients could discharge themselves at any time on seventy-two hours notice. A person could be admitted as a temporary patient for up to six months if they could not express either their willingness or unwillingness to enter the asylum but were likely to benefit from temporary treatment. In practice the provision was less widely used than the other two. However, voluntary admissions and, to a lesser extent, temporary admissions increased rapidly as Table 25 shows. The Mental Treatment Act also required changes in terminology; an asylum was to be called a mental hospital; a pauper a 'rate-aided person' or a 'rate-aided patient'; and a lunatic a 'person of unsound mind', a 'person' or a 'patient'. And local authorities were given powers 'to make arrangements, whether by the provision of institutions or otherwise, for treatment as out-patients, either gratuitously or on such terms of payment as they think fit, of persons suffering from mental illness' and also 'to make provision for the after-care of any

Table 25   Direct admission to county and borough mental hospitals by legal status (percentages)

	Voluntary	Temporary	Certified
1931	7.1	1.8	91.1
1932	10.3	1.5	88.2
1933	13.1	1.8	85.1
1934	17.4	3.0	79.6
1935	24.1	5.2	70.7
1936	26.9	5.3	67.8
1937	31.3	5.2	63.5
1938	35.2	5.5	59.3

Source: Annual Reports of the Board of Control 1932–9.

persons who have undergone treatment for mental illness and to contribute to the funds of voluntary associations formed for that purpose'.[50]

Following the act a number of out-patient centres funded by local authorities began to be opened, although the numbers of patients served was relatively small. By the end of 1938 the Board of Control reported that there were some 177 clinics including the ones already established at voluntary hospitals.[51] Incomplete statistics showed more than 19,000 patients who had come for treatment, making a total of more than 74,000 attendances.[52] But in the early years the new local authority clinics differed from the old clinics, apparently following more closely the intended policy of seeing potentially severe cases early:

Unless established in general hospitals, they received few patients from other hospital departments. And when the clinic was located in a general hospital, the liaison between the visiting psychiatrist (whose contacts with the hospital were limited to his weekly or bi-weekly attendances) and the rest of the hospital was sometimes imperfect. In some areas, the fear wherein the Mental Hospital is still held could extend to the newly established clinic; the appropriate type of patient, it was thought, to send there was not so much the neurotic who needed psychotherapy as the early psychotic who might be required to be admitted to a Mental Hospital as a Voluntary patient . . . the typical psychiatric clinic established by a Local Authority differs from the typical clinic under the sole auspices of a Voluntary Hospital in holding fewer sessions, in dealing with fewer new patients, in seeing fewer return cases, in handling a smaller proportion of neurotics and a larger of psychotics.[53]

Progress both in the provision of separate facilities at mental hospitals for voluntary patients and in after-care services, which were largely in the hands of voluntary associations, was far slower.[54]

Nevertheless, although local authorities and mental hospitals were sometimes slow to make use of the powers assigned them, the Mental Treatment Act finally gave legislative expression to the wishes of reformers that steps should be taken to facilitate the early treatment of acute cases of insanity, wishes that had been overridden in the 1890 Lunacy Act. What brought about the shift from the legalism and custodialism of the 1890 Act to the medicalism of the 1930 Act? Why were the wishes of medical men like Maudsley ignored in 1890 but accepted in 1930? The answers to these questions lie in two areas. First, they are to be found in what was happening in psychiatry outside the asylums during this period – in the ideas and practice developed in relation to private patients who consulted private physicians and usually remained outside the walls of any institution – a sector that can be conveniently referred to as office psychiatry. Second, they are to be found in changes that occurred during the early decades of the twentieth century in the overall policies towards the poor and dependent; in changes in the poor law system and the state's welfare provisions.

Office psychiatry

Reformist initiative and state legislation throughout the eighteenth and nineteenth centuries directed its attention almost exclusively towards lunatics, to the more severe cases of mental disorder that appeared to pose a problem for the social order of society either by virtue of the attendant social and economic dependency or by virtue of the potential violence and destructiveness they could engender. No major policy initiatives concerned themselves with making any provision, medical or otherwise, for those who might be merely troubled in mind, and their problems were left to the vagaries of the market in healing, the charitable activities of neighbours or the support of friends. Moreover, although interest in these milder mental troubles did not disappear entirely either among scholars or healers in the nineteenth century the attention of official medicine was increasingly directed towards lunatics in asylums who were readily available subjects for research, not least because the severe forms of insanity appeared to be readier to yield to the increasingly dominant search for the specific pathological lesion engendered by new ideas about the localization of disease.

Medical practitioners, however, who depended in whole or in part on practice outside the asylums and madhouses often did not wish to avoid the problem of offering some treatment for milder mental disturbances. Some set themselves up as specialists in nervous disorders, a phrase that embraced a wide diversity of conditions of both physical and psychological origin.[55] Commonly described as neurologists, a term with a wider meaning then than now, these specialists and other private physicians offered a variety of therapies to their patients.[56] Some continued with the Galenic remedies of bleeding, vomits and purges, although by the second half of the nineteenth century these had tended to fall into desuetude.[54] Phrenology, which had provided the intellectual foundation on which behavioural prescriptions could be based, also fell into disrepute.[58] Some practitioners prescribed drugs, especially the opiates. Yet others, both within and outside the ranks of official medicine, used mesmerism or (as it was later to be called) hypnotism in the treatment of less severe mental problems.

Mesmerism, named after the eighteenth-century Viennese physician Anton Mesmer, who first developed the technique, was derived from his ideas about a force in animate nature that he termed animal magnetism, which he contended arose from the reciprocal influence of heavenly bodies and living things on earth.[59] He considered this force to be responsible for nervous illnesses and his object was to restore harmonious balance by the use of his own animal magnetism. This he found he could do by stroking or passing his hand over the other person's body. His ideas about animal magnetism, published in a book in 1779, were widely attacked by medical men, and the mesmeric phenomenon he identified, (which his critics were forced to recognize), was attributed to the exercise of imagination. The new term hypnotism, shortened from neuro-hypnotism (that is, nervous sleep), was introduced in 1843 by James Braid, a Manchester surgeon, in an attempt to dissociate the therapeutic technique from the discredited principles of animal magnetism.[60] Mesmerism and hypnotism were widely used both within and outside official medicine (for instance, prior to the introduction of chloroform, to induce anaesthesia), but they never gained complete respectability within official medicine.[61] In the case of mental disorders hypnotism was largely used for directive therapy: to suggest the disappearance of symptoms. Braid found the technique of particular value in cases of hysteria:

The most striking cases . . . for illustrating the value of the hypnotic mode of treatment, are cases of hysterical paralysis . . .. In such cases, by . . . substituting a salutary idea of vigour . . . the patients are found to have acquired . . . voluntary power over their hitherto paralysed limbs, as if by a magical spell or witchcraft.[62]

However its therapeutic efficacy was debatable. Freud, who used it in his early days in clinical practice, found its effects short lasting: 'If, after a short time, one had news of the patient once more, the old ailment was back again or its place had been taken by a new one.'[63] During the nineteenth century, however, the technique became both fashionable and popular and there was a widespread demand for it.[64]

Another fashionable treatment in the closing decades of the nineteenth century was the so-called rest cure, introduced in the 1890s by an American physician, S. Weir Mitchell, in which the patient remained in bed, usually for six weeks, received no visitors, was not allowed to read, but was given bodily massages and 'excessive feeding'.[65] The treatment developed out of Mitchell's attempt to deal with soldiers suffering from battle fatigue after the Civil War. Too much strain and too little relaxation appeared to tax the limited resources of the individual and rest was an obvious solution to what he viewed as an essentially bodily problem; food was seen as a way of counteracting the weight loss associated with nervous exhaustion, and massage a means of exercise without exertion. The extension of the treatment to a broad range of nervous complaints was seen by Mitchell as a desirable antidote to heroic medical treatment and far preferable to the excessive administration of drugs. The treatment sounds only a variant (more systematic and longer in length) of the sort of medical advice as regards the management of their social and physical environment that doctors following Galenic principles had continually meted out (the novelty was in eschewing more heroic interventions). However, the treatment effectively excluded patients from active management of their day to day activities or from attempts to ameliorate their social situation (which many would now argue was the source of their nervous problems) and so involved and encouraged a passivity and invalidism for which it has subsequently been much criticized. From the doctors' point of view the treatment probably had a number of advantages. A psychoanalyst writing in 1953, who had begun his psychiatric career some forty years earlier, gives this retrospective assessment in psychodynamic terms:

It provided a consoling form of treatment for both physician and patient. It relieved the doctor of the burden of investigating integral psychological factors responsible for the psychic disturbance and also of unwelcome reminders of his general ineffectiveness in handling the phobias and compulsions of which patients annoyingly complained. It pandered to the patient in allowing him to regress to an earlier state of helplessness and dependency for which most neurotics unconsciously yearn. The prescribed forced feeding in the rest cure indulged an infantile need for attention and importance; the isolation released him from the stern demands of reality and external conflict to center his interest on himself . . . It transiently relieved the patient of some of his symptoms and the responsibility for them which had now been condoned by the authoritative physician. At the same time the isolation carried with it some elements of punitive incarceration which would assuage the patient's feeling of guilt.[66]

More recently feminists, drawing attention to the fact that many of those with nervous complaints were women while the physicians were usually men, have seen the rest cure as symbolic of male power and sexuality in the way in which it forced women into dependence: 'The cauterizer, with his injections, leeches, and hot irons seems suggestive of a veiled but aggressively hostile male sexuality and superiority, and the rest-cure expert carried this spirit to a sophisticated culmination.'[67] The problem with this analysis is not the attention to dependency (though it should be noted that dependency is a pervasive characteristic of the doctor–patient relationship), but the argument that the specific form of treatment can be accounted for in terms of the dynamics of hostility and sexuality, whether it be the earlier heroic and harsh interventions or the later milder but none the less controlling use of the rest cure.[68] Undoubtedly gender (including female dependence) was a salient dimension of the practitioner–patient encounter which could be exploited to serve the practitioner's interests; and undoubtedly medical men usually accepted and affirmed contemporary values in the way they treated their female patients and the expectations they had of them. But neither aggression nor sexual politics need to be invoked to explain the nature of medical interventions – even though women's passivity and invalidism may have often been encouraged by them. The introduction of the rest cure must be accounted for in terms not only of the earlier discrediting of the intellectual foundations of Galenic medicine and the rather later discrediting of heroic therapies more generally, but also of the continuing economic motives of practitioners who needed to offer some form of therapy if they were to make a living. It was economic interest, including the benefits of securing and keeping their female as well as male clientele, rather than hostility towards women *per se* , that was the key.

There were developments, too, in the concepts used to refer to some of these less severe complaints. Of especial importance was the concept of neurasthenia introduced in 1869 by G. M. Beard, another American neurologist, in an attempt to bring together and systematize the diverse, ill-defined symptoms of which his patients complained.[69] He argued that these symptoms were but varying manifestations of a single condition, neurasthenia or nervous exhaustion. Its symptoms were numerous:

Insomnia, flushing, drowsiness, bad dreams, cerebral irritation, dilated pupils, pain, pressure and heaviness in the head, changes in the expression of the eye, neurasthenic asthenopia, noises in the ears, atonic voice, mental irritability, tenderness of the teeth and gums, nervous dyspepsia, desire for stimulants and narcotics, abnormal dryness of the skin, joints and mucous membranes, sweating hands and feet with redness, fear of lightning, or fear of responsibility, of open places or of closed places, fear of society, fear of being alone, fear of fears, fear of contamination, fear of everything, deficient mental control, lack of decision in trifling matters, hopelessness, deficient thirst and capacity for assimilating fluids, abnormalities of the secretions, salivation, tenderness of the spine, and of the whole body . . ..[70]

And so on, for this is but half the list. Beard contended that the condition, which he believed was especially common in America and was on the increase, was due to a lack of nerve force and was essentially a physical state that had its origins in the demands of modern civilization. Steam power, the telegraph, the periodical press, and the sciences, in all of which he held America to be most advanced, led to the pressures of time-keeping, specialization, fast communication, noise, new discoveries, an increase in business and risk taking. And all could tax the limited quantum of nerve force that supplied the organs of the body (whose level was set by heredity). Hence, it was among the professional and business classes and in America in particular that neurasthenia was most commonly found.

Beard's remedies followed traditional paths. He believed in

drugs and instruments, and in anything that would help to cure. He had a long list of special and often ingenious and unusual formulas which were put up for him in certain drug stores . . . . He used deep injections into the urethra, cold sounds and local electralization.[71]

Similarly his theorizing about the causes of neurasthenia built on earlier ideas. Civilization had often been invoked as the explanation for any increase in insanity.[72] And Beard moulded the ideas to fit the class characteristics of his clientele. His patients were from the professional and business classes and he devised a theory that could account for a nervous disability apparently specific to them, a theory that exalted them and their civilization above other people – neurasthenia was a mark of superiority. However, although the evidence suggests that more women than men made use of the new specialists in nervous disorders, Beard did not view neurasthenia as a typically female problem.[73] He mentions one or two causes specific to women – parturition, for example – but many of the factors he listed as causes of neurasthenia were arguably ones affecting the lives of men more than women, and initially at least neurasthenia seems to have been a label more often applied to men. Yet in as far as more women did seek help from medical specialists for nervous complaints, the introduction and acceptance of this new medical category helped to give legitimacy to medical work in this area, and must have encouraged other women to seek medical help for their problems. Indeed the importance of medical work like Beard's lay in the development of new ideas and practice that gave professional status and respectability to these encounters between patient and healer. They encouraged a sense that this was a field of professional knowledge and competence. Freud's contribution to psychiatry was to add, through his development of psychoanalysis, new concepts and new treatments that facilitated and strengthened professional (largely medical) work in relation to less severe mental disorders, and encouraged individuals to turn to specialists in mental disorders, usually medical men, for help with their problems.

Freud and psychoanalysis

Freud's ideas, like those of other medical men, were shaped by the economic and social aspects of his work. On the one hand psychoanalysis was suited to the social and educational skills of his patients; on the other hand it was suited to his own material needs as a private practitioner working as a free market entrepreneur.

The opportunities and challenges, both academic and clinical, in the field of nervous illness had, Freud reports, been pointed out by Charcot when Freud went to Paris in 1885 to study with him: 'Charcot used to say that, broadly speaking, the work of anatomy was finished and that the theory of the organic diseases of the nervous system might be said to be complete: what had next to be dealt with was the neuroses.'[74] Freud's initial concerns were academic and he hoped to do medical research; he became especially interested in hysteria, which Charcot had been studying, and planned a comparative study of hysterical and organic paralyses. However, on his return to Vienna, his financial and domestic circumstances (he was keen to marry after a four year engagement) led him to set up in private practice and to abandon academic circles. He established himself as a specialist in nervous diseases. His immediate problem was to provide his patients with some treatment and thereby earn himself a living. His initial choice of therapies was conventional enough, and we have already encountered his disarming comment on his early motives and endeavours (see p. 128) in which electrotherapy and hypnosis were initially favoured in preference to hydrotherapy, since the latter did not offer a means of earning his own living.[75]

Though he does not mention them, the prescription of drugs and medicines to his patients would have been an equally poor foundation for developing a specialist practice outside the asylum context, since they could be and readily were prescribed by non-specialist physicians. Consequently Freud found himself relying heavily on hypnosis: 'in the first years of my activity as a physician my principal instrument of work, apart from haphazard and unsystematic psycho-therapeutic methods, was hypnotic suggestion'.[76] Initially he was pleased with the method: 'there was something positively seductive in working with hypnotism. For the first time there was a sense of having overcome one's helplessness; and it was highly flattering to enjoy the reputation of being a miracle-worker'.[77] Patients too, he found, were not hard to come by and their 'number seemed further multiplied by the manner in which they hurried, with their troubles unresolved, from one physician to another'.[78]

With time Freud began to find a number of problems with hypnosis: he could not manage to hypnotize every patient, nor put them into as deep a state of hypnosis as he wished. However, a reluctant clinician, he also used the method to follow up his academic interest in the origin of symptoms 'questioning the patient upon the origin of his symptom, which in his waking state he could often describe only very imperfectly or not at all', and it was from this questioning, based on a procedure described by Breuer, that first the cathartic method, and then psychoanalysis itself was developed.[79]

The term psychoanalysis refers at one and the same time to an explanation of symptoms and behaviour, to a technique for the exploration of mental processes, and to a method of therapy.[80] Its basic assumptions are well known and I shall not describe them at length. At its centre is the assumption of psychic determinism, that 'ideas are effective in the genesis, in the maintenance, and in the extirpation of the symptoms'.[81] This, together with the notion of the unconscious – the belief that wishes, ideas and feelings may remain 'hidden from the consciousness of men' through the mechanism of repression – and the assumption of infantile sexuality, which offers a reason for the repression, provides a framework in which symptoms can be given meaning and become intelligible.[82] Symptoms are related to the unconscious wishes and to the childhood experience of the patient. Freud, tracing the link between a patient's delusion and her own feelings, wishes and experiences, comments on what the endeavour achieves:

Firstly, the delusion has ceased to be absurd or unintelligible; it had a sense, it had good motives and it fitted into the context of an emotional experience of the patient's. Secondly, the delusion was necessary, as a reaction to an unconscious mental process which we have inferred from other indications, and it was precisely to this connection that it owed its delusional character and its resistance to every logical and realistic attack. It itself was something desired, a kind of consolation. Thirdly, the fact that the delusion turned out to be precisely a jealous one and not of another kind was unambiguously determined by the experience that lay behind the illness.[83]

Hence Freud's approach directs attention to the content and meaning of the individual's thoughts and feeling, to what goes on within the mind – albeit that mental events are placed within a social context. In that respect it offered an internalist, individual psychology to parallel the internalist individualist biology and physiology of the nineteenth century.

Freud himself did not see psychoanalysis as an alternative to the organic theories of mental pathology that dominated official medicine at the end of the nineteenth century. He contended 'that the mental is based on the organic', and he attempted, at least initially, to describe the organic basis of the psychological processes he analysed.[84] Moreover, even later, when he recognized that these attempts had been unsuccessful, 'he did not discard the hope that psychological explanations might eventually be replaced by physiological ones'.[85] Nevertheless, psychoanalytic explanations and psychoanalytic therapies did direct attention away from the physiological to the psychological, as Freud himself recognized in his observations about psychiatry. Hence, despite his continued use of medical categories of mental disease, his conception of mental illness differed considerably from that suggested by nineteenth-century ideas about localized, structural organic pathology. Freud located pathology at the psychological not the organic level (this is of course also what the terms mental disease or mental illness suggest, but what those who emphasized brain pathology as the cause of mental illness in fact denied). Moreover, by pointing to the continuity between normal and abnormal mental functioning, psychoanalytic ideas also undermined the assumption of a qualitative break between health and disease and between different diseases which the notion of disease entities based on germ theory had involved.[86]

Not surprisingly psychoanalysis was much criticized by the medical profession, as hypnosis had been. Freud commented: 'until recently they have met it with everything possible that could damage it, from the shallowest ridicule to the gravest calumny'.[87] Yet it gradually gained some adherents within the medical profession and, especially in the United States, came to play an important part in psychiatric thought and practice.[88] Its adoption as a therapeutic technique and its partial modification (both in terms of treatment objectives and precise techniques) came primarily in psychiatric work outside the asylums, more specifically in the private realm of office psychiatry in which it had originated. Its adoption in this sphere can be explained in terms of its marked attractions for both therapist and patients as the basis for privately paid office practice. Its attractions to the affluent, high status patients were several.[89] First, it was designed around the type of mental complaints such patients were most likely to bring: psychoanalysis largely dealt with the realms of the less severe rather than the more severe psychiatric problems, with neuroses rather than psychoses. Indeed Freud gave new meaning to the term neuroses. Initially it had been used to refer to disorders of the nerves; Freud, however, distinguished psycho-neuroses – disorders with a psychogenic origin – from actual neuroses, and the term soon came to refer only to this more restricted group of psychoneuroses.[90] Freud did direct some theoretical attention towards the psychoses and one or two subsequent psycho-analysts have made psychoses a specific object of concern; but the neuroses have received the bulk of attention from psychoanalysts, especially as far as therapy is concerned, many arguing for the nigh impossibility of using psychotherapeutic techniques on psychotic patients.[91]

Second, the content of the method itself had obvious attractions to the type of patient with less severe mental troubles who could afford to request help from a medical practitioner. These educated and articulate patients were offered a therapy that called upon, and made use of, their verbal and intellectual capacities, and allowed them to participate in the therapeutic process, albeit not on exactly equal terms, but as thinking, talking persons.(Psychoanalysts tend to regard a certain level of verbal facility as a precondition of successful therapy.)[92] The fact that psychoanalytic ideas might seem to point to unconscious processes outside their rational control and assert the strength of their emotions does not undermine this point, for they also asserted the potential for change and required the active participation of the individual as an intellectual as well as emotional being in order to achieve this end. Hence the brief label of psychoanalysis as the 'talking cure' identifies its attractions for patients.[93] A third attraction related to this is to be found in the fact that what were undoubtedly experienced as a psychological problem – that is a problem of feelings, thoughts and emotions – were being met at the same level. Those who brought complaints of a neurotic nature were concerned about their fears, anxieties and depressions and they were allowed, indeed encouraged, to give them expression; like was met with like. In this respect psychoanalysis was potentially more attractive than hypnosis since the attempts at direct removal of symptoms by suggestion did not permit the patient to 'indulge' in the analysis of their experiences to the same extent.

The novelty in the content and nature of the doctor–patient relationship in psychoanalysis was not without its problems. From the practitioner's point of view distance and authority had to be maintained if the relationship were to continue in a professional manner. However, a number of procedures followed by orthodox psychoanalysts helped to ensure the continuing authority and detachment of the analyst. The asymmetry of the relationship was affirmed by the analyst's refusal to talk about his or her own feelings or personal life.[94] The authority of the analyst's explanation of the patient's psychopathology was defended by the notion of resistance to interpretation which deflected the possibility of the patient's undermining the accuracy of the analyst's account. Furthermore the notion of transference was of especial value in maintaining a proper distance between analyst and patient.[95] The concept refers to the displacement of the patient's feelings, generated in earlier personal relationships, on to the analyst; the recognition by psychoanalysts not only of the importance of transference but of the need to analyse and deal with it provided a device which allowed the doctor–patient relationship and the feelings it engendered to become the object of analytic interest and attention. As a result both patient and analyst were more able to cope intellectually and emotionally with a potentially intense relationship. Freud and Breuer alike had found in their early psychotherapeutic endeavours that the relationship could be a seductive one for the patient (and the analyst) and eventually recognized the extent of the problem this type of treatment had to face.[96] The use of a couch with the analyst seated behind the patient is a further example of the distancing techniques used by analysts. There is a parallel in the problem faced by the early male midwives of creating a framework in which they could escape the sexual and seductive connotations of a male stranger's presence at a woman's delivery – one stratagem they used being to work with the woman's body hidden from view.[97]

Psychoanalysis had equal attractions for the private practitioner. First and foremost it provided other practitioners, as it had Freud himself, with a new and economically viable method of treatment that could offer them a relatively secure living. Here its novelty was less important, despite the dearth of alternatives at the time, than the fact that proper psychoanalysis required lengthy, intensive treatment. Treatment five days a week for fifty minutes a day over three years or more might make psychoanalysis prohibitive for all but the affluent (as it has done) and totally unsuitable for the public sector; but it offered the prospect of a stable if not extravagant living for its practitioners in a situation where the vagaries of market competition could make it difficult to secure a regular living from medical practice. Though patients need to be affluent to afford psychoanalysis, not many patients are required to keep an analyst in full-time work.

Second, psychoanalysis was attractive to practitioners as a method of therapy because it was based on a new and specialized set of ideas that facilitated the professionalization of therapeutic work.[98] Hypnosis was a reasonably simple technique that could be quickly learned, so that it was relatively easy for anyone to offer the treatment. Psychoanalysis, as advocated by Freud, was founded on a complex body of ideas and required a lengthy training (a personal training analysis with supervision of early cases) so that claims to professional expertise could be made and defended more forcefully. This is not to say that psychoanalysis was not vulnerable on this score, and descriptions of it as the talking cure and suggestions that all the therapist has to do is simply listen and make occasional encouraging comments are evidence of the problems. Third, the detailed theoretical framework of psychoanalysis offered practitioners a comprehensive and systematic way of thinking about their patient's problems that not only made them seem intelligible but also provided a therapeutic technique to deal with them. The specialist language and ideas could serve both to enhance the practitioner's professional status, and to provide a secure and comforting intellectual apparatus that had and still has obvious attractions for the practitioner.[99]

Psychoanalysis flourished, therefore, in the sphere of private practice in relation to the neurotic problems of the more affluent members of society. When the level of affluence did not permit such lengthy, intensive forms of treatment; when the problems to be dealt with were more severe (psychotic or organic rather than neurotic); and when the state was involved in the provision of medical services, psychoanalysis was not adopted as a form of therapy in its orthodox form (shortened, more directive psychodynamic therapy was used somewhat more widely). Hence the contrast between the role of psychoanalysis in the United States and Britain where private and public medicine have had such different trajectories.[100] It is illuminating that paying for treatment (i.e. a fee for service organization of its practice) has come to be regarded by psychoanalysts as important to the maintenance and success of therapy itself.[101] They argue that if patients have to pay for their treatment they will be more committed to it and will be more likely to be motivated to change. Whether true or not the proposition serves as a legitimation of private practice (and indirectly of the restriction of the treatment to those who can afford to pay for it).

Psychoanalysis has had, of course, a major impact on psychiatric work in institutions as well as outside them and on work in the public as well as the private sector, even where it has not been adopted as a method of therapy. On the one hand it has had a direct effect on ideas about the neuroses. Many psychiatrists during this century have accepted the general validity of psychodynamic explanations of the neuroses even if they have not accepted some of the specific details of Freudian ideas or used psychodynamic therapies. (There has not been and does not need to be a necessary symmetry between explanation and treatment.) In that respect Freudian thought encouraged a 'psychologization' of ideas about less severe mental illnesses. On the other hand it has had a more indirect and mediated effect on psychiatric ideas and practice. By establishing the (psycho-) neuroses as an important focus of therapeutic interest it helped to draw attention to the less severe mental disorders and gave them a more important place on the psychiatric map. It neither problematized them for the first time (being troubled in mind, melancholic or mopish were old categories) nor made them the object of medical attention for the first time (healers have long offered remedies for such problems); rather it reconceptualized these troubles, setting them in a new theoretical framework that helped to secure them greater status in some psychiatric and medical spheres. Psychoanalysis also created a new sense that such conditions were treatable. It therefore encouraged public demand for professional help with such problems – this help in practice being largely medical, since medicine to a great extent monopolized psychoanalytic practice. Equally important, it led to new ideas about the interrelation of mind and body, and by pointing to the continuity between normal and abnormal psychological functioning, psychoanalytic ideas also facilitated a situation in which the demand for treatment for more minor psychological problems would increase.

Freud's early work was published in the 1890s and was quickly translated into English, but it was not until the second and third decades of this century that it began to attract wide attention in psychiatric circles in America and England (a turning point being marked by Freud's trip to the United States in 1909 to lecture at Clark University).[102] The precise spread of psychoanalytic ideas in England has been little studied, but they appear to have influenced writers on shell-shock and on war neurosis and by the 1920s were beginning to be widely discussed amongst educationalists, social scientists, writers and critics as well as psychiatrists.[103] Hence they helped to generate ways of thinking about mental disorder, especially in its milder forms, that made the response to insanity embodied in the 1890 Lunacy Act seem less and less adequate.

The breakdown of the poor law system

The policies advocated in the Report of the Macmillan Commission, like those put forward by medical critics of the second half of the nineteenth century, were in almost all respects directly contrary to the spirit of the nineteenth-century poor law system. The Macmillan Report urged patients to seek treatment in the early stages of illness; the poor law system was founded on principles of deterrence. The Macmillan Report urged local authorities to expand their facilities for the mentally ill, to set up out-patient clinics, improve after-care facilities and make provision for voluntary cases in the public mental hospitals; the poor law system sought above all to keep expenditure levels to a minimum. The Macmillan Report gave a greater emphasis to non-residential forms of care; the poor law system saw the institution as the preferred locus of relief. The Macmillan Report sought to break the asylums' links with the poor law; it was a keystone of the poor law system that it should be the sole source of public relief to the dependent. Consequently the enactment of the policies put forward by the Macmillan Report in the Mental Treatment Act can only be fully explained by the large scale collapse of the poor law during the first three decades of the twentieth century.

The reforms of the Liberal Government of 1906–11 marked the first crucial stage of the system's collapse.[104] These reforms, spearheaded by the National Insurance Act of 1911, introduced an insurance based system of public welfare.[105] Individuals covered by the legislation (the system was by no means comprehensive) were required to insure themselves against the event of unemployment, sickness, and disability, with the support of contributions from the state and their employers. The insurance schemes not only provided financial benefit in lieu of wages (at relatively low levels) but also certain types of non-institutional medical service. Participants to the health insurance scheme had to sign up with a general practitioner who was registered with the scheme. Three years earlier the government had introduced the first old age pensions to the poor and respectable over-70s.[106] Unlike the schemes for sickness and unemployment it was non-contributory, though means tested (a contributory, insurance based scheme being introduced in 1925).[107] The Liberal reforms effectively side-stepped the issue of direct reform of the poor law, which had become a matter of great controversy. A Poor Law Commission had been set up in 1905 as a result of pressure for reform of the poor law but there was disagreement among its members.[108] The Majority and Minority Reports of the Commission produced in 1909 condemned the existing poor law system and recommended the end of a separate poor law: they emphasized the need to prevent poverty, and argued for the need to develop further specialized services. However, the Minority Report recommended 'the break-up of the Poor Law' proposing that different categories of need be dealt with separately, largely locally, whereas the Majority Report argued for the replacement of the poor law guardians with local public assistance authorities that would include members of voluntary organizations. Reform in either direction was, however, held back by the lack of agreement about the direction of change, the need for reform of local government finance, and by opposition from the Local Government Board, the central authority of the poor law system.[109] Meanwhile the new pensions and insurance schemes introduced by the Liberal government laid the basis for a system of welfare that began to supplant the poor law system, since persons covered by the new provisions were less likely to be forced to turn to the poor law for assistance. And as new schemes were introduced or their coverage extended, the numbers falling into the net of the poor law declined. Between 1910 and 1914 the total numbers of paupers declined from 916,377 to 748,019, the most marked decline occurring in those on outdoor relief.[110]

The introduction of the Liberal reforms not only started to undermine the poor law system by providing public benefits outside its framework so that its role was diminished; equally, if not more importantly, it undermined the poor law by striking at the very principles on which it was founded. On the one hand insurance based schemes helped to undermine the principle of institutional deterrence. For while the philosophy of deterrence continued to be embodied in the poor law system itself, the development of provision outside the poor law meant that there was some, albeit limited, provision for dependency on an 'outdoor' basis without the pressure towards institutional care. Indeed the insurance system was designed to reduce the resort to just such institutional dependency. On the other hand, by introducing the philosophy of self-protection aided by the state and employers, the reforms helped to undermine the whole idea that benefit was a matter of last resort.

The Liberal reforms were brought about by a number of factors.[111] Not least was the growing power and consciousness of the working class.

The male working class had been enfranchised in 1884 and the period witnessed a resurgence of class consciousness, and the development of socialist ideas and policies, that demanded a new response by the state to the needs of the working class. The Liberal reforms sought to stem the tide of any potential revolutionary spirit by dealing more effectively with some of those needs. Balfour had commented in 1895:

Social legislation, as I conceive it, is not merely to be distinguished from Socialist legislation but it is its more direct opposite and its most effective antidote. Socialism will never get possession of the great body of public opinion . . . among the working class or any other class if those who wield the collective forces of the community show themselves desirous to ameliorate every legitimate grievance and to put Society upon a proper and more solid basis.[112]

The presence of the Labour Party in Parliament (there were fifty-three Labour MPs in the 1906 Parliament) was 'the symbol of the distress of the masses which, if not placated, would in the long term destroy the Liberals'.[113]

But it was not just fear of the potential radicalism of the working class that led to the Liberal reforms. There was, too, concern for the economic and military status of the country. The rapid and easy economic growth of the first phases of industrialization had passed and with it the clear economic lead Britain had over other countries.[114] The United States and Germany began to move ahead in industrial productivity introducing mass production and mechanizing processes such as machine making, and had the advantage, in the case of the United States, of an enormous domestic market. Britain's relative economic stagnation had important consequences. In particular it helped to generate a new concern for national efficiency and a desire to make the country more productive, and this in turn led to a concern for the health and welfare of all social groups. As Asquith commented

What is the use of talking about Empire if here, at its very centre, there is always to be found a mass of people, stunted in education, a prey of intemperance, huddled and congested beyond the possibility of realising in any true sense either social or domestic life.[115]

Concern about the condition of the labouring population was reflected in and gained documentary support from a range of empirical studies of the population that detailed the full extent of poverty in parts of England in the second half of the nineteenth century. Mayhew's study of *London Labour and the London Poor* in the early 1850s was paralleled by Charles Booth's *Life and Labour of the People in London* in the late 1880s and Seebohm Rowntree's study of York in *Poverty: a Study of Town Life*, published in 1901.[116] Even more important, however, was the information provided about the poor health of recruits during the Boer War since this seemed to be a direct reflection on the military strength of the nation, already beginning to be concerned about its performance in the war. According to one estimate some 40 per cent of recruits had to be rejected on health grounds, and concern was such that an interdepartmental committee on physical deterioration was established.[117] Its report, published in 1904, devoted much of its attention to the welfare of infants and children.[118] It led to one of the first of the Liberal reforms, the 1906 Education (Provision of Meals) Act, introduced by a Labour back-bencher, which empowered local authorities to provide free school meals to children in need. An act passed the following year established medical inspection in schools, also recommended in the physical deterioration report. But while new attention and specific legislative provisions were directed at the health of children, there was also concern for the more general problems of poverty arising from the 'accidents' of unemployment and ill-health since they affected the family as a whole and were related to the health and welfare of both children and adults. There needed, Lloyd George argued, to be:

provisions against the accidents of life which bring so much undeserved poverty to the hundreds and thousands of homes, accidents which are quite inevitable such as the death of the breadwinner or his premature breakdown in health. I have always thought that the poverty which was brought upon families owing to these causes presents a much more urgent demand upon the practical sympathy of the community than even Old Age Pensions. With old age the suffering is confined to the individual alone; but in these other cases it extends to the whole family of the victim of circumstances.[119]

The sickness and unemployment schemes were designed to deal with just such contingencies.

The First World War in turn led to further pressure for reform, and a new spirit of reconstruction generated further legislation that broadened welfare provision outside the poor law, and in so doing helped to destroy the principles and practices of the poor law system. In the first instance the War fuelled anxieties about the high levels of infant mortality, especially among males. The Local Government Board in its report for 1915–16 argued that 'at a time like the present there is urgent need for taking all possible steps to secure the health of all mothers and children and to diminish ante-natal and post-natal mortality'.[120] A Carnegie Trust Report on Maternal and Child Welfare in 1917 commented:

The value of population has never been appreciated as it is today, and regrets at the unheeded wastage of infant life in bygone years are as sincere as they are useless, a simple calculation shows that had the annual wastage of male infant life during the last 50 years been no greater than it is at present, at least 500,000 more men would have been available for the defence of the country today.[121]

The Maternal and Child Welfare Act that followed in 1918 required local authorities to establish maternal and child welfare committees with powers – permissive but not mandatory – to provide a full maternal and child welfare service with midwives, health visitors, day nurseries, free milk, etc.[122]

Of more immediate importance in the mental health field was the creation of a Ministry of Health in 1919, which took over the powers of the Local Government Board. A Ministry of Health had originally been proposed as a wartime measure to bring together government activity in the health field, but was finally accepted as part of post-war reconstruction.[123] In 1920 the new ministry took over powers over lunacy and mental deficiency that had been invested in the Home Office – an event of considerable symbolic significance for it gave administrative expression to the view that lunacy was now, as far as the state was concerned, a matter of health rather than of public order.[124] The ideological realm of welfare, care and service could replace that of control and deterrence and the foundation of the subsequent expansion of state mental health services had been laid. The establishment of a new Ministry of Health with powers over lunacy did not, however, get rid of the immediate association of mental health services with the poor law for at this point 'the Poor Law remained intact within the Ministry of Health'.[125]

The war did, however, lead to direct pressures for reform of the mental health services away from their poor law mould. In the first place it strengthened pressures for provision of publicly funded mental health services outside the confines of the poor law. Pathological mental states arising from war service were seen as qualitatively different not only in symptomatology – 'shell-shock' was first defined and identified in this period – but also in their moral aetiology, since they had arisen in service to the country.[126] A writer to *The Lancet* put the argument like this:

Cases which in civilian life would be uncertifiable should not when in the
army be treated as lunatics. The cause of the loss of balance is quite
definite. The injury has been sustained in fighting for their country. Are
they for this to be penalised? . . . These soldiers should on no account be
placed in an asylum atmosphere and under lunacy authorities.[127]

A similar case was also made for civilians whose mental pathology could
be attributed to the stresses of war. It was these arguments that underlay
the first bill put forward to Parliament in 1915, designed to encourge
early treatment, whose stated purpose was 'to facilitate the early
treatment of mental disorders of recent origin, arising from wounds,
shock and other causes'.[128] Although this bill was withdrawn in 1917 the
Ministry of Pensions did agree that discharged soldiers should be treated
as private patients in asylums and that the cost should be met by the
state, and, as we have seen, private patients could be more readily
admitted to asylums on a voluntary basis.[129]

Furthermore, as the desire for reconstruction increased as the war
ended, there were more general demands for lunacy reform. In 1918 the
Board of Control, which had taken over the functions of the
Commissioners in Lunacy under the Mental Deficiency Act of 1913,
produced a report for the Government Reconstruction Committee
arguing for the introduction of voluntary admission, and facilities for
early treatment and after-care.[130] But the bill introduced in 1922, which
was rather more restricted than the Mental Treatment Act of 1930, failed
to get through Parliament.[131] By then reconstruction had already
stagnated largely as a result of the government's deflationary attempts to
cut back public expenditure in the face of financial pressures as the post-
war boom disappeared.[132] The so-called 'Geddes axe' curtailed a variety
of social programmes including housing and education and the financial
costs of lunacy reform ensured the failure of the bill. The establishment
of the Royal Commission the following year helped, however, to create a
stronger pressure for reform, and in their report the commission
specifically sought to counter financial anxieties about the implementation of their proposals. They rehearsed the standard arguments of the
nineteenth century lunacy reformers that the long-term economic gains
would outweigh the short-term financial costs:

If our recommendations are adopted, local authorities will be trusted with
powers and duties involving new expenditure. It will not be wholly
unremunerative. The provision of facilities for early treatment in out-patient
clinics or in reception houses and the extension of the voluntary boarder

system will, we believe, result in many cases regaining their mental stability before the illness reaches a stage which would necessitate prolonged institutional treatment. Thus cases will be deflected temporarily or permanently from the public mental hospitals. This must have an important bearing on the question of providing further accommodation. It appears that the demand for accommodation in public mental hospitals is rapidly overtaking the supply; and the authorities are confronted with the necessity for extending asylum accommodation forthwith in some areas. But, for the reasons suggested above, the adoption of our proposals may modify substantially the extent of need for such further provision. The extension of after-care cannot fail to consolidate the recovery of many patients and prevent relapses. The encouragement of research holds the gratest hope for the discovery of new possibilities of cure. It may be some years before the results of these measures are reflected in a diminution of the population in mental hospitals. But, as we have indicated, there is this credit side to the account which must be borne in mind when the financial implications of our proposals are considered.[133]

The argument about the prospects of cure and potential economic gains are more cautious than their nineteenth-century predecessors, but they are invoked none the less in order to make the financial investment seem worthwhile. The commission argued, too, that the cost of maintaining lunatics should be transferred from the poor rate to the county or borough rate, a provision that would have meant not only that the lunacy system would have been further separated from the poor law but also that the financial burden would be borne by the local authority, making further expenditure ideologically and practically easier.[134]

In the event reform of the poor law, which the commission had expected, occurred before the Mental Treatment Act was passed. And the reform, along with the fact that a Labour government was returned to power in June 1929, undoubtedly facilitated the successful passage of the Mental Treatment Act. The reform was incorporated into the Local Government Act of 1929, which was the work of Neville Chamberlain, then Minister of Health, and was passed when the Conservative government was still in power.[135] The act, which marked an important step in the breakdown of the poor law system, abolished the poor law Boards of Guardians and vested their powers in new Public Assistance Committees that were to be set up by local authorities for the relief of the destitute. Paupers were at the same time re-termed 'rate-aided persons'. Local authorities were encouraged to allocate activities, other than those concerned with the relief of able-bodied, to other appropriate committees so that a greater separation of these services from the relief of destitution could be achieved (as the Minority Report of the Poor Law Commission had recommended in 1909). Hence, although to the unemployed 'the new P.A.C.s were merely the old guardians writ large', the provision of health services, including those of mental health, were further separated from issues of public assistance as the Macmillan Commission had advocated.[136] Significantly, too, the act introduced for the first time an element of central funding into local authority finance so strengthening its financial base and permitting some expansion of services.

The inclusion of the poor law in the local government reform of 1929 was bound up with the government's difficulties in dealing with the problem of long-term unemployment (which was increasing) outside the confines of the poor law system, since the poor law could not cope with the extra numbers of people involved.[137] The government's attempts to deal with this problem without totally abandoning the insurance principle and without pushing the unemployed on to the poor law, led to pressure for greater control of the poor law system. The government wanted to ensure that the poor law guardians, who had acquired a considerable degree of autonomy, acted in line with their policies, and did not offer, as some local guardians did, more generous levels of relief that undermined the unemployment benefit schemes they devised.

The introduction of voluntary in-patient treatment for 'persons of unsound mind' and the granting of powers to local authorities to develop special facilities for early treatment had to await, therefore, the major steps in the breakdown of the poor law system and the development of systems of welfare built on different principles and practices from those of the nineteenth-century poor law. The principles embodied in the Mental Treatment Act marked a significant departure from those embodied in the lunacy system of the second half of the nineteenth century and in the 1890 Lunacy Act, and the new act laid the foundations for the pattern of mental health services of the second half of the twentieth century.

Notes and references

1 See Jones, 1979.
2 The use of the term community care is discussed more fully in the following chapter.
3 Unfortunately continuous time series data over this period are lacking due in part to frequent changes in the organization and administration of mental health services. Some of the limitations of official statistics on mental health are discussed in *Trends in British Society since 1900* (Halsey, 1972), Section 11.
4 Bott's analysis of the pattern of admissions to a single hospital from its

opening in 1905 showed that in that particular hospital first admission rates grew more rapidly in the decade 1945 to 1955 than in the decade up to 1965 (1976, p. 103).

5   General Register Office, 1962, Chapter III; Royal College of General Practitioners 1974.

6   Some 43 per cent of those admitted to a psychiatric bed are diagnosed as having a psychotic or organic disorder; in contrast less than one per cent of consultations with general practitioners for conditions diagnosed as mental disorders are for psychotic or organic disorders (Department of Health and Social Security, 1984, Table A2.2, Royal College of General Practitioners, 1974, Table 11).

7   Most are intended to provide treatment and care for those with long-term problems; see Kramer, 1963. The first day hospital in England was opened in 1946 (Farndale, 1963).

8   See Chapter 5.

9   *Special Report of the Commissioners in Lunacy on the Alleged Increase in Lunacy*, 1897; Department of Health and Social Security, 1984; Goldberg and Huxley, 1980, Chapters 4, 5 and 7.

10   Maudsley, *The Physiology and Pathology of Mind*, 1867, p. 501.

11   See Chapter 8, pp. 276–9.

12   Maudsley, 1867.

13   Tuke, in his historical account of the Retreat, referring to the year 1799, commented that 'The experience of the Retreat, had already proved the great importance of placing the insane under proper care, in an early stage of the disorder' (1813, p. 57). A little later he quotes the Report of the General Meeting held in 1800 which stated that 'Experience has this year abundantly convinced us, of the advantage to be derived from an early attention to persons afflicted with disorders of the mind.' See also Hodgkinson, 1967, Chapter 4, p. 59.

14   Hunter and MacAlpine, 1974, p. 52.

15   Granville, *The Care and Cure of the Insane*, 1877.

16   ibid., Vol. II, p. 152.

17   ibid., Vol. II, p. 218.

18   ibid., p. 219.

19   Quoted in Jones, 1960, pp. 22–3.

20   Maudsley, 1867, pp. 494–5.

21   Lewis, 1967.

22   Hunter and MacAlpine, 1963, p. 1073.

23   Royal Commission, 1957, p. 72.

24   ibid., p. 72.

25   Royal Commission, 1926, p. 45; p. 49.

26   Jones, 1960, p. 103. Royal Commission, 1926, pp. 45–6.

27   Jones, 1960, p. 104.

28   Blacker, 1946, p. 17.

29   Jones, 1960, pp. 98 and 124; Blacker, 1946.
30   Royal Commission, 1926, p. 48.
31   ibid., pp. 43–4.
32   Jones, 1960, p. 97; Bean, 1980, pp. 39–40; Royal Commission, 1926, p. 49.
33   Jones, 1960, pp. 106–12; Bean, 1980, pp. 23–5.
34   Lomax, 1921.
35   Jones, 1960, p. 100.
36   Bean, 1980, p. 23.
37   Royal Commission, 1926, p. 17.
38   Bean, 1980, p. 23.
39   Royal Commission, 1926, p. 15.
40   ibid., pp. 15-6.
41   ibid., p. 20.
42   ibid., pp. 18–9.
43   ibid., p. 47.
44   ibid., p. 17.
45   ibid., p. 17.
46   ibid., pp. 21–2.
47   ibid., p. 23; pp. 56–7.
48   Jones, 1960, Chapter 8.
49   Mental Treatment Act, 1930, Section 1.
50   ibid., Section 6.
51   Board of Control, 1939, p. 2.
52   ibid., p. 2.
53   Blacker, 1946, p. 18.
54   Jones, 1960, pp. 125–6.
55   For an early attempt to define the category of nervous disorders, see Robert Whytt's *Observations on the Nature, Causes and Cure of those disorders which have been called nervous, hypochandriac, or hysteric*, 1765 (Hunter and MacAlpine, 1963, pp. 391–2).
56   Rosenberg, 1968, p. 60.
57   Shryock, 1947, chapter 9.
58   For an interesting discussion of phrenology, see Cooter, 1981.
59   Hunter and MacAlpine, 1963, pp. 480–6.
60   ibid., pp. 906–10.
61   ibid., pp. 481–2; Zilboorg, Chapter 9.
62   Hunter and MacAlpine, 1963, pp. 906–7.
63   See his lecture 'Analytic Therapy', in his *Introductory Lectures on Psychoanalysis* (1974, p. 502).
64   Hunter and MacAlpine, 1963, p. 909.
65   Wood, 1974, p. 19. The phrase is Mitchell's own. See also Morantz, 1974; Smith-Rosenberg, 1972.
66   Obendorf, 1953, p. 51.

67 Wood, 1974, p. 9.
68 Morantz, 1974.
69 For a discussion of Beard's ideas, see Rosenberg, 1976; see also Sicherman, 1981; Haller, 1971.
70 G. M. Beard, *American Nervousness*, 1881, p. 7.
71 Recollections of a contemporary, Charles L. Dana, quoted in Rosenberg, 1976, pp. 103–4.
72 See, for instance, Brigham's comments in *Remarks on the influence of mental cultivation upon health*, 1832 (Hunter and MacAlpine, 1963, pp. 821–5).
73 Wood, 1974, pp. 2–3; Morantz, 1974, p. 43; Smith-Rosenberg, 1972, p. 665.
74 Quoted in Wollheim, 1971, p. 20.
75 Freud, 1935, pp. 26–7.
76 ibid., p. 28.
77 ibid., p. 29.
78 ibid., pp. 28–9.
79 ibid., p. 32.
80 On psychoanalysis as a technique for the exploration of mental processes, see Farrell, 1970.
81 Wollheim, 1971, p. 23.
82 Freud, 1935, p. 29.
83 The quotation is from Freud's Lecture 'Psychoanalysis and Psychiatry', in his *Introductory Lectures on Psychoanalysis* (1974, p. 292).
84 Quoted by Rieff, 1965, p. 6.
85 ibid., p. 6.
86 See Chapter 2.
87 Freud, 1962, p. 146.
88 For its impact in the US, see Mannoni, 1971, Appendix; Obendorf, 1953; Hale, 1971.
89 The impact of the socio-economic background of Freud's patients on his ideas is discussed by Ansbacher, 1959. Ansbacher adopts an earlier estimate of the socio-economic composition of Freud's patients which assigned 74 per cent of them to the category 'wealthy'; 23 per cent to the 'middle class' and only 3 per cent to the 'poor (working class)'.
90 See, for instance, his lecture 'The Common Neurotic State', in his *Introductory Lectures on Psychoanalysis* (Freud, 1974).
91 On psychoanalytic approaches to psychosis see, for instance, Searles (1964), as well as the work of Melanie Klein (Segal, 1964; and 1979). On the *de facto* focus on the neuroses, see Freud, 1974, p. 512 and Kovel, 1978, pp. 118–9.
92 Kovel, 1978, p. 119.
93 A term Freud himself sometimes used. See his *Five Lectures on Psychoanalysis* (1962, p. 45).

94   For a rationale for this see Storr, 1966, p. 80.
95   Freud, 1974, Lecture 27; see also Szasz's comments in 'The concept of transference' (1963b).
96   Freud, 1935, p. 46.
97   Donnison, 1977, p. 11.
98   Scull comments 'the Freudian system possessed a combination of almost unsurpassable virtues as a professional ideology. It had the great merit of being non-testable, and hence non-refutable; and, like Marxism, it lent itself to simplification for the simple and sophistication for the sophisticated. Requiring prolonged and costly training, it developed in its devotees a presumptive expertise which readily justified the rejection of outside, non-professional interference . . ..' (1979, pp. 258–9).
99   Notwithstanding the advantages for practitioners, psychoanalysis's all-embracing nature gives rise to many of the criticisms of its scientific status; see, for instance, Popper, 1963, p. 35.
100 On the relationship between psychoanalysis and psychiatry in the United States in the mid-1960s, see Rogow, 1970. A more recent (1973) study of private office psychiatry in the United States is Marmor, 1975.
101 Insurance coverage for psychotherapy is limited though increasing; see Marmor, 1975, Chapter 5; Bodenheimer *et al.*, 1977.
102 See Hale, 1971; Obendorf, 1953; Jones, 1958, Vol. II.
103 On shell shock see Smith and Pear, 1917; see also MacCurdy, 1918.
104 On Liberal reforms see Hay, 1975; Fraser, 1984, Chapter 7; Thane, 1982, Chapter 2.
105 Thane, 1982, pp. 84–7, pp. 91–6.
106 ibid., pp. 82–3.
107 ibid., p. 198.
108 ibid., pp. 88–91.
109 Fraser, 1984, p. 146.
110 Thane, 1982, p. 91.
111 Hay, 1975, *passim*.
112 Quoted in Fraser, 1984, p. 139.
113 ibid., pp. 147–8.
114 Hobsbawm, 1969, Chapter 9; Landes, 1969, Chapters 4 and 5.
115 Quoted in Hay, 1975, p. 31.
116 For an account of these studies, see Rose, 1972, Chapter 4.
117 Lewis, 1980, p. 15; Thane, 1982, p. 58; Fraser, 1984, p. 179.
118 Lewis, 1980, p. 15.
119 Quoted in Fraser, 1984, pp. 161–2.
120 Quoted in Lewis, 1980, p. 29.
121 ibid., p. 29.
122 ibid., p. 34.

123   Fraser, 1984, pp. 179–80.
124   Jones, 1960, p. 99.
125   Fraser, 1984, p. 180.
126   ibid., p. 182.
127   Quoted in Bean, 1980, p. 40.
128   ibid., p. 39.
129   ibid., p. 40.
130   Jones, 1960, pp. 97–8.
131   It proposed a single new category of 'temporary treatment of mental disorder without certification' for those willing to submit to treatment and capable of volition, a category closer to the 1930 Mental Treatment Act's status of voluntary patient than the latter Act's 'temporary treatment' provisions.
132   Fraser, 1984, p. 182.
133   Royal Commission, 1926, p. 144.
134   ibid., p. 143.
135   Fraser, 1984, p. 188.
136   ibid., p. 188.
137   ibid., pp. 184–98.

10 Community care

The post-war policy shift towards community care has been explained in a number of different ways. A standard account, often favoured by psychiatrists, relates it to the therapeutic developments of the post-war years, more especially to the introduction of psychotropic drugs in the 1950s, and, to a lesser extent, to the impact of the sustained and vocal critiques of institutional care that came from both within and outside psychiatry during the same decade.[1] The chemically synthesized drugs of the 1950s, the first of which, like chlorpromazine and reserpine, were used as anti-psychotic drugs, permitted, it is contended, a greater number of patients to be treated outside the hospital and facilitated the earlier discharge of those who did have to be admitted. This, together with an increasing recognition of the anti-therapeutic nature of institutional care (highlighted by a diverse range of studies of institutionalization publicized in books like psychiatrist Russell Barton's *Institutional Neurosis* and sociologist Erving Goffman's *Asylums*), led, it is argued, to general support for policies of shifting care away from the mental hospital towards the community.[2] Put simply we can characterize the policy change and the explanation that is offered of it in terms of the simple model set out in Figure 3. The model suggests a polarization of spheres, the mental hospital and the community, as well as a

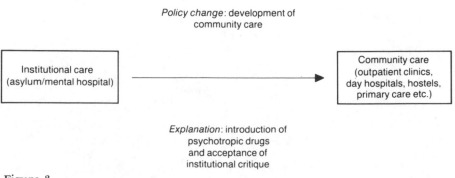

Figure 3

polarization of values, with the mental hospital viewed as bad and undesirable, and the community as good and beneficent.

There are, however, a number of problems with this explanation of the shift to community care, grounded as it is in the liberal–scientific view of medical work, as Scull in his book *Decarceration*, and others, have indicated.[3] First, it is defective on grounds of timing. The decline in the size of the resident population of psychiatric beds was apparent in national statistics for this country and the US in the mid 1950s (see Table 22 above) and in the statistics for particular hospitals from at least the beginning of the 1950s, yet the chemically synthesized drugs were only just beginning to be introduced in the mid 1950s.[4] The first to be developed was chlorpromazine compounded by the Rhône-Poulenc research laboratories in France in 1951.[5] It was initially used to try and prevent the common nauseas of pregnancy and its potential as an anti-psychotic drug did not begin to be tested until 1953. And it was the following year before it was first marketed for psychiatric patients under the brand name Largactil in England, and Thorazine in the United States. Hence, although its psychiatric use spread rapidly it followed rather than preceded the first signs of a reduction in mental hospital populations.

Scull presents a second objection to the thesis: that there is little evidence that the psychotropic drugs have been very effective in curing mental disorders. In his words there is 'a growing volume of evidence which suggests that claims about the therapeutic effectiveness of so-called "anti-psychotic" medication – mainly the phenothiazines – have been greatly exaggerated'.[6] This may be so; however, as he recognizes, they may have helped to control symptoms and so facilitated a move to management of patients in the community, instead of in the hospital. Moreover, in as far as they created a new therapeutic optimism (whether mistaken or not), they played a part in the acceptance of the policy of community care, even though its roots are to be found in earlier developments.

Scull has, however, presented us with an alternative description of the policy transition and an alternative explanation that questions the benevolent assumptions of the liberal explanation. For Scull, the key policy change is a negative one: the rejection of the asylum; he uses the term decarceration as a 'shorthand for a state-sponsored policy of closing down asylums, prisons and reformatories', a policy more commonly described as deinstitutionalization.[7] According to Scull this represents a movement away from what he calls 'an institutionally based system of segregative control'.[8] He measures the adoption of this policy by the decline in the number of resident patients in state mental hospitals in the US and the UK since the mid 1950s, a decline more substantial in the US than in the UK and one that he recognizes is far from complete in either country. The results, he contends, are, however, clear enough. There has been a run down of facilities provided for the mentally ill and an indifference to their problems that has often been far from benign:

Clearly a certain proportion of the released inmates are able to blend unobtrusively back into the communities from whence they came. After all, many of those subjected to processing by the official agencies of social control have all along been scarcely distinguishable from their neighbours who were left alone, and presumably they can be expelled from institutions without appreciable additional risk. But for many other ex-inmates and potential inmates, the alternative to the institution has been to be herded into newly emerging 'deviant ghettoes', sewers of human misery and what is conventionally defined as social pathology within which (largely hidden from outside inspection or even notice) society's refuse may be repressively tolerated. Many become lost in the interstices of social life, and turn into drifting inhabitants of those traditional resorts of the down and out, Salvation Army hostels, settlement houses, and so on. Others are grist for new, privately-run, profit-oriented mills for the disposal of the unwanted – old age homes, halfway houses, and the like. And yet more exist by preying on the less agile and wary, whether these be 'ordinary' people trapped by poverty and circumstance in the inner city, or their fellow decarcerated deviants.[9]

Scull's description of the transition is not, therefore, of a move from mental hospital care to community care but from segregation in the asylum to neglect and misery within the community. This description of the nature of the transition generates its own explanation: that the main reasons for the adoption of the new policy were economic. Decarceration was introduced because 'segregative modes of social control became, in relative terms, far more costly and difficult to justify'.[10] This meant that in the face of the rapid expansion of the state's activities in the post-war period and its consequent financial problems – the fiscal crisis of the state – policy makers were forced to adopt less costly policies.[11] For him the anti-institutional ideology of the 1950s may have facilitated decarceration but was not in itself sufficient to account for its adoption. As evidence he points to the critique of institutional care in the nineteenth century, which he asserts had little real impact. Portrayed graphically, Scull's interpretation of decarceration and its explanation is shown in Figure 4.

Scull's explanation has all the problems of the Marxist–functionalist approach he adopts which I have outlined in Chapter 4. Moreover, like

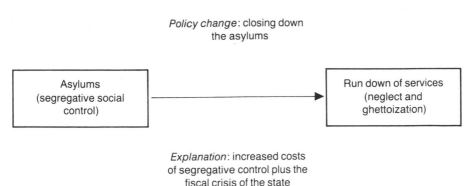

Figure 4

the liberal–scientific explanation he rejects, his own account is defective on grounds of timing. The fiscal crisis of the state to which he refers is a phenomenon of the early 1970s and later, and not of the 1950s, when, although public expenditure was increasing, rapid economic growth and greater prosperity helped to ensure that there was comparatively little anxiety about the increase.[12] In addition his explanation ignores the changes that have occurred in the pattern of mental health service expenditure during this century. In particular it ignores the development and expansion of psychiatric services outside the mental hospital, especially in the field of primary care. While, therefore, Scull is right to draw attention to the dangers attendant on a policy of community care that can hide a failure to make provision for the mentally ill under a gloss of the apparent humanity of putting people back in the communities to which they belong; and while he is right to point out that during the last two decades or more there has been a mystification and distortion of a reality of neglect and lack of resources to those discharged from mental hospitals; nevertheless he cannot account for the introduction of the policy of running down mental hospitals in the 1950s and 1960s in simple economic terms.[13] As we shall see Scull's argument fits events of the mid 1970s onwards much better than it does those of the 1950s and 1960s.

As I indicated in the previous chapter the move towards community care has been associated with a significant reorientation of services away from the chronic long-stay patients, towards those with less serious, shorter-term problems, who were formerly little catered for by public mental health services. It is not, therefore, that all mental health services have been run down under the guise of community care, rather that resources have largely gone into selected community services, those for acute, less serious mental disorders, and not into those dealing with chronic, more serious complaints. As a result aggregate expenditure on mental health services has increased, but this has largely been at the expense of those in need of some form of residential support, whether in a mental hospital or 'in the community'. Community services for the acute and milder forms of mental illness have by and large expanded over the post-war period. Community services for chronic, long-term mental illness, which have always been meagre, have not.[14] Hospital provision for them has been reduced, and little has been put in its place. The issue is not therefore of a reduced overall expenditure on the mentally ill to be accounted for by governmental reluctance to increase or maintain particular levels of public expenditure, though there is plenty of recent evidence of this in the last decade, but of the direction and form that expenditure has taken in the post-war period. Scull, in his concern to account for decarceration in economic terms fails to attend to the ideas, beliefs and objectives of those who formulate and implement policy, which have structured and mediated the economic concerns of the state. To account for the post-war pattern of expenditure we need to return to the changes that occurred in the mental health services during the 1930s.

The immediate antecedents of community care

The decades of the 1930s and 1940s were crucial to the development of mental health services in England. In the first place the policy changes introduced by the 1930 Mental Treatment Act contributed to a change in the perception of the mental hospital, especially concerning its relation to the surrounding community. Second, it was a period that witnessed an increasing therapeutic interventionism of an obviously medical character which not only began to generate a new wave of therapeutic optimism, unparalleled since the first half of the nineteenth century, but also helped to affirm the view that psychiatry could and should be a proper part of medicine. And third, the establishment of a publicly funded and centrally administered National Health Service which included the mental health services not only brought about the administrative and financial integration of the mental health services with the health services as a whole, but also broadened the range of medical services provided by the state with important consequences for mental health services in particular. The introduction of the NHS was but part of a general expansion of state-funded welfare provisions that itself affected the structures and models of service provision including those adopted in the mental health field.

In certain respects the introduction of voluntary admission in the public mental hospitals did little to change the custodial character of asylums. Despite their new designation and the voluntary status of a fair proportion of patients on admission, the hospitals continued to play a custodial role in relation to the majority of their inmates as measured by the character of the resident population. At any point in time the bulk of residents continued to be people detained on a compulsory basis; the proportion of long-stay patients showed little sign of declining; and the proportion of elderly patients continued to increase as it had done during the earlier part of the century. Some of the figures for the mid 1950s are given in Table 26. There is some evidence, too, that in the early years of the National Health Service infirm and mentally defective people, who would otherwise have been directed to social welfare homes, were increasingly sent to mental hospitals

partly because of the general shortage of accommodation and partly because of the policy of sorting out the various types of people who had previously been accepted into public assistance institutions [the old workhouses] and of providing them with more specialized forms of care.[15]

Nevertheless, although the mental hospitals continued to play a largely custodial role in relation to many of their inmates, the widespread introduction of voluntary admission, as well as the general concern to turn asylums into proper hospitals, did lead to important changes in the management of patients. In the first place the custodial

Table 26   Characteristics of residents of psychiatric beds in England and Wales in selected years

(a) Legal status of mentally ill patients resident in National Health Service hospitals and Broadmoor, excluding long-stay annexes, on 31 December 1955.

	Voluntary	*Temporary*	*Confined*	*Other*
31 Dec 1955	25.4%	0.3%	70.4%	3.9%

(b) Length of stay of patients resident in designated mental hospitals on 31 December, 1954

	Less than 1 year	*1–2 years*	*2–5 years*	*5 or more years*
31 Dec 1954	17%	7%	15%	61%

(c) Age of patients resident in designated mental hospitals in the NHS on 31 December, 1954

	0–15 yrs	*16–34 yrs*	*35–44 yrs*	*45–54 yrs*	*55–64 yrs*	*65 and over*
31 Dec 1954	0.1%	12.3%	14.7%	20.8%	21.4%	31.7%

Source: Report of the Royal Commission on the Law Relating to Mental Illness and Mental Deficiency, 1954–7. Appendix IV

trappings of the mental hospitals seemed increasingly inappropriate and some were abandoned, as part of the so-called 'open door' policies. Compulsory detention of asylum inmates had been given both concrete and symbolic force in nineteenth century asylums by the practice of locking wards: 'Nursing and medical staff were accustomed to walk the hospital to the accompaniment of jangling bunches of keys, and for a nurse to lose his or her keys was the swiftest road to dismissal' (just as allowing patients to escape had initially led to fines for the staff responsible).[16] In the 1920s, however, a few institutions began to introduce one or two open wards and systems of 'parole', allowing better behaved patients freedom of the grounds and some freedom to go into the surrounding community. Such practices were advocated not only on grounds of the desirability of giving patients more liberty but also for ease of management, the argument being that if patients no longer felt they were being locked away they often became more amenable.[17] In addition some argued that harsh and cruel treatment of patients by staff would be reduced because the institution would be open to the public. A Member of Parliament, discussing the Mental Deficiency Bill in 1927, put the case like this:

However excellent your institution may be, however carefully you may select the matrons and managers in charge, so long as you have a lock on the door, you cannot prevent suspicion of those minor cruelties, injustices and acts of arbitrary authority which may embitter the life of the inmates of these institutions. Once you have got rid of the lock, why then, your institutions, even without so much inspection, will improve, because freedom – publicity – is the cure for any inhumanity and injustice.[18]

During the 1930s and 1940s more mental hospitals began to adopt open-door policies for some of their wards, and some writers began, at the end of the 1940s to urge that the practices could be extended to the whole hospital. Dingleton Hospital at Melrose in Scotland was the first to do so in 1949, when G. M. Bell was medical superintendent.[19] By the 1950s most hospitals had some, if not the majority, of their wards without their former locks and keys, although few extended this to the whole hospital. This symbolic opening of the wards often went along with dismantling the prison-like railings around the mental hospital and attempts to eradicate the prison-like controls and constraints of daily life: permitting freedom of movement around the hospital and its grounds, allowing male and female patients to mix with one another, making the physical environment more pleasant, encouraging people to visit the hospital, and improving the arrangements for visiting.[20] Hence, not only did the open-door policies involve an attempt to make asylums more like hospitals and less like prisons, they also involved emphasizing the links between asylum and community.[21]

The innovations in therapy of the 1930s and 1940s stemmed primarily from developments within medicine, although their adoption was almost certainly encouraged by the therapeutic orientation embodied in the Mental Treatment Act and the new spirit of progress and optimism it began to generate.[22] Of especial importance in the psychiatric sphere were the new physical treatments developed at the end of the 1930s. These included new forms of the shock therapies of the eighteenth century. Insulin coma therapy, usually termed a shock therapy, was the first.[23] Insulin had been isolated in 1922 by Canadian physicians Banting and Best following developments in endocrinology, and was successfully used in the treatment of diabetics in the 1920s. In Vienna in the early 1930s Sakel used insulin to induce states from mild hypoglycaemia to deep coma in psychiatric patients and the technique was first used in Britain at the Edinburgh Royal Mental Hospital in 1936. The principle underlying the treatment is said to have been derived from Weir Mitchell's rest cure and the technique involved a daily dose of insulin (some forty to sixty comas constituting a course of treatment). The treatment was used for a variety of conditions including anorexia nervosa, the symptoms of drug withdrawal, wartime psychiatric casualties, as well as the functional psychoses such as schizophrenia and endogeneous depression. It was, however, relatively costly in terms of medical and nursing time even in its later modified (reduced) form because of the dangers associated with coma, and was abandoned in the late 1950s.

The controversial chemically, and then electrically induced convulsion therapies were also introduced in the late 1930s. The induction of convulsions using either camphor or electricity had been tried intermittently since the second half of the eighteenth century (Freud, for one, arguing that electrical treatment had little effect).[24] In 1934 a Hungarian psychiatrist, Meduna, reported the use of Cardiazol (metrazol), a soluble component of the synthetic camphor preparations, to induce convulsions, and the technique began to be adopted elsewhere.[25] It was first used in Britain in 1937, and was considered less dangerous, but more unpleasant, than insulin therapy. It was initially used for both schizophrenia and depression, although fairly early on it was held to be more effective with the latter than the former, as electro-convulsion therapy is today. Meduna based his use of chemically induced

convulsions on the idea of a biological antagonism between schizophrenia and epilepsy, which he derived from the observation of a
number of researchers that epilepsy and schizophrenia were rarely
found together – an idea that has subsequently been discredited.

Cerletti and Bini, the Italian psychiatrists who introduced a new form
of electrical treatment in 1938, applying electrodes to the head, also
accepted the idea of biological antagonism.[26] The advantages of the new
electro-convulsion therapy or ECT – which was first used in Britain the
following year – over the chemically induced convulsions were said to be
in terms of resources and convenience rather than therapeutic
effectiveness. An article published in *The Lancet* in 1939 by the physician
at a mental hospital and his colleagues asserted:

From the technical point of view there can be no doubt that the electrical
method is greatly superior to any hitherto employed for the production of
severe convulsions. For the operator only a small amount of training and
experience is necessary and a knowledge of physics, though desirable on
general grounds, is not essential. It was thought at first that the conditions
for inducing a fit in safety would be very critical, but this does not appear
to be so, and it is possible that the method may eventually be made
simpler than that described here. In any case the apparatus is comparativly
cheap and portable, and preparation of the patient need take no more than
a minute.

The psychological reaction of the patient is mild. The absence of pain
and fear may be accounted for by supposing that a great part of the brain is
instantaneously stunned by the shock, so that the pain impulses set up in
the head arrive at the thalamic centres too late to be consciously
integrated.[27]

Then, as now, its precise mode of operation was unknown, and its
effectiveness has been a matter of continual debate.[28] It has, however,
continued to be widely used by psychiatrists, especially in the treatment
of depression.[29]

Another equally controversial physical treatment developed in the
latter part of the 1930s was psychosurgery, known variously as lobotomy
or leucotomy.[30] First used in 1890, the treatment was further developed
in 1936 by a Portuguese neurologist Egaz Moniz, who used a steel cutter –
a leucoteme – to cut pre-frontal lobe fibres, following work on animals
that suggested that the destruction of these lobes reduced fear, anxiety
and obsessional behaviour. The procedure was introduced by two
surgeons (Freeman and Watts) into the United States and began to be
used in Britain in the early 1940s, the first operation occurring in Bristol

in 1941 (some 10,365 were carried out between 1942 and 1954). In the 1950s increasing concern about side effects and developments in psychopharmacology led to a decline in its use (and in some hospitals its complete abandonment). More recently modified procedures have been developed which involve less destruction of brain tissue and there has been something of a resurgence of interest.

The precise spread of these new forms of physical treatment has not been well documented. Indeed the available quantitative data on forms of treatment in English mental hospitals is poor. Some of the public mental hospitals did not use any of them until the 1940s. Napsbury Hospital, St Albans, a psychodynamically oriented hospital from the early 1950s, first used ECT in 1944, insulin therapy in 1947 and transorbital lobotomies the same year.[31] The hospital abandoned insulin therapy in 1958 and ECT was not used very frequently (unlike other hospitals). Tranquillizers were introduced to the hospital in 1956–7. Bexley Hospital in Kent introduced Cardiazol therapy as the first shock therapy in 1936–7, ECT in 1939–40, and prefrontal leucotomies in 1941–2. It did not use insulin therapy until 1948–9.[32]

Two other therapeutic developments were of some importance in the 1930s and the 1940s. The first concerned chronic patients and stemmed directly from concern about the custodial nature of mental hospitals. The end of the 1930s saw the beginnings of a renewed critique of asylums as therapeutic environments, which was to receive broader public attention during the 1950s.[33] Many of the new critics were themselves medical superintendents and mental hospital psychiatrists and though the critiques that they offered paralleled in many respects those of the nineteenth century, they gave a new emphasis to the detrimental psychological consequences of long-term stays in mental hospitals. It was not just that mental hospitals provided a regime of custody rather than treatment, but that the routine and regimentation, the environmental and social poverty of hospital life were themselves creating additional problems: they were adding insult to injury. A range of terms were used to describe the effects of long term stay on inmates: 'prison stupor', 'prison psychosis', 'psychological institutionalism', 'institutionalization', and 'institutional neurosis'. The critiques drew particular attention, therefore, to the problems of long-stay chronic patients, to the need for more active treatment programmes, and to the need for a physical and social environment with more freedom and more contact with community life. These critiques, therefore, not only encouraged the adoption of open-door policies, but they were also associated with specific therapeutic interventions designed to rehabilitate chronic patients and allow them to return to community life. Chronic patients were, for instance, given 'habit training' to encourage them to regain basic skills.[34]

These early attempts to rehabilitate patients were followed in the late 1940s and 1950s by attempts to develop 'therapeutic communities', separate units of not more than 100 patients, often within the larger hospitals.[35] In these units staff and patients were encouraged to participate in the creation of a more active therapeutic environment and attempts were made to break down the traditional hierarchy of authority between staff and patients, the latter being urged to 'become active participants in their own therapy'. Much of this work was stimulated and developed by psychiatrists called upon during the war to develop rehabilitation programmes for disabled civilians and members of the armed forces. Therapeutic community principles tended to be introduced, however, not for chronic patients, but for those with behavioural problems and neurotic complaints. The Henderson Hospital, begun as the Industrial Neurosis Unit of the Belmont Hospital, where Maxwell Jones developed his ideas about therapeutic communities, was initiated by the Ministries of Health, Labour and Pensions as a treatment unit for 'social misfits'.[36] In 1962 Maxwell Jones moved to Dingleton Hospital, Melrose in Scotland, where G. M. Bell had set up the first open-door hospital in 1949 and established a therapeutic community. Although there are certain parallels between therapeutic community principles and those of moral treatment – most obviously the importance attached to the institution as a therapeutic environment – there are also striking differences.[37] The emphasis in the former on the community as a democratic, egalitarian social organization, on permissiveness, and on the importance of meetings to talk through difficulties and tensions (a form of group psychotherapy) are among the most striking. Therapeutic communities were never, however, widely introduced. They were established in one or two places where the commitment of a particular psychiatrist overcame the opposition of nursing staff and Hospital Management Committees to the innovation.[38] And sometimes one or two wards in a hospital might have regular ward meetings with staff and patients run along therapeutic lines. But the large size of most mental hospitals and the attitudes of staff and management militated against their more general introduction.

While the therapeutic innovations of the 1930s and 1940s and their increasing use in the 1950s helped to create a climate of therapeutic optimism, the introduction of the National Health Service brought about a fuller integration of mental health services with other health services, as well as broadening the availability of a range of publicly funded medical services. The inclusion of psychiatric services in the new National Health Service was a matter of some debate. In April 1943 when discussions were under way between the Ministry of Health and the various interested parties, the Minister of Health, Ernest Brown, stated in Parliament that the mental health services would not be included in the new scheme for a National Health Service.[39] Later that year, however, after representations from the Royal Medico-Psychological Association, he agreed to include them and the White Paper of 1944 that set out the detailed proposals for the new health service did incorporate them.[40] The argument used in the White Paper and by others who advocated their inclusion followed the Macmillan Commission's claim as to the inseparable relationship between mental and physical health and the need for mental illness to be treated like physical illness.[41] Aneurin Bevan, the Minister of Health responsible for negotiating the introduction of the NHS, put the point like this: 'The separation of mental from physical treatment is a survival from primitive conceptions and is a source of endless cruelty and neglect.'[42]

From the point of view of psychiatrists, integration of mental health services with other health services was likely to tighten the links between psychiatry and the rest of medicine and improve the status of psychiatrists. As a group they were strong advocates of inclusion, although their own specific proposals on the organization of psychiatric services within a national health service did not go as far as the government's final plans. The Royal Medico-Psychological Association's report published in 1945, *The Future Organisation of the Psychiatric Services*, recommended the establishment of separate mental health authorities in each area throughout the country to co-operate with other local bodies running other parts of the health services including the local hospitals. (It envisaged continuing local rather than central control of hospitals that was introduced in the National Health Service Act.)[43] Hence, the degree of administrative and financial integration effected by the National Health Service was greater than the psychiatrists anticipated.

The tripartite organizational structure established for the NHS of hospital, general practitioner, and local authority services, put the mental hospitals under the control of Regional Hospital Boards, each with their own university medical school.[44] 'This brought the practice and the teaching of psychiatry closer together, and enabled the mental hospitals, which generally existed in geographical and professional isolation, to form closer contacts with the teaching facilities of the Region.'[45] The Hospital Management Committees that directly administered small groups of hospitals or a single large hospital could group mental hospitals with one or two other hospitals or administer them separately, but even when the latter occurred there was still integration at the regional level for hospitals in a particular area.[46] However, health and welfare services outside the hospital, other than general practitioner services, were not only under a separate administrative structure but were also, unlike the other two sectors of the health services, to be funded locally and not through the overall system of National Health Service finance. As a result the forms of mental health service for which they were responsible – residential homes, half-way houses, social work support (mainly services concerned with after care) – were at a disadvantage since they had to compete with many other calls on local authority money.[47]

Attempts to remedy the administrative and planning difficulties created by the tripartite organization of the NHS through reorganization in 1974 and then again in 1982 have not solved this particular problem, although some services formerly funded by local authorities are now funded through the NHS, and there have also been efforts in the joint funding of projects by NHS and local authorities.[48] The organization of the NHS both in its original and in its modified forms has, therefore, created particular problems about the financing of certain types of service, especially those provided outside the hospital. None the less, the introduction of the NHS by virtue both of the fuller integration of mental health services into the overall health services of the country and the provision of medical services offering primary, hospital and after care to a far broader range of people has had an important impact on the mental health services of the country. In particular it facilitated the move towards community care since it provided a broader range of alternatives to in-patient care.

The policy of community care

The first official use of the term community care apparently came in the 1930 Annual Report of the Board of Control when it was used to refer to a policy then being put forward, of making provision for the mentally handicapped to live outside hospitals wherever possible.[49] This policy paralleled that advocated by a number of nineteenth-century critics of asylums of making provision through the poor law system for chronic and incurable cases by boarding them out with friends or relatives under supervision. The National Association for the Promotion of Social Science had pointed to the advantages of such policies when discussing the treatment of pauper lunatics in 1869:

Now . . . the question may properly be asked, whether . . . we cannot recur, in some degree, to the system of home care and home treatment; whether, in fact, the same care, interest, and money which are now employed upon the inmates of our lunatic asylums, might not produce even more successful and beneficial results if made to support the efforts of parents and relations in their humble dwelling . . . . If only one-twentieth of inmates of our asylums could by any machinery whatever, be restored to their relations, we should have strengthened the bonds of family affection and enlarged the sphere of individual liberty. Moreover, such a mode of treatment would form a fitting extension of the non-restraint system.[50]

Underlying these suggestions was the concern for the swelling numbers of asylum patients and the way in which chronic and incurable cases blocked up the asylums and stopped them from being real hospitals. However, in the second half of the nineteenth century the asylum was still the preferred locus of therapeutic intervention; care outside the hospital was to be a supplement to the asylum, freeing it for its proper role, not providing an alternative to it.

The policy of community care that developed in the twentieth century not only sought to free the hospital for its proper therapeutic purposes but no longer viewed the hospital as the ideal locus of treatment: the community was to be the place where treatment should take place wherever possible. The Report of the 1954–7 Royal Commission on the Law relating to Mental Illness and Mental Deficiency (the Percy Report) marks the turning point in official policy concerning mental health services from a hospital to a community-based system of care and therapy.[51] The commission had been appointed in October 1953 'to inquire . . . into the existing law and administrative machinery governing the certification, detention, care (other than hospital care or treatment under the National Health Service Acts, 1946–52) . . .' of the mentally ill.[52] It had, therefore, a dual brief. First to examine the law relating to certification and compulsory detention of the mentally ill, with a view to considering 'the extent to which it is now, or should be made, statutorily possible for such persons, to be treated, as voluntary patients, without certification'; and second, to examine the administrative machinery governing the provision of services outside NHS hospitals.[53] This second objective arose from the problems that had been created for the planning of mental health services on a local basis by the introduction of the NHS and the inclusion of mental health services within it. Indeed it seems to have been the inclusion of mental health services within the NHS that occasioned the establishment of the commission, since it not only highlighted the contrasting legal status and position of patients in hospitals under the same regional administration, but also generated new problems about the co-ordination and funding of services at the local level.[54]

The commission, which first met in 1954, was under the chairmanship of Lord Percy who had served for a short period on the 1924–6 Royal Commission.[55] It was composed of eleven members, one of whom was a woman. The balance of the new commission was more strongly medical than the earlier one. It included four medical men: a neurologist, Sir Russell Brain, then President of the Royal College of Physicians; T. P. Rees, a psychiatrist, President of the Royal Medico-Psychological Association in 1956–7; and two other doctors. In addition, a male nurse, who was President of the Confederation of Health Service Employees, and a lay member of the Central Health Services Council were members. Of the remaining five, two were from the legal profession. The commission's report, published in 1957, extended and developed the arguments of the earlier commission that a mentally disordered person should be treated where possible like a person with a physical illness. Its starting point was not, however, an assertion of the close interconnection of mental and physical illness, but the related claim that mental disorder was an illness and should be treated as such: 'Disorders of the mind are illnesses which need medical treatment.'[56] An assertion of identity replaced that of interconnection.

The recommendations concerning the use of legal procedures followed from this assertion of the proper identity of mental disorder as an illness. The 1930 Mental Treatment Act had moved in the direction of treating the mentally ill on comparable terms to the physically ill by introducing the possibility of voluntary admission. But the act still required that those with mental disorder should 'be well enough to sign an application form expressing a positive wish to receive treatment'.[57] Such a formality was not required of the physically ill. The Percy Report urged, therefore, that

the law should be altered so that whenever possible suitable care may be provided for mentally disordered patients with no more restriction of liberty or legal formality than is applied to people who need care because of other types of illness, disability or social difficulty.[58]

The commission did not believe that compulsory powers could be entirely abandoned, but felt they should be used 'only when they are positively necessary to override the patient's own unwillingness or the unwillingness of his relatives, for the patient's own welfare or for the protection of others'.[59] They recommended, however, that the term 'certification' should no longer be used in connection with any legal procedures; instead the report spoke of 'formal' and 'informal' admission.[60]

Although the requirement for compulsion in certain cases prevented the complete assimilation of the procedures governing admission and discharge of the mentally ill to those of the physically ill, both the definition of mental illness and the necessity for formal admission were to be matters for medical judgement alone.[61] The report argued that the supposed safeguard of the magistrate's order in cases involving compulsory detention, retained in the 1930 Act, was of little value: 'Stronger safeguards would be provided by requiring more than one medical opinion, by extending the powers of discharge and by providing new opportunities for review by a strong independent body consisting of both medical and non-medical members.'[62] Matters concerning the admission and discharge of the mentally ill, both on a formal and informal basis, were to be placed squarely in the hands of the medical profession, with new tribunals to protect the patient's interests where compulsion was involved.[63]

The commission's assertions about community care likewise followed from the commitment to treating mental illness as an illness. Mental illness was seen as a broad category covering 'a much wider range of forms and degrees of mental disorder than the term of "unsound mind" (which it was to replace), and the appropriate form of treatment must be correspondingly diverse'.[64] As with sickness generally, in-patient treatment might not be necessary. 'The majority of mentally ill patients . . . do not need to be admitted to hospital as in-patients. Patients may receive medical treatment from general practitioners or as hospital out-patients and other care from community health and welfare services.'[65] Such treatment outside the hospital was embraced under the loose term community care, a term which was not given any precise definition in the report but was used to refer to services and benefits provided by the state for the mentally ill, whether specific to them or not, which did not involve in-patient admission.

But the report did not stop at pointing to the availability and appropriateness of forms of public provision for the mentally ill outside the hospital: it argued for a change of emphasis; community care was now preferable to hospital care:

The recommendations of our witnesses were generally in favour of a shift of emphasis from hospital care to community care. In relation to almost all forms of mental disorder, there is increasing medical emphasis on forms of treatment and training and social services which can be given without bringing patients into hospital as in-patients, or which make it possible to discharge them from hospital sooner than was usual in the past.[66]

The hospital (asylum) was no longer the ideal locus of care, and if admission were necessary, the patient should be discharged as soon as possible. In part this was a reiteration of the old argument of ensuring that hospitals should be used for their proper therapeutic purposes and not end up merely providing a home for those with no suitable place to live: 'Patients should not be retained as hospital in-patients when they have reached the stage at which they could return home if they had reasonably good homes to go to.'[67] Local authorities should, therefore, take on the responsibility of providing residential accommodation for elderly mentally ill or infirm patients 'who need to be provided with a home and some help and advice but do not need psychiatric training or nursing care in hospital', as well as for others recovering from mental illness.[68] More importantly, however, the emphasis on community care involved a new model of therapeutic provision for the mentally ill in which the institution no longer had pre-eminence as the best place for the treatment. The new model of care aimed to provide services for every stage of the illness, and for prevention as well as cure: primary care facilities, acute hospital beds, hospital beds for chronic patients who still needed medical or psychiatric care, residential hostels, half-way houses, day hospitals, social work support as well as the health and welfare services more generally. This model of care contrasts very markedly with the model that underlay the establishment of the nineteenth-century asylums. It is not simply that the old asylum was now to be supplemented by a diverse range of public services that did not involve in-patient admission, but that the asylum was no longer considered the ideal therapeutic environment. Integration into the community rather than separation from it had become the new ideal. How do we account for such a change in the model of care between the nineteenth and twentieth centuries? Why did the nineteenth-century view of the therapeutic asylum no longer seem appropriate? Why were institutions no longer to be given the same pre-eminence?

The changing models of care

Underlying the change in the model of care were a number of important factors. First, were changes in the content of therapeutic ideas about the causes and treatment of mental disorders. The nineteenth-century model of care with its emphasis on the asylum was sustained and supported not only by the institutional bias of the poor law system but also by the principles and practices of moral treatment. The advocates of moral treatment emphasized the advantages of movement into a separate, segregated asylum as a retreat from the pressures of ordinary life and as a place that could be ordered and regulated in a way that would have positive therapeutic benefit. In the twentieth century professionals concerned with the treatment of mental disorder – mainly medical practitioners – have generally operated with theories and therapies that focus on the inner workings of the individual – whether physical or psychological – and have paid little attention to the social environment in which the individual is located. (The obvious exception are those who espouse the principles of the therapeutic community.) Hence the positive therapeutic value attached to the institution and its social organization has largely disappeared. This is not to say that the belief has entirely vanished that the pressures of normal everyday situations may precipitate, exacerbate, or even cause mental disorder, but the focus on physical aetiologies has directed attention away from such social processes. Moreover, even when there is an emphasis on the social aetiology of illness, removing the individual from environmental pressures is no longer seen as necessarily the best remedy. For instance, the focus on the pathological nature of family interactions and their role in the genesis of mental illness in the late 1950s was more often associated with demands for family therapy than with demands that the individual should be removed from the family.[69] In sum the redirection of therapeutic activity away from moral treatment, which gave positive value to the social order of the asylum, towards psychological and physical methods of treatment, which focus on the individual, has led to a reconceptualization of asylum care which has facilitated the shift to community care. This reconceptualization was enhanced by the increasingly vocal critique of mental hospitals that became especially forceful at the end of the 1950s.[70]

Second, there is the matter of the state's provision of a broader range of medical and social services outside the asylums and the hospitals. Here it is not so much, as Scull suggests, that the movement away from segregative patterns of care is encouraged by the provision of welfare services in the form of direct payments to dependents – the elderly, sick and unemployed – thereby making institutional provision seem increasingly costly (it could be argued that such benefits in fact lessen the cost since the alternative is no longer institutional care or nothing but institutional care versus 'outdoor' relief), as that the value attached to institutions for purposes of policing the poor has declined and the provision of state medical and social work services has made institutional care seem less necessary and less appropriate.[71] General practitioners can, at least in theory, monitor medical progress; psychiatrists can provide specialist help in out-patient clinics; social workers can help to ameliorate family and social pressures; health visitors and peripatetic nurses can provide nursing care and advice; and social security benefits can provide a material and physical environment that is not itself negative to health. As a result what was only available within the institution is now available outside it and institutional care has come to seem increasingly redundant. Consequently the Liberal reforms of 1906–14, the expansion of health and welfare provisions during the inter-war years, and the Beveridge Reforms of 1944–8 have all helped to change the perception of the place and value of the asylum and the hospital in the pattern of medical care.[72] The institutional bias of the whole system of public welfare has been undermined.

Third, there is the long-standing desire of certain elite members of the medical profession to transform psychiatry into a proper specialism of medicine whose practice would be fully consonant with medical values. This had been one motive underlying the introduction of voluntary admission as well as the inclusion of mental health services into the National Health Service. It has also underlain medical support for the reorientation of psychiatry towards community care. Psychiatry had suffered, both within and outside the medical profession, from its identification with the custodial work of asylums, from its association with patients of low status, whose chronic complaints required little medical intervention, and from its institutional separation from other medical services and from the community. Community care, with out-patient clinics attached to general hospitals and psychiatric units in them, meant greater integration with the rest of medicine and more opportunities for work with acute patients of higher social standing. Hence, although particular psychiatrists might oppose the reorientation to community care, for the psychiatric profession as a whole the new model of care offered obvious professional advantages.[73]

Fourth, and finally, the formulation and broad acceptance of the policy of community care was based on the new therapeutic optimism of the 1940s and 1950s.[74] This optimism, heightened though not initiated by the introduction of psychotropic drugs, stemmed from a number of sources: from the therapeutic developments of the period; from the increasing numbers of voluntary patients and those with less severe complaints using the mental hospitals; from the administrative reorganization of the services; and from the general climate of optimism of the period associated with post-war recovery and economic growth. New treatments not only encouraged a belief that those who did have to be admitted to mental hospital could be more readily discharged, markedly improved, to the community, but also that in many cases in-patient admission might not be necessary at all.

In sum we can offer an alternative description of the policy change termed deinstitutionalization, and an alternative explanation of it. It views the key policy change as the adoption of a new model of care for the mentally disordered, with services designed to cover all stages of the patient career and the full range of disorders, acute and chronic, severe and mild. This policy is in direct line of descent from the desire of medical reformers in the second half of the nineteenth century to encourage the early treatment of mental illness, and to transform the asylum into a mental hospital. A number of factors contributed to the adoption of this new model of care. First, the emergence of new medical ideas about the causes and treatment of mental illness undermined the support for and commitment to institutions as the desirable locus of care explicit in earlier environmentalist thinking about insanity. Second, the development of a broader range of state-funded services and benefits not only eliminated the institutional bias of the welfare system, but also increasingly made institutional care seem neither necessary nor appropriate. Third, the new model of care offered opportunities to

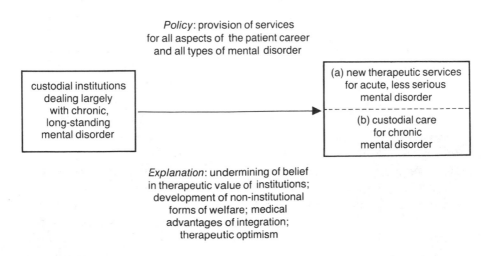

Figure 5

psychiatrists for a fuller integration of their specialism with the rest of medicine and a close approximation of their practice to that of the parent discipline. Fourth, the therapeutic optimism generated by the therapeutic innovations of the 1930s, 1940s and 1950s made shorter stays in hospital and adequate out-patient care seem a practical proposition. The alternative description and explanation is set out in Figure 5. I shall consider the implementation of the policy and its consequences in the following section.

Community care redefined

The clear commitment of the Percy Commission to the policy of community care was not matched by the legislative provisions of the Mental Health Act of 1959 that followed. The Percy Commission had made a number of practical suggestions designed to facilitate the shift in the balance of services from the hospital to the community, such as the awarding of special grants to local authorities to cover the necessary capital expenditure for new services.[75] The Mental Health Act, passed by the Conservative government when Derek Walker-Smith was Minister of Health, neither made the provision of local authority services mandatory nor made financial provision for additional capital expenditure. Kathleen Jones comments that the local authorities 'could do a great deal; but they were actually required to do very little'.[76] Instead the act was largely directed to giving legislative effect to the Royal Commission's proposals concerning the legal procedures governing admission and discharge, including the establishment of Mental Health Review Tribunals to which appeals against continued detention could be brought (albeit only for certain categories of compulsory detention).[77] The main sections of the act dealt respectively with admission for observation and assessment for up to twenty-eight days (Section 25); for treatment initially for up to one year (Section 26); and in cases of emergency for up to seventy-two hours (Section 29).[78] Affirmation of the policy of extending community services came not in the Mental Health Act itself but in a circular from the Ministry of Health to all local authorities in May 1959 which drew attention to the Royal Commission's recommendation for a reorientation towards community services.[79]

The lack of legislative teeth to back up the new community care policy was, however, no immediate obstacle to hospital administrators, medical superintendents and mental hospital doctors who wished to commence, continue or strengthen a policy of ensuring more rapid discharge of patients recently admitted to mental hospitals and the rehabilitation and discharge of those who had been in the institution many years. As a result, the total number of residents of psychiatric beds continued to decline from their high point in 1954 of some 148,000 in England and Wales, as Table 22 above showed. Indeed, despite some warning comments about the policy of community care, a distinct policy of running down the old mental hospitals and even of closing them down altogether began to emerge.[80] This is the policy that Scull terms decarceration, and in many respects it was the logical outcome of the new model of community care and the optimism surrounding it: for if the community services were expanded, if there was ample provision for the transition between mental hospital and ordinary life, if the mental hospitals themselves no longer encouraged dependency, and were able to rehabilitate old long-stay patients, then there might be little need in the long run for the mental hospitals.[81] All that would be needed would be some psychiatric beds for the acutely sick requiring short-term hospitalization. These could be attached to general hospitals, as some had already advocated, with the added advantage of further integrating psychiatric services with general health services and so reducing the stigma of mental illness.[82]

Consequently, from the early 1960s plans were put forward for reducing the total number of psychiatric beds and even of phasing out mental hospitals altogether, initially on the basis of statistical projections of the decline already occurring in the resident psychiatric population. In 1961, for instance, statisticians at the General Register Office projected a future need of some 0.9 beds per 1000 population for psychiatric patients staying less than two years, and the same number again for long-stay patients (in comparison to the 1954 figure of 3.4 per 1000 which in 1960 was lowered to 3.1 per 1000).[83] They also suggested on the basis of their projections that none of the patients then in hospital would, if present trends continued, still be there in sixteen years.[84] Enoch Powell, then Minister of Health in the Conservative government, transformed projections into policy when he announced to MIND's annual conference the same year that the old mental hospitals 'isolated, majestic, imperious, brooded over by the gigantic watertower and chimney combined, rising unmistakable and daunting out of the countryside' should be run down over the next fifteen years, and that people requiring in-patient treatment should be looked after in units in local hospitals where they would remain more closely in touch with their own community.[85]

Sir Keith Joseph, Minister of Health in the 1970 Conservative administration, reaffirmed the policy of running down the old mental hospitals. His 1971 Memorandum, *Hospital Services for the Mentally Ill*, argued that the eventual level of psychiatric beds could be even lower than that suggested in 1962.[86] But he added a more cautious note: 'the Department is trying to do something in itself difficult'.[87] The problems were two-fold. On the one hand a number of studies had begun to indicate that expectations about eliminating chronic mental illness were over-optimistic and had identified a group of 'new' long-stay patients.[88] On the other hand the adequacy of some of the community services, especially those designed to facilitate rehabilitation by providing supportive residential accommodation, was being called into question, and the absence of mandatory powers in the mental health legislation to establish local authority community services was becoming more apparent.[89] The lack of investment in residential accommodation outside the hospitals was both organizational and financial in origin (savings on mental hospital beds could not be readily directed to community services, given the separate organizational and financial structures of the hospital and community services).[90] The needs of mental patients in the community had to compete with education and housing and other social services for local authority budgets. And in the early 1970s the financial pressures on local authorities began to increase with the government's attempts to control public expenditure.[91] In 1973, after two rounds of cuts in expenditure on health and welfare services, the prospects of closing down mental hospitals and expanding publicly funded community services seemed more remote.[92]

The 1975 White Paper, *Better Services for the Mentally Ill*, issued when Barbara Castle was Secretary of State for Social Services in the Labour government, reflected this sense of caution even more strongly and pointed to the limitations of what had been achieved:

although it is sixteen years since the Mental Health Act of 1959 gave legislative recognition to the importance of community care, supportive facilities in a non-medical, non-hospital setting are still a comparative rarity. In 1973–4 nearly £300 million was spent on hospital services for the mentally ill; by comparison just over £15 million was spent on personal social services of which some £6.5 million was on day and residential facilities. In March 1974, 31 local authorities, as then constituted, had no residential accommodation for the mentally ill, and 63 no day facilities.[93]

And it was pessimistic about the future: 'It is clear that the scope for making progress during the next few years will be very limited' because of the 'present state of financial stringency'.[94] Significantly, moreover, it recognized that in the meantime there was already anxiety that mental hospitals would be run down while little was done to replace them, and asserted that its objective was not to close down mental hospitals until community facilities had been provided.[95]

Concern about the lack of resources going to services for the mentally ill (as well as to services for the mentally handicapped, the elderly and children) was also expressed in the Department of Health and Social Security's consultative document, *Priorities for Health and Social Services in England*, published the following year, 1976.[96] The document held services for the mentally ill to be a major priority and again pointed to deficiencies in existing provision, especially in the area of community services:

The most serious deficiencies in existing services for the mentally ill are in the local authority social services, where in 1974 there were fewer than 4,000 residential places, and only just over 5,000 day places, against an estimated national requirement of 12,000 and 30,000 respectively.[97]

And it went on to point to the need for capital expenditure if adequate community services were to be provided:

Even with the prospect of a sharp reduction overall in local authority capital schemes, it is essential that capital expenditure for mental illness should be increased, not only as a proportion of the total but in absolute terms, if there is to be any real progress either in meeting existing urgent needs or in developing the new pattern of services.[98]

It, too, was aware of concern about premature mental hospital closure and reiterated that mental hospitals would not be closed down unless alternatives had been provided

The possibility of closing a hospital depends both on the existence of the necessary range of health and local authority facilities and on the length of time for which care must be provided for the hospital's remaining long-stay patients.[99]

It is evident from both these documents that financial restrictions up to the mid 1970s proved a very real obstacle to the move towards community care that the Percy Commission had advocated. They were not, *contra* Scull's analysis in *Decarceration*, its major cause. This is because the notion of community care with which the authors of the Priorities document, like the Percy Commission, operate is one that treats the provision of publicly funded community services, such as day hospitals and after-care residential units, as well as general practitioner services, home help, social security benefits and so forth, as the *sine qua non* of community care. Scull, however, points to the possibility of using the term community care as a gloss for a reduction in hospital services without any compensating expansion in community services – a fear that those working in the field had already expressed. He points, indeed, to the dangers of the way in which the term community care can mean simply care in the community, whatever happens to publicly funded community services. It can mean private care not public care; care by private individuals (usually family members and usually women) in the home, or in the private health and residential care market.[100] It is this care which offers the cheap alternative to the public mental hospital for any government bent on cutting public expenditure. And in as far as this private care can be presented, as it often is, as care within the family then it can be made to seem therapeutically advantageous as well as desirable, and standard institutional critiques can be used to support it, just as they can the provision of public community services.[101]

And there is evidence that from the mid 1970s onwards the demands to cut public expenditure and the ideological reorientation of the state's attitudes to welfare have increasingly meant that the notion of community care has been reinterpreted from its meaning at the time of the Percy Commission and earlier as the development of public community services to that of private care in the community. The emotional and social support that can be provided by private individuals in the community is held to be all important, and the long-standing recognition of the need for public community services – care by the community – is forgotten. A privatized model of care replaces that of public community services. And as a result financial constraints hasten rather than delay the move to community care.

Certainly recent government and other official pronouncements point to a new emphasis attached to care within and by the family, and in the private sector – voluntary or commercial – rather than through public services. The 1979 Report of the Royal Commission on the National Health Service, when discussing community care, made it clear that community care meant largely private care in the community; public services were to provide back-up support and were not the essence of community care: 'Community care is provided primarily by families or neighbours, with the support of the health and personal social services.'[102] No such assertion is to be found in the Percy Report.[103] The NHS Commission did, however, recognize the need for further expansion of public community services but suggested that care in the community might well be cheaper, thereby encouraging a belief that costs could and should be cut in the move to community care and, indeed, suggesting that the very purpose of introducing community care is to cut costs.[104] The 1981 consultative document, *Care in the Community*, issued by the Department of Health and Social Security concerned itself with those requiring long-term care (those most in need of support services).[105] It suggested that local authorities should look to the private and voluntary sector to provide such services, asserting that 'Progress depends on making better use of what is already available, including the important contribution of the voluntary and private sectors.'[106] And it, too, pointed to the financial savings that might be achieved:

Although the cost to the community health and personal social services of providing care for people transferred from hospital is difficult to assess, there are good reasons for believing that in many cases it would both be lower and better value.[107]

Such claims depend of course on ignoring the private costs, emotional, financial and physical, to those women and men who provide private care (if such care is available).[108]

But the ideological and financial retrenchment of the past decade from publicly funded community services, like the services themselves, have not occurred evenly. It is the services for those with chronic long-term complaints, including the elderly, which have never been properly developed and are most under attack – day hospitals, residential homes, home helps, district nursing and so forth.[109] In contrast, services for those with acute, less severe problems are less threatened by ideological and financial pressures. General practitioner services (whose spending, alone in the NHS, is at present not directly controlled), and out-patient services, which have expanded in the post-war period, have survived relatively unscathed, as have the psychiatric units in general hospitals.[110] The result has been, therefore, the development of a two-tier stratified mental health service. The Report of the Royal Commission on the National Health Service made the point in connection with the development of psychiatric units in district general hospitals:

the creation of these units, dealing mainly with the acute and more easily treatable problems, has led to what amounts in many places to a two-tier service, a first-rate service for the acutely ill and a second-rate service for the remainder; and to much resentment in the mental hospitals.[111]

But the division is wider than this, and it reflects broader divisions within society. The upper tier, largely located outside the mental hospitals, which deals with the acute, less serious problems, consists not only of the psychiatric units in general hospitals, but also of the out-patient clinics, general practitioner primary care services, as well as short-stay units at mental hospitals. The patients in this sector are a largely new population as far as public mental health services are concerned, with a higher proportion of younger adults, women and the middle classes than those dealt with formerly by state funded mental health services.[112] There is then a lower tier made up of the bulk of wards in the old mental hospitals and the special geriatric hospitals where the chronic, more intractable problems are to be found. Here the patients are more likely to be old, male and working class, and the proportion of elderly patients in all psychiatric beds has now reached the high figure of over 50 per cent.[113]

The recent amendment of the Mental Health Act – an Amendment Act was passed in 1982 and a consolidated act passed in 1983 – does little to redress this balance.[114] Much of the new legislation is concerned with the legal safeguards surrounding compulsory detention in response to evidence of misuses and abuses of various sections of the 1959 Act. In addition, some attention is paid to the rights of detained patients in hospital to refuse treatment, and to the voting rights of informal patients. But the act does not require either local authorities or the NHS to make any improvements in services, nor does it make any alterations in the financial provisions that might facilitate such improvements: 'Throughout there is a clear sense that anything with cost implications has been carefully avoided.'[115] Hence while the act can be seen as introducing certain small limits on medical powers in relation to formal patients, it does not address itself to the character or limitations of existing services.

Sedgwick, in his book *Psycho Politics*, identifies a strong civil–libertarian interest underlying the pressure for reform of mental health legislation during the 1960s and 1970s which helped to determine the character of this recent legislation.[116] The civil–libertarian ethic, he suggests, views a legalistic framework that secures patients' rights as a means of controlling and limiting medical power. Yet the ethic, though it has a long ancestry and an essential role,

has the crucial defect of being unable to focus therapeutic policy on any question other than the misuse of medical power. Consequently, civil libertarians find themselves cast in the role of a permanent reforming opposition to the main structures of authority and decision in psychiatry. Because their voice is essentially reactive, they depend on medical practitioners to initiate and conduct treatment before they themselves can appear in the next phase of the cycle as protestors and resisters.[117]

The ethic, consequently 'blocks the formulation of fresh demands and programmes'.[118] It ignores, for instance, the marked inequalities in the provision and standard of mental health services. And, by implication, it permits governments to pass legislation with precisely the same deficiencies.

To point to inequalities, and the consequent uneven burdens for private individuals in terms of class and gender, as well as to the failure to develop publicly funded community services along the lines envisaged by the Percy Commission, is not to assert that the funnelling of more public resources into community mental health services is necessarily the best way of dealing with the problem of the mentally ill.[119] To do so would be to accept the liberal–scientific view of psychiatric activity, in which the major problems of existing services are the lack of resources, such as buildings, qualified staff and so forth, and the failure of governments to follow medically formulated policies. Rather it is to point to the way in which mental health services continue to be structured not by social needs but by the social and political power (or rather lack of it) of patients and their families, by the interests of the medical profession, and by the reluctance of the state to finance expansions in welfare services. In the move towards community care the medical interest in divesting itself of its custodial (caring) role in favour of therapeutic (medical) intervention combined with the powerlessness of those with long-term needs, the chronic, elderly and persons of low status, has made such patients an easy target for public expenditure cuts. That such needs may themselves originate from the social conditions in which many people live, and are not necessarily best met under medical supervision in a hospital context does not invalidate the argument. In the following chapter I shall consider some of the alternatives to medical intervention.

Notes and references

1 See for instance Jones, 1960, p. 166. Scull (1977, Chapters 5 and 6) discusses such explanations in some detail.
2 Barton, 1959; Goffman, 1968; Wing, 1962.
3 Scull, 1977, Chapters 5 and 6.
4 ibid., p. 82.
5 Chain, 1963, p. 444; Ayo and Blackwell, 1970.
6 Scull, 1977, p. 86.
7 ibid., p. 1.

8   ibid., p. 64.

9   ibid., pp. 152–3.

10   ibid., p. 135.

11   O'Connor defines a fiscal crisis as the 'tendency for government expenditures to outrace revenues' (1973, p. 2).

12   ibid., p. 41.

13   Sedgwick makes a similar point in his *Psycho Politics* (1982, pp. 200–205).

14   See p. 351 below; see also MIND, 1974. Sedgwick attacks the 1960s critics of psychiatry for their 'almost unanimous abdication from the task of proposing and securing any provision for a humane and continuous form of care for those mental patients who need something rather more than short-term therapy for an acute phase of their illness' (1982, p. 213).

15   Royal Commission on the Law relating to Mental Illness and Mental Deficiency, 1957, p. 205.

16   Jones, 1960, p. 128.

17   ibid., p. 128.

18   ibid., p. 79.

19   Bell, 1955; see also the Mental Hospital Reports in *The Lancet* of the 1920s and 1930s.

20   ibid.

21   ibid.

22   The wide-ranging developments in drug therapies during the 1930s and 1940s are outlined by Chain, 1963.

23   Strecker, 1937; Wilson, 1936.

24   Freud, 1935, pp. 26–7.

25   Strecker, 1937; Wilson, 1936.

26   Fleming *et al.*, 1939; see also Clare, 1976, Chapter 6.

27   Fleming *et al.*, 1939, pp. 1354–5.

28   Clare, 1976, pp. 250–62.

29   ibid., p. 241.

30   ibid., Chapter 7.

31   Bott, 1976.

32   Norton, 1963.

33   Myerson, 1939; see also Bettelheim and Sylvester, 1948.

34   Myerson, 1939; Bennett and Robertson, 1955.

35   Main, 1946; Jones, 1952.

36   Maxwell Jones briefly details his career in the introduction to *Social Psychiatry in Practice*, 1968.

37   T. P. Rees delivering the Presidential Address to the Royal Medico-Psychological Association (now the Royal College of Psychiatrists) in 1956 argued that occupational therapy, recreational therapy and socio-therapy (i.e. the treatments provided by all members of a therapeutic

community – see Jones, 1968, pp. 98–102) are the modern equivalents
of moral treatment (1957, p. 309).

38 Again, unfortunately, the timing of their introduction and the pattern
and extent of their use have not been well documented.
39 Jones, 1960, p. 148.
40 Ministry of Health, 1944.
41 Jones, 1960, p. 148.
42 Foot, 1975, p. 137.
43 Royal Medico-Psychological Association, 1945. The Memorandum
asserted that 'the argument for treating psychiatry in all essential
respects like other branches of medicine' was 'strong and conclusive.
There is everything to be said for making the administrative structure
of psychiatry exactly the same in principle and even in major detail as
that of other branches of medicine.' (Quoted in Hoenig and
Hamilton, 1969, p. 6.)
44 See Levitt, 1976, pp. 17–19.
45 Jones, 1960, p. 151.
46 ibid.
47 See, for instance, the comments made by MIND, 1974, p. 9 and p.
20.
48 On the 1974 reorganization see Levitt, 1976. Joint funding is
discussed in the Department of Health and Social Security's *Care in the
Community*, (1981, pp. 5–7).
49 This claim is made by Hunter and MacAlpine (1974, p. 67). Titmuss
(1963, p. 221) said that he had been unable to find the exact origins
of the term.
50 Quoted in Hunter and MacAlpine, 1974, p. 66.
51 Royal Commission, 1957.
52 ibid., p. 1.
53 ibid., p. 1.
54 The Minister of Health announcing the membership of the
Commission spoke of 'the out of date and unsatisfactory state of the
law' (Jones, 1960, p. 179).
55 The composition of the committee is detailed by Jones (ibid., p. 183).
56 Royal Commission, 1957, pp. 3–4.
57 *Mental Treatment Act*, 1930.
58 Royal Commission, 1957, pp. 3–4.
59 ibid., p. 4.
60 ibid., p. 133.
61 See the Introduction to Gostin (1975) for some comments about the
powers the Mental Health Act of 1959 gave to the medical profession.
See also Bean, 1980, p. 27.
62 Royal Commission, 1957, pp. 11–12.
63 ibid., pp. 148–53.

64   ibid., p. 5.
65   ibid., p. 5.
66   ibid., p. 207.
67   ibid., p. 207.
68   ibid., p. 211.
69   Much of the work was concerned with schizophrenia and is summarised by Mishler and Waxler, 1968. On family therapy see Poster, 1978, Chapter 5, and Walrond-Skinner, 1981.
70   Barton, 1959; Goffman, 1968; Martin, 1955.
71   Scull, 1977, p. 135. See also Sedgwick, 1982, pp. 203 and 205.
72   Fraser, 1984; Thane, 1982.
73   Psychiatrists complained in particular about their isolation from the rest of medicine; see the *Lancet*, 11 December 1943, p. 745.
74   For a contemporary flavour of that optimism, see the comments in Tooth and Brooke, 1961, p. 710. See also Bennett and Morris, 1983, p. 7; and Gostin, 1975, p. 6.
75   Royal Commission, 1957, pp. 242–5.
76   Jones, 1960, p. 188.
77   A study of the operation of Mental Health Review Tribunals in their early years was carried out by Greenland (1970); see also Gostin, 1975, Part II. The Mental Health Act 1983 has broadened the range of cases that can be brought to tribunals (Gostin, 1982, p. 1131).
78   The Mental Health Act, 1959.
79   Jones, 1960, p. 191.
80   ibid., pp. 188–90.
81   See pp. 335–6 above.
82   The Memorandum issued with the Mental Health Act of 1959 expressed the hope that there would be a substantial increase in psychiatric facilities in general hospitals (Brook and Stafford Clark, 1963, p. 111). The history and role of psychiatric units in general hospitals is examined by Hoenig and Hamilton, 1969.
83   Tooth and Brooke, 1961; see also Baker, 1961.
84   They would, however, be replaced by new long-stay patients (Tooth and Brooke, 1961, p. 713).
85   Quoted in MIND, 1974, p. 1.
86   Department of Health and Social Services, 1971.
87   ibid., p. 1, quoted in MIND, 1974.
88   Magnus, 1967; Measey and Smith, 1973.
89   MIND, 1973.
90   MIND, 1974, p. 17.
91   Fraser, 1984, Postscript.
92   MIND, 1974, p. 1, and pp. 21–3.
93   Department of Health and Social Security, 1975, p. ii.
94   ibid., p. iii.

95 ibid., pp. 83–4.
96 Department of Health and Social Security, 1976a.
97 ibid., p. 57.
98 ibid., p. 57.
99 ibid., p. 55.
100 Finch and Groves, 1983; Equal Opportunities Commission, 1982; Land, 1978.
101 Barton, 1959; Goffman, 1968; Wing, 1962.
102 Royal Commission, 1979, p. 58. The Department of Health and Social Security's paper *A Happier Old Age*, asserted that community care 'envisages the use of family resources, volunteers, and informal effort whenever possible rather than the expansion of domiciliary services' (1978a, p. 3).
103 Royal Commission, 1957.
104 Royal Commission, 1979, pp. 58–9.
105 Department of Health and Social Security, 1981.
106 ibid., pp. 1–2.
107 ibid., p. 3.
108 Finch and Groves, 1983.
109 Department of Health and Social Security, 1976, pp. 57–8.
110 General practitioners are independent contractors within the NHS and there are, as a result, fewer financial controls over their activities than over the work of hospital practitioners.
111 Royal Commission, 1979, p. 139.
112 Unfortunately official statistics on psychiatric in-patients do not provide information as to the social class of patients and information about the social characteristics of out-patients is even more limited. However, a range of smaller scale studies provide some information on the social characteristics of different patient populations. Much of this data has been collected together by Goldberg and Huxley (1980). For the social characteristics of patient populations in the United States see Hollingshead and Redlich, 1958; Redlich and Kellert, 1978; Mollica and Redlich, 1980.
113 ibid.
114 See Pilling, 1983; Gosta, 1982.
115 Pilling, 1983, p. 96.
116 Sedgwick, 1982, Chapter 7.
117 ibid., p. 217.
118 ibid., p. 219.
119 This point is also made by Sedgwick (ibid., pp. 195–6).

11 Conclusion

Contemporary mental health services and psychiatric ideas and practices have been moulded and fashioned by the complex interplay of two interrelated but often opposing spheres of influence. First, and most obviously there is medicine itself. It is the ideas and practices of the medical profession that have structured and continue to structure some of the most fundamental features of contemporary ways of thinking about the phenomena that fall within the category of mental illness: the idea that there are discrete, separately identifiable mental illnesses with distinctive symptom syndromes and causes, as well as typical modes of onset, course and prognosis; the idea that an understanding of the physical processes associated with these symptoms can offer the most satisfactory analysis of the illness in question; the idea that physical treatments can generally offer a, if not the, most valuable tool in the care and treatment of mental illnesses. It is the medical profession too, by virtue of the power, status, and authority it has achieved, that ensures that psychiatrists are at the top of the hierarchy of the occupational groups involved in the care of the mentally ill; that gives certain exclusive legal powers to psychiatrists *vis-à-vis* their patients – to prescribe drugs, to admit and discharge from hospital against their patients' wishes if necessary, to offer treatment within the NHS and so forth; and it is their identity as doctors that gives psychiatrists a key role in determining the content and character of mental health services, both directly via medical and psychiatric representation on key policy making bodies and indirectly via the impact of their ideas and practices. For example, the development of psychotropic drugs and their presentation as a valuable therapeutic tool for a wide range of mental disorders has undoubtedly encouraged the resort to medical practitioners for a range of phenomena which the practitioners themselves consider mental illnesses.

However, the content and character of medical ideas and practices is not itself unchanging. Much of what we now take as typical of medicine both as a body of ideas and practices and as a profession is relatively new. The immediate origins of contemporary medical ideas about illness are to be found in nineteenth-century developments: in the localization of diseases associated with the Paris school in the early decades of the nineteenth century; in the development of germ theory through the work of Koch and Pasteur in Germany and France in the middle of the nineteenth century, as well as in twentieth-century scientific and technological developments that had a marked impact on diagnosis and treatment – the introduction of X-rays around the turn of the century, the development of electro-cardiographic techniques, the chemical synthesis of drugs in the 1930s and 1940s and so forth. Institutionally it was the rapid and increasing importance of hospitals in the nineteenth century, following their emergence as distinctively medical institutions (that is, places specifically concerned with the treatment of illness by medical practitioners) that gave medicine much of its present-day character. The hospitals contributed to medicine's reliance on science and technology as the basis of its expertise and, thereby, facilitated the successful professionalization of its practice, as well as giving shape to the pattern of health service provisions.

The professional power of medicine in the clinical field is, likewise, relatively new. It was only in the nineteenth century, partly as a result of developments associated with the rise of hospital medicine, that the competing groups of authorized healers formed themselves into what can be regarded as a single profession with a single register of qualified and licensed practitioners. Divisions of course remained: between specialists of varying status and prestige, and between hospital doctors and the newly emerging general practitioners, and the continuing existence of different colleges of medicine reflects this; but there is much that is shared including many of the legal powers which registered practitioners have acquired over the last century. Over the same period the increasing role played by the state in the provision of health care has diminished the profession's direct power to control the social and economic organization of its work, and has changed the nature of the economic and organizational constraints on medical practice. However, since the development of state health services has also led to an expansion of medical activity, the impact of medicine on the ways in which people think about, make sense of, and deal with events and experiences in their lives must have also increased.

In the sphere of lunacy and mental disturbance the changing character of medical ideas and practices and the growing professionalization of medicine have had a profound effect. On the one hand they contributed to and encouraged the establishment of new hospitals for lunatics paralleling the general hospitals. In so doing they facilitated the development of a new medical specialty focused on the care of lunatics in asylums, a specialty of official medicine whose legal powers, although contested, were more firmly established in the nineteenth century. On the other hand the nineteenth-century changes in medical knowledge encouraged and strengthened the interest in the organic aspects of lunacy and mental disorder, which was reflected in the search for physical lesions and the high levels of autopsy common in the second half of the nineteenth century. These medical changes also contributed to the therapeutic nihilism of the latter part of the century as the old faith in moral treatment and the positive value of institutional care declined. And then, in turn, the development of new physical treatments for mental disorders in the twentieth century led to a new wave of therapeutic optimism which began at the end of the 1930s with the introduction of insulin therapy, ECT and psychosurgery. To describe these nineetenth- and twentieth-century changes as the medicalization of insanity or mental disorder is to say little more than that healing activities in this sphere, like other healing activities, increasingly took on the character and shape that we now take to be distinctively medical. For medical interest in mental disorder was not new nor did it extend to entirely new territories. Rather the character of medical work in this field changed. First, it became increasingly professionalized, with psychiatrists extending their legal powers, organizing themselves as a group more effectively, and developing their professional expertise. Second, medical work increasingly concentrated on physical processes and physical treatments and the former environmentalism largely disappeared. And third, the number of medical interventions increased and their balance changed, as the mechanisms for providing medical care without direct cost to the patient developed and people from all social backgrounds with all types of complaints became patients of registered psychiatric practitioners.

Mental health services and psychiatric ideas and practices are also moulded and fashioned by the policies and activities of the state and its attendant bureaucratic structures. It is the state that has acceded to and licensed medical practitioners' claims for professional power and professional autonomy and given them legislative backing; it is the state that has given institutions powers to control and confine lunatics considered dangerous or in need of treatment; it is the state that has given medical practitioners, sometimes in conjunction with magistrates, sometimes without, powers to certify and decertify patients; it is the state that has first permitted and then required local authorities to make separate institutional provision for pauper lunatics; and it is the state that has developed and funded a broader range of mental health services, out-patient clinics, day hospitals, psychiatric units in general hospitals, primary care facilities, home helps, district nursing and so forth. Undoubtedly during the nineteenth and twentieth centuries, the state's involvement in this as in so many other spheres of social policy widened, although there has been some retrenchment during the past decade. The state's initial role was confined to that of statutory regulation, at first indirectly and then directly. It gave powers to a range of authorities to license healers and to attempt to suppress the activities of irregular healers; later it gave powers to physicians and magistrates to inspect private madhouses and to admit and discharge persons from them. In the nineteenth century first permissive and then mandatory legislation broadened the state's involvement from regulation to that of specific service provision, initially in relation to a narrow category of pauper lunatics and, during this century, to a wide range of persons from all social classes, for all types of mental disorder.

Indeed, the state, by virtue of the services it makes available and by its interventions and activities in the economic and social realm, plays an important part in helping to determine the use of health services. This is because by its legislative enactments and its ideological apparatuses it helps to create and structure both social dependence and psychological distress and, in consequence, the 'demand' for mental health services. As we have seen, for instance, the institutional bias of the New Poor Law, and the reluctance to provide outdoor relief during much of the nineteenth century, helped to create the 'demand' for asylum care and the enormous expansion in numbers confined within public asylums during the nineteenth century. Similarly the state's reluctance since the Second World War to provide much in the way of publicly funded community services in the form of purpose-built residential homes, home helps, district nurses and so forth, and its recent willingness to see an expansion in the use of poorly regulated and inadequate private residential care while running down the old mental hospitals, is likely to affect the perception of the old mental hospitals, and we could see a new demand for greater investment in these decaying institutions on the grounds that even they are preferable to virtually non-existent public community services. In a similar fashion, decisions about issues such as the age of retirement, the level of pensions, housing, unemployment, industrial investment, all help to structure and create the sorts of social dependence or psychological difficulties that may lead to medical intervention. This is most obvious in the case of the over-65s, who can expect little in the way of employment in the labour market, material benefits or social status, and who are forced into greater social and economic dependence as well as greater psychological distress. Not surprisingly the result is high levels of 'demand' on the mental health services among this group.

Viewed historically we can see three major phases in the development of services for those with mental disorders which highlight the complex interaction of medical ideas and practices with state policies in determining the character of psychiatry and the mental health services. First, the period of commercial and charitable healing – a period in which cures and advice for mental problems could be purchased in the market or might be given on a charitable basis to those in need. The range of conditions for which remedies were sought was as diverse as the healers themselves and the ideas and practice on which their healing art was based. Healing, like many other commercial activities, was stratified, with the most affluent receiving help from higher status, academically better educated practitioners and calling more freely on their services for more minor as well as more severe conditions. Among the poor, where lower status practitioners would find their market, a problem would generally need to be more severe to merit the cost of the services of any commercial healer, or to call upon itself a healer's charity.

It was in this commercial and charitable context that the first moves to segregate the insane began with the establishment of private madhouses on a commercial basis in the seventeenth century, followed by the charitable voluntary asylums in the middle of the eighteenth. At this point the only public institutions that confined the insane were more general places of confinement, the workhouses and common goals, largely developed during the eighteenth century as a means of policing and containing the consequences of economic dependency, although some paupers were sent to the private madhouses under the auspices of the poor law system. While the first separate institutions for the insane were prompted by motives of profit and professional interest and played upon a family's concern to deal with a difficult family member both humanely and effectively, public asylums were developed as a solution to the problems of social and economic order created by economic, social and personal dependency and had a clear motive of collective social control.

It was in the nineteenth century that the second phase, the segregation of the insane in separate institutions, developed fully with the establishment and rapid growth of public asylums. The factors underlying the state's funding of these new institutions were numerous. There were the difficulties that had been encountered in funding the charitable asylums which were beginning to serve as the model for institutional provision for lunatics. There were the widespread criticisms of private madhouses where the motive of profit was considered to be at the root of the problem of wrongful detention. There were the new concerns about the harsh treatment of pauper lunatics in workhouses and private madhouses that a changing consciousness about insanity, especially pauper insanity, was beginning to engender. There was the new optimism about the curability of insanity associated with the principles of moral treatment; and there was, too, the increased power of the bourgeoisie, the class especially sympathetic to the case for lunacy reforms, and willing, if necessary, to accept the necessity for central intervention.

That state intervention in respect of the problem of lunacy should have taken an institutional form was overdetermined. First, there was the keen and strengthening medical interest in hospital care. The relocation of medical practice had important professional and material advantages for medical men in terms of access to new patients, a broader range of clinical experience, more adequate training, contact with other medical men, and clinical research. Second, the elaboration of the principles of moral treatment provided a positive institutional ideology that justified and legitimated the development of separate institutional provision for lunatics. The ideology asserted both the need to remove the individual from existing environmental pressures and the merits of creating a special, well-ordered institution which would have its own therapeutic properties. Third, there was the institutional bias of the poor law system itself, heightened in the nineteenth century with the publication of the Poor Law Report in 1834. Although outdoor relief was not abolished following the 1834 Poor Law Amendment Act, the philosophy of the New Poor Law embodied a view of institutions as a convenient and appropriate way of deterring the economically dependent from seeking poor law relief, which would not only keep the numbers in receipt of relief to a minimum, but also instill proper social attitudes and values amongst inmates. Hence in the establishment of public asylums professional advantage, humanitarian concerns and the economic and political interests of the state combined.

It was, however, primarily poor law concerns, in conjunction with the power of public asylums to legally detain their inmates (first established in relation to lunatics considered dangerous), that contributed to the custodial character of the public asylums. Medical ideals of therapy, reinforced and amplified by the apparent potential of moral treatment, could not flourish in the large-scale, understaffed and poorly funded institutions, despite the presence of a medical superintendent, when saving an extra halfpenny on the weekly cost of care counted for more than rates of cure or individual attention to inmates. Public asylums for lunatics functioned, despite their original therapeutic intent, like other poor law institutions as places of last resort where those for whom little could be hoped in the way of improvement were to be found, largely because the poor law did not provide any alternative means of economic or social support.

During the second half of the nineteenth century, public asylums, like the private madhouses and charitable asylums that preceded them, came to be widely criticized and there were new demands for lunacy reform. The aim was to transform the asylums from custodial into therapeutic institutions by ensuring that persons disturbed in mind were given treatment in the early stage of the disease. This was to be achieved both by allowing voluntary admission and by setting up special facilities for early, acute cases. Very little reform, however, occurred in the public sector until the passing of the Mental Treatment Act in 1930. By that time the poor law system, which constituted the main obstacle to reform, had largely been supplanted by a range of welfare provisions developed outside the framework of the poor law which heralded the beginnings of the welfare state and the end of the poor law system.

The beginning of the third phase of services for those with mental disorders – of the movement away from the asylums and mental hospital and the development of a policy of community care – can be dated back to the same period. The new policy objectives were brought about as much by the changing character of welfare provisions as by changing medical ideas. The expansion in a broad range of state welfare provisions, both in the form of financial benefits and in the form of services, created a new context in which care outside the mental hospital was not only more feasible but also more acceptable. The undermining of the poor law system and the expansion of welfare provisions based largely on insurance principles meant that publicly funded care was now to be provided outside the institution, and indeed the whole institutional bias of public provision was undermined.

It might seem, therefore, that in the move to community care in many respects state welfare policies had more impact than medical ideas and practices. Indeed, it might be argued that the general medical bias towards the institution – the hospital – has remained as strong as it was in the nineteenth century. Certainly the hospital is still the preferred locus for major medical interventions. Nevertheless, not only has the hospital increasingly become the centre of a diverse range of services, and in the process the ideal model of health services has changed; but also in the field of psychiatry the mental hospital had particular disadvantages as a locus for professional medical activity, so that there has been greater pressure to adopt models of care in which the mental hospital is no longer centre stage. For instance, although the mental hospitals' formal associations with the poor law system have disappeared, the physical plant remains largely the same. More important, the mental hospital separated psychiatry from the rest of medicine and compounded and enhanced rather than minimized status differentials between the two, largely because of the custodial nature of mental hospitals. Hence models of care have been developed in which mental health services are fully integrated with general health services; in which there are small psychiatric units in general hospitals, and in which there is an expansion of work with acute, early cases outside the mental hospital. Equally importantly the shift of psychiatric interest towards physical pathology and physical methods of treatment and the attendant decline in the principles of moral treatment led to the collapse of the ideology which viewed the institution as having positive therapeutic potential in its own right, an ideology which had sustained the initial commitment to institutional care. Hence the drug revolution of the 1950s, following on the development of ECT, insulin therapy, and psychosurgery at the end of the 1930s, facilitated the acceptance and implementation of community care policies, not only because they created a climate of optimism about the treatment of mental illness and the prevention of chronicity, but also because they represented methods of care that did not attach any intrinsic therapeutic value to the institution in itself.

However, while these factors contributed to the adoption of a policy of community care, others acted as a brake on its effective implementation. Nineteenth-century investment in the physical plant of mental hospitals, the lack of resources for the development of new community services, and the problem of divided responsibility between health and local authorities, all contributed to the slow implementation of the new policy throughout the 1950s and 1960s despite the steady expansion of public expenditure. In the 1970s the cutbacks in public expenditure which marked the state's fiscal crisis were followed by the ideological transformation of government policies when the Conservative government came into power in 1979, and by continuing economic recession; together they produced an even greater reluctance to invest more resources in mental health services. The result was not, as it might have been, a return to old institutional policies of deterrence but a renewed enthusiasm for the policy of community care, not in its initial guise of publicly funded community services, but in a new guise of private care in the community. Community care now largely means care in the home, by women, and care by private and charitable agencies. Financial concerns, consequently, now strengthen rather than inhibit the move away from the mental hospital.

These basic stages in the development of mental health services have been associated with and contributed to changing conceptualizations of insanity and mental disorder which highlight the way in which such concepts are socially and historically constituted. In the sixteenth, seventeenth and eighteenth centuries insanity and lunacy were narrow, primarily societal categories, albeit usually imprecisely defined, but they were only the most extreme of a range of mental states that might be considered problematic and might be brought to the attention of a healer if circumstances (particularly the family's material circumstances) allowed. Official as well as irregular healers dealt with a broad spectrum of problems of the mind and had a range of concepts to differentiate them. Then as now the judgements of individual behaviour, whether by family or healers, took into account a person's social characteristics and reflected normative assumptions about appropriate and rational conduct for persons of a particular age, class and gender. When, however, institutions began to set up, and particularly when public asylums were introduced and expanded in the nineteenth century, much of the attention, especially in the discussion of public policy, focused on lunacy and insanity alone, and the less severe disorders were largely ignored. This was because the more minor problems of mind were far less likely to produce the degree of social dependency or difficulty that was held to merit the dominant form of public intervention – institutional care. In this process, however, the more restricted notions of lunacy and insanity (real madness) were themselves broadened, as concepts such as those of partial insanity and moral insanity were introduced and developed by medical men in their effort to categorize and treat the full range of cases that ended up in institutions. But the more minor problems – that did not typically fall within the compass of asylum care which provided the basic core of the work of the emergent psychiatric profession – received far less academic attention and political comment. Healing activity continued outside the asylums in relation to a broader range of mental disorders, but it was not at the centre of the public and political interest in mental disease.

Towards the end of the nineteenth century and during the twentieth century, however, the milder forms of mental disorder have attracted increasing interest and new concepts, new theories and new treatments have been introduced which have modified our understanding of them. Initially this medical interest existed largely in the private sector and found its best-known examplar in the work of Freud and the development of psychoanalysis. But with the expansion of publicly funded services outside the mental hospital as welfare services were transformed, and with the development of relatively cheap forms of the treatment suitable for wide-scale therapy, interest in the realm of psychiatric activity broadened once more, and the balance of psychiatric work began to change. As a result the less severe forms of mental disorder, the neuroses and behaviour disorders, of people from all social backgrounds, not just the affluent, have become a major feature of medical and psychiatric work and of public and political concern.

This shift in the character of psychiatric work has led to new tensions and contradictions for psychiatry as a profession. In the second half of the nineteenth century the major tension was between the curative orientation of medicine and the increasing custodialism of psychiatric work in asylums. While this contradiction has not entirely disappeared during this century, and has been a major motive of endeavours to transform the character of asylums, a new contradiction has emerged. This is the contradiction between the increasing emphasis within medicine on physical causes of illness and physical treatments and the visibly social and psychological character of the neuroses and behaviour disorders which play so large a part in medical and psychiatric work.

Freud wished to establish psychoanalysis as a separate science, in practice largely directed towards the neuroses, which was to exist outside medicine, though closely linked with it. His desire to do this was but one reflection of, and attempt to resolve this new contradiction. The 1960s critiques of Szasz, Laing and Scheff were but a more recent assertion of psychiatry's neglect of the social and psychological as the new scientific medicine has taken its hold. It is not, therefore, surprising that these latter critiques attracted widespread public interest at a time when the balance of psychiatric and medical activity in relation to mental disorders was changing very markedly. For it is precisely in relation to the less severe mental disorders that questions about the nature and appropriateness of medical intervention are most obvious.

The response to this tension within the mental health field has been two-fold. On the one hand many psychiatrists have incorporated elements of psychological and sociological thought into their ideas and practice, but they have done so in a selective manner and have transformed and moulded them into a form that is more consistent with their own ideological perspective. For example, much research on the social aspects of mental illness is largely carried out within an epidemiological framework which does not call into question the conceptual basis of medical practice, and examines the social in an atomized, individualized manner. For example, the work on so-called stressful life events and mental illness is largely of this type. It examines the impact of situational factors such as unemployment and divorce at the level of the individual and makes little attempt to study the broader social and cultural context in which these events are located. Similarly, certain psychoanalytic ideas have been adopted in a modified form by psychiatrists as a basis for understanding neurotic behaviour, although they are largely neglected when it comes to treatment. Of the psychological approaches the more recently developed behaviour therapy is more acceptable to psychiatrists because of its positivist foundations and is used in the treatment of behaviour disorders and some neuroses.

On the other hand, there has been a proliferation of new professionals within the mental health services in the areas of potential expertise that fall outside the current boundaries of psychiatric knowledge and practice – a proliferation encouraged by the development of mental health services to new patient groups in new locations. In Britain these new mental health professionals, clinical psychologists, psychotherapists, counsellors and social workers, who clearly pose a potential threat to the authority and status of the psychiatric profession, have emerged historically largely within the medical ambit and have in many respects been contained as subordinate groups within the medical hierarchy. None the less there has been a marked expansion in the employment of such professionals within the NHS in the post-war period, much of their work being with the expanding sector of out-patients rather than with in-patients. For example, between 1964 and 1975 the number of psychologists employed in mental illness hospitals and units for out-patient and in-patient work increased some ten fold. In the United States this proliferation of mental health professionals has been even more extensive, and many of them have more status, independence and authority than in this country. Moreover, the ideas of these new mental health professionals are by no means mirror images of those of psychiatrists to whom they may be formally subordinate and this, too, can create problems for the domination of psychiatric ideas and practices. Undoubtedly, however, both the selective incorporation of psychological ideas and the proliferation of new mental health professionals have served to contain and cover over the tension arising from the contradiction of a specialism whose expertise and ideas have come increasingly to be drawn from the natural sciences, which attempts to deal with a broad range of mental disorders, the origin and character of which are linked to a diversity of structural and cultural features of society. None the less, neither development tackles what many critics view as the fundamental limitation of the mental health services, and of psychiatry and the other mental health professions, which is that their orientation is almost entirely curative. As we have seen, psychiatry (like its parent medicine), and the mental health services in which its practice is carried out, focus on the care and treatment of specific individuals who, for whatever reason, have become psychologically disturbed. Their mode of action is almost entirely responsive.

To contend that curative individualism is the fundamental limitation of psychiatry and of the mental health services is to move beyond debates as to the precise causes of mental illness. It also calls into question the nature and form of social intervention in the complex interplay of forces that may lead to what society now regards as mental health problems. The argument is that instead of directing all our resources and attention on to disturbed individuals, important though it is to ameliorate their situation, we need also to look beyond the individual to the forms and levels of intervention which would make mental disorders less likely for the population as a whole, or for particular groups within it. Consider, for example, senile dementia. At present the way of dealing with the problem of senile dementia is to offer care and treatment to specific individuals who have been medically identified as demented, and research into the causes of senile dementia underpins this type of intervention by concentrating on the physical changes to the brain associated with dementia. There is, however, very little attempt to look at other factors which may contribute to this problem. Factors such as social isolation, the lack of family and social support, and the lack of material resources, meaningful work and status, may, as I have already suggested, make it difficult for the growing numbers of those over 65 to lead independent lives; and may help to generate dependence, distress and confusion, which may consequently make a diagnosis of dementia more likely. Nor is there much in the way of social intervention aimed to strengthen and ensure the independence of the over 65s, which would arguably do more for that group as a whole than simply trying to cope with the ever increasing numbers of those already identified as demented.

Or consider the problem of heroin addiction. Faced with the recent moral panic about heroin abuse, the temptation is to focus all our resources and energies on trying to wean the addicted off their drugs or on trying to control the availability of heroin, by increasing the penalties for drug pushing and so forth. But while the latter may seem a somewhat more preventively oriented 'solution' to the problem of heroin addiction than the former, both ignore crucial questions about why individuals turn to heroin use and why they are tempted by the activities of the drug pushers. Forms of social intervention that might involve more radical social change, such as dealing with the boredom, alienation and frustration of many young people are consequently ignored.

Of course, as these examples illustrate, preventive social interventions, like curative interventions, make assumptions about the causes of mental health problems. Our knowledge of these causes is, however, often fragmentary, whether we examine the causal assumptions that underpin curative, individualist intervention or those on which preventive, public intervention is founded. In the case of the latter the inadequacy of our understanding is itself in part the result of the curative bias of our contemporary orientation to health which ensures that resources largely go on research that justifies and legitimates curative interventions and not on research that would facilitate preventive interventions at the social level. More importantly, however, the absence of preventive social interventions is usually a matter of the lack of political will and not of the deficiencies of existing knowledge. As the classic instance of cholera made clear, effective preventive action, like effective curative intervention, can be accomplished without precise knowledge of the causal mechanisms involved. Public health campaigns in the nineteenth century were instituted with some success on the basis of subsequently discredited miasmatic theories of cholera transmission.

As developments in the field of public health also demonstrate, successful preventive intervention requires collective action by the state and cannot usually be effected by individuals acting on their own. Nor, indeed, can we expect it to be effected by medical practitioners whose expertise and ideology are narrowly clinical and who work in services organized to deliver care and cure to individuals who are already disturbed. Without doubt the curative character of these services and of their work has served the interests of medical practitioners and has contributed to their successful professionalization. But it is the state that has ultimate responsibility for the curative character of mental health services and has the necessary powers to generate the sort of collective interventions that effective prevention requires. That it does not do so is, therefore, a political matter and requires debate and action in the political arena. It is political interests and political opposition to more radical social interventions that maintains the curative approach.

Much of the intervention that would be required to tackle health problems in a preventive manner would not be of a 'medical' character, or at least not medical in the sense that we now understand that word, as examples from the field of physical health demonstrate. Legislation requiring the wearing of seat belts, although designed to prevent death and physical injury, does not involve any provision of medical services. Nor is much in the way of medical expertise required to establish whether or not the wearing of seat belts does lower mortality and physical injury in car accidents. In contrast, in the case of smoking and lung cancer medical expertise has been involved in initial research which has established the deleterious consequences for health of smoking. But preventive intervention designed to reduce smoking does not require the expertise of medical practitioners, especially if it occurs at the societal rather than individual level. If intervention takes the form of strong restraints on the publicity and lobbying of the tobacco industry or serious use of mechanisms such as taxation to reduce tobacco consumption, then the services of medical practitioners or other caring professionals are not required. If it is restricted to exhorting individuals to stop smoking then the public may well turn to professional carers and healers in their efforts to do so, in the face of the relatively low cost, general acceptability, and high promotion of cigarette smoking.

Issues about the desirable forms of intervention to deal with the high levels of mental disorder now manifest in our society cannot, therefore, be settled simply by resort to the facts about the causes of mental disorder. For decisions as to the most appropriate forms of intervention involve matters of political judgement. Contrary to existing medical beliefs, it is not that knowledge as to the precise causes of mental disorders determines the way in which we intervene to deal with the problem of mental disorder. Rather, as the force of the argument in Chapter 3 suggested, it would be more accurate to say that the political acceptability of particular forms of intervention determines what we choose to emphasize as *the* causes of the different types of mental disorder. Consequently, the contribution of sociology and history to our understanding of mental disorder is, above all, to challenge the belief that psychiatric interventions are value free and to illumine the way in which existing ideas and practices about mental disorder are shaped by social, political and economic forces.

Bibliography

B. Abel-Smith, *The Hospitals, 1800–1948*, London: Heinemann, 1964.

P. Allderidge, 'Management and mismanagement at Bedlam, 1547–1633', in C. Webster (ed.), *Health, Medicine and Mortality in the Sixteenth Century*, Cambridge: Cambridge University Press, 1979, pp. 141–6.

L. Althusser, 'Contradiction and Overdetermination', in his *For Marx*, Harmondsworth: Penguin, 1969.

American Psychiatric Association, *Diagnostic and Statistical Manual of Mental Disorders, Third Edition*, Washington: American Psychiatric Association, 1980.

A. Anastasi, *Psychological Testing*, New York: Macmillan, 1961.

M. Anderson, *Family Structure in Nineteenth Century Lancashire*, London: Cambridge University Press, 1971.

H. L. Ansbacher, 'The significance of the socio-economic status of the patients of Freud and of Adler', *American Journal of Psychotherapy*, **13**, 1959, pp. 376–82.

D. Armstrong, 'Medical knowledge and modalities of social control', unpublished.

S. E. Asch, 'Effects of group pressure upon the modification and distortion of judgements', in H. Guetzkow (ed.), *Groups, Leadership and Men*, Pittsburg: Carnegie Press, 1951.

V. Aubert, *Elements of Sociology*, London: Heinemann, 1967.

F. J. Ayo and B. Blackwell (eds.), *Discoveries in Biological Psychiatry*, Philadelphia: Lippincott, 1970.

N. H. Azrin and T. Ayllon, *The Token Economy: A Motivational System for Therapy and Rehabilitation*, New York: Appleton-Century-Crofts, 1968.

A. A. Baker, 'Pulling down the old mental hospital', *The Lancet*, 25 March 1961, pp. 656–7.

R. Barton, *Institutional Neurosis*, Bristol: John Wright, 1959.

G. Bateson, D. D. Jackson, J. Haley and J. Weakland, 'Toward a theory of schizophrenia', *Behavioural Science*, 1, 1956, pp. 251–64.

W. Battie, *A Treatise in Madness*, introduced by R. Hunter and A. MacAlpine, London: Dawsons, 1962.

P. Bean, *Compulsory Admissions to Mental Hospitals*, Chichester: Wiley, 1980.

H. Becker, *Outsiders*, New York: The Free Press, 1963.

H. Becker, B. Geer, E. C. Hughes and A. L. Strauss, *Boys in White: Student Culture in Medical School*, Chicago: Chicago University Press, 1961.

A. L. Beier, *The Problem of the Poor in Tudor and Early Stuart England*, London: Methuen, 1983.

G. M. Bell, 'A mental hospital with open doors', *International Journal of Social Psychiatry*, 1, 1955, pp. 42–8.

R. Benedict, 'Anthropology and the abnormal', *Journal of General Psychology*, 1, 1934, pp. 59–80.

R. Benedict, *Patterns of Culture*, London: Routledge, 1935.

D. H. Bennett, 'Social Forms of Psychiatric Treatment', in J. K. Wing (ed.), *Schizophrenia: Towards a New Synthesis*, London: Academic Press, 1978.

D. H. Bennett and I. Morris, 'Deinstitutionalization in the United Kingdom', *International Journal of Mental Health*, 11, 1983, pp. 5–23.

D. H. Bennett and J. P. S. Robertson, 'The effects of habit training on chronic schizophrenic patients', *Journal of Mental Science*, 101, 1955, pp. 664–72.

E. Benton, *Philosophical Foundations of the Three Sociologies*, London: Routledge and Kegan Paul, 1977.

E. Benton, *The Rise and Fall of Structural Marxism*, London: Macmillan, 1984.

P. L. Berger and T. Luckman, *The Social Construction of Reality*, London: Allen Lane, 1966.

J. L. Berlant, *Profession and Monopoly: a study of medicine in the United States and Great Britain*, Berkeley: University of California Press, 1975.

G. Best, *Mid-Victorian Britain, 1851–1879*, London: Fontana, 1979.

B. Bettelheim and E. Sylvester, 'A therapeutic milieu', *American Journal of Orthopsychiatry*, 18, 1948, pp. 191–206.

W. H. Beveridge, *Full Employment in a Free Society*, London: George Allen and Unwin, 1944.

G. Bignami, 'Disease models and reductionist thinking in the biomedical sciences', in S. P. R. Rose (ed.), *Against Biological Determinism*, London: Allison and Busby, 1982.

J. Birtchnell, 'Social class, parental social class and social mobility in psychiatric patients and general population controls', *Psychological Medicine*, 1, 1971, pp. 209–21.

C. P. Blacker, *Neurosis and the Mental Health Services*, London: Oxford University Press, 1946.

H. Blumer, *Symbolic Interactionism: perspective and method*, Prentice Hall: Englewood Cliffs, 1969.

B. E. Blustein, ' "A hollow square of psychological science": American neurologists and psychiatrists in conflict', in A. Scull (ed.), *Madhouses, Mad-Doctors, and Madmen*, London: Athlone Press, 1981, pp. 241–70.

Board of Control, *Twenty-fifth Annual Report*, London: HMSO, 1939.

T. Bodenheimer, S. Cummings and E. Harding, 'Capitalizing on illness: the health insurance industry', in V. Navarro (ed.), *Health and Medical Care in the US: A Critical Analysis*, New York, Baywood, 1977, pp. 69–84.

C. Boorse, 'On the distinction between disease and illness', *Philosophy and Public Affairs*, **5**, 1975, pp. 49–68.

C. Boorse, 'What a theory of mental health should be', *Journal for the Theory of Social Behaviour*, **6**, 1976, pp. 61–84.

E. Bott, 'Hospital and society', *British Journal of Medical Psychology*, **49**, 1976, pp. 97–140.

T. B. Bottomore, *Elites and Society*, Harmondsworth: Penguin, 1966.

J. Breuer and S. Freud, *Studies on Hysteria*, Harmondsworth: Penguin, 1974.

Brighton Women and Science Group, 'Technology in the lying-in room', British Women and Science Group, *Alice through the Microscope*, London: Virago, 1980.

C. P. B. Brook and D. Stafford-Clark, 'Psychiatric treatment in general wards', in H. Freeman and J. Farndale (eds.), *Trends in the Mental Health Services*, Oxford: Pergamon Press, 1963.

J. Brotherston, 'Evolution of medical practice', in G. Maclachlan and T. McKeown (eds.), *Medical History and Medical Care*, London: Oxford University Press, 1971.

I. K. Broverman, D. M. Broverman, F. E. Clarkson, P. S. Rosenkrantz, and S. R. Vogel, 'Sex role stereotypes and clinical judgements of mental health', *Journal of Consulting and Clinical Psychology*, **34**, 1970, pp. 1–7.

A. F. J. Brown, *Essex at Work, 1700–1815*, Chelmsford: Essex County County Council, 1969.

G. W. Brown and T. Harris, *Social Origins of Depression: A Study of Psychiatric Disorder in Women*, London: Tavistock, 1978.

R. Brown, 'Physical illness and mental health', *Philosophy and Public Affairs*, **7**, 1977, pp. 17–38.

A. Brundage, *The Making of the New Poor Law, 1832–39*, London: Hutchinson, 1978.

J. Busfield, 'Gender, mental illness, and psychiatry', in M. Evans and C. Ungerson (eds.), *Sexual Divisions: Patterns and Processes*, London: Tavistock, 1983.

J. Busfield and N. Hart, 'Which is the healthier sex? The contrasting health experiences of men and women', paper given at the *BSA Medical Sociology Group Annual Conference*, September 1978.

A. Bussutic, I. W. Kemp and M. A. Heasman, 'The accuracy of medical certificates of cause of death', *Health Bulletin*, **39**, 1981, pp. 146–52.

W. F. Bynum, 'Rationales for therapy in British psychiatry, 1780–1835', in A. Scull (ed.), *Madhouses, Mad-Doctors and Madmen*, London: Athlone, 1981.

J. Cairns, *Cancer: Science and Society*, San Francisco: W. H. Freeman, 1978.

K. Campbell, *Body and Mind*, London: Macmillan, 1971.

M. Carpenter, 'Asylum nursing before 1914: a chapter in the history of labour', in C. Davies (ed.), *Rewriting Nursing History*, London: Croom Helm, 1980.

A. M. Carr-Saunders and P. A. Wilson, *The Professions*, London: Frank Cass, 1964.

A. Cartwright, *The Dignity of Labour? A study of childbearing and induction*, London: Tavistock, 1979.

F. F. Cartwright, *A Social History of Medicine*, London: Longman, 1977.

E. Cassirer, *The Philosophy of the Enlightenment*, Boston: Beacon Press, 1955.

R. B. Cattell, *The Scientific Analysis of Personality*, Harmondsworth: Penguin, 1965.

R. H. Cawley, 'The present status of physical methods of treatment of schizophrenia', in A. Cooper and A. Walk (eds.), *Recent Developments in Schizophrenia*, London: Royal Medico-Psychological Association, 1967.

E. B. Chain, 'Academic and industrial contributions to drug research', *Nature*, 2 November 1963, supplement, pp. 441–51.

S. G. and E. O. A. Checkland, *The Poor Law Report of 1834*, Harmondsworth: Penguin, 1974.

A. Clare, *Psychiatry in Dissent: Controversial Issues in Thought and Practice*, London: Tavistock, 1976.

Sir George Clark, *A History of the Royal College of Physicians of London*, vols. 1 and 2, Oxford: Oxford University Press, 1964 and 1966.

R. A. Cloward and F. F. Piven, 'Hidden protest: the channelling of female innovation and resistance', *Signs*, 4, 1979, pp. 65–9.

S. Cobb, *Foundations of Neuropsychiatry, Sixth Edition*, 1958.

A. L. Cochrane, *Effectiveness and Efficiency: Random Reflections on Health Services*, London: Nuffield Provincial Hospitals Trust, 1972.

R. Cochrane, *The Social Creation of Mental Illness*, London: Longman, 1983.

R. Cochrane and M. Stopes-Roe, 'Factors affecting the distribution of psychological symptoms in urban areas of England', *Acta Psychiatrica Scandanavica*, 61, 1980, pp. 445–60.

W. C. Cockerham, 'Labelling theory and mental disorder: a synthesis of psychiatric and social perspectives', *Studies in Symbolic Interaction*, 2, 1979, pp. 257–80.

A. Collier, *R. D. Laing: The Philosophy and Politics of Psychotherapy*, London: Harvester Press, 1977.

D. Cooper (ed.), *The Dialectics of Liberation*, Harmondsworth: Penguin, 1968.

R. Cooperstock, 'Sex differences in the use of mood-modifying drugs: an explanatory model', *Journal of Health and Social Behaviour*, 12, 1971, pp. 238–44.

R. Cooter, 'Phrenology and British alienists, ca. 1825–1845', in A. Scull (ed.), *Madhouses, Mad-Doctors, and Madmen*, London: Athlone, 1981.

R. Cooter, 'Anticontagionism and history's medical record', in P. Wright and A. Treacher (eds.), *The Problem of Medical Knowledge*, Edinburgh: Edinburgh University Press, 1982.

J. Coulter, *Approaches to Insanity*, London: Martin Robertson, 1973.

P. R. Cox, *Demography*, 4th edn., London: Cambridge University Press, 1970.

W. A. Creasey, *Cancer: An Introduction*, Oxford: Oxford University Press, 1981.

M. A. Crowther, *The Workhouse System, 1834-1929*, London: Batsford, 1981.

N. Dain, *Concepts of Insanity, 1789-1865*, New Brunswick: Rutgers, 1964.

J. M. Davis, 'Treatment of affective disorders in clinical practice: implications for education and research; and the biogenic amine hypothesis', in T. Rothman (ed.), *Changing Patterns in Psychiatric Care*, London: Vision Press, 1971.

K. Davis, 'Mental hygiene and the class structure', *Psychiatry*, 1, 1938, pp. 55–64.

Department of Health and Social Security, *Hospital Services for the Mentally Ill*, Hospital Memorandum, no. 97, London: DHSS, 1971.

Department of Health and Social Security, *Better Services for the Mentally Ill*, London: HMSO, 1975.

Department of Health and Social Security, *Priorities for Health and Personal Social Services: A Consultative Document*, London: HMSO, 1976a.

Department of Health and Social Security, *Prevention and Health: Everybody's Business*, London: HMSO, 1976b.

Department of Health and Social Security, *A Happier Old Age*, London: HMSO, 1978a.

Department of Health and Social Security, *Review of the Mental Health Act 1959*, London: HMSO, 1978b.

Department of Health and Social Security, *Care in the Community: a Consultative Document on Moving Resources for Care in England*, London: DHSS, 1981.

Department of Health and Social Security, *In-patient Statistics from the Mental Health Enquiry for England 1981*, London: HMSO, 1984.

K. Doerner, *Madmen and the Bourgeoisie: A Social History of Insanity and Psychiatry*, Oxford: Blackwell, 1981.

B. P. Dohrenwend and B. S. Dohrenwend, *Social Status and Psychological Disorder: A Causal Inquiry*, New York: Wiley, 1969.

M. Donnelly, *Managing the Mind: A Study of Medical Psychology in Early Nineteenth Century Britain*, London: Tavistock, 1983.

J. Donnison, *Midwives and Medical Men: A History of Inter-Professional Rivalries and Women's Rights*, London: Heinemann, 1977.

R. P. Dore, 'Function and cause', *American Sociological Review*, 26, 1961, pp. 843–53.

L. Doyal, *The Political Economy of Health*, London: Pluto, 1979.

L. Doyal, 'A matter of life and death: medicine, health and statistics', in J. Irvine, I. Miles, and J. Evans (eds.), *Demystifying Social Statistics*, London: Pluto, 1979.

R. Dubos, *Mirage of Health: Utopias, Progress, and Biological Change*, New York: Harper, 1959.

G. S. Duckworth and H. B. Kedward, 'Man or Machine in psychiatric diagnosis', *American Journal of Psychiatry*, **135**, 1978, pp. 64–8.

H. Eckstein, *The English Health Service: Its Origins, Structure and Achievements*, Cambridge, Mass.: Harvard University Press, 1959.

B. Ehrenreich and J. Ehrenreich, *The American Health Empire: Power, Profits, and Politics*, New York: Vintage Books, 1971.

B. Ehrenreich and D. English, *Witches, Midwives, and Nurses: A History of Women Healers*, London: Compendium, 1974.

B. Ehrenreich and D. English, *Complaints and Disorders: The Sexual Politics of Sickness*, London: Writers and Readers Publishing Cooperative, 1976.

B. Ehrenreich and D. English, *For Her Own Good: 150 Years of the Experts' Advice to Women*, London: Pluto Press, 1979.

G. L. Engel, 'The need for a new medical model: a challenge for biomedicine', *Science*, **196**, 1977, pp. 129–36.

D. Ennals, *Out of Mind*, London: Arrow, 1973.

Equal Opportunities Commission, *Caring for the Elderly and Handicapped*, Manchester: Equal Opportunities Commission, 1982.

G. Erwin, *Behaviour Therapy: Scientific, Philosophical and Moral Foundations*, Cambridge: Cambridge University Press, 1978.

H. J. Eysenck, *Handbook of Abnormal Psychology*, New York: Basic Books, 1960a.

H. J. Eysenck, *Behaviour Therapy and the Neuroses*, London: Pergamon Press, 1960b.

H. J. Eysenck, *The Future of Psychiatry*, London: Methuen, 1975.

J. Farndale, 'British Day Hospitals', in H. Freeman and J. Farndale (eds.), *Trends in the Mental Health Services*, Oxford: Pergamon Press, 1963.

B. A. Farrell, 'Psychoanalysis: The Method', in S. G. M. Lee and M. Herbert, *Freud and Psychology*, Harmondsworth: Penguin, 1970.

K. Figlio, 'The historiography of scientific medicine: an invitation to the human sciences', *Comparative Studies in Society and History*, **19**, 1977, pp. 262–86.

K. Figlio, 'Chlorosis and chronic disease in 19th century Britain: the social constitution of somatic illness in a capitalist society', *International Journal of Health Services*, **8**, 1978, pp. 589–619.

K. Figlio, 'How does illness mediate social relations? Workmen's compensation and medico-legal practices, 1890–1940', in P. Wright and A. Treacher (eds.), *The Problem of Medical Knowledge*, Edinburgh: Edinburgh University Press, 1982.

J. Finch and D. Groves (eds.), *A Labour of Love: Women, Work and Caring*, London: Routledge and Kegan Paul, 1983.

G. B. A. M. Finlayson, *England in the Eighteen Thirties: Decade of Reform*, London: Edward Arnold, 1969.

F. J. Fish, *Schizophrenia*, Bristol: John Wright and Son, 1962.

G. W. T. H. Fleming, F. L. Golla, and W. G. Walter, 'Electric-convulsion therapy of schizophrenia', *The Lancet*, 30 December 1939, pp. 1353–5.

A. Flew, *Crime or Disease?*, London: Macmillan, 1973.

M. W. Flinn, 'Medical services under the New Poor Law', in D. Fraser (ed.), *The New Poor Law in the Nineteenth Century*, London: Macmillan, 1976.

M. Foot, *Aneurin Bevan, 1945–1960*, St Albans: Paladin, 1975.

R. F. Fortune, *Sorcerers of Dobu*, New York: Dutton, 1932.

M. Foucault, *Madness and Civilization: A History of Insanity in the Age of Reason*, London: Tavistock, 1967.

M. Foucault, *The Order of Things*, London: Tavistock, 1970.

M. Foucault, *The Archaeology of Knowledge*, London: Tavistock, 1972.

M. Foucault, *The Birth of the Clinic: An Archaeology of Medical Perception*, London: Tavistock, 1973.

M. Foucault, *Discipline and Punish: The Birth of the Prison*, London: Allen Lane, 1977.

M. Foucault, *The History of Sexuality, Volume I: An Introduction*, London: Allen Lane, 1979.

D. Fraser (ed.), *The New Poor Law into the Nineteenth Century*, London: Macmillan, 1976.

D. Fraser, *The Evolution of the British Welfare State*, 2nd edn, London: Macmillan, 1984.

H. Freeman, 'Pharmacological treatment and management', in J. K. Wing (ed.), *Schizophrenia: Towards a New Synthesis*, London: Academic Press, 1978.

E. Freidson, *Profession of Medicine*, New York: Dodd, Mead, 1970a.

E. Freidson, *Professional Dominance*, Chicago: Aldine, 1970b.

S. Freud, *An Autobiographical Study*, London: Hogarth Press, 1935.

S. Freud, *Two Short Accounts of Psychoanalysis*, Harmondsworth: Penguin, 1962.

S. Freud, *Introductory Lectures on Psychoanalysis*, Harmondsworth: Penguin, 1974.

S. Freud, 'The Loss of reality in neurosis and psychosis', in *On Psychopathology*, Harmondsworth: Penguin, 1979.

E. Z. Friedenberg, *Laing*, London: Fontana, 1973.

E. Gamarnikow, 'Sexual division of labour: the case of nursing', in A. Kuhn and A. M. Wolpe (eds.), *Feminism and Materialism*, London: Routledge and Kegan Paul, 1978.

J. Gardiner, 'Women's domestic labour', *New Left Review*, **89**, 1975, pp. 47–58.

H. Garfinkel, *Studies in Ethnomethodology*, Englewood Cliffs: Prentice Hall, 1967.

P. Gay, *The Enlightenment: An Interpretation*, vols. I and II, London: Wildwood House, 1973.

General Register Office, *Morbidity Statistics from General Practice, 1956-7*, vol. III, London: HMSO, 1962.

General Register Office, *A Glossary of Mental Disorders*, London: HMSO, 1968.

M. D. George, *London Life in the Eighteenth Century*, Harmondsworth: Penguin, 1966.

H. H. Gerth and C. W. Mills, *From Max Weber: Essays in Sociology*, London: Routledge and Kegan Paul, 1948.

A. Giddens, *A Contemporary Critique of Historical Materialism, Vol 1: Power, Property and the State*, London: Macmillan, 1981.

E. Goffman, *Asylums: Essays on the Social Situation of Mental Patients and Other Inmates*, Harmondsworth: Penguin, 1968.

E. Goffman, 'The insanity of place', the Appendix to his *Relations in Public*, London: Allen Lane, 1971.

D. Goldberg and P. Huxley, *Mental Illness in the Community: the Pathway to Psychiatric Care*, London: Tavistock, 1980.

E. M. Goldberg and S. C. Morrison, 'Schizophrenia and social class', *British Journal of Psychiatry*, **109**, 1963, pp. 785–802.

L. Gostin, *A Human Condition: The Mental Health Act from 1959 to 1975. Vol. I*, London: MIND (National Association for Mental Health), 1975.

L. Gostin, 'A review of the Mental Health (Amendment) Act', parts I, II and III, *New Law Journal*, December 1982, pp. 1127–31, 1151–5, 1199–1203.

I. Gough, *The Political Economy of the Welfare State*, London: Macmillan, 1979.

W. R. Gove, 'The relationship between sex roles, marital status and mental illness', *Social Forces*, **51**, 1972, pp. 34–44.

W. R. Gove, 'Labelling and mental illness: a critique', in W. R. Gove (ed.), *The Labelling of Deviance*, New York: Halsted, 1975, pp. 33–81.

W. R. Gove, *Deviance and Mental Illness*, Beverly Hills: Sage Publications, 1982.

W. R. Gove and T. Herb, 'Stress and mental illness among the young: a comparison of the sexes', *Social Forces*, **53**, 1974, pp. 256–65.

W. R. Gove and P. Howell, 'Individual resources and mental hospitalization: a comparison and evaluation of the societal reaction and psychiatric perspectives', *American Sociological Review*, **39**, 1974, pp. 86–110.

W. R. Gove and J. F. Tudor, 'Adult sex roles and mental illness', *American Journal of Sociology*, **78**, 1972, pp. 812–35.

C. Greenland, *Mental Illness and Civil Liberty*, London: G. Bell and Sons, 1970.

V. Greenwood and J. Young, *Abortion in Demand*, London: Pluto, 1976.

G. N. Grob, *Mental Institutions in America: Social Policy to 1875*, New York: The Free Press, 1973.

W. Haase, 'The role of socio-economic class in examiner bias', in F. Reissman *et al.* (eds.), *Mental Health of the Poor*, Free Press, 1964.

N. J. Hale, *Freud and the Americans: The Beginnings of Psychoanalysis in the United*

States, 1876–1917, New York: Oxford University Press, 1971.

E. Halevy, *A History of the English People in the Nineteenth Century*, vol. I, *England in 1815*, London: Ernest Benn, 1960.

J. S. Haller, 'Neurasthenia: the medical profession and the "new woman" of late nineteenth century', *New York State Journal of Medicine*, 15 February 1971, pp. 473–82.

A. H. Halsey (ed.), *Trends in British Society since 1900*, London: Macmillan, 1972.

C. Ham, *Health Policy in Britain*, London: Macmillan, 1982.

J. Hanmer and P. Allen, 'Reproductive engineering: the final solution?', Brighton Women and Science Group, *Alice Through the Microscope*, London: Virago, 1980.

E. Hare and J. K. Wing, *Psychiatric Epidemiology*, London: Oxford University Press, 1970.

R. Harré, *The Philosophies of Science*, London: Oxford University Press, 1972.

H. A. L. Hart and A. M. Honoré, *Causation in the Law*, Oxford: Oxford University Press, 1959.

J. R. Hay, *The Origins of the Liberal Welfare Reforms, 1906–14*, London: Macmillan, 1975.

U. Henriques, *Before the Welfare State: Social Administration in early Industrial Britain*, London: Longman, 1979.

C. Hill, *Intellectual Origins of the English Revolution*, Oxford: Clarendon Press, 1965.

C. Hill, *Reformation to Industrial Revolution*, Harmondsworth: Penguin, 1969.

E. J. Hobsbawm, *Industry and Empire*, Harmondsworth: Penguin, 1969.

R. G. Hodgkinson, *The Origins of the National Health Service: the Medical Services of the New Poor Law, 1834–1871*, London: The Wellcome History Medical Library, 1967.

J. Hoenig and M. W. Hamilton, *The Desegregation of the Mentally Ill*, London: Routledge and Kegan Paul, 1969.

A. B. Hollingshead and F. C. Redlich, *Social Class and Mental Illness*, New York: Wiley, 1958.

S. W. F. Holloway, 'Medical education in England, 1830–1858: a sociological analysis', *History*, 4, no. 9, 1964, pp. 299–324.

S. W. F. Holloway, 'The Apothecaries Act, 1815: a reinterpretation', Parts I and II, *Medical History*, 10 July 1966, pp. 107–29; 11 July 1966, p. 221–36.

A. Horwitz, 'The pathways into psychiatric treatment: some differences between men and women', *Journal of Health and Social Behaviour*, 18, 1977, pp. 169–78.

M. Howarth-Williams, *R. D. Laing: His Work and Its Relevance for Sociology*, London: Routledge and Kegan Paul, 1977.

H. S. Hughes, *Consciousness and Society: the Reorientation of European Social Thought, 1890–1930*, New York: Random House, 1958.

R. Hunter and I. MacAlpine, *Three Hundred Years of Psychiatry, 1535–1860*, London: Oxford University Press, 1963.

R. Hunter and I. MacAlpine, *George III and the Mad Business*, London: Allen Lane, 1969.

R. Hunter and I. MacAlpine, *Psychiatry for the Poor: 1851 Colney Hatch Asylum. Friern Hospital 1973*, London: Dawsons, 1974.

S. Hyman, *Supplies Management for Health Services*, London: Croom Helm, 1979.

M. Ignatieff, *A Just Measure of Pain: The Penitentiary in the Industrial Revlution, 1750–1850*, London: Macmillan, 1978.

I. Illich, *Medical Nemesis: the Expropriation of Health*, London: Marion Boyars, 1975.

I. Illich, *Limits to Medicine*, Harmondsworth: Penguin, 1977a.

I. Illich, 'Disabling Professions', in I. Illich, I. K. Zola, J. McKnight, J. Caplan and H. Shaiken, *Disabling Professions*, London: Marion Boyars, 1977b.

D. Ingleby, 'The social construction of mental illness', in P. Wright and A. Treacher, *The Problem of Medical Knowledge*, Edinburgh: Edinburgh University Press, 1982, pp. 123–43.

L. L. Iverson, 'Biochemical and pharmacological studies: the dopamine hypothesis', in J. K. Wing (ed.), *Schizophrenia: Towards a New Synthesis*, London: Academic Press, 1978.

M. Jahoda, 'Towards a social psychology of mental health', in A. M. Rose (ed.), *Mental Health and Mental disorder*, London: Routledge and Kegan Paul, 1956.

K. Jaspers, *General Psychopathology*, London: Manchester University Press, 1963.

R. Jessop, *The Capitalist State: Marxist Theories and Methods*, Oxford: Martin Robertson, 1982.

N. D. Jewson, 'Medical knowledge and the patronage system in eighteenth century England', *Sociology*, 8, 1974, pp. 369–85.

N. D. Jewson, 'The disappearance of the sick man from medical cosmology, 1770–1879', *Sociology*, 10, 1976, pp. 225–44.

T. J. Johnson, *Professions and Power*, London: Macmillan, 1972.

E. Jones, *Sigmund Freud: Life and Work*, vol. II, London: Hogarth, 1958.

K. Jones, *Lunacy, Law and Conscience, 1744–1845*, London: Routledge and Kegan Paul, 1955.

K. Jones, *Mental Health and Social Policy, 1845–1959*, London: Routledge and Kegan Paul, 1960.

K. Jones, 'Integration or disintegration in the mental health services', *Journal of the Royal Society of Medicine*, 72, 1979, pp. 640–8.

M. Jones, *Social Psychiatry: A Study of Therapeutic Communities*, London: Tavistock, 1952.

M. Jones, *Social Psychiatry in Practice: The Idea of the Therapeutic Community*, Harmondsworth: Penguin, 1968.

W. K. Jordan, *Philanthropy in England, 1480–1660*, London: Allen and Unwin, 1959.

L. Jordanova, 'Conceptualising power over women' (review of Barbara Ehrenreich and Deirdre English, *For Her Own Good*), *Radical Science Journal*, 12, 1982, pp. 124–8.

R. Keat and J. Urry, *Social Theory as Science*, London: Routledge and Kegan Paul, 1975.

R. E. Kendell, *The Role of Diagnosis in Psychiatry*, Oxford: Blackwell, 1975a.

R. E. Kendell, 'The concept of disease and its implications for psychiatry', *British Journal of Psychiatry*, 117, 1975b, pp. 305–15.

L. S. King, 'What is disease?', *Philosophy of Science*, 21, 1954, pp. 193–203.

P. Kline, *Fact and Fantasy in Freudian Theory*, London: Methuen, 1972.

K. Koch, 'The New Marxist theory of the state or the rediscovery of the limitations of the Structural–Functionalist paradigm', *Netherlands Journal of Sociology*, 16, 1980, pp. 244–57.

M. L. Kohn, 'Social class and schizophrenia: a critical review', in D. Rosenthal and S. Kety (eds.), *The Transmission of Schizophrenia*, Oxford: Pergamon Press, 1968.

J. Kovel, *A Complete Guide to Therapy: from Psychoanalysis to Behaviour Modification*, Harmondsworth: Penguin, 1978.

J. Kovel, 'The American mental health industry', in D. Ingleby (ed.), *Critical Psychiatry*, Harmondsworth: Penguin, 1981.

B. M. Kramer, 'The Day Hospital: partial hospitalization in psychiatry', in H. Freeman and J. Farndale (eds.), *Trends in the Mental Health Services*, Oxford: Pergamon Press, 1963.

F. Kraupl Taylor, *The Concepts of Illness, Disease and Morbus*, Cambridge: Cambridge University Press, 1979.

D. E. Kreisman and V. D. Joy, 'Family response to the mental illness of a relative: a review of the literature', in O. Grusky and M. Pollner (eds.), *The Sociology of Mental Illness*, New York: Holt, Rinehart and Winston, 1981.

N. Kreitman, P. Sainsbury, J. Morrisey, J. Towers and J. Scrivener, 'The reliability of psychiatric assessment: an analysis', *Journal of Mental Science*, 107, 1961, pp. 887–908.

T. S. Kuhn, *The Structure of Scientific Revolutions*, Chicago: University of Chicago Press, 1962.

M. Lader, 'Drug research and mental health services', in M. Meacher (ed.), *New Methods of Mental Health Care*, Oxford: Pergamon, 1979.

R. D. Laing, *The Divided Self: An Existential Study in Sanity and Madness*, London: Tavistock, 1960.

R. D. Laing, *Self and Others*, London: Tavistock, 1961.

R. D. Laing, 'Series and nexus in the family', *New Left Review*, 15, 1962, pp. 7–14.

R. D. Laing, *Sanity, Madness and the Family, Vol. I: Families of Schizophrenics*, London: Tavistock, 1964.

R. D. Laing, *The Politics of Experience and The Bird of Paradise*, Harmondsworth: Penguin, 1967.

R. D. Laing and D. G. Cooper, *Reason and Violence: A Decade of Sartre's Philosophy, 1950–1960*, London: Tavistock, 1964.

H. Land, 'Who cares for the family?', *Journal of Social Policy*, 7, 1978, pp. 257–84.

D. S. Landes, *The Unbound Prometheus: Technological Change and Industrial Development in Western Europe from 1750 to the Present*, Cambridge: Cambridge University Press, 1969.

R. Lapouse, M. Monk and W. Terris, 'The drift hypothesis and socio-economic differentials in schizophrenia', *American Journal of Public Health*, 46, 1956, pp. 968–86.

J. Larrain, *Marxism and Ideology*, London: Macmillan, 1983.

J. Leff, 'Social and Psychological causes of the acute attack', in J. K. Wing (ed.), *Schizophrenia: Towards a New Synthesis*, London: Academic Press, 1978.

H. M Leichter, *A Comparative Approach to Policy Analysis: Health Care Policy in Four Nations*, Cambridge: Cambridge University Press, 1979.

E. M. Lemert, *Social Pathology*, New York: McGraw Hill, 1951.

R. Levitt, *The Reorganised National Health Service*, London: Croom Helm, 1976.

A. Lewis, 'Health as a social concept', *British Journal of Sociology*, 4, 1953, pp. 109–24.

A. Lewis, 'Henry Maudsley: his work and influence', in his *The State of Psychiatry*, London: Routledge and Kegan Paul, 1967.

J. Lewis, *The Politics of Motherhood: Child and Maternal Welfare in England 1900–39*, London: Croom Helm, 1980.

T. Lidz, 'Schizophrenia, and the family', *Psychiatry*, 21, 1958, pp. 21–7.

T. Lidz and S. Fleck, 'Schizophrenia, human interaction and the role of the family', in D. Jackson (ed.), *The Etiology of Schizophrenia*, New York: Basic Books, 1960.

D. Lockwood, 'The weakest link in the chain? Some comments on the Marxist theory of action', *Research in the Sociology of Work*, 1, 1981, pp. 435–81.

M. Lomax, *Experiences of an Asylum Doctor, with Suggestions for Asylum and Lunacy Law Reform*, London: George Allen and Unwin, 1921.

C. M. MacBryde, *Signs and Symptoms*, Philadelphia: Lippincott, 1964.

J. T. MacCurdy, *War Neuroses*, London: Cambridge University Press, 1918.

M. MacDonald, *Mystical Bedlam: Madness, Anxiety, and Healing in Seventeenth*

Century England, Cambridge: Cambridge University Press, 1981.

A. MacIntyre, *The Unconscious: A Conceptual Study*, London: Routledge and Kegan Paul, 1958.

A. MacIntyre, 'A mistake about causality in social science', in P. Laslett and W. G. Runciman (eds.), *Philosophy, Politics and Society*, Oxford: Blackwells, 1962.

T. McKeown, *The Modern Rise of Popoulation*, London: Edward Arnold, 1976a.

T. McKeown, *The Role of Medicine: Dream, Mirage or Nemesis?*, London: Nuffield Provincial Hospitals Trust, 1976b.

R. V. Magnus, 'The new chronics', *British Journal of Psychiatry*, **113**, 1967, pp. 555–6.

T. F. Main, 'The hospital as a therapeutic institution', *Bulletin of the Menninger Clinic*, **10**, 1946, pp. 66–70.

M. Mann, 'State and Society, 1130–1815: an analysis of English state finances', *Political Power and Social Theory*, **1**, 1980, pp. 165–208.

O. Mannoni, *Freud: the Theory of the Unconscious*, London: New Left Books, 1971.

T. Marmor, *Psychiatrists and their Patients: a National Study of Private Office Practice*, Washington, DC: American Psychiatric Association, 1975.

D. Martin, 'Institutionalisation', *The Lancet*, **2**, 1955, pp. 1188–90.

R. Matthews, ' "Decarceration" and the fiscal crisis', in B. Fine *et al.* (eds.), *Capitalism and the Rule of Law*, London: Hutchinson, 1979.

L. Measey and H. Smith, 'Patterns of new chronicity in a mental hospital', *British Journal of Psychiatry*, **123**, 1973, pp. 349–51.

D. Mechanic, 'Problems and prospects in psychiatric epidemiology', in E. H. Hare and J. K. Wing (eds.), *Psychiatric Epidemiology*, London: Oxford University Press, 1970.

D. Mechanic, *Medical Sociology, Second Edition*, New York: The Free Press, 1978.

B. N. Meltzer, J. W. Petras and L. T. Reynolds, *Symbolic Interactionism: Genesis, Varieties and Criticism*, London: Routledge and Kegan Paul, 1975.

K. Menninger, *The Vital Balance: the Life Process in Mental Health and Illness*, New York: The Viking Press, 1963.

R. K. Merton, *Social Theory and Social Structure*, Revised Edition, Glencoe, Ill.: The Free Press, 1968.

R. Miliband, *The State in Capitalist Society: the Analysis of the Western System of Power*, London: Weidenfeld and Nicholson, 1969.

C. W. Mills, *The Power Elite*, New York: Oxford University Press, 1959.

MIND, *Community Care Provisions for Mentally Ill and Mentally Handicapped Adults*, MIND Report No. 11, London: MIND, 1973.

MIND, *Co-ordination or Chaos? The Run-down of Psychiatric Hospitals*, MIND Report No. 13, London: MIND, 1974.

Ministry of Health, *A National Health Service*, London: HMSO, 1944.

E. G. Mishler, L. R. Anarasingham, S. T. Hauser, R. Liem, S. D. Osherson,

N. E. Waxler, *Social Contexts of Health, Illness and Patient Care*, Cambridge: Cambridge University Press, 1981.

E. G. Mishler and N. E. Waxler, 'Family interaction processes and schizophrenia: a review of current theories', in G. Handel (ed.), *The Psychosocial Interior of the Family*, London: Allen and Unwin, 1968.

R. F. Mollica and F. Redlich, 'Equity and Changing Patient Characteristics – 1950 to 1975', *Archives of General Psychiatry*, **37**, 1980, pp. 1257–63.

M. Molyneux, 'Beyond the domestic labour debate', *New Left Review*, **116**, 1979, pp. 3–27.

M. S. Moore, 'Some myths about "mental illness" ', *Inquiry*, **18**, 1975, pp. 233–65.

R. Morantz, 'The Lady and her physician', in M. Hartman and L. W. Banner (eds.), *Clio's Consciousness Raised*, New York: Harper and Row, 1974.

J. N. Morris, *Uses of Epidemiology*, Edinburgh: Livingstone, 1964.

R. J. Morris, *Class and Class Consciousness in the Industrial Revolution, 1780–1850*, London: Macmillan, 1979.

A. Myerson, 'Theory and principles of the "total push" method in the treatment of chronic schizophrenia', *American Journal of Psychiatry*, **95**, 1939, pp. 1197–204.

V. Navarro, *Medicine Under Capitalism*, New York: Prodist, 1976.

V. Navarro, *Class Struggle, the State and Medicine: An Historical and Contemporary Analysis of the Medical Sector in Great Britain*, London: Martin Robertson, 1978.

A. Norton, 'Mental hospital ins and outs: a survey of patients admitted to a mental hospital in the past 30 years', in H. Freeman and J. Farndale (eds., *Trends in the Mental Health Services*, Oxford: Pergamon Press, 1963, pp. 40–59.

A. Oakley,'Wisewoman and medicine man: changes in the management of childbirth', in J. Mitchell and A. Oakley (eds.), *The Rights and Wrongs of Women*, London: Harmondsworth, 1976.

A. Oakley, 'Women and Health Policy', in J. Lewis (ed.), *Women's Welfare Women's Rights*, London: Croom Helm, 1983.

C. P. Obendorf, *A History of Psychoanalysis in America*, New York: Grune and Stratton, 1953.

J. O'Connor, *The Fiscal Crisis of the State*, London: St James Press, 1973.

D. Ogg, *Europe in the Seventeenth Century*, 8th edn, London: A. and C. Black, 1965.

D. Owen, *English Philanthropy, 1660–1960*, Cambridge, Mass.: Harvard University Press, 1965.

G. W Oxley, *Poor Relief in England and Wales, 1601–1834*, Newton Abbott: David and Charles, 1974.

F. Parkin, *Marxism and Class Theory*, London: Tavistock, 1979.

N. Parry and J. Parry, *The Rise of the Medical Profession: A Study of Collective Social Mobility*, London: Croom Helm, 1976.

W. Parry-Jones, *The Trade in Lunacy: A Study of Private Madhouses in England in the Eighteenth and Nineteenth Centuries*, London: Routledge and Kegan Paul, 1972.

T. Parsons, *The Social System*, London: Routledge and Kegan Paul, 1951.

M. Pelling and C. Webster, 'Medical Practitioners', in C. Webster (ed.), *Health, Medicine and Mortality in the Sixteenth Century*, London: Cambridge University Press, 1979, pp. 165–235.

H. J. Perkin, *The Origins of Modern English Society, 1780–1880*, London: Routledge and Kegan Paul, 1969.

D. L. Phillips, 'Social class and psychological disturbance: the influence of positive and negative experiences', *Social Psychiatry*, **3**, 1968, pp. 41–6.

D. L. Phillips and B. F. Segal, 'Sexual status and psychiatric symptoms', *American Sociological Review,* **34**, 1969, pp. 58–72.

S. Pilling, 'The Mental Health (Amendment) Act 1982: reform or cosmetics?', *Critical Social Policy*, **7**, 1983, pp. 90–6.

J. Plamenatz, *Ideology*, London: Macmillan, 1970.

K. Plummer, 'Misunderstanding labelling perspectives', in D. Downes and P. Rock (eds.), *Deviant Interpretations*, London: Martin Robertson, 1979.

K. Popper, *Conjectures and Refutations: The Growth of Scientific Knowledge,* London: Routledge and Kegan Paul, 1963.

R. Porter, 'Being mad in Georgian England', *History Today*, **31**, 1981, pp. 42–8.

R. Porter, *English Society in the Eighteenth Century*, Harmondsworth: Penguin, 1982.

M. Poster, *Critical Theory of the Family*, London: Pluto, 1978.

J. Pound, *Poverty and Vagrancy in Tudor England*, London: Longman, 1971.

A. Powell, *The Metropolitan Asylums Board and its Work, 1867–1930*, London: Metropolitan Asylums Board, 1930.

F. Redlich and S. R. Kellert, 'Trends in American mental health', *American Journal of Psychiatry*, **135**, 1978, pp. 22–8.

T. P. Rees, 'Back to moral treatment and community care', *Journal of Mental Science,* **103**, 1957, pp. 303–13.

D. D. Reid, *Epidemiological Methods in the Study of Mental Disorders*, Geneva: World Health Organisation, 1960.

P. Rieff, *Freud: The Mind of the Moralist*, London: Methuen, 1965.

B. Rimland, 'Psychogenesis versus biogenesis: the issues and the evidence', in S. C. Plog and R. B. Edgerton (eds.), *Changing Perspectives in Mental Illness*, New York: Holt, Rinhart and Winston, 1969.

J. Robson, 'The NHS Company Inc.? The social consequences of the professional dominance in the National Health Service', *International*

Journal of Health Services, **3**, 1973, pp. 413–26.

A. A. Rogow, *The Psychiatrists*, New York: Delta, 1970.

M. Rokeach, *The Open and Closed Mind*, New York: Basic Books, 1960.

A. M. Rose, (ed.), *Human Behaviour and Social Processes: An Interactionist Approach*, London: Routledge and Kegan Paul, 1962.

M. E. Rose, *The Relief of Poverty, 1934–1914*, London: Macmillan, 1972.

S. P. R. Rose, 'Disordered molecules and diseased minds', paper given at the WHO Conference on Biological Markers in Mental Disorders, Milan, 1983.

C. E. Rosenberg, *The Trial of The Assassin Guiteau: Psychiatry and Law in the Gilded Age*, Chicago: University of Chicago Press, 1968.

C. E. Rosenberg, *No Other Gods: On Science and American Social Thought*, Baltimore: Johns Hopkins University Press, 1976.

D. L. Rosenhan, 'On being sane in insane places', *Science*, **179**, 1973, pp. 250–8.

D. Rosenthal and S. Kety (eds.), *The Transmission of Schizophrenia*, London: Pergamon Press, 1968.

D. J. Rothman, *The Discovery of the Asylum: social order and disorder in the new republic*, Boston: Little, Brown and Co., 1971.

Royal College of General Practitioners, *Morbidity Statistics from General Practice, 1970–1971*, London: HMSO, 1974.

Royal Commission on Lunacy and Mental Disorder, *Report*, London: HMSO, 1926.

Royal Commission on the Law Relating to Mental Illness and Mental Deficiency, 1954–1957, *Report*, London: HMSO, 1957.

Royal Commission on the National Health Service, *Report*, London: HMSO, 1979.

Royal Medico-Psychological Association, *A Memorandum on the Future Organisation of the Psychiatric Services*, London: Royal Medico-Psychological Association, 1945.

J. G. Scadding, 'Diagnosis: the clinician and the computer', *The Lancet*, **2**, 1967, pp. 877–82.

T. J. Scheff, 'Decision rules, types of error, and their consequences in medical diagnosis', *Behavioural Science*, **8**, 1963, pp. 97–107.

T. J. Scheff, *Being Mentally Ill*, London: Weidenfeld and Nicholson, 1966.

E. M. Schur, *Labelling Deviant Behaviour*, New York: Harper and Row, 1971.

A. Schutz, 'The dimensions of the social world', in *Collected Papers II: Studies in Social Theory*, The Hague: Nijhoff, 1964.

A. T. Scull, 'From madness to mental illness: medical men as moral entrepreneurs', *Archives Européenes de Sociologies*, **16**, 1975, pp. 218–61.

A. T. Scull, *Decarceration: Community Treatment and the Deviant – A Radical View*, Englewood Cliffs: Prentice Hall, 1977.

A. T. Scull, *Museums of Madness: The Social Organization of Insanity in 19th Century England*, London: Allen Lane, 1979.

A. T. Scull, 'Moral treatment reconsidered: some sociological comments on an episode in the history of British psychiatry', in his *Madhouses, Mad-Doctors, and Madmen*, London: The Athlone Press, 1981.

H. F. Searles, *Collected Papers on Schizophrenia and Related Subjects*, London: Hogarth Press, 1964.

W. Seccombe, 'The housewife and her labour under capitalism', *New Left Review*, 83, 1974, pp. 3-24.

P. Sedgwick, 'R, D. Laing: self, symptom and society', in R. Boyers (ed.)., *Laing and anti-Psychiatry*, Harmondsworth: Penguin, 1972.

P. Sedgwick, *Psycho Politics*, London: Pluto Press, 1982.

H, Segal, *Introduction to the Work of Melanie Klein*, London, Heinemann, 1964.

H. Segal, *Klein*, London: Fontana, 1979.

M. Shepherd (ed.), *Psychiatrists on Psychiatry*, Cambridge: Cambridge University Press, 1982.

M. Shepherd, B. Cooper, A. C. Brown and G. W. Kalton, *Psychiatric Illness in General Practice*, London: Oxford University Press, 1966.

A. Sheridan, *Michel Foucault: The Will to Truth*, London: Tavistock, 1980.

M. Sherif, *The Psychology of Social Norms*, New York: Harper, 1936.

J. Shields, 'Genetics', in J. K. Wing (ed.), *Schizophrenia: Towards a New Synthesis*, London: Academic Press, 1978.

R. H. Shryock, *The Development of Modern Medicine*, New York: Knopf, 1947.

B. Sicherman, 'The paradox of prudence: mental health in the Gilded Age', in A. Scull (ed.), *Madhouses, Mad-Doctors and Madmen*, London: The Athlone Press, 1981.

M. Siegler and H. Osmond, *Models of Madness, Models of Medicine*, New York: Macmillan, 1974.

M. Silverman and P. R. Lee, *Pills, Profits and Politics*, Berkeley: University of California Press, 1974.

T. Silverstone and P. Turner, *Drug Treatment in Psychiatry*, London: Routledge and Kegan Paul, 1974.

V. Skultans, *English Madness: Ideas on Insanity, 1580–1890*, London: Routledge and Kegan Paul, 1979.

E. Slater and M. Roth, *Clinical Psychiatry, Third Edition*, London: Ballière, Tindall and Cassell, 1969.

D. E. Smith, 'A version of mental illness', unpublished article, Department of Sociology, University of Essex, 1967.

D. E. Smith, 'The statistics on mental illness: what they will not tell us about women and why', in D. E. Smith and S. J. David (eds.), *Women Look at Psychiatry*, Vancouver: Press Gang, 1975.

D. E. Smith, ' "K is mentally ill": the anatomy of a factual account', *Sociology*, 12, 1978, pp. 23–53.

G. E. Smith and T. H. Pear, *Shell Shock and Its Lessons*, Manchester: The University Press, 1917.

C. Smith-Rosenberg, 'The hysterical woman: sex roles and role-conflict in nineteenth century America', *Social Research*, 39, 1972, pp. 652–78.

M. Spector, 'Legitimizing homosexuality', *Society*, **14**, 1972, pp. 52–6.

L. Srole, T. S. Langner, S. T. Michael, P. Kirkpatrick, M. K. Opler, and T. A. C. Rennie, *Mental Health in the Metropolis*, revised edn, books 1 and 2, New York: Harper, 1975.

D. Stafford-Clark, *Psychiatry Today*, 2nd edn, Harmondsworth: Penguin Books, 1963.

A. Storr, 'The concept of cure', in C. Rycroft (ed.), *Psychoanalysis Observed*, London: Constable, 1966.

A. Strauss and B. Glaser, 'Patterns of dying', in C. Cox and A. Mead (eds.), *A Sociology of Medical Practice*, London: Collier Macmillan, 1979.

J. S. Strauss, 'Diagnostic models and the nature of psychiatric disorder', *Archives of General Psychiatry*, **29**, 1973, pp. 445–9.

J. S. Strauss, 'A comprehensive approach to psychiatric diagnosis', *American Journal of Psychiatry*, **132**, 1975, pp. 1193–7.

H. P. Strecker, 'A comparison of insulin and cardiazol convulsion therapies in the treatment of schizophrenia', *The Lancet*, 12 February 1938, pp. 311–73.

D. Sudnow, 'Normal Crimes: sociological features of the penal code in a public defender office', *Social Problems*, **12**, 1965, pp. 255–76.

T. S. Szasz, *The Myth of Mental Illness: Foundations of a Theory of Personal Conduct*, New York: Hoeber-Harper, 1961.

T. S. Szasz, *Law, Liberty and Psychiatry*, New York: Macmillan, 1963a.

T. S. Szasz, 'The concept of transference', *International Journal of Psychoanalysis*, **44**, 1963b, pp. 432–43.

T. S. Szasz, *The Ethics of Psychoanalysis: The Theory and Method of Autonomous Psychotherapy*, New York: Basic Books, 1965.

T. S. Szasz, 'The myth of mental illness', in his *Ideology and Insanity*, New York: Doubleday, 1970a.

T. S. Szasz, 'Involuntary mental hospitalization: a crime against humanity', in his *Ideology and Insanity*, New York: Doubleday, 1970b.

T. S. Szasz, *The Manufacture of Madness: A Comparative Study of the Inquisition and the Mental Health Movement*, London: Routledge and Kegan Paul, 1971.

T. S. Szasz, *Ceremonial Chemistry: The Ritual Persecution of Drugs, Addicts and Pushers*, New York: Doubleday, 1974.

T. S. Szasz, *Psychiatric Slavery*, New York: The Free Press, 1977.

T. S. Szasz, *Schizophrenia: The Sacred Symbol of Psychiatry*, Oxford: Blackwell, 1979.

T. S. Szasz, 'Anti-psychiatry: the paradigm of the plundered mind', in O. Grusky and M. Pollner (eds.), *The Sociology of Mental Illness*, New York: Holt, Rinehart and Winston, 1981.

A. J. Taylor, *Laissez-faire and State Intervention in Nineteenth century Britain*, London: Macmillan, 1972.

C. Taylor, *The Explanation of Behaviour*, London: Routledge and Kegan Paul, 1964.

M. K. Temerlin, 'Suggestion effects in psychiatric diagnosis', *Journal of Nervous and Mental Disease*, **147**, 1968, pp. 349–53.

P. Thane, 'Women and the Poor Law in Victorian and Edwardian Britain', *History Workshop Journal*, **6**, 1978.

P. Thane, *The Foundations of the Welfare State*, London: Longman, 1982.

K. Thomas, *Religion and the Decline of Magic*, Harmondsworth: Penguin, 1973.

E. P. Thompson, *The Making of the English Working Class*, New York: Random House, 1963.

C. Thunhurst, *It Makes you Sick: The Politics of the NHS*, London: Pluto, 1982.

L. A. Tilly and J. W. Scott, *Women, Work and Family*, New York: Holt, Rinehart and Winston, 1978.

R. A. Titmuss, 'Community care – fact or fiction', in H. Freeman and J. Farndale (eds.), *Trends in the Mental Health Services*, Oxford: Pergamon Press, 1963, pp. 221–5.

G. C. Tooth and E. M. Brooke, 'Trends in the mental health population and their effect on future planning', *The Lancet*, 1 April 1961.

B. Towers, 'The influence of medical technology on medical services' in G. McLachlan and T. McKeown (eds.), *Medical History and Medical Care*, London: Oxford University Press, 1971.

P. Townsend, 'Inequality and the health service', *The Lancet*, 15 June 1974, pp. 1179–90.

P. Townsend and N. Davidson (eds.), *Inequalities in Health: The Black Report*, Harmondsworth: Penguin, 1982.

W. Tudor, J. F. Tudor and W. R. Gove, 'The effect of sex role differences on the social control of mental illness', *Journal of Health and Social Behaviour*, **18**, 1977, pp. 98–112.

R. J. Turner and M. O. Wagenfeld, 'Occupational mobility and schizophrenia: an assessment of the social causation and social selection hypotheses', *American Sociological Review*, **32**, 1967, pp. 104–13.

J. Vaizey, *Britain in the Sixties: Education for Tomorrow*, Harmondsworth: Penguin Books, 1962.

I. Veith, *Hysteria: The History of a Disease*, Chicago: University of Chicago Press, 1965.

M. C. Versluysen, 'Old wives tales? Women healers in English history', in C. Davies (ed.), *Rewriting Nursing History*, London: Croom Helm, 1980.

I. Waddington, 'The role of the hospital in the development of modern medicine: a sociological analysis', *Sociology*, **7**, 1973, pp. 211–24.

S. Waldrond-Skinner (ed.), *Developments in Family Therapy*, London: Routledge and Kegan Paul, 1981.

A. Walk, 'Gloucester and the beginnings of the R.M.P.A.', *The Journal of Mental Science*, **107**, 1961, pp. 603–32.

V. Walsh, 'Contraception: the growth of a technology', in the Brighton Women and Science Group, *Alice through the Microscope*, London: Virago, 1980.

V. Walters, *Class Inequality and Health Care: The Origins and Impact of the National Health Service*, London: Croom Helm, 1980.

J. Walton, 'The treatment of pauper lunatics in Victorian England: the case of Lancaster Asylum, 1816–1870', in A. Scull (ed.), *Madhouses, Mad-Doctors, and Madmen*, London: Athlone, 1981.

M. Weber, *The Theory of Social and Economic Organisation*, New York: Free Press, 1964.

C. Webster, *The Great Instauration: Science, Medicine and Reform, 1622–1660*, London: Duckworth, 1975.

H. J. Wegrocki, 'A critique of cultural and statistical concepts of abnormality', *Journal of Abnormal and Social Psychology*, **34**, 1939.

D. Widgery, *Health in Danger: The Crisis in the National Health Service*, London: Macmillan, 1979.

I. G. H. Wilson, *Study of Hypoglycaemic Shock Treatment in Schizophrenia*, London: HMSO, 1936.

J. K. Wing, 'Institutionalism in mental hospitals', *British Journal of Social and Clinical Psychology*, **1**, 1962, pp. 38–51.

J. K. Wing, *Reasoning About Madness*, Oxford: Oxford University Press, 1978.

J. K. Wing, J. L. T. Birley, J. E. Cooper, P. Graham and A. D. Isaacs, 'Reliability of a procedure for measuring and classifying "Present Psychiatric State" ', *British Journal of Psychiatry*, **113**, 1967, pp. 499–515.

J. K. Wing, J. E. Cooper and N. Sartorius, *Description and Classification of Psychiatric Symptoms*, London: Cambridge University Press, 1974.

R. Wollheim, *Freud*, London: Fontana, 1971.

J. Wolpe, *Psychotherapy by Reciprocal Inhibition*, Stamford: Stamford University Press, 1958.

A. D. Wood, ' "The fashionable diseases": women's complaints and their treatment in nineteenth century America', in M. Hartman and L. W. Banner (eds.), *Clio's Consciousness Raised*, New York: Harper and Row, 1974.

J. Woodward, *To do the Sick no Harm: A Study of the British Voluntary Hospital System to 1875*, London: Routledge and Kegan Paul, 1974.

B. Wootton, *Social Science and Social Pathology*, London: Allen and Unwin, 1959.

World Health Organisation, *Mental Disorders: Glossary and Guide to their Classification*, Geneva: World Health Organisation, 1978.

E. A. Wrigley and R. S. Schofield, *The Population History of England, 1541–1871*, London: Edward Arnold, 1981.

L. C. Wynne, I. Ryckoff, J. Day and S. Hirsch, 'Pseudo-mutuality in the family relations of schizophrenics', *Psychiatry*, 21, 1958, pp. 205–20.

R. Young, *Mind, Brain and Adaptation in the Nineteenth Century: Cerebral Localisation and its Biological context from Gall to Ferrier*, Oxford: Clarendon Press, 1970.

R. Young, 'Science *is* social relations', *Radical Science Journal*, 5, 1977, pp. 65–129.

M. Zax and E. L. Cowen, *Abnormal Psychology*, 2nd edn, New York: Holt, Rinehart and Winston, 1976.

E. Zigler and L. Phillips, 'Psychiatric diagnosis: a critique', *Journal of Abnormal and Social Psychology*, 63, 1961, pp. 607–18.

G. Zilboorg, *A History of Medical Psychology*, New York: Norton, 1941.

Name index

Subject index